WITHDRAWN

The American Dream
and the
Public Schools

The American Dream and the Public Schools

JENNIFER L. HOCHSCHILD

and

NATHAN SCOVRONICK

CALVIN T. RYAN LIBRARY
U. OF NEBRASKA AT KEARNEY

OXFORD
UNIVERSITY PRESS

OXFORD
UNIVERSITY PRESS

Oxford   New York
Auckland Bangkok Buenos Aires
Cape Town   Chennai Dar es Salaam Delhi Hong Kong Istanbul
Karachi Kolkata Kuala Lumpur Madrid Melbourne Mexico City Mumbai
Nairobi São Paulo Shanghai Taipei
Tokyo Toronto

Copyright © 2003 by Jennifer L. Hochschild and Nathan Scovronick

First published by Oxford University Press, Inc., 2003
198 Madison Avenue, New York, New York 10016
www.oup.com
First issued as an Oxford University Press paperback, 2004
ISBN-13 978-0-19-517603-2 (pbk.)

Oxford is a registered trademark of Oxford University Press

All rights reserved. No part of this publication may be reproduced,
stored in a retrieval system, or transmitted, in any form or by any means,
electronic, mechanical, photocopying, recording, or otherwise,
without the prior permission of Oxford University Press.

The Library of Congress has cataloged the hardcover edition as follows:
Hochschild, Jennifer L., 1950–
The American dream and the public schools / Jennifer L. Hochschild
and Nathan Scovronick.
p.   cm.
Includes bibliographical references and index.

1. Education and states—United States.
2. Educational equalization—United States.
3. Public schools—United States.
I. Scovronick, Nathan B., 1945–
II. Title.
LC89 .H63 2003
371.01′0973—dc21   2002027848

7 9 8

Printed in the United States of America
on acid-free paper

To Tony, Lea, and Raphe
—*J.L.H.*

To Lily
—*N.S.*

In America, when a problem is too hard for adults, we pass it on to schools.

—*Patricia Graham, 1996*

CONTENTS

PREFACE AND ACKNOWLEDGMENTS

ALMOST TWO DECADES AGO, Jennifer Hochschild published a book on race in public education, and since then she has worked on several court cases involving school desegregation. Almost twenty years ago, Nate Scovronick was policy director of the New Jersey General Assembly, and later he worked on education issues for the state's governor. Both of us have taught university courses on schooling and have consulted and worked with public school educators. Both of us have children who have been entirely educated in public school systems. We have discussed the issues in this book with each other, with students, and with other colleagues for years.

So when we decided to write this book, we thought that we saw things the same way and that we knew most of what we needed to know in order to write it—it was to be the product of hard but pleasant labor over a few summers and Christmas vacations. Seven years, many arguments, and innumerable drafts later, we have learned our lesson the hard way. This book proved more difficult—and rewarding—to write than we anticipated, for reasons that are directly relevant to the actual making of education policy.

We began with some general but very important questions. Why is education policy so contentious? Why are there so many arenas of contention? Does the array of seemingly disparate issues have something in common that might help explain the level of controversy and lead us to some overall policy conclusions? We quickly discovered that we did agree on almost everything but also differed on a few important points. We agreed, and we hope that the book makes this case strongly, that public education is a unique treasure in the array of American public policies and that it deserves to be maintained and cherished, though not everywhere in its present form. We agreed that the great flaw in the American public school system is its systematic and pervasive denial to poor (and disproportionately nonwhite) children of the chance to get a good education. We agreed that much can be done within the contours of public schooling to overturn this egregious inequity and that such a change can also foster other goals of public education—eliminating racial discrimination, training children to be democratic citizens, promoting respect for difference along with appreciation of commonality, opening up an array of new dreams for children to consider, seeking to ensure that all children are taught as much as they can learn. And we agreed that the coming demographic transformation will change much of what we think we know about schooling, among many other things.

Our differences were limited, but real. One of us, for example, saw tracking and almost all forms of ability grouping as powerful engines of unequal opportunity; the other believed grouping could be reformed to contribute to the learning of all students. One of us had more sympathy with racial, religious, and linguistic identity politics; the other was more concerned with its potential to fragment the schools and divide the country. One of us was more willing to experiment with carefully designed forms of private and parochial school vouchers than the other. In retrospect it was not surprising that we had some disagreements. Most people who write about education policy focus on one or two contentious issues, but our questions required us to consider a broad range of issues—just as educators must do every day. It was inevitable that we would differ on some. Moreover, it was not surprising that we had these particular disagreements; these issues are among the most difficult for Americans to resolve. We hope that the resolution of our differences, and the effort to bring our policy recommendations together within one framework, will help people to understand the issues, see how they are linked, and work together on productive reforms.

To come to our resolution, we had to go back to fundamental questions about the purposes of education in this country and its connection with our dominant national ideology (or the closest thing we have to one), the American dream. There is plenty wrong with the American dream. It has justified the narrow pursuit of material gain and encouraged a national obsession with competition rather than cooperation; it has allowed too many people to believe that the wealth of the advantaged is evidence of virtue and the poverty of the disadvantaged evidence of sin; it has made it difficult for most people to understand stasis and change as the product of social structures and processes rather than individual choices and actions. But there is also a lot that is right with the dream—its egalitarian premise, its open definition of success, its optimism, and its mandate to the government to assure fair play and the continued vitality of democratic institutions. Good or bad, however, there is no denying the power of the dream for most Americans; reformers must work with it rather than against it if they hope to be any more successful than King Canute trying to stop the incoming tide. In the end we could resolve our differences and reach coherent policy recommendations only by considering all education issues in the context of the common goals and widely shared beliefs captured by the idea of the American dream, as well as by reviewing the willingness of Americans to act on behalf of them. With this approach we could aim for a consistent viewpoint, tethered strongly to political reality, and identify reasonable policy directions even when empirical research could not point the way.

Despite the recent explosion of writing about education policy, research is simply not definitive on many important educational issues. This occurs partly because research is distorted by political motives, has flaws in its design, or is simply unable to capture the complexity of the teaching and learning process. The paucity of clear research results also occurs because of the nature of academic debate itself, a process of analysis and conclusion, criticism and reevaluation, that can leave policymakers in the lurch and educators looking for a framework to guide their actions. Nevertheless, recent research has dramatically improved what we know about how children learn, how schools can help children disadvantaged by poverty or racial discrimination, and how communities can promote inclusion and equality without jeopardizing the pursuit of individual success. We have done our best to point to the newest research of the highest quality and to use it when possible as a basis for our conclusions; we also have tried to provide a framework to make decisions when public officials and citizens still do not know enough about issues on which crucial policy choices must be made. We hope that our approach helps people to determine policy based on knowledge and principle rather than on fear, ambition, or pious hope.

Education is a deeply political enterprise, regardless of how much people try to hide that point behind professionalism, nonpartisanship, or abdication to the market. How could it be otherwise? One of our nation's most important tasks is to teach the members of the next generation how to maintain a democracy while pursuing their own life goals, and the schools are our only collective way of doing it. This book was written in the hope of helping people to understand how important and exciting that political enterprise is, and also to see how they can help to push it in the right direction—toward making the practice of the American dream come a little closer to its promise, for all Americans.

We could not have written this book without the help and advice of many people. First and foremost is Smriti Belbase, who worked with us through one of the most intense and tortuous periods of composition and whose calm, humor, insights, information, and dedication to the task were invaluable in keeping the project moving. Scott Abernathy, Elaine Bonner-Tompkins, Jennifer Chen, Michael Fortner, Christopher Mackie, Bryan Shelly, and especially Francesca Petrosino were also invaluable research assistants and sounding boards. Linda Taylor and Jayne Bialkowski did heroic work keeping us, and the growing manuscript, reasonably on track.

Other colleagues read most or all of various drafts and gave terrifically helpful suggestions. We took that advice very seriously, even if we did not always do what they recommended, and we trust that the book is much improved as a result. Above all, we appreciate their willingness to give us their time—the one resource that cannot be increased. These colleagues include Rainer Baubock, Thomas Corcoran, Steven Elkin, Patricia Graham, Jeffrey Henig, Christopher Jencks, Richard Kahlenberg, David Kirp, Ellen Lagemann, Kathryn McDermott, Lorraine McDonnell, Jal Mehta, Kristen Monroe, Richard Murnane, Marion Orr, David Paris, Harry Stein, Clarence Stone, and Michael Timpane. Participants in seminars at Princeton University, Harvard University, the Cambridge Forum, the Russell Sage Foundation, and the Institute for Advanced Study in the Behavioral Sciences made clear to us what was controversial, contradictory, underdeveloped, and even—on occasion—persuasive about our particular arguments and general framework.

Tim Bartlett at Oxford University Press gave excellent editorial advice that nudged us out of our tendencies to be excessively academic or excessively curt. He was the paradigmatic reader—smart, thoughtful, open-minded about the issues, and without the burden of an expert's knowledge of their details. If we could make him understand and agree with the way we looked at the issues, we believed that others would do the same. Jim Erdman was a solicitous copyeditor, and Catherine Humphries a wonderfully helpful and adept production editor. Anonymous readers for several presses made very useful suggestions; we thank them for the care and attention that keeps the business of academia flowing reasonably smoothly and raises the quality of the discourse.

Finally, our families. Jennifer Hochschild dedicates this book to her husband and children, in the faith that they share her values and know how she feels about them. Nate Scovronick wants to thank his wife and children for their remarkable patience, and to dedicate this book to his mother, who taught in a poor urban high school with enthusiasm and dignity.

The American Dream
and the
Public Schools

INTRODUCTION

We have a great national opportunity—to ensure that every child, in every school, is challenged by high standards, . . . to build a culture of achievement that matches the optimism and aspirations of our country.

—*President George W. Bush, 2000*

There is nothing wrong with America that cannot be cured by what is right with America.

—*President Bill Clinton, 1993*

THE AMERICAN DREAM IS A POWERFUL CONCEPT. It encourages each person who lives in the United States to pursue success, and it creates the framework within which everyone can do it. It holds each person responsible for achieving his or her own dreams, while generating shared values and behaviors needed to persuade Americans that they have a real chance to achieve them. It holds out a vision of both individual success and the collective good of all.

From the perspective of the individual, the ideology is as compelling as it is simple. "I am an American, so I have the freedom and opportunity to make whatever I want of my life. I can succeed by working hard and using my talents; if I fail, it will be my own fault. Success is honorable, and failure is not. In order to make sure that my children and grandchildren have the same freedom and opportunities that I do, I have a responsibility to be a good citizen—to respect those whose vision of success is different from my own, to help make sure that everyone has an equal chance to succeed, to participate in the democratic process, and to teach my children to be proud of this country."

Not all residents of the United States believe all of those things, of course, and some believe none of them. Nevertheless, this American dream is surprisingly close to what most Americans have believed through most of recent American history.

Public schools are where it is all supposed to start—they are the central institutions for bringing both parts of the dream into practice. Americans expect schools not only to help students reach their potential as individuals but also to make them good citizens who will maintain the nation's values and institutions, help them flourish, and pass them on to the next generation. The American public widely endorses both of these broad goals, values public education, and supports it with an extraordinary level of resources.

Despite this consensus Americans disagree intensely about the education policies that will best help us achieve this dual goal. In recent years disputes over educational issues have involved all the branches and levels of government and have affected millions of students. The controversies—over matters like school funding, vouchers, bilingual education, high-stakes testing, desegregation, and creationism—seem, at first glance, to be separate problems. In important ways, however, they all reflect contention over the goals of the American dream. At the core of debates over one policy or another has often been a conflict between what is (or seems to be) good for the individual and what is good for the whole; sometimes the conflict revolves around an assault on the validity of the dream itself by certain groups of people. Because education is so important to the way the American dream works, people care about it intensely and can strongly disagree about definitions, methods, and priorities.

Sustained and serious disagreements over education policy can never be completely resolved because they spring from a fundamental paradox at the heart of the American dream. Most Americans believe that everyone has the right to pursue success but that only some deserve to win, based on their talent, effort, or ambition. The American dream is egalitarian at the starting point in the "race of life," but not at the end. That is not the paradox; it is simply an ideological choice. The paradox stems from the fact that the success of one generation depends at least partly on the success of their parents or guardians. People who succeed get to keep the fruits of their labor and use them as they see fit; if they buy a home in a place where the schools are better, or use their superior resources to make the schools in their neighborhood better, their children will have a head start and other children will fall behind through no fault of their own. The paradox lies in the fact that schools are supposed to equalize opportunities across generations and to create democratic citizens out of each generation, but people naturally wish to give their own children an advantage in attaining wealth or power, and some can do it. When they do, everyone does not start equally, politically or economically. This circle cannot be squared.

Many issues in education policy have therefore come down to an apparent choice between the individual success of comparatively privileged students and the collective good of all students or the nation as a whole. Efforts to promote the collective goals of the American dream through public schooling have run up against almost insurmountable barriers when enough people believe (rightly or wrongly, with evidence or without) that those efforts will endanger the comparative advantage of their children or children like them. At that point a gap arises between their belief that every child deserves a quality education and their actions to benefit their own children over the long run.

Because most Americans now believe that the American dream should be available to all American citizens, public schools in the United States have made real progress toward enabling everyone to pursue success as they understand it. Compared with a few decades ago, dropout rates have fallen, achievement scores have risen, resources are more equally distributed, children with disabilities have the right to an appropriate education, and black children are not required by law to attend separate and patently inferior schools.

Yet this progress has met limits. Hispanics and inner city residents still drop out much more frequently than others, the gap between black and white achievement rose during the 1990s after declining in the previous decade, the achievement gap between students from lower- and higher-class families has barely budged, and poor students in poor urban schools have dramatically lower rates of literacy and arithmetic or scientific competence. Most importantly, life chances depend increasingly on attaining higher education, but class background is as important as ever in determining who attends and finishes a four-year college.

The gap between belief and action has emerged in different school districts at different times over different issues; education policy has therefore been not only contentious but confusing. Policymakers have pursued, with considerable support, one goal or set of goals for a while and then stopped or shifted emphasis; some policymakers have pursued a direction in one jurisdiction while their counterparts elsewhere have moved strongly in another. Some schools and districts seized upon orders to desegregate as an opportunity to institute desired reforms; others fought all efforts at desegregation and sought to minimize the changes it entailed. Some districts and states embrace public school choice and charter schools; others (or the same ones under different leadership) resist or ignore them. Some districts focus on basic skills while neighboring districts emphasize the teaching of higher-order thinking.

The gap between beliefs and actions not only leads to contention and confusion, it also generates policies that are irrational in the sense that they are inconsistent with evidence of what works or are not based on any evidence at all. At times policymakers have abandoned proven reforms or have promoted them only over stiff opposition. Desegregation enhanced the long-term life chances of many African American students and rarely hurt white students, but the movement to complete or maintain it has largely been over for 25 years. School finance reform broadens schooling opportunities for poor children without harming those who are better off, but equity in funding has depended mostly on the intervention of the courts. At other times policymakers have adopted reforms for which there is no empirical support or on the basis of conflicting assessments. There is at best mixed evidence of the benefits of separating students according to academic achievement or language ability, but the former is almost universal and the latter is widespread. And charter schools or private school choice programs have been widely advocated without convincing evidence that they make any difference at all.

Irrational policymaking can be explained by the fact that public officials have made their choices at least partly on the basis of claims that pursuing collective goals of the American dream could endanger or has endangered the individual achievement of privileged children. Under pressure they have been willing to sacrifice the wider objectives or put them at risk for the sake of the narrower ones, whether or not there was good evidence that the objectives really were in conflict.

This irrationality is most apparent when it comes to reforms that could have the greatest impact and that have the soundest research support. Where it has been tried, educating poor children *with* students who are more privileged, or educating them *like* students who are more privileged, has improved their performance and long-term chance of success. Quality preschool, individual reading instruction, small classes in the early grades, and consistently challenging academic courses have been demonstrated to help disadvantaged children achieve, just as they enable middle-class children to achieve. Similarly, it helps all children to have peers who take school seriously, behave in ways that help them learn, and are backed by parents who have the resources to ensure that schools satisfactorily educate their children. Most importantly, qualified, knowledgeable teachers make a difference. Well-off children almost always attend schools that have most of these features; poor children too frequently do not.

An honest attempt to secure a good education for poor children therefore leaves policymakers with two difficult choices. They can send them to schools with wealthier children, or they can, as a reasonable second best, seek to give them an education in their own neighborhood that has the features of schooling for well-off students. The former has proved so far to be too expensive politically, and the latter has often been too expensive financially. Americans want all children to have a real chance to learn, and they want all schools to foster democracy and promote the common good, but they do not want those things enough to make them actually happen.

Decisions about schooling also take place in a context that makes it hard to change anything and especially difficult to alter the structure of privilege. Unlike schooling in every other major industrialized country, public education in this country is democratic and deeply local. Despite the rhetoric of presidential candidates, it is not the federal government but states and localities that carry most of the burden of public education. Until recently local property taxes provided the bulk of the financing for public schools, and local officials still make most decisions about personnel and pedagogy. School assignments for students are based on local district or community residence; when com-

munities are divided not only by geography but also by race and class, as they
are in much of the United States, the schools will mirror these divisions.

Americans want neighborhood schools, decentralized decision making, and
democratic control. They see these devices in part as ways to ensure that schools
can accommodate distinctive community desires, and to give parents a greater
say about what goes on in them. Despite the fact that participation in school
elections is very low and information on which to base a vote is often scarce,
Americans will not surrender local control without a fight. They simply will
not permit distant politicians or experts in a centralized civil service to make
educational decisions. The reasons for this preference are complicated, including the incredible diversity of the population and the huge size of the country. Not least important, however, is the fact that local districts mirror and
reinforce separation by class and race. Democratic control, therefore, not only
provides support for public education but also creates a forum for the occasional exercise of bigotry and xenophobia; localism not only accommodates
community idiosyncrasies but also serves as a barrier to changes in the distribution of students and resources.

As these observations about localism suggest, the gap between belief in the
American dream and its practice has demographic and historical as well as individual and structural causes. In the United States, class is connected with race
and immigration; the poor are disproportionately African Americans or recent
immigrants, especially from Latin America. Legal racial discrimination was
abolished in American schooling during the last half century (an amazing accomplishment in itself), but prejudice and racial hierarchy remain, and racial
or ethnic inequities reinforce class disparities. This overlap adds more difficulties to the already difficult relationship between individual and collective
goals of the American dream, in large part because it adds anxieties about diversity and citizenship to concerns about opportunity and competition. The
fact that class and race or ethnicity are so intertwined and so embedded in the
structure of schooling may provide the greatest barrier of all to the achievement of the dream for all Americans, and helps explain much of the contention,
confusion, and irrationality in public education.

Public schools are essential to make the American dream work, but schools
are also the arena in which many Americans first fail. Failure there almost certainly guarantees failure from then on. In the dream, failure results from lack
of individual merit and effort; in reality, failure in school too closely tracks
structures of racial and class inequality. Schools too often reinforce rather than
contend against the intergenerational paradox at the heart of the American
dream. That is understandable but not acceptable.

The first chapter of this book expands on the themes we have introduced here;
it more closely examines the dilemmas created by the American dream, the education system in which those dilemmas must be addressed, and the structures

of inequality that make their amelioration so difficult and contentious. After that, the organization follows a rough chronology of major educational controversies over the last half century: we discuss school desegregation in chapter 2, school funding in chapter 3, school reform in chapter 4, school choice in chapter 5, the separation of students with distinctive characteristics in chapter 6, and challenges to the American dream by particular groups in chapter 7.

As we will see, some controversies such as those over racial integration and ability grouping show these goals in conflict; others, like those over creationism or Afrocentrism, can raise questions about the very legitimacy of the ideology itself. In this limited space, we cannot discuss any of these issues comprehensively. Instead we provide a brief history of each, analyze current controversies in light of the goals of the American dream, and evaluate evidence about the likely impact of particular changes in education policy. Each of the substantive chapters looks at how the tensions and paradox within the American dream affect not only the way people think about educational disputes but also the way they act on them, which is often very different. In the final chapter, we draw together our recommendations and assess the impact of the changing racial and ethnic makeup of the United States on the future of these issues.

This is not the usual approach to considering education policy in this country. Most books on education are written about one subject considered in isolation. Most politicians focus on one or two issues that rise to the top of the polls, have some kind of symbolic value, or reinforce the overall image they wish to convey. The education debate in recent years has mostly focused on two such issues, first vouchers and then standards and accountability. The first is largely a false and marginal issue, involving very few students and not fully embraced even by many of its advocates, who do not really want city children to be able to attend suburban schools. The push for vouchers is mainly part of a broader attempt to redefine the relationship between individuals and the state, to make people think more like consumers in a market than citizens in a democracy. We seek here to bring the emphasis back to the role of public schools in creating both good citizens and successful people.

The second recent debate, about standards and accountability, is central to the concern of most people for the quality of their schools and the progress of their children. The standards movement is a reasonable attempt to bring coherence to a system shaken by the substantive and financial reforms of the 1970s and 1980s; the creation of standards in all states but one has enabled a much higher level of accountability throughout the system. It has also, however, created the temptation for politicians to talk tough and test incessantly, sometimes with high stakes for the students who are least responsible for their poor education. So far the debate has too often ignored the hard issues raised when equal demands are made on students who have unequal chances to meet them. Those issues require serious consideration of the structure and purposes of education in this country, and the consequences of wealth inequality as well as ethnic and racial inequality. This book tries to bring those issues back to the table.

Like everyone who writes about schooling in the United States, we start from a set of beliefs. American educators should promote both core values—success for each one and the collective good of all. (In any case, the goals are so deeply embedded in American beliefs and practices that it does not make sense to try to contest them.) We do not believe that either core value should be completely dominant: too much attention to individual success leads to atomistic selfishness, and too much attention to the collective good can lead to populist despotism. We share some of the concerns of those who seek distinctive group treatment or who reject the American dream, but we find their alternatives to be deeply problematic; too much attention to group identity can lead to fragmentation, harm to the groups most in need of help, and mutual antagonism.

We also start from a conviction that the *public* nature of public education needs to be protected and strengthened. With a few tragic exceptions, parents can be trusted to promote the interests of their children. Some will succeed more than others, fairly or not, but the value of individual success will not lose its motivating force. Similarly, advocates can be trusted to work energetically on behalf of their group, whether they seek fuller inclusion of "their" students in, or treatment separate from, the mainstream. They too will enjoy varying degrees of success, but their commitment and pressure will persist. In contrast, there are by definition few whose principal concern is to promote the collective good. Fostering the community aspects of the American dream is the job of policymakers and public officials, despite the fact that they too have mixed incentives and competing values. Representatives of the government have a special duty to cultivate community goals, both to preserve the ability of government to act and to keep the good of the nation as a whole from being submerged by self-interest and unfairly distributed power.

In short, even if one supports the two core values equally or supports group values as well, we believe that public officials and public-spirited citizens should work to improve the quality of education for everyone while placing priority on the collective aspects of public education—on policies that promote mutual respect and interaction among students from different backgrounds, provide for greater inclusion, allocate resources more fairly in order to overcome disadvantage, and train students for democratic citizenship. We recognize that there are severe political limitations on some initiatives along these lines; despite those limitations, this is the right direction.

Though predictions are risky, we have a sense that coming demographic transformations may make policies to promote the collective good not only more urgent but also more feasible. As the much larger number of recent immigrants join African Americans in a slow move up economic and political ladders, they are likely to remain more connected to the disadvantaged in our society and to strengthen the movement for greater opportunity. As Americans see the possibility of real social fragmentation, many may become convinced of the need for education policies that help unite people and strengthen democratic values and practices. Americans have always asked public schools to be the main institution bringing together all the goals of their dream; the schools can never fully succeed in doing this, but they can do much better. In the new America, they can do more to help the dream function not at its mean-spirited worst but at its open-hearted best.

We do not expect to persuade every reader of our views or to settle all the controversial issues in education policy. Our central argument, after all, is that the widely accepted but conflicting goals of education are all legitimate, and that placing a priority on one or another is a matter of interest, conviction, and public position rather than truth. More than anything else, we seek to establish a framework that makes sense of the debate on these issues; in the end the relevant policy decisions can and should be made only through democratic deliberation.

I

WHAT AMERICANS WANT
FROM PUBLIC SCHOOLS

Nothing can more effectually contribute to the Cultivation and Improvement of a Country, the Wisdom, Riches, and Strength, Virtue and Piety, the Welfare and Happiness of a People, than a proper Education of youth, by forming their Manners, imbuing their tender Minds with Principles of Rectitude and Morality, [and] instructing them in . . . all useful Branches of liberal Arts and Science.

—Benjamin Franklin, 1749

I do not see any way to achieve a good future for our children more effectively than debating together and working together on how we educate the next generation. Children may be about 20 percent of the population, but they are 100 percent of the future.

—David Tyack, educational historian, 2001[1]

AMERICANS CONTINUE TO FOLLOW the advice of Benjamin Franklin in making "the proper education of youth" the most important American social policy. Public education uses more resources and involves more people than any other government program for social welfare. It is the main activity of local governments and the largest single expenditure of almost all state governments. Education is the American answer to the European welfare state, to massive waves of immigration, and to demands for the abolition of subordination based on race, class, or gender.

Although public schools in the United States are expected to accomplish a lot for their students, underlying all of these tasks is the goal of creating the conditions needed for people to believe in and pursue the ideology of the American dream. Our understanding of the American dream is the common one,[2] described by President Clinton this way: "The American dream that we were all raised on is a simple but powerful one—if you work hard and play by the rules you should be given a chance to go as far as your God-given ability will take you." The dream is the unwritten promise that all residents of the United

States have a reasonable chance to achieve success through their own efforts, talents, and hard work. Success is most often defined in material terms, but everyone gets to decide what it is for himself or herself. The first man to walk across Antarctica talks about this idea in the same way as people who make their first million: "The only limit to achievement," he said, "is the limit you place on your own dreams. Let your vision be guided by hope, your path be adventurous, and the power of your thoughts be directed toward the betterment of tomorrow."[3]

The American dream is a brilliant ideological invention, although, as we shall see, in practice it leaves much to be desired. Its power depends partly on the way it balances individual and collective responsibilities. The role of the government is to make the pursuit of success possible for everyone. This implies strict and complete nondiscrimination, universal education to provide the means for pursuing success, and protection for virtually all views of success, regardless of how many people endorse them. The state also has to create and preserve democratic institutions, including schools. Public schools must teach in ways that are broad enough to enable children to choose among alternative definitions of success, thorough enough to provide the skills they need to pursue their goals, and democratic enough to give them the habits and values needed to maintain the institutions and sustain the ideology of the dream. The polity, in short, has to create the conditions that make the dream appealing, possible, and viable for future generations.

Once the government provides this framework, individuals are on their own, according to the ideology. If schools teach the basics well, then there is no excuse for illiteracy; if schools provide civic education and democratic training, there is no excuse for bad citizenship. Put more positively, once the polity ensures a chance for everyone, it is up to individuals to go as far and fast as they can in whatever direction they choose. As President Clinton continued in the speech quoted above, "Most of all, we believe in individual responsibility *and* mutual obligation; that government must offer opportunity to all and expect something from all, and that whether we like it or not, we are all in this battle for the future together."

The direct question "Do you believe in the American dream?" elicits a positive response from at least three-fourths of the population.[4] People define the fruits of the dream in various ways, but almost all include enough money to care for themselves and their family, freedom and opportunity to choose their life course, good family relationships and friends, a meaningful job, and the feeling that they are "making or doing things that are useful to society."[5] Individual goals predominate in these surveys, but collective goals have strong support. Ninety percent of Americans agree that "equal opportunity for people regardless of their race, religion, or sex" is "absolutely essential" as an American ideal, and the same huge proportion agree that "our society should do what is necessary to make sure that everyone has an equal opportunity to succeed."[6] Questions measuring belief in democracy, diversity, and citizenship training also elicit strong support. Just as many young as old claim to "believe in the American dream," and those under 50 agree slightly more than those over 50 that our society should ensure everyone an equal opportunity to succeed.

Americans want the educational system to help translate the American dream from vision to practice. Campaign rhetoric, results from public opinion polls, and advertisements constantly make the connection. A recent ad for Amway Corporation, for example, featured a photogenic 13-year-old immigrant declaring that the American dream is "starting over, a new life. Exploring. And enjoying it!" To get there, he said, "you need hope. You have to know how to learn." President George W. Bush made the same point, less succinctly: "The quality of our public schools directly affects us all—as parents, as students, and as citizens. . . . If our country fails in its responsibility to educate every child, we're likely to fail in many other areas. But if we succeed in educating our youth, many other successes will follow throughout our country and in the lives of our citizens." Americans rank "prepar[ing] people to become responsible citizens" and "help[ing] people to become economically self-sufficient" highest among various possible purposes of public schooling.[7]

Schools are intended to benefit each person—as Benjamin Franklin put it, to provide "wisdom, riches, and strength, virtue and piety, welfare and happiness"—as well as to foster the "cultivation and improvement of a country." But even this is not all that Americans expect. At various points in American history and especially during the past decade, some people have also demanded that schools fulfill a third goal, satisfying the distinctive needs of particular groups. The desire to help some, even at the expense of one or all, rests on the belief that members of certain racial, ethnic, religious, or gender groups cannot be full participants in American society unless their group identity is publicly recognized and they are treated differently from other citizens. Sometimes members of a group believe that they cannot pursue their dreams unless they are separated from others profoundly different from themselves, and in a few cases group members reject the American dream altogether. For these reasons, for example, African American citizens obtained Afrocentric schools for black students in cities such as Milwaukee and Detroit, and the Plymouth Brethren Church in Michigan sought separate public school entrances, classrooms, and lunchrooms in order "to provide for the instruction and well-being of our children in the face of the continuing decline in moral judgment and values."[8] Most Americans, however, show little support for this goal, and it is the most controversial in practice. (Afrocentric schools have been picketed and threatened, and the Plymouth Brethren were denied their request.) Nevertheless, the goal of fostering the good of a particular group affects public schools out of proportion to its support because of the passion of its advocates and broader sympathy for their grievances.

For the last half century, controversies over education policy have largely resulted from the efforts of Americans to put all three goals into educational practice.[9] Most people believe in the two core goals and seek to balance or reconcile them, but different people place priority on one or the other. A few people place priority on helping a particular group that resists the American dream, and then citizens must weigh the dream against some other set of ideals. Some conflicts created by these multiple goals may reflect the contradictory or hypocritical views of individual Americans, but those are beyond our focus here. There is more than enough to concern us if we treat these disagreements as honest attempts to deal with competing values, as we will see when we look more closely at the goals themselves.

The Success of Individuals

Good schools should and can help individuals attain success. Virtually all Americans share that belief. Almost everyone sees the mastery of basic skills as the core of schooling, endorses teachers and principals who will "push students to . . . excel," and wants every student to be given a chance to complete high school.[10]

Beyond that, however, "success" has several meanings. It may be *absolute*—reaching some level of well-being higher than where one started. Absolute success is, in principle, available to everyone. In schooling it would consist in teaching all students some of the skills they need to live satisfactory adult lives, such as literacy and numeracy, the ability to find and use information, the ability to plan and discipline oneself, and the pleasure of exercising one's mind. For all individuals to achieve absolute success would be a triumph indeed; no society has attained it. Pursuing this goal can be controversial because it can require providing more educational resources to some students than others so that all may succeed regardless of initial talent or family resources.

For most people, however, absolute success is not enough. They seek *relative* success—attaining more than someone else such as one's parents or classmates. Relative success is egalitarian if it applies an equal standard of measurement to all, but it is not egalitarian in the sense that some individuals will do better than others. Most Americans assume that if schools are doing their job, their children will end up better off than their parents or most classmates. (They seldom consider the possibility of ending up worse off.)

Some parents go even farther and expect schools to provide their children with an advantage over other children. As one parent argued during a dispute in Boulder, Colorado, "No one active in his or her child's education . . . needs to apologize for trying to get what they want for their kid. . . . If the school district has a problem with that, so be it."[11] School district boundaries help to provide such an advantage when they follow neighborhood lines that separate wealthy children from those who are poor and often nonwhite; school financing schemes have this effect when they are based on local property value and thereby create or maintain a privileged competitive position for wealthier children at the expense of the others. Tracking provides advantages when the best teachers or the most resources are devoted to a high track disproportionately filled with wealthier students. Such practices produce *competitive* success, in which the success of some implies the failure of the others. Competitive success may include an initially equal chance to seek victory, but beyond that starting point, opportunities are taken and advantages used, not redistributed to those with fewer.

Americans also disagree on what counts as success, and thus on what curricula and other school activities will help their students achieve it. In the view of some people, schools are supposed to nurture the thirst for knowledge while teaching students how to slake it. They share the Puritans' view that "the mind of man is a vast thing, it can take in, and swallow down Heaps of Knowledge, and yet is greedy after more; it can grasp the World in its conception." In a recent survey, three in five Americans in fact agreed that schools must seek "to increase people's happiness and enrich their lives culturally and intellectually." In the same survey, however, fully four out of five also agreed that "help[ing] people to become economically self-sufficient" was a very important purpose of public schools. In this view schools are supposed to give students the tools they need to improve their status. This is more in tune with Benjamin Franklin, for whom "the Encouragements to Learning are . . . great . . . [because] a poor Man's Son has a chance, if he studies hard, to rise . . . to gainful Offices or Benefices . . . and even to mix his Blood with Princes."[12] Most schools try to satisfy both views, to fulfill both purposes of education, but must constantly balance their competing demands. The ideology of the American dream is agnostic on what counts as success, but this very neutrality leads to controversy over appropriate policy choices.

The Collective Good

Achieving one's dream would not be possible past one generation, or for many even within the first generation, if the ideology of the American dream did not include prescriptions for pursuing collective goals.[13] Creating and maintaining even a flawed democracy is hard work. The framework of the American dream depends on more than transmitting knowledge and skills; it depends on teaching students how to be good citizens and to work together for the common good.

One collective goal holds that schools must help to *provide equal opportunity* for all children. As we show in later chapters, surveys and budget decisions alike show that most Americans now agree, at least in principle, that schools should help offset the unfair disadvantages caused by disability, and should provide at least equal treatment to those with other difficulties such as those occasioned by poverty, lack of facility in English, or membership in a disfavored racial group. For some people this is a matter of simple justice and should not be controversial: "You'd be hard-pressed to find a single member of Congress who doesn't believe in full funding of IDEA [the Individuals with Disabilities Education Act]," says the Republican spokesman for the education committee of the House of Representatives. Others calculate that they do not want their children to have to confront the specter of second-class citizens and be asked to compensate for their social, economic, and political liabilities. A mother of an autistic child in California warns, "For the people who think, 'This is not my problem': it is. . . . We should spend our tax dollars in helping these families, not hindering their needs, so these children one day can be responsible tax-paying citizens, not burdens to our communities." [14]

To ensure that all can pursue their dreams, schools also have to help students acquire the *ability to deal with diverse others in the public arena.* Individual dreams and actions always vary and may conflict; schools need to teach people to respect the way other people view success. When our nation was founded, the most volatile dimensions of diversity were different Christian faiths and varying views of monarchical government. Since then, we have come to expect students to learn to cope with and even show consideration for visions of success affected by political views, class, region, race, ethnicity, gender, sexual orientation, and disability. Most people now agree with George Washington, who "greatly wished to see a plan adopted . . . [which], by assembling the youth . . . Will contribut[e] . . . from their intercourse and interchange of information to the removal of prejudices"—in modern language, to teach mutual respect by having students learn in the same classroom with others unlike themselves.[15] That is why public schools have always been under great pressure to admit all students within their designated districts; private schools were permitted to be parochial and selective, but public schools were not. (The greatest exception to this pattern, as we will see, was racial segregation.) Many schools are now expected to teach through a multicultural curriculum so that children will not merely tolerate each other, but also understand and appreciate varying backgrounds and aspirations.

Americans also want schools to turn individuals into democratic citizens who will act so that the necessary political, social, and economic conditions persist for future generations to pursue *their* dreams.[16] "Sadly," wrote one columnist, "most American young people know little about their heritage of freedom, and have little grasp of the responsibilities of citizenship." At least 70 percent of Americans agree that schools must "teach such values as honesty, respect, and civility," that "the percentage of high school graduates who practice good citizenship" is a very important measure of schools' success, and that schools should teach that "democracy is the best form of government." Seven out of ten endorse "requiring democracy education in Service and Civics as a graduation requirement" for all high school students.[17]

To turn students into democratic citizens, educators must provide students with *a common core of knowledge*. Americans abhor the (apocryphal?) boast of the French administrator that at 10:00 A.M. he could know just which page of Virgil all students of a certain age were construing throughout the nation. But they do generally agree that all students in the United States should end their schooling with some shared learning; almost all Americans agree that high school graduates must be able "to show they understand the common history and ideas that tie all Americans together."[18] Educators concur that graduates should not only know the outlines of American history, but also be able to communicate in English, be literate and arithmetically competent, and understand basic rules of politics and society, such as the purpose of elections and the meaning of the rule of law.

Closely allied with a common core of knowledge is the desire for students to graduate with a *common set of democratic values and practices*. After all, as the great sociologist Emil Durkheim put it, "School is the only moral agent through which the child is able systematically to learn to know and love his country. It is precisely this fact that lends pre-eminent significance to the part played by the school . . . in the shaping of national morality." The idea of common values can be controversial; nevertheless, almost two-thirds of people in the United States think schools must "promote cultural unity among all Americans" (and most of the rest think they should do so). More tellingly, studies of community meetings consistently find that "discussion of citizenship values . . . —the values and behaviors which are at the very core of the practice of democracy— . . . have the greatest potential for creating common ground" even among people bitterly divided over policy goals, according to a scholar at Northeastern University in Boston.[19] Americans typically want students to acquire political values such as loyalty to the nation, a belief in the rule of law and the Constitution, and an appreciation that rights sometimes trump majority rule and majority rule sometimes overrules intense desire. They want students to acquire social values such as the work ethic, self-reliance, and trustworthiness, and they want them also to acquire democratic habits like following fair rules, negotiating rather than using violence to secure their desires, respecting those who disagree, taking turns, expressing their views persuasively, organizing with others for change, competing fairly, and winning (or losing) gracefully. They also want students to incorporate, and practice, the tenets of the American dream itself.[20]

As with the pursuit of all three forms of individual success, these collective commitments have never been fully achieved for all students. Strong efforts to promote one or several of the community-oriented goals are likely to conflict with strong efforts to promote others of them; schools that focus on teaching all students a core curriculum, for example, may not be very adept at teaching students how to be active democratic citizens, and vice versa. But the deepest dilemmas for public schools lie not within but between the individual and collective goals for the schools, despite the fact that the goals for one and all are paired elements of the ideology of the American dream. And both core goals can conflict with a third, more contentious, demand focused on the special conditions of some.

The Welfare of Groups

Particular groups make claims to distinctive treatment in schools for two reasons. First, those acting on behalf of children who were treated unfairly because of some shared characteristic have demanded the right to have the group recognized and treated differently, so that in the end all groups will end up with equal opportunity for schooling. In the nineteenth century, reformers made the radical claim that girls deserved access to public schooling as much as boys did, and a few even asserted that African Americans or Native Americans had the same right. In the mid-twentieth century, *Brown v. Board of Education* held that black children in a public education system had a constitutional right to participate on the same terms as white children. This demand for equal opportunity, inclusion, and respect fits squarely within the American dream.

At other times, however, people have insisted that a particular group must be treated *differently* if it is to get an equal education. In some cases this has meant separate schooling within the public system to fit the group's perspectives, in others changing the practices of existing schools in deference to the group. In the nineteenth century, Catholic leaders protested the Protestant pedagogy of the new "public" schools; if schools would not be religiously neutral, they should teach Catholic doctrine to Catholic children or provide funds for a parallel system of Catholic schools. A century later, some people call for separate, extended bilingual education to help immigrant children maintain their native culture. Some African Americans argue that only if members of their race run their schools or only if curricula are designed specifically for their children will blacks enjoy the same autonomy, respect, and cultural self-definition that whites have always had.

Whether claims for differential treatment fit comfortably within the ideology of the American dream depends on the specific views of the claimants. To the degree, for example, that Afrocentrists are motivated by a rejection of European-American values, their separatism will be in opposition to the ideology of the dream. To the degree, conversely, that proponents believe that immigrant children will best achieve their dreams as Americans by learning in their native language, they may fit within the flexible boundaries of the ideology. But a strong demand that one group's identity be respected is highly volatile. Sooner or later (probably sooner), it is likely to be discordant with the demands of other groups; it is certain to conflict at some point with the priorities of the majority who remain focused on the core collective and individual goals.

The Goals in Practice

Americans who have thought most carefully about the purposes of public education have generally believed, in accord with the American dream, that neither core goal should supersede the other. Thomas Jefferson offered six "objects of primary education" that included both goals in order "to instruct the mass of our citizens in these, their rights, interests, and duties, as men and citizens." The first three objects identify types of individual success: "to give to every citizen the information he needs for the transaction of his own business"; "to enable him to calculate for himself, and to express and preserve his ideas, his contracts and accounts, in writing"; and "to improve, by reading, his morals and faculties." Two focus on participation in the public arena: "to understand his duties to his neighbors and country, and to discharge with competence the functions confided to him by either"; and "to observe with intelligence and faithfulness all the social relations under which he shall be placed." The final one combines both goals: "to know his rights; to exercise with order and justice those he retains; to choose with discretion the fiduciary of those he delegates; and to notice their conduct with diligence, with candor, and judgment."[21] Jefferson used these principles to design an elaborate system of public elementary and secondary education for all (white, male) children of Virginia. It was to be publicly subsidized for those who could not afford it.

Almost 200 years later, the Supreme Court echoed Jefferson in a court case called *Plyler v. Doe*: the American people "have recognized 'the public schools as a most vital civic institution for the preservation of a democratic system of government,' and as the primary vehicle for transmitting 'the values on which our society rests.' . . . In addition, education provides the basic tools by which individuals might lead economically productive lives." More recent court cases use similar language. "[A] thorough and efficient [education] means more than teaching the skills needed in the labor market," said the New Jersey supreme court in a landmark 1990 decision on school finance. "It means being able to fulfill one's role as a citizen, a role that encompasses far more than merely registering to vote."[22]

Some school practices can in fact foster the two basic values, or even all three, simultaneously. Helping students to learn as much as they can both enables them to pursue their dreams and increases the chance that the brightest will benefit the nation through discoveries, insights, or leadership. Ensuring that all students are verbally and mathematically competent helps them to live satisfying lives at the same time that it makes them better democratic citizens.

Teaching immigrant students to speak English makes them more likely to succeed in mainstream society and reinforces the cultural core so essential to a huge and diverse democracy. Showing respect for those outside the racial or cultural mainstream encourages them to pursue their own distinctive dreams while broadening the sensibilities of all students. Providing resources to incorporate children with disabilities in regular classrooms might be the best way to offset their disadvantages as well as to teach other students to accommodate difference.

In the day-to-day practice of schooling, however, fostering what is good for all may divert resources from one or some; what shows respect for the identity of some may violate the convictions of others or reduce the commitment of students to the common core; what encourages success for the brightest or luckiest may deny opportunity for the slowest or unluckiest. When priorities must be determined—under pressure from demographic change, political demands, fiscal limits, global competition, competing values, or fear—one goal or another is likely to win out.

Previous trade-offs themselves shape the context within which new choices must be made. In the first decades of the last century, many citizens saw immigration as a frightening challenge to the American way of life and demanded that schools be transformed in order to "Americanize" these future citizens. In the 1950s anxieties about the Soviet Union led to a focus on enhancing achievement for the apparently brightest students. By the 1960s emphasis shifted to creating equality of opportunity. In the 1980s, with many people fearing economic challenges from abroad and reduced opportunities for success at home, attention shifted again to individual achievement and parents engaged in ever more intense competition for advantage in educational or fiscal resources. Most recently demands for group respect that started as a drive for integration in the 1960s have sometimes been transformed into advocacy for separate schools or distinct treatment within common schools.

Regardless of the motivations behind each movement, the combination of multiple goals, competing interests, and a fragmented governance structure has often made policies incoherent and decisions unstable. As one goal takes precedence and then is replaced by another, some policies, institutions, and practices continue to function well in the new environment. Others, however, become relics that create an inappropriate policy emphasis, use a disproportionate amount of resources, or otherwise distort the system. Too much bureaucracy may remain from Progressive era attempts to deal with demographic change; too much willingness to accept inequality, or to jettison public schooling entirely, may be the legacy of fear of international competition from the 1980s; too much separatism may be the consequence of the newest demand for group rights and respect. Each particular goal fits within, or at least need not contradict, the overall ideology of the American dream. But they can get in each other's way and generate intense conflict when priorities have to be set. In particular, the individual goals too often take precedence over the collective goals, as we shall demonstrate over the next five chapters.

The Centrality of Public Education

The intensity of conflicts over how to balance shared but competing goals is a good barometer of how much Americans care about public education. They care so much, as we have said, because education is at the core of the dominant American ideology; it is essential both to create the democratic structure of which Americans are so proud and to provide the tools for the success that Americans seek so passionately. By no coincidence education is also a huge public undertaking, and the size of the enterprise itself increases the opportunities for disagreement, raises the stakes, and heightens the level of concern.

Because the United States does not provide the kind of family support, employment assistance, health insurance, or public child care available in France or Germany or Sweden, social scientists often describe America as a welfare laggard. In those countries these services were established sooner, encompass more of the population, and absorb more of the national wealth than in the United States. But the United States is a welfare leader with regard to schooling; here public schools started earlier and have always included more people and taken a larger share of resources. This difference in approach reflects a crucial difference in ideology. Europeans believe more strongly that the state should ensure a decent standard of living for all its citizens; Americans believe more strongly that it is the duty of the state to provide opportunity and then the job of each citizen to earn an appropriate standard of living.[23]

In the middle of the nineteenth century, the United States' elementary school enrollment rate was roughly double that of every European country except Germany. By the turn of the twentieth century, when the largest European nations had caught up to the United States in early schooling, the United States began to move ahead on high schools. As two Harvard economists point out, "When, during World War II, President Roosevelt formulated the GI Bill of Rights to fund college for millions of Americans, his counterpart in Great Britain, Prime Minister Churchill, was given a bill that granted youth the right to free secondary school education."[24] By now virtually all developed nations have caught up to or even passed the United States in secondary schooling, but Americans are still more likely to attain higher education than are residents of most other countries. Just over a quarter of adult Americans have completed college, compared with only 14 percent of Germans, 9 percent of Italians, and 19 percent of Canadians.[25]

The United States remains one of the highest spenders on education even as its rank in spending on other social welfare policies has slipped over the past few decades. In fact, the United States ranks higher than all but three nations

(Denmark, Switzerland, and Austria) in annual expenditures per K-12 student. In choosing to spend so much on schooling, American policymakers are acting exactly in accord with public preferences; education is the only issue in the arena of social welfare policies for which Americans are much more supportive than residents of other welfare states.[26] Americans are also much more likely than Europeans to rank as "essential" almost any school subject that they are asked to evaluate. They are especially focused on skills needed for individual achievement, but they also want schools to teach citizenship skills more than do Europeans.[27] Americans pay a lot for education, and they expect a lot.

Schools in the United States absorb a huge share of the nation's public outlay of funding, employment, and contracting. In 1999, almost seven million people held full- or part-time jobs in public elementary and secondary schools; they constitute more than half of all local governmental employees.[28] This also represents a large share of all the jobs in many cities; public schools are the second-largest employment sector in Los Angeles County and Gary, Indiana, and the largest employer in Baltimore.[29] Since most public school employees are highly organized, and since policy choices have high stakes for them, schooling can involve all of the special-interest advocacy, all the lobbying, and all the political maneuvering of any other big business.

And schooling is big business. *Fortune* magazine publishes an annual list of the largest companies in the United States; if the public school system of California alone were one of those companies, it would rank twenty-second. That is slightly higher than Metropolitan Life Insurance and slightly lower than Hewlett-Packard. About 47 million children are in public K-12 schools, almost 90 percent of the school-age children in the United States. In 2001, it cost about $390 billion a year from all sources to educate them—more than defense and not too much less than social security.[30] Almost a quarter of all state expenditures go to K-12 schools.[31]

Unlike in other comparable nations, education in the United States is intensely local. There are over 92,000 public schools, located in almost 15,000 school districts in every community in the country. Districts are governed by local board members who are either elected or appointed by elected officials. America's geographic and demographic diversity, its citizens' distrust of central government, its preference for local democracy, and the grassroots origin and development of its public schools have led to this fragmented and decentralized educational governance system. The Supreme Court has provided its most elegant justification: "The public educator's task is weighty and delicate indeed. It demands particularized and supremely subjective choices among diverse curricula, moral values, and political stances to teach or inculcate in students, and among various methodologies for doing so. Accordingly, we have traditionally reserved the 'daily operation of school systems' to the states and their local school boards."[32] In the early 1990s, 60 percent of Americans agreed that it is "very important for educational decisions to be made by the schools themselves"; in the other member nations of the Organization for Economic Cooperation and Development (OECD, the most developed nations), comparable percentages ran from 17 in Spain to 49 in France and Portugal.[33]

Local districts raise almost half the money used to support schools, and most of the rest comes from state revenues. In contrast to most other nations, unlike most other social policies in the United States, and despite the claims of presidents and presidential candidates, the federal government is not a major actor here; it provides only 8 percent of the money spent on schools and dedicates barely 2 percent of its budget to schooling. At this level it can issue mandates for change and provide some help, but it cannot implement programs or provide services that make a difference to a large number of students; states and local districts have to do those things.

In this context conflicts over educational policies, priorities, and practice are inevitable. Because schooling is so central to cherished values in this country, people care intensely about the outcome of educational disputes; because it is so expensive, powerful interest groups have high stakes in the way disputes are resolved. Public officials at three or four levels of government often have different views of the same policy problem; school officials in thousands of districts are affected differently by the solutions. Since school district boundaries are so deeply entangled in patterns of race and class, issues of educational inequality and separation are volatile and sometimes intractable. It is, however, the structure of inequality in the United States that presents the most direct educational challenge to the American dream.

The Structure of Inequality in Education

Some schools provide a first-rate education. But some are terrible: "For years, it was like storming the Bastille every day," says one urban teacher.[34] Some schools are blessed with well-fed children; others struggle to teach children who lack the basic amenities. In some districts virtually all students are at least second-generation Americans; in others many of the students have recently immigrated from dozens of nations. Some districts have their pick of the best teachers; others count themselves lucky to have any warm body in front of the classrooms come September. Huge disparities in education spending persist, and some states or districts spend twice as much as others.

In Newton North High School in Massachusetts, the students are mostly affluent and white. Ninety-nine percent graduate, 88 percent take the SATs, 80 percent plan to attend a four-year college, 32 students were National Merit finalists or semifinalists in one year, and an additional 45 won National Merit letters of commendation. The school offers courses in 5 languages (as well as English as a second language), 14 Advanced Placement or college credit courses, and 34 fine arts courses. It has 3 student-run publications, 26 sports teams, and a wide variety of other extracurricular programs ranging from Amnesty International to a ski club and ROTC. Students at Newton North have the opportunity to pursue their dreams.

On the other side of the country, a school in San Diego presents a different picture. Ninety percent of the children in this school are poor, 40 percent have limited English proficiency, many move frequently. A third of the teachers are brand new, and two of the twenty are out on "stress disability" leave. A recent evaluation of the school found that it needed a nurse, a counselor, facilities for parents and preschool children, and an adult literacy program. The principal claims that "we've pulled together, and we're going to do the best we can,"[35] but her chances of success seem slim. The children in her school will probably have little chance to pursue their dreams.

This kind of variation across students and districts is not random; students live in a system of nested inequalities. The first level is statewide. Students' educational outcomes depend a lot on which state they are born in. Children in Massachusetts, like those in Iowa, New Jersey, or North Dakota, have more than a 50 percent likelihood of enrolling in college by age 19, but children in Florida, Arizona, Alaska, and Nevada have less than a 30 percent chance. The discrepancy in college attendance by state is even greater for children from low-income families.[36] In 1998–1999, schools in Massachusetts spent an average of $8,750 per student, schools in New Jersey over $10,700. But schools in California spent only $6,050 per student, and those in Utah just under $4,500. Fewer than 3 percent of students in Iowa, North Dakota, and Wisconsin drop out of school; more than 7 percent do in Louisiana, Arizona, Georgia, New Mexico, and Nevada. Overall, in fact, at least 30 percent of the variation in students' achievement is related to the state in which they live.[37]

Inequalities within a state can be just as great as those between the states. Newton is a high-spending district even for Massachusetts. In neighboring Connecticut the school district that spends the most per pupil provides almost twice as much funding as the district that spends the least. Districts vary a lot both in available resources and student needs; the poorest town in Connecticut has 150 times as many poor students as the wealthiest town. These differences have consequences for schooling outcomes. The district with the highest scores on the Connecticut Mastery Test does almost three times as well as the district with the lowest scores. In one district 40 percent of high school students drop out before graduating, but in others none do. In some districts almost all students continue their education beyond high school, but in others fewer than half do.[38]

In Connecticut as in other states, many, although not all, of these indicators of advantage or disadvantage are highly correlated. Districts with a lot of poor students have lower average test scores and higher dropout rates; districts with a lot of minority students, or a lot whose native language is not English, also have lower average test scores. (These districts are often the same.) The highest-spending districts report high test scores, and some of the lowest-spending districts report the lowest test scores, although the pattern in the middle-wealth districts is less clear.[39]

Schools vary greatly even within districts. In California in 1990, schools varied more within a given district than they did across districts as a whole. In Yonkers, New York, the subject of an important lawsuit over school and housing desegregation, schools in the city's northern and eastern section were built relatively recently and have beautiful grounds and excellent facilities; some schools in its southwestern section were built a century ago and have tiny playgrounds of cracked and slanted cement (or none at all) and dismal laboratories and libraries. In New York City, funding for regular students in elementary and middle schools varied by several thousand dollars per student in the late 1990s; per capita operating funds were particularly low in schools with many poor or immigrant students. In some New York grade schools, almost all of the teachers are certified, and in a few the pupil/teacher ratio is well below ten; in others only two out of five teachers are certified, or the ratio of students to teachers is close to 20. Schools with a lot of poor students or limited English speakers had significantly fewer certified teachers and higher student/teacher ratios. In some New York schools, most students perform at least at the fiftieth percentile in reading tests, but in others barely one-seventh do.[40]

Finally, the classes taken within a school matter a lot. Most high schools sort students by perceived or measured ability, and well-off children almost always dominate the high groups. Children with disabilities or students with limited English proficiency are not likely to be in high-ability groups regardless of their actual abilities. Typically the best teachers, the smallest classes, and the most resources go to the high groups, and to mainstream or English-speaking classes.

Students therefore sit at the center of four or more nested structures of inequality and separation—states, districts, schools, classes, and special needs. Well-off or white parents usually manage to ensure that their children obtain the benefits of this structure; poor and non-Anglo parents have a much harder time doing so.

Inequalities in family wealth are a major cause of inequalities in schooling, and inequalities of schooling do much to reinforce inequalities of wealth among families in the next generation—that is the intergenerational paradox described in the introduction. The effects are far-reaching; by the 1980s economic class mattered as much as race or ethnicity in determining who attended a four-year college, and who was admitted to the most selective among them.[41] The effects may even be increasing. Parents' income became less important in determining how much schooling a child received until roughly 1980, but its impact has grown since then. For example, 29 percent of the poorest quarter of high school graduates enrolled in a four-year college in the early 1980s, compared with 55 percent of the richest quarter. By a decade later, however, the proportion of poor students who enrolled in college had declined marginally while the proportion of the well-off who enrolled had increased considerably, to 66 percent.[42]

Class differences affect not only college attendance but also basic reading ability. A recent literacy test in OECD nations revealed that the gap between the best and worst readers was wider in the United States than anywhere else; the bottom fifth in America read more poorly than the bottom fifth in every other nation except Canada.[43]

Outcomes of schooling increasingly matter because they are becoming linked more closely to a person's financial and political success. In 1979 college-educated men who worked full time earned 29 percent more than full-time workers with only a high school diploma; by 1998 that gap had increased to 68 percent. (Among women the comparable wage gap increased from 43 percent to 79 percent.) Over this period men who graduated from college enjoyed real wage gains of 8 percent, but men who only graduated from high school *lost* 18 percent of what they would have earned formerly. The wage gap is growing in most nations, but in almost all cases at a lower rate than in the United States. In the late 1990s, only Portugal, Hungary, and the Czech Republic among OECD nations showed greater inequality than the United States between earnings of high school dropouts and earnings of college graduates.[44]

California provides a good example of how much more schooling matters now than it used to. In 1969 dropouts earned about $31,000; by 1996 their wages had dropped to $17,000—a loss of almost half their yearly earnings. But workers with a postgraduate degree saw their incomes rise from about $58,000 in 1969 to about $73,000 27 years later—a gain of about a quarter.[45] That is a big difference in both directions.

Education also powerfully affects people's involvement with politics and their community, thereby creating another link between the nested structure of inequalities in schooling and the American dream. As one of our nation's foremost scholars of political participation concludes, "The best predictor of political activity is education. . . . Education fosters activity through its effect on information, skills, values, resources, networks, and more. No wonder it is so potent. Furthermore, the potency grows after education ends." Well-educated citizens, not surprisingly, show greater understanding of the principles of democratic government than others. They are better able to identify local and national leaders and more likely to know current political facts. They pay much closer attention to political life and are more tolerant of those with unpopular political views. They are also much more likely to vote than those with little education; the disparity in voting between high school dropouts and graduates has widened since the 1960s.[46] The relationship between education and the likelihood of engaging in political activity is, in fact, closer in the United States than in almost all other industrialized democracies.[47]

Education, then, makes a difference in realizing both core goals of the American dream, in some ways more than ever. The deep and growing structural inequalities embedded in the system represent a powerful challenge to its realization.

The Biggest Challenge

Not surprisingly, the structure of nested inequalities creates the worst problems in the schools in large, poor central cities (and in some small rural schools as well). In the 100 largest school districts, almost 70 percent of the students are non-Anglo (compared with 40 percent of students nationally), and over half are poor or near-poor (compared with fewer than 40 percent nationally).[48] Cities often have fewer resources to help those students than do wealthier suburbs. They have larger schools and larger classes, as well as less adequate buildings, classrooms, and technology. Compared with suburban districts, teachers in city schools are less likely to be certified or to have studied in the areas that they teach, have less experience, and are more likely to leave before the end of the school year. These schools suffer from much more administrative and behavioral turmoil and have a higher level of disruption, violence, and anxiety about safety. All of the districts with high dropout rates are in large cities. Urban children have much lower test scores than nonurban children, and they perform less well on measures of civic training.[49] For young non-Anglo men in Philadelphia in the 1990s, attending a neighborhood public high school rather than a magnet school had a "devastating effect" on their incomes as adults, according to two urban sociologists. It is not hard to see why when we listen to the ruling of the trial court in the ongoing school finance case in New York City:

> City public school students' graduation/dropout rates and performance on standardized tests demonstrate that they are not receiving a minimally adequate education. This evidence becomes overwhelming when coupled with the extensive evidence, discussed above, of the inadequate resources provided the City's public schools. The majority of the City's public school students leave high school unprepared for more than low-paying work, unprepared for college, and unprepared for the duties placed upon them by a democratic society. The schools have broken a covenant with students and with society.[50]

In short, the worst-off students and schools have a completely different educational experience from the best-off, and the outcomes are predictably very different. Those differences are growing, and racial and class inequalities remain intertwined. During the 1970s and 1980s, the gap in the quality of schools attended by blacks and whites worsened, entirely because poor inner-city schools and schools with fewer than 20 percent of whites deteriorated so much. In fact, black students in nonurban schools actually did better during this period, even while black students in urban schools were doing worse. Similarly, during the 1990s, the most accomplished quarter of fourth grade readers improved their test scores on the National Assessment of Educational Progress (NAEP), while the least accomplished quarter lost even more ground. The top scorers were mostly white, the low scorers were disproportionately black and Latino boys in poor urban schools.[51]

Class disparities among school districts are growing as communities and even whole regions become more economically homogeneous. In 1970 the typical affluent American lived in a neighborhood where two-fifths of the residents were also affluent; 20 years later that figure had climbed to over half. Conversely, the proportion of poor people living in poor neighborhoods in inner cities has increased. In the two decades after 1970, in every one of 48 cities in the largest metropolitan areas, from the poorest in comparison to its suburbs (Hartford, Connecticut) to the wealthiest (Greensboro, North Carolina), the disparity in wealth between city and suburbs grew worse.[52] Most importantly here, in the decade after 1982 economic disparities between school districts rose, whether measured by household income, poverty rates, or rates of housing vacancy. There remains a close relationship between the number of poor people and the number of African Americans and Hispanics in a community. Nevertheless, separation by income has grown substantially in American communities during the same decades that separation by race and ethnicity has declined, at about the same rate.[53]

High and growing economic similarity within communities undermines the collective goals of the American dream for all students as well as individual goals for students in poor districts. It makes it much more difficult, in many cases impossible given district boundaries, for poor students to be educated with middle-class students. They therefore miss out on the good facilities and high-quality teachers that students in middle-class districts are more likely to enjoy, and they are denied the benefits of middle-class peers. That is a severe loss; one of the few things we know for certain about schooling is that the class background of a student's classmates has a dramatic effect on that student's level of success. The sociologist James Coleman said it first and best almost 40 years ago: "A pupil's achievement is strongly related to the educational backgrounds and aspirations of the other students in the school. . . . [C]hildren from a given family background, when put in schools of different social compositions, will achieve at quite different levels." This finding has been documented over and over in various countries and schools and with different methodologies and sets of data. In one dramatic example, well-off students in mostly poor schools performed worse on reading tests than did poor students in mostly middle-class schools.[54] Direct efforts to integrate poor and better-off students, nevertheless, have been few and far between and have proven very difficult to accomplish.[55]

It is the schools attended mostly by poor, disproportionately black and Latino, urban children that provide the evidence for those who see an educational crisis in the United States, and the schools of the more affluent, mostly white, children that provide most of the success stories. Despite Americans' belief in the collective goals of public education, and despite the importance of those goals to maintaining the American dream, disparities in outcomes among schools may have worsened in recent years even as absolute levels of educational attainment and achievement have improved. In the words of one careful urban sociologist, "Whether intentional or not, the process [of class concentration] represents a retreat from the concept of community and has very serious long-run implications for American society."[56] Those implications begin in school.

2

SCHOOL DESEGREGATION

[In America,] nature and liberty affords us that freely, which in England we
want. . . . Every man may be master and owner of his owne labour and land.
[Colonists] thinke it but reason, . . . [that] no Lawes . . . should bee inacted
here without their consents, because they onely feele them, and must live under them. [Here, a man] out of every extremity, . . . found himselfe now borne
to a new life.

—Captain John Smith, 1616

We didn't land on Plymouth Rock, my brothers and sisters—Plymouth Rock
landed on *us*.

—Malcolm X, 1965[1]

RACIAL DOMINATION WAS, FROM THE OUTSET, the most glaring flaw in
the ideology of the American dream. It began when the dream began,
with Captain John Smith's move to the "New World" in 1607. In his
comments are all the elements of the American dream: equal opportunity for
all, a chance of success for each, control over our nation's political and economic future, and virtue, since America was "as God made it when hee created
the world." But enslaved Africans, who arrived in Virginia soon after Smith
did, were not "borne to a new life"—or at least not one that allowed participation in the American dream. They were brought into, not out of, "every extremity." And that terrible irony, the simultaneous invention of American
slavery and American freedom,[2] has shaped American society ever since. It has
shaped its public schools as well.

Desegregation has been our nation's most direct effort since Reconstruc-
tion to come to grips with the evils of racial domination in public schooling.
Beginning in the mid-1960s, it was the first as well as one of the largest postwar efforts to make America's schooling practices fit its ideals. Many of the issues that we discuss in later chapters, such as funding equalization, school
reform, the separation of children, and distinctive group treatment, are in part

extensions of the successes of school desegregation or reactions to its perceived failures. Controversy over desegregation showed the difficulty in trying to satisfy both the individual and collective goals of the American dream; the experience demonstrated both the power of the ideology and the intractability of its internal conflicts. It continues to reverberate throughout American schooling and society.

School desegregation was, on balance, an educational success. Its accomplishments were smaller than its advocates promised and less than they hoped for, but except when done irresponsibly or very unwisely, it improved the chances for black children to attain their dreams and did not diminish the chances for white children. Members of both races usually gained socially from the interaction. If it were politically feasible, a continued effort along these lines would be educationally beneficial. Ending legal segregation in schools and other public facilities, fostering real, not just legal, desegregation, did more to move the American dream from ideology to practice than has any other public policy or private effort.

Nevertheless, the effort to desegregate schools is largely over; mandatory desegregation was a political failure. A member of the education committee for the Minnesota senate speaks for many when he says, "I don't think it's worked anywhere that it's been tried."[3] The evidence clearly shows that he is wrong; the social and educational benefits were real. The serious efforts to desegregate the schools that began in the mid-1960s, however, ended barely a decade later, and many school districts are now undoing the changes they made then.

Arguments about the virtues and flaws of desegregation have revolved around the two basic goals of the American dream in public schooling. Advocates argued that denying the opportunity for integration to African Americans harmed their individual chances for success. The Supreme Court in the 1954 decision of *Brown v. Board of Education* made the most famous observation on the individual costs of segregation: "To separate [children in schools] from others of a similar age and qualifications solely because of their race generates a feeling of inferiority as to their status in the community that may affect their hearts and minds in a way unlikely ever to be undone." The Court held, therefore, that separate education was "inherently unequal." Later proponents focused on the fact that separate education was not only inherently unequal, but also inevitably worse for those in the minority: "No matter what people say, when schools are one race, blacks get the bottom of the barrel. That cannot be acceptable," as a black resident of Richmond, Indiana, points out.[4]

Supporters of desegregation have also consistently argued that it was essential to the realization of the collective goals of the American dream, that it would benefit all of us, that it would remove an unforgivable barrier to equal opportunity and full participatory citizenship for all Americans. Recently the changing demography of this country has added additional force to these classic claims. "It's critical that we continue our desegregation effort," said a school official in Montclair, New Jersey. "The world is becoming a blacker, browner, poorer place where people speak more languages. It's important to prepare our kids to get along with people who are not like them." A recent graduate of the St. Louis schools makes the same point: "I hope in my heart that it [the inter-district transfer program] continues. If not, you're going to have kids who are all the same going to certain schools, and they're not going to be ready to go out into the world." A white investment banker concurs: "I didn't want our kids to grow up thinking their biggest decisions are whether to go to Bermuda or Cancún for Easter break. [In a desegregated school,] my kids have seen both sides."[5]

Opponents of desegregation have focused mostly on the individual harm that could be done to those forced to mix with black children, or poor black children, or urban black children. Most desegregation occurred within urban or suburban districts and was volatile enough; some occurred across district lines and was particularly explosive because it involved a threat to the local structure of privilege as well as long-standing practice. "I don't know how many kids could leave [urban schools] without compromising [our] suburban schools. How far am I willing to go [on desegregation]? Not real far," says one unusu-ally frank parent. Other critics have argued that it would undermine the col-lective goals of the American dream as well. David Armor, a sociologist who is a prominent opponent of mandatory desegregation, concludes that "while vir-tually all social scientists would agree that forced racial segregation is both un-constitutional and immoral, it has not been demonstrated that . . . desegregated schools by themselves produce consistent social and educational benefits; in some cases the consequences of desegregation may be harmful to race relations and black self-esteem."[6]

Some opponents believe that desegregation has centered on the wrong problem: "My issue is focusing on how to improve education for all children in this city," said the Boston school superintendent recently, "and not be dis-tracted or have a lot of energy and resources going into debates around stu-dent assignment." And finally, some still cherish the old ideal of the neighborhood school. "I'd love to have my child able to walk to school," says a mother in Boston. "I think it's important that you have that sense of com-munity. I'd have more involvement with the school if it's close to home."[7] Most poignantly, a man in Oklahoma City who has watched several generations of his family attend various kinds of schools, reflects that

we have happier children in this neighborhood without busing. If people are honest, they'll say there was some good to busing—the children got to meet other people. But in the educational arena, well, I think we had more prob-lems. Black teachers who nurtured the children, who put the emphasis on good behavior, discipline and doing schoolwork were gone. There was not training to show white teachers how to handle black kids. We integrated but there was no change in the hearts and minds of Caucasians.[8]

In short, to many Americans, desegregation was a failed social experiment. "No one who lived through the 1970s can forget the busing wars: the irate mothers, the innocent-looking black children, the bitter white teenagers throwing bottles and screaming, 'Niggers, go home,'" wrote journalist Tamar Jacoby recently. "Looking back a quarter century later, we'd like to think it was somehow worth it—or, at the very least, that busing's failure taught us something. But the tragic irony is that busing turns out to have been largely irrelevant, a monumental distraction from the real progress we've made on race and from the task, as daunting as ever, of improving the school performance of impoverished black children." Even Supreme Court Justice Anthony Kennedy observed during oral arguments in an important case that he saw "no advantages to have been brought about by busing."[9]

In fact, desegregation was not a failure, but it *was* hugely controversial. It challenged prejudice and racial hierarchies as old as the country. It required change in the way education had always been organized, particularly in the South. It threatened the preferences of whites to attend school with people like themselves, and sometimes the preferences of members of both races to attend particular schools. It also helped millions of students to pursue their dreams, and enhanced citizens' ability to participate in shared democratic governance.

Most centrally, it was a moral fight made for the sake of social justice; on that level it was necessary, long overdue, and a real victory. Listen to President Kennedy, after officials in Alabama unleashed the dogs and turned the fire hoses on the protesters in Birmingham demanding desegregation:

> We are confronted primarily with a moral issue. It is as old as the scriptures and as clear as the American Constitution. The heart of the question is whether all Americans are to be afforded equal rights and equal opportunities. . . . We face, therefore, a moral crisis as a country and as a people.

"If we want a segregated society," reflected Christopher Jencks, the preeminent academic analyst of these issues, soon thereafter, "we should have segregated schools. If we want a desegregated society, we should have desegregated schools."[10]

Desegregation created a high level of discord in society because it brought the values of the American dream into conflict. If Americans had not sincerely believed in the collective goals of the American dream, if they were not willing to make sacrifices for them, there would have been no victories. If the majority of Americans did not eventually come to believe that the risks to their individual goals were too high, the fight would not be over.

De Jure and De Facto Segregation

To understand how and why things developed in this way, we have to look first at the complicated evolution of the law on desegregation. This evolution profoundly affected how desegregation was implemented and therefore how well it satisfied the individual and collective goals of the American dream. Together federal courts and executive branch created the possibility of desegregated schools; at the same time, however, they constrained its impact and framed a volatile controversy over it.

Federal judicial decisions revolved around the legal distinction between schools segregated by law or government action (de jure) and those segregated by individual choices or social practices (de facto). Throughout the first half of the twentieth century, segregation was explicit in the constitutions of southern and some border states, and in the ordinances of some northern and western school districts or communities; these places were ultimately the subject of court orders to desegregate. Although segregation by individual decision and social practice was widespread, including in the North, the courts never assumed responsibility to remedy it, despite arguments before them that it too was ultimately the result of state action intended to separate the races. By the end of the process of judicial and executive decision making on this issue, two rules had emerged: the Constitution required schools to be desegregated where the law had previously required racial separation, and it did not require desegregation where it had not. By creating and maintaining this distinction, the courts made it possible for many black children to be treated fairly and gain educationally—and also restricted the places where that change was likely to occur.

It took a long series of court decisions and regulations for this distinction to be put firmly in place and for its implications for schooling to become clear. Attorneys for the National Association for the Advancement of Colored People (NAACP) began in the 1930s to try to persuade the Supreme Court to overturn *Plessy v. Ferguson*, the 1896 case that permitted "equal but separate accommodations" in transportation (and by extension in schools and other public facilities). In 1954, in *Brown v. Board of Education*, the Supreme Court finally and unanimously repudiated *Plessy* and made its bold assertion that "separate educational facilities are inherently unequal." A year later, in *Brown II*, the Court held that school systems must admit blacks "on a nondiscriminatory basis, . . . with all deliberate speed."[11]

In a moment of elation, attorney Thurgood Marshall predicted the next day that it might take "up to five years" for all schools to be integrated, and nine years for all of American society. The Cincinnati *Enquirer* opined that "what the Justices have done is simply to act as the conscience of the American nation."[12] To supporters of *Brown*, it looked like the American dream might soon be more than a cruel taunt to African Americans.

Desegregation, however, took place with a great deal of deliberation and very little speed, and the dream was delayed once again. The rest of the 1950s and early 1960s saw responses ranging from substantial desegregation in some border states to massive resistance in Virginia and elsewhere. Most states with de jure segregation found ways to avoid anything beyond trivial compliance. In 1957 President Eisenhower sent national troops to ensure token desegregation in Little Rock, Arkansas, but undermined that message with his statement that "no single event has so disturbed the domestic scene in many years as did the Supreme Court's decision of 1954." He urged the Attorney General to "avoid predictions that the law [of integration] will necessarily be permanent."[13]

The 1960s were different; they made the American dream appear increasingly accessible to blacks. Civil rights marches caught the attention of the nation, and television forced people to confront the horrors of black children being bombed in church. Under great pressure from President Lyndon Johnson and demonstrators, Congress passed three civil rights laws (two with real enforcement powers) and two substantial school laws between 1964 and 1971. The 1964 Civil Rights Act permitted the federal government to cut off funds from school districts that discriminated and enabled the attorney general to sue districts on behalf of individual students. The 1965 Elementary and Secondary Education Act (ESEA) provided federal funds (over $1 billion a year initially—then a huge amount) for schools with many poor children. The executive branch began writing regulations for schools seeking ESEA support and soon progressed to requiring school districts to submit plans for complete desegregation. The Voting Rights Act (1965) and, to a lesser extent, the Housing Rights Act (1968) extended the breadth of civil rights legislation.

In 1968, with enforcement of their decisions now much more likely, the Supreme Court reentered the fray, declaring that the time for "deliberate speed was over." It began to order more serious and immediate remedies for desegregation, culminating in a 1971 decision that permitted mandatory busing to achieve desegregation on the grounds that "desegregation plans cannot be limited to the walk-in school."[14] Congress responded with the 1972 Emergency School Aid Act (ESAA), which provided federal aid to school districts embarking on desegregation. In 1973 the Court began to require mandatory remedies in northern cities that had taken official actions to segregate.[15] This was the high-water mark in attempts by the federal government to secure the American dream for black Americans through desegregation.

By then, however, resistance to "forced busing," was fierce, for complicated reasons we will explain later on. White parents stoned school buses carrying black children in Boston and bombed buses carrying black children in Pontiac, Michigan. "I'll never forget the hatred I saw in those faces in Boston," the psychologist Kenneth Clark recalled later. Many whites who could afford to do so fled cities that had desegregative court orders, or were likely to have them, or were rumored to be likely to have them. Local officials sometimes called on people to obey the law, but mostly said little and did less. Opponents attacked the Supreme Court for exceeding its legitimate authority. The new president, Richard Nixon, elected with southern support largely because of his stated opposition to broad interpretations of civil rights laws, began criticizing what he called "extreme" court orders that "have raised widespread fears that the nation might face a massive disruption of public education, that wholesale compulsory busing may be ordered and the neighborhood school virtually doomed."[16] He also began appointing much more conservative justices to the Supreme Court.

Until 1973 the courts had focused on the first rule—where students were separated by law, the schools had to be desegregated. Afterward the Supreme Court focused on articulating the second rule—where there was only de facto school segregation, no action needed to be taken to change racial separation. In 1974, in the most important decision since *Brown*, a deeply divided Court decided the case of *Milliken v. Bradley I*, which was brought to remedy segregation in the overwhelmingly black school district of Detroit. A lower court had attempted to frame a solution that would mix children in the city with those in the largely white suburbs, but the Supreme Court declared that suburbs could not be required to participate unless plaintiffs could show that "racially discriminatory acts of the state or local school districts . . . have been a substantial cause of interdistrict segregation."[17] If the city were segregated by action of its board, as Detroit was, the city would have to do the best it could to fix the problem within its own borders.

Milliken shut off effective school desegregation for most northern cities, where more and more African Americans and Latinos were living. Except in southern states where segregation was written into law, it was very hard to prove that city or district boundaries were drawn purposely to separate the races; courts could therefore rarely impose cross-district remedies. Only in two border cities, Indianapolis and Wilmington, Delaware, were the *Milliken* criteria satisfied.[18] By this ruling the Supreme Court set almost insuperable limits on the extent to which schooling policies could promote the American dream by challenging racial hierarchy and separation in northern metropolitan areas. Soon after *Milliken* the other branches of the federal government moved in the same direction. Even some liberal representatives and senators began to oppose busing, and in 1974 Congress prohibited the use of federal funds for it.

Although judicial decisions to end de jure segregation gave an enormous boost to the chances of southern (and some northern) black children to achieve their dreams, the limits set by *Milliken* made things worse in much of the country. It prohibited movement of students, teachers, and resources across district lines unless state governments intervened, and it reinforced the effects of racial and class isolation in housing. The possibility that cities might be desegregated under *Brown* and its successors helped send whites to suburbs that *Milliken* then absolved from any role in a solution. At the same time, economic trends sent poor blacks (and later, immigrants) into the cities. As industries then moved out, cities became much poorer, resources for city schools became more limited as their need became more urgent, and urban schools got much worse. Their decline further justified whites' (and middle-class blacks') retreat into suburbia or private schools. By 1992 even the liberal Democratic president was sending his daughter to a private school.

In this way the same Court and political processes that enabled progress also restricted the potential gains from desegregation and limited its possible success. Substantial desegregation in many northern metropolitan areas did not fail: it was never tried. Under these circumstances it could never live up to the educational expectations of its advocates nor to their promises of real integration.

By the 1980s desegregation orders had largely addressed instances of de jure segregation, and the Supreme Court began to develop guidelines to release districts from court supervision. The increasingly conservative Court followed the principle that a court's oversight of local school districts "[f]rom the very first . . . was intended as a temporary measure to remedy past discrimination." While the Court of 1968 had declared that segregation must be "eliminated root and branch," the Court by 1991 announced that discrimination must only be "eliminated to the extent practicable." A year later it held that a district could be released from judicial oversight "in incremental stages, before full compliance ha[d] been achieved in every area of school operations" in order to promote the "ultimate objective" of returning "schools to the control of local authorities at the earliest practicable date." Again the Court relied on the distinction between de jure and de facto segregation, reiterating that "[o]nce the racial imbalance due to the de jure violation has been remedied, the school district is under no duty to remedy imbalance that is caused by demographic factors." Finally, in 1995 the Court ruled that states have no federal constitutional requirement to fund efforts to promote students' achievement once de jure segregation has been remedied.[19] It has not spoken on the question of school desegregation since then.

A number of districts, especially large ones, successfully appealed during the 1990s to be released from judicial oversight. Most have returned to neighborhood school assignments, often at the cost of predicted increases in racial imbalance among schools. These districts include Wilmington, Miami, Jacksonville, Denver, Buffalo, Mobile, Cleveland, Las Vegas, Nashville, Minneapolis, San Jose, San Francisco, Boston, and Seattle.[20] Segregation between blacks and whites in schools increased slightly in the 1990s, and the relationship between housing and school segregation increased dramatically over the decade. That increase occurred, argues David Rusk of the Urban Institute, because "federal courts dismantled school busing programs in many metro areas and black children reverted to (black) neighborhood schools."[21]

In districts still under desegregation orders, courts are largely inactive. But in the past few years, some courts have followed a line of legal argument descending from debates over affirmative action and ruled that school districts may not, even if they want to, require racial balance among students in magnet and other selective schools. A Massachusetts judge held that a program to balance admissions by race in the prestigious Boston Latin School "offends the

Constitution's guarantee of equal protection." The legal debates are complex and the legal issues differ from other desegregation cases, but the political and psychological implications of these new cases are clear: the movement toward racial mixing in schools has not only been halted but partly reversed. "Thirty years ago, school districts were getting sued for not promoting diverse learning environments," says an attorney at a prominent law firm. "Now they're getting sued for actually doing [it]."[22]

Although some existing mechanisms for desegregation will remain in place and a couple of new initiatives have begun, mainly at the state level, it is very unlikely that there will be any new wave of litigation or new desegregative laws. This effort is largely over; black children must pursue the American dream by a different route.

The Impact of Desegregation

Students in Schools. The first half of this history, the effort to abolish de jure segregation, was a stunning success. It started slowly but eventually transformed education throughout the South and in northern districts that had clearly violated the Constitution. Although in the first decade after *Brown*, with little support from any level or branch of government, virtually no black children attended school with whites in the South (where three-fifths of African Americans lived), attendance patterns changed dramatically during the next few decades. Federal courts and agencies squeezed legal segregation, federal funds provided inducements to school districts, and civil rights activists heightened the moral sensitivity and prudential anxiety of white Americans. By 1968 fewer than two-thirds of black children attended all-black schools, and by the end of the 1980s, fewer than one-third did. Conversely, the proportion of black students in majority white schools in the South rose from zero to 44 percent over the same period.[23]

As a matter of routine, many white children began to go to school with classmates of a different race (and therefore usually class). Some of their parents accepted this eagerly, some fearfully, some furiously—but they did it. Over about a decade, the average black student shifted from learning in an all-black environment to learning in a racially mixed environment, and that change has remained in place. There can be no better evidence that Americans are capable of putting into practice their shared belief in the collective values of the ideology of the American dream.

Mandatory desegregation—"forced busing"—largely succeeded in the South because school districts typically encompassed city, suburban, and rural communities. Before 1954 children had been required to attend segregated schools within a single district, in some cases riding past the neighborhood school to another, of the "right" race, a good deal farther from their home. (In at least four southern states, busing for desegregation *reduced* the time, mileage, or transportation costs required by segregation.)[24] Thus the abolition of de jure segregation in the South usually took place within the boundaries of a single school district but across class lines and urban borders.

The North was different. School districts were typically smaller and followed—or created—neighborhoods that were fairly homogeneous by race and class. Since federal law did not permit mandatory reassignment across district lines, and separation across districts was assumed to be de facto, racial transformation halted and has even partly reversed, as we noted above. By 1999 the proportion of black students in almost all-minority schools had slid back up to 37 percent across the nation from a low of 33 percent in the 1980s, while the proportion of black students in majority white schools in the South declined from a high of 44 percent a decade ago to 33 percent.[25]

Most racial and ethnic separation is now *between*, not *within*, districts; except in very unusual situations, it is beyond challenge in federal courts or any agency that follows the lead of federal courts. Over a third of African American children live in very large cities. Schools in Chicago, Philadelphia, Detroit, Prince Georges County, Baltimore, Milwaukee, New Orleans, Washington, Columbus, Atlanta, and Cleveland all have more than 50 percent black students (and many of the rest are Hispanic). In contrast, most of the 5,300 communities with populations under 100,000 are at least 90 percent white, and almost half are at least 98 percent white.[26] Metropolitan areas with a lot of relatively small school districts have especially high levels of racial separation between districts since it is relatively easy in such circumstances to work in one district and move your family to another. While racial separation within cities declined during the 1990s, racial separation in the suburbs increased, especially though not only across district lines.[27]

The distinction between de jure and de facto segregation is actually much less clear than the courts have made it seem. Segregation resulted in part from political choices such as zoning rules, public agency mortgage guidelines, highway location decisions, mass transit access, and above all from school district boundaries and the placement of schools. As the pre-*Milliken* Supreme Court pointed out, "People gravitate toward school facilities. . . . The location of schools may thus influence the patterns of residential development of a metropolitan area and have important impact on composition of inner-city [and other] neighborhoods."[28]

State legislatures could change most of these decisions: they could consolidate school districts, alter boundaries, provide transportation, and create financial or other incentives to encourage greater integration across district lines. But they will not.[29] The courts have deemed the location of boundaries and other such policies to be beyond their jurisdiction on this issue, and most legislators and governors do not want to touch it. Since *Milliken*, probably no white elected official has promoted vigorous efforts to desegregate the schools; it is politically too dangerous.

Pursuing Individual Success. Schools were desegregated in part for moral reasons and with very broad social objectives, but also in order to give individual black students, who had been receiving a second-class education by law, the chance to learn more and thereby pursue success. In general, they did. Some people opposed desegregation because they thought it would mean that white students would learn less. With few exceptions, they did not. So far as one can tell from the evidence,[30] desegregation succeeded not only in moving children into integrated settings but also benefited them educationally.

In some school districts, white hostility and resistance made school desegregation disruptive and frightening for a while. In Boston, for example, in a public meeting held to discuss specific problems in implementing an early desegregation plan, parents who sought to testify "time and again . . . were interrupted by jeers and yells from the group of ROAR [Restore Our Alienated Rights, a white antibusing group] supporters. . . . Printed material that had been distributed was shredded with Afro combs and thrown around the auditorium. Signs protesting 'Communist busing' were paraded in front of ever-present TV cameras." Within a short time, however, protests like these ceased; from that point on, there is no convincing evidence that most white students were harmed academically by desegregation. Twenty of 23 studies conducted through the mid-1980s of white achievement after desegregation showed improvement or no effect.[31] Harm occurred only when, atypically and irresponsibly, a desegregation plan sent a few white students to a predominantly black school with a high concentration of children who were poor and from single-parent families (these schools were also often harmful to their black attendees, but few had worried about that).

Across the nation whites gained years of schooling during and after the period of most desegregative activity. The proportion of white adults with at least a high school education doubled from 1960 to 2000 (from 43 to 88 percent), and the proportion with at least a college degree more than tripled, from 8 to 28 percent. Whites' NAEP scores generally rose in the 1970s and 1980s and were flat in the 1990s. This rise is particularly notable since more white students were staying in high school during this period (and thus more of the generally less able students were available for testing), and an increasing proportion of students categorized as white on these assessments were immigrating from nations where they did not speak English or where schooling was poorer.[32] The proportion of white students taking the SAT and ACT has almost doubled since the early 1970s, at the same time that the average white's score on both tests also rose—suggesting both that more whites were aspiring to college and that whites were learning more material appropriate for college aspirants.[33] Although the reasons for these improvements were complex, nothing here suggests that desegregation inhibited the pursuit of individual success by white students.

African Americans also made clear gains during the period after schools were desegregated. In 1960 fewer than one-fourth of black adults had at least a high school education; by 2000 more than three-fourths did. At the same time, the proportion of blacks with college degrees quadrupled, from 4 to 17 percent. Black students are still more likely than white students to drop out, but the rate is only half that of 1970. Blacks living in less segregated cities are much more likely to graduate from high school than blacks in more segregated cities. The racial gap in college attendance, although not college graduation, has also narrowed.[34]

Black students not only are remaining in school longer than did their parents and grandparents, they are also learning more. Their test scores improved steadily in reading, math, and science during the 1970s and 1980s, the two decades that blacks and whites increasingly attended school together—and did not improve during the 1990s, when school desegregation stopped and was even partly reversed. African Americans' SAT and ACT scores, like whites', have increased over the past 30 years even though almost twice as many black students take the tests now—again demonstrating both higher schooling aspirations and better preparation for college.[35] Because so much else was changing at the same time, scholars do not agree on the extent of the impact on achievement of desegregation alone,[36] although almost all agree that it did not hurt.[37] The most recent study, the only one with nationwide data on achievement in the 1990s, found that, even controlling for family background and prior achievement, blacks' and Latinos' reading scores are substantially closer to those of whites in integrated elementary schools than in segregated ones.[38] In short, school desegregation helped black children to acquire the tools they need to pursue their dreams.

Desegregation, of course, was done differently in different places, and the way it was handled affected its impact. Blacks gained most when they participated in metropolitan plans that involved a city and its surrounding suburbs; examples include Charlotte-Mecklenburg, North Carolina, and Louisville, Kentucky. They also gained most when they were desegregated in the early grades, and when they formed about a quarter to a third of a school's enrollment. Black students who attended school in wealthier districts did better than those who moved within their own or similarly poor districts; as we will see in the next chapter, wealthier districts, not surprisingly, have more of the elements that enhance achievement. In St. Louis, the subject of one of the best studies, black students who transferred to white suburban high schools during the early 1990s learned more, compared with their own starting points, than did black students who transferred into specialized, well-funded, and predominantly black city magnet schools. They were also more likely to graduate from high school. Indianapolis and San Francisco found similar results: black high school students bused to the suburbs attained higher test scores than their peers remaining in city schools. Parents in the *Gautreaux* program, which moves poor, inner city black families into middle-class, predominantly white suburbs around

Chicago, consistently prefer their children's new schools despite concerns about occasional racist treatment. Their children have done better on all measures of educational and job outcomes than a comparison group of children in families who moved within the city to predominantly black and fairly poor neighborhoods. As one *Gautreaux* mother reflected, "They go to school with all nationalities—it's like the UN out here in DuPage [a suburban county]. They got to learn different lifestyles and it makes them want a better lifestyle. . . ." Another mother reports simply, "The level of everything is so much higher than it was in the city. . . . Everything is just more advanced."[39]

The American military provides a striking illustration of how effective integrated schools can be. The Army is the most integrated institution in American society, and the Department of Defense runs over 150 schools in 15 overseas nations for 75,000 children of military personnel. About 16 percent of these students are African Americans. White students in these schools score about the same on the SAT as whites in all public and private schools in the United States. But even controlling for family characteristics, poverty, mobility among schools, and other variables that affect test scores, black students consistently show higher achievement than their counterparts in American schools. Almost the same percentage of black as white graduates of overseas military schools go directly to college.[40]

Schools that changed their teaching techniques to include cooperative learning in heterogeneous classrooms, higher standards, and more rigorous evaluations also showed good results from desegregation. A student in Hoagland, Indiana, who experienced a change in teaching techniques at the same time as desegregation, for example, called cooperative learning "one of the funnest things we have. When you're just sitting in a classroom, they try to put a label on you like you're smart or not, but everybody is good at something. It kind of brings that out. And believe me, the spelling grades have gone way, way up since we started." Schools that included black students in accelerated classes and did not put them disproportionately in special education or low-track classes produced—no surprise here—the best results. Magnet schools with the highest level of integration are also the most likely to offer the highest-quality education.[41]

Black students, like white ones, need more than good test scores to be able to pursue success. And desegregation has helped them to do well in the racially mixed adult world. Compared with racially isolated black students, those from desegregated schools have higher job aspirations, hold job goals more realistically related to their schooling, usually do better in college, have more racially mixed social and professional networks in adult life, and are somewhat more likely to hold white-collar and professional jobs in the private sector.

There is no mystery about these results. Children who have had racially integrated experiences when young are likely to continue to do so as they get older. And once black teens get access to social and informational networks that expand their horizons beyond their own neighborhoods, they use them just as whites do—to get better jobs, find out about higher education, meet new people, and otherwise get on in the world. Almost the only way for disproportionately poor urban African Americans in particular to meet typically more affluent whites and blacks from the suburbs is to go to school, and into classes, with them.[42]

School desegregation, in short, made black students better able to pursue and attain their dreams—and possibly even to seek competitive success against whites. Except in unusual circumstances, it did not harm the ability of whites to pursue *their* dreams. With successful desegregation, of course, whites are more likely to face the kind of competition from blacks that they face from everyone else. But if they believe in the American dream, they cannot legitimately complain about that.

Fostering Community Goals. Desegregation has almost always promoted the collective goals of the American dream in education. Reformers initially hoped that simply putting black and white students into the same schools or classes would lead to more interracial friendship and respect—that other children would follow the lead of the white student in Columbus, Ohio, who said, "When you first go into school you're easily influenced by what you're told about black people, but after you get to know some of them, you're influenced by their niceness." An array of systematic studies, however, shows that simply mixing students of different races can increase rather than decrease tension. One of the nine students who desegregated Central High School in Little Rock, Arkansas, looked back on her experience 40 years later with no illusions: "We thought that once the [whites] saw that black people are not devils, we don't carry knives or guns, we can read and write, they would accept us. But after they knew us, they still didn't like us."[43]

But some practices do help children to become friends. These include school policies that promote equal status for all students, principals and teachers who signal the importance of interracial tolerance and respect for clear rules and practices, and classrooms and extracurricular activities that encourage cooperative interaction. On balance these practices work: over the long run, desegregated children are more likely than others to become desegregated adults. Both black and white adults from integrated schools have more close friends and casual acquaintances of the other race than do adults from racially isolated schools. They are more likely to attend desegregated colleges, live in (or at least accept) integrated neighborhoods, hold jobs in integrated work settings, and be comfortable with racially mixed work groups.[44] As one young political activist put it, "We are the generation of integration and desegregation, and we have friends that are Jewish, Asian, Irish. We really do understand the power of collaboration." African Americans do not always feel as comfortable as that comment suggests, but the experience of desegregation teaches

them that "you went into this new place and you made it okay and, you figure, it'll be okay next time, too." White Americans are now more likely to tell
pollsters that they have black friends and coworkers, to abjure prejudice and
racial discrimination, and to endorse measures to enhance racial equality than
their counterparts were before schools were desegregated.[45] Again, many other
things besides school desegregation were happening at the same time, so it is
hard to make a direct connection. From the evidence, however, it would be
impossible to claim that desegregation worsened American race relations.

School desegregation may also make communities better off. Successfully
desegregated schools contributed to greater economic success, social integration, and the building of political coalitions in the metropolitan areas of Wilmington, Delaware, and Charlotte, North Carolina. In Charlotte even the man
who had chaired the school board in its unsuccessful appeal against the first
desegregation orders, back in the late 1960s, recently declared that the way
people came together to implement desegregation "generated an era of racial
good will in this community. . . . Our compliance with court orders . . . and
the general positive attitude of people here in race relations has contributed
tremendously to the economics of the community." Desegregation efforts can
also lead to increases in residential integration. In Jefferson County (Louisville),
the Kentucky Human Rights Commission published the location of neighborhoods that blacks could move into so that neighborhood could avoid busing;
white suburbanites began recruiting black families, and the number of naturally desegregated schools increased.[46]

Most importantly, the commitment to desegregate schools is the visible
center of Americans' expressed commitment to abolish racial hierarchy and promote equal rights. As President Lyndon Johnson put it, "All our citizens must
have . . . not just legal equity but human ability, not just equality as a right and
a theory but equality as a fact and equality as a result."[47] Americans who seek
to make the American dream more than a fraud have been able to point to
school desegregation as the best evidence that others share their views.

Across the board, then, school desegregation has harmed no group, and it has
helped African Americans to pursue their dreams. It has fostered the collective
goals of equal opportunity, interracial engagement, and equal rights. It has only
rarely created a legitimate direct conflict between success for some and that of
others, or between the individual and collective goals of schooling. In fact, when
properly implemented, desegregation has enabled the core goals of schooling to
be mutually reinforcing. School desegregation, in short, worked pretty well.

The Politics of School Desegregation

Experience and Values. If we can believe polls on the subject of race, most Americans also believe that school desegregation has on balance worked. To begin

with the individual goals, up to two-thirds agree that integration has "improved the quality of education received by black students." The younger the respondents, the more likely they are to have had experience with desegregation and the more likely they are to agree. By 1999 fully 80 percent of young adults, compared with 63 percent of the elderly, thought desegregation had helped blacks' education. Just as many whites as blacks concur. This marks a big shift: in 1971 only 42 percent of all Americans thought desegregation helped black students.[48]

Furthermore, up to half of Americans agree that integration "improved the quality of education received by white students," and that number too has slowly but steadily risen through the 1990s. Here too the younger the respondents, the more positive they were; by 1999, 70 percent of young adults, compared with 45 percent of the elderly, believed that whites' education had improved as a result of school desegregation. On this question, however, unlike the previous one, the races split; a majority of blacks but a minority of whites agreed throughout the 1990s that desegregation improved the education of whites.[49]

Americans mostly believe that school desegregation has fostered the collective goals of schooling. By the mid-1990s two-thirds agreed that it has "improved relations between blacks and whites." A principal in Charlotte, North Carolina, put it this way: "It's hard to remember the pain and agony of those first few years because we've now replaced it with something else. . . . We don't have a perfect society here. But we've come a long way." More blacks than whites—74 to 62 percent—hold this view, but that is still a solid majority of whites. Americans under age 50 are more likely to agree than those over 50. These results also mark a big shift; in 1971 only two-fifths of all Americans thought desegregation had improved race relations, and almost as many thought it had "worked against better relations."[50]

Most Americans not only believe that desegregation works, but also claim to believe in the principle behind it. By 1995 fully 96 percent of whites agreed that black and white children should attend the same rather than separate schools (up from half in 1956). Only 12 percent of whites claimed in 1997 that they would object if half of the children in their own child's school were black (down from 47 percent in 1958). As one white mother in Charlotte put it, desegregation "hasn't upset my child like I expected. And though I'm surprised to hear myself saying this, I think in years to come, we'll see that it's something that had to be done." Blacks began and remain virtually unanimous on the principle.[51]

Principles and Practices among Whites. If Americans generally agree that desegregating schools is better for individuals, good for the nation, and the right thing to do, are they committed to actually doing it? For most, the answer is no. On this issue a lot of Americans change their views when it comes to putting principles into practice. Whites' support for federal government intervention to "see to it that black and white children are allowed to go to the same schools" peaked at only 48 percent in 1966 and declined to 31 percent by 2000. At most a third of whites support busing to achieve racial balance, up from roughly a tenth in the early 1970s. Even questions stipulating that the amount of busing would not increase with mandatory desegregation attain support from fewer than a fifth of white Americans.[52]

Opposition to mandatory busing does not necessarily imply opposition to desegregation. Busing sometimes frightened children or disrupted families who had chosen to live in a particular neighborhood because of the local school. The mayor of the small town of Leonia, New Jersey, which faced district consolidation and busing, expressed it this way: "I moved to a school district I am happy with. Why does the state have to come in and change it? . . . Leonia wants to be left alone. If Englewood and Englewood Cliffs [the nearby towns] have problems, let them fix them themselves."[53] People sometimes object to long bus rides or believe that buses are more dangerous than walking or riding in private vehicles. Many people value local neighborhood attachments and see busing as intrusive or too expensive.

These are reasonable concerns, but they were not at the core of many objections to "forced busing." Desegregation sometimes reduced the amount or cost of busing and increased white students' average transportation time only marginally.[54] Buses are safer than cars or walking.[55] And Americans have no problem in general with putting their children on a bus to go to school, as waves of district consolidation in the decades after World War II demonstrated. Only 15 percent of children rode school buses in 1940, when there were 117,000 school districts, but 43 percent did by 1970, when there were only 18,000 districts. In 1972, on survey questions that had nothing to do with school desegregation, almost 90 percent of respondents found it "convenient" for their children to ride a school bus or were "satisfied" with the school's bus system.[56] But at the same time, almost no whites endorsed busing to desegregate schools, and few supported any other mandatory state interventions to accomplish it. Only 20 percent were willing to "create more housing for low-income people in middle-income neighborhoods," and only about 30 percent were willing to consider changing school district boundaries. (The rest were roughly evenly split among those who favored "do[ing] something other than" those proposals, those opposed to school desegregation, and those with no answer.)[57]

It is unlikely that these solutions are any more popular today. White Americans endorse school desegregation in principle, and believe that it has benefited blacks, the nation as a whole, and arguably whites. They support voluntary measures to achieve it but are not willing to take the necessary actions to make it happen. As one schooling expert put it recently, "Today a bipartisan consensus holds that integrated schools are a good thing but we shouldn't do much of anything to promote them."[58]

Whites in fact sometimes take fairly drastic steps to avoid putting their children in racially mixed schools. Many have moved or changed schools to avoid it, and white parents consistently choose schools with very few non-Anglo students, even in cases in which the quality of more racially mixed schools is demonstrably higher. Whites who lack other public school choices are more likely to send their children to private school as the proportion of blacks in their schools increases. Whites who move out of cities usually choose suburbs whose schools are "whiter"; these results hold firm even when studies control for family characteristics, school quality, and the economic status of classmates. It is no longer laws, restrictive covenants, or violence that explains the continuing high level of segregation in the United States,[59] but rather the fact that many whites are willing and able to pay more to live in a predominantly white neighborhood or send their children to a predominantly white school.

This issue has not lost its volatility, despite the dramatic change in perceptions and principles. In 1990 in the small, 85 percent white, suburban school district of East Allen County, Indiana, the superintendent transferred a few grade school classes of black students to a white school. He also planned a more extensive program that would move children of both races and close two underpopulated schools. After protests and petitions, the school board approved a softer proposal in a public meeting at which people in the audience called the swing voter a "traitor" and shouted that "we've got to take . . . [him] out." Police escorted him home through a hostile crowd. The superintendent was advised to get police protection, and his seventh-grade son "revealed that boys at school wanted to smash a truck into the superintendent's house." The superintendent resigned and moved.[60]

Whites avoid racially mixed schools for various reasons, all focused on concerns about the individual goals of education. Despite decades of evidence to the contrary, some worry that their children will suffer educational harm from mixing with even some students from central cities or other districts. As one parent put it in a recent focus group, "*This* is the fear: you want to lower the quality of my child's education to raise the quality of the inner-city education." Some whites fear losing their advantage in the competition for success: as another parent put it in a similar group, when it comes to schooling, changes are all right "as long as our kids get to go first." Some may simply be hypocrites who never really believed in desegregation, or racists despite their statements to pollsters and others. Others may genuinely endorse the idea of desegregation but, despite greater societal understanding of how it is best implemented, they find its personal costs to be unacceptable. Finally, some may believe in desegregation but think it too marginal to distract from a focus on individual achievement. As the educational critic Chester Finn put it, "[My opponent in a debate over desegregation] must be the only American who still thinks that integration for its own sake is an important societal goal. Almost everybody else is interested in whether kids are going to good schools where they are safe and learning to read. The price of forced busing and other forms of social engineering is too high to pay when there are more urgent crises facing this country's schools."[61]

Any of these reasons may hold. From the politician's viewpoint, the explanation matters much less than the fact that most white Americans are not willing to risk desegregating their schools, and they will punish at the next election anyone who tries to do so.

Recent Court Action. The most important recent case on desegregation, *Sheff v. O'Neill,* shows all of these dynamics at work. Unlike most earlier cases, its setting was a state court rather than the federal judicial system. Plaintiffs brought the case in Connecticut, focusing on the city of Hartford and its suburbs. Economic, racial, and ethnic differences between city and suburbs were greater than in almost any metropolitan area in the country, and the schools in Hartford had performed terribly for years. In 1994, for example, 1,500 fourth graders in Hartford attended schools where fewer than 1 percent of the children met the state math and reading goals.[62]

Several years before the case was filed, Connecticut's commissioner of education had issued an "impassioned report" calling school segregation "educationally, morally, and legally wrong." He called for "collective responsibility" in planning a remedy but also suggested that the state board of education "be empowered to impose a mandatory desegregation plan" should voluntary planning fail. As the commissioner later reported, "All hell broke loose." One legislator called for his resignation; another deemed him "despicable"; the governor abjured mandatory solutions; and the next year's report did not mention desegregation.[63]

Nevertheless, a few years later, with a lawsuit threatened, the state legislature set up regional planning groups to propose voluntary desegregative measures for the area around Hartford—although the mandate neither set numerical goals nor mentioned the word "desegregation." After six months of deliberation, regions proposed such changes as interactive videos, " 'non-face-to-face interaction' via distance learning, cooperative projects, and visits involving urban and suburban schools." None came close to proposing an extensive desegregation plan. As the chair of Glastonbury's town council pointed out, "Towns are willing to put up a certain amount, but we still have our taxpayers to account to, and our kids." In 1993, by a margin of two to one, residents of Connecticut reported that they would vote against a legislator who supported "regional school districts."[64] Plaintiffs representing poor minority children in Hartford went to court.

In 1996 the state supreme court responded by requiring the state to end the racial and ethnic isolation of the schoolchildren in Hartford and required desegregation in some form between the city and its suburbs. "When children attend racially and ethnically isolated schools," said the court, these " 'shared values' . . . through which social order and stability are maintained . . . are jeopardized." Current school assignments violated "the legislature's affirmative constitutional obligation to provide a substantially equal educational opportunity to all of the state's schoolchildren."[65] The court left it to the governor and legislature to design an appropriate plan to change the situation.

Initial public response was heartening. Half of the respondents to a state poll agreed that "more should be done to integrate schools throughout . . . Connecticut"; three-fifths agreed that racial imbalance is a serious problem, and three-fifths agreed that public officials should "do their best to improve racial integration even if that means doing more than the Court requires," rather than "try[ing] to figure out the smallest change the Court will accept." But within four days of the *Sheff* decision, the governor ruled out mandatory transportation: "The Supreme Court did not say they wanted forced busing, and we know that forced busing is not an alternative. It's not acceptable to the legislature, it's not acceptable to the people." Asked for an alternative proposal, he responded,

> We have got to be creative and thoughtful and compassionate in figuring out other ways to try to resolve the issue. . . . Just because the solution is not before us at this very moment, doesn't mean it doesn't exist. . . . But I thought it was important to put a line in the sand and say we're not going to do forced busing because that's the issue that will ignite the emotions.[66]

The signal was clear, and a year later the state legislature responded in kind. It reorganized the management structure of the Hartford district, expanded early childhood education and reading programs for poor children, instituted a few voluntary or symbolic programs for desegregation, and stopped. The most substantive of its actions was to provide financial support for magnet schools across district lines and a small program of interdistrict choice for students from the biggest cities. The focus of legislators on school reform rather than integration was responsive to their constituents, at least those outside Hartford. Few members of the public saw racial isolation as the main cause of Hartford students' poor performance, and citizens urged a focus on educational quality and better parenting rather than on busing or redistricting.[67] At least one critic called the legislature's actions "dismal," but a newly configured court supported the legislature's actions. The judge to whom the plaintiffs turned said that the legislature's plan must be given more time to work and that the only alternative would have been mandatory reassignment, which would have generated even more white flight.[68]

Hartford's schools are now more racially and ethnically segregated than they were before the lawsuit began a decade ago. As of 2000, about 1,400 students participated in the interdistrict choice program—no more than 3 percent of the students in Hartford, New Haven, or Bridgeport. Several suburban districts that accepted students during the first year of the program no longer do.

Combined with the new interdistrict magnet program and a few charter schools, perhaps 2 percent of students in Connecticut move across district lines for schooling (and some of them are white students transferring out of cities or minority students transferring in).[69] A few students have benefited from these reforms; the rest are left without a serious program for desegregation.

Consistent with public opinion, the legislature has focused instead on a new round of ambitious reforms for Hartford, including curricular changes, teacher training, computer access, health clinics, new accountability systems for administrators, and an end to social promotion. Hartford's superintendent is ambitious and energetic, and the powerful teachers' union is newly focused on student learning. These are hopeful developments, but there is nothing realistically on the table that would desegregate the schools, and the courts have up to this point declined further intervention.[70] In this matter, despite the eloquent language in the *Sheff* decision about "shared values . . . through which social order and stability are maintained," the individual goals of the American dream have swamped the collective ones.

Principles and Practices among Blacks. Like the plaintiffs in *Sheff,* most African Americans have strongly supported school desegregation during the last 40 years. Throughout the 1970s and 1980s, over 95 percent agreed that blacks and whites should attend the same schools. More blacks than whites agree that "black children do better if they go to schools which are racially mixed," and at least 85 percent (compared with about half of whites) agree that "more should be done to integrate schools throughout the nation." About two-thirds of African Americans, compared with about two-fifths of whites in this survey, endorse racially mixed student bodies "even if it involves some school busing."[71]

But the intensity of African Americans' support for school desegregation is waning. More than four out of five supported federal intervention in the schools until the early 1970s, but by 1994 fewer than three in five did. In 1995 barely half of African Americans agreed that racial integration in schools, homes, and work was important; to the rest integration mattered little so long as all races received equal opportunities and fair treatment. (Whites and Asian Americans held the same views; slightly more Latinos endorsed integration.) On all recent surveys, blacks rank greater funding for minority schools over desegregation when asked to choose.[72] Among African Americans, slightly more prefer allowing students to attend local schools, even at the cost of greater racial separation, than prefer transferring students to other schools to promote integration. African Americans are still twice as likely as whites (60 to 34 percent) to agree that a racially diverse student body is "absolutely essential" for a good school, but, like whites, they rank racial diversity eleventh out of twelve proffered characteristics of a good school.[73]

Blacks' political activity has tracked these survey responses. From the 1930s through the 1980s, the NAACP fought intensely to desegregate schools throughout the nation. In the mid-1990s, however, local chapter heads in Yonkers, New York, and Bergen County, New Jersey, publicly declared that busing for desegregative purposes had "outlived its usefulness." They were deposed, but their position has gained strength within the organization; President Kweisi Mfume has observed that while "the NAACP stands by its founding proposition of a single, fully integrated society," it must "at the same time [be] fighting to guarantee educational equality for students within our existing public schools." In that context "busing is but one of several tools that can be used to achieve the goal of desegregation of our public schools."[74]

African American elected officials increasingly opt for a black-controlled neighborhood school system that they believe will bring funds and positions of authority into their community. "In Cleveland," according to *Emerge* magazine, "an initiative by Mayor Michael White helped to convince a federal judge to minimize crosstown busing and allow the city to focus on retooling its own schools. In Seattle, Mayor Norman B. Rice has led the charge to replace busing with school choice and magnet school programs. Meanwhile, Mayor Wellington Webb has tried to end busing in Denver. So has St. Louis Mayor Freeman R. Bosley, Jr. He favors pouring more resources into programs to boost the quality of city schools." Mayor Rice is quoted in the same article to say that "we had better turn off the racial issues and begin talking about quality education."[75]

African Americans are ambivalent about school desegregation for as many reasons as whites are. To some, desegregation is not necessary to increase the chances for individual black students to achieve success. In the words of one African American mother in Denver, "You don't have to send a child across town to teach them to read a book." To others desegregation has not sufficiently advanced the collective goals of schooling. Robert Carter, one of the chief litigators in the original *Brown v. Board*, put it this way:

> We believed that the surest way for minority children to obtain their constitutional right to equal educational opportunity was to require the removal of all racial barriers in the public school system, with black and white children . . . together exposed to the same educational offerings. Integration was viewed as the means to our ultimate objective, not the objective itself.

Others believe that African Americans as a group will gain benefits from schools within their own neighborhoods. An official in the Denver public schools argues that keeping children close to home "will give students a sense of community at their school. We lost that when we were busing students. And . . . it will let parents and adults in the community reconnect with the schools. . . . This is an excellent opportunity for the Latino [or black] community to refocus and set a new agenda and promote the concept of community at our schools."[76]

A few African Americans express ideological objections to integration in favor of a racially separate community, which they believe will be morally or emotionally preferable or politically more powerful. The most famous, although not the most vehement, defender of racially separate schools is Justice Clarence Thomas. In the Supreme Court's decision in *Missouri v. Jenkins*, he complained that many plaintiffs in school desegregation cases "assume that anything that is predominantly black must be inferior, [that] segregation injures blacks because blacks, when left on their own, cannot achieve." That view produces "a jurisprudence based upon a theory of black inferiority. . . . [B]lack schools can function as the center and symbol of black communities, and provide examples of independent black leadership, success, and achievement." Finally, others have simply lost patience with whites' anxieties and defensiveness. A young veteran of New York City's public schools puts it this way: "White people are still protecting their babies, because these are going to be the power people in the future. . . . I cannot ever see them bringing white kids and putting them into what they call danger zones, with the 'dangerous, inferior people.'" A senior litigator in the American Civil Liberties Union (ACLU) concludes simply, "In school desegregation, it's not that people disagree with the goals or objectives. It's just that 'I'm tired. Enough. I give up.'"[77]

Among African Americans as among whites, politicians care less about the explanations than the fact itself. Black constituents are not demanding school desegregation anywhere nearly as much as they used to; many support the desegregative practices now in place, but that is all. Some of the most energetic black political activists have abjured it. Most black and white elected officials concur on this point if on nothing else about school desegregation: at the beginning of the new millenium, in the political arena, this game is over.

"It should go without saying," said the Supreme Court in *Brown II*, "that the vitality of these constitutional principles [mandating desegregation] cannot be allowed to yield simply because of disagreement with them." But that is precisely what happened. Twenty years later a disillusioned Justice Thurgood Marshall, in dissent, declared that the *Milliken* decision was "more a reflection of the perceived public mood that we have gone far enough in enforcing the Constitution's guarantee of equal justice than it is the product of neutral principles of law." By 1999, with the courts removing themselves and school districts from involvement on this issue and political leaders abandoning it, the president of the Association of American Medical Colleges described our society as "being hammered by a mean-spirited backlash." "Race," he said, "has once again become a wedge issue that is being very cynically exploited by politicians arguing that our ugly legacy of racial discrimination is behind us."[78] Backlash or not, concerns about the effects of school desegregation on individuals and groups have taken precedence over America's commitment to the collective goal of integrated education. That has resulted partly from the mistaken view that there had to be a tradeoff, that equality for and incorporation of the minority could only be accomplished by sacrificing individual achievement of the majority. That false presumption led to an unwarranted retreat from our nation's most impressive effort in the past half century to bring the practice of the American dream closer to the ideal.

Winston Churchill once described democracy as the worst system of governance except for all of the others. School desegregation was like that. Few people outside the black community wanted it badly and districts sometimes did it poorly, but done well desegregation was always and still is the policy best suited to help all students pursue success and learn how to live in the multiracial and multiethnic future that will be theirs. Integration is not guaranteed to follow desegregation, but it is impossible without it.

Most racially isolated black students are now in school districts deemed by the courts to be segregated by (legal) practice rather than by (illegal) mandate, and many of them suffer from the worst schools anywhere. Although academic achievement for poor urban children was never certain to follow desegregation, it has proved very difficult to achieve without it. For these children the connection between education and the American dream remains very weak and must be strengthened some other way. We turn therefore to school funding and then to school reform—efforts to make more equal education that will remain separate.

3

SCHOOL FINANCE REFORM

The State's constitutional duty . . . embraces broad educational opportunities
. . . to equip our children for their role as citizens and as potential competitors in today's market as well as in the marketplace of ideas. Education . . .
must prepare our children to participate intelligently and effectively in our
open political system to ensure that system's survival, . . . and it must prepare
them to be able to inquire, to study, to evaluate and to gain maturity and understanding. . . . The mandate of the Constitution . . . is addressed to the State
and requires, as a first priority, fully sufficient funds.
— *Seattle v. State of Washington, 1978*

If the educational fare of the seriously disadvantaged student is the same as
the "regular education" given to the advantaged student, . . . the students in
the poor urban districts will simply not be able to compete. A thorough and
efficient education requires such level of education as will enable all students
to function as citizens and workers in the same society, and that necessarily
means that in poor urban districts something more must be added.
— *Abbott v. Burke (New Jersey), 1990*

We've never aspired to be average here. If our costs are a little high, it reflects
the fact that we want our children to be able to compete.
— *Parent from a wealthy school district, 1999*[1]

I N A WEALTHY NORTHEASTERN STATE, two schools are near each other ge-
ographically but far apart in every other way. The school in the city sits be-
side an abandoned lot in a community that has lost most of its industrial
jobs. "The physical appearance of the school is bleak, depressing. The hall is
dark and dingy. . . . The playground outside is all brown wood and it is completely surrounded by hard pavement." The library has not been used for 13
years; even the faculty bathrooms have no toilet paper or soap. The gym leaks.
There is one computer for every 35 students, and none of the classrooms is
wired for the Internet. The principal has trouble attracting qualified teachers in
many fields and has none trained in computer instruction; according to the

scholar who looked at these schools, teachers mainly use the computers to keep the students busy playing games when they have completed their worksheets. In this school 98 percent of the students are non-Anglo, more than two-thirds are eligible for free or reduced-price school lunches, almost three in ten are in special education. The residents of the district have a per capita income of $17,000 a year.

In the suburb nearby, the school is "housed in a modern building and surrounded by large, well-maintained athletic fields. [It] boasts such amenities as a spacious school library furnished with rows upon rows of book stacks, and a high-ceilinged auditorium with theater-style seating and a grand piano on stage. Not only does the school have computers in every classroom, it also has a fully equipped computer lab, staffed by an instructor." There is one computer for every four students, all wired for Internet use. Teachers have aides as well as access to "resource teachers" who specialize in various academic fields, help with curricula, and give "guest lectures" in classrooms. Most students participate in the orchestra, chorus, or specialized bands (or perhaps all three). One fourth-grade teacher, a graduate of Vassar College, was chosen over more than 200 competitors for her job, and along with the others in the school is paid considerably more than the state average. In this school 95 percent of the students are Anglo, fewer than one percent are eligible for free or reduced-price lunches, and only 5 percent are in special education. Residents of the district have a per capita income of $70,000.

Despite the fact that it receives much less financial aid from the state, the suburban school spends $1,200 a year more on each of its students than the one in the city. The urban students receive 10 percent less instructional time each year, including less time for science, social studies, and language arts, and no time for computer instruction. Test scores in the city school, especially in reading, are dramatically lower than in the suburban school, and many more city students repeat a grade. In most years *none* of the fourth-graders in the city school pass all three components (reading, writing, and mathematics) on the state standardized test; typically, more than half of the students in the suburban school pass all three.

These are not extreme examples. This urban school is not at the bottom of its state in achievement scores, and the suburban school is not at the top; these schools are in neither the lowest-spending city district nor the highest-spending suburb.[2] More money is not the only thing that urban students need to be able to compete, but it is surely one thing. Money pays for the people who educate, it pays for the things they need to do their job, and it pays for decent, safe facilities in which they can do it. For every child, more money can buy things that really matter, like better teaching. For poor children it can pay for preschool programs, smaller classes, and tutoring that can improve their performance. Poor children need money, and it cannot come from the poor residents of the community.

Inequalities in funding result from a school district arrangement with a longer history even than residential racial separation. Because education in this country is delivered through school districts based on residence, and residence is based largely on wealth, the structure of schooling in America is inseparable from the structure of class. Local taxes fund almost half of school district expenditures. Districts with expensive houses and correspondingly high rates of return from taxation can raise money relatively easily, while property-poor districts, with children who need more help, have trouble raising the money to provide it. As a result, children in affluent (predominantly white) districts receive a better education than do children in poor (disproportionately minority) districts, and children in this country do not approach adulthood with anything like an equal chance to pursue their dreams.

In this way, the egalitarian side of the American dream is betrayed. Class, often closely connected with race, matters at the beginning, in the middle, and at the end of primary and secondary education. Average SAT scores exactly track income, and well-off children are seven times more likely to complete four years of college than are their poor peers.[3] For class to affect so strongly both the quality and quantity of education, despite the promise of the American dream, is not acceptable.

At the same time that the Supreme Court in *Milliken I* was upholding the boundaries between districts segregated by race, reform-minded lawyers therefore began another round of litigation to make districts that were to remain racially separate at least equal in resources. They took a financial rather than a racial approach to securing the equality of opportunity promised by the American dream, giving up, at least for a while, the collective goals of integration and training for democratic citizenship. This reform movement continues. "This is like the South in the 1950s," says one advocate. "This is our desegregation battle. Economic issues are the race issues of the 1990s"[4]—and of today.

The Impact of More Money

Some Americans argue that more money will not improve students' outcomes. They point out that spending on education has increased threefold since the 1960s, but that test scores only inched upward in the 1970s and 1980s and stalled during the 1990s. As educational economist Eric Hanushek puts it, "It takes very little effort to see the contrast between the growing resources . . . and the flat student performance." He argues that instead of pouring more money into schools, policymakers should focus on "radically different incentives for students and for school personnel" involving "more extensive experimentation with alternative practices and incentive schemes." In several recent surveys, about three in ten Americans also had questions about the impact of money, believing that the amount spent on public education affects its quality "not too much" or "not at all."[5] A representative of the Education Commission of the States observes that "we're hearing a drumbeat of voters saying that just putting more money into the problem is not the solution"; the conservative magazine the *Weekly Standard* casually comments that "everyone who cares to know has known for years that money spent on education does not correlate with results."[6]

Opponents of increasing or equalizing funding provide examples to show how resources spent on schools are often wasted. Their most frequently cited evidence includes the facts that four of the five states with the highest increases in expenditures in recent decades have shown below-average increases on SAT scores, and that the number of guidance counselors, support staff, and other jobs they label "administrative bloat" has increased much more than the number of teachers over the past few decades.[7]

These critics can be answered. Although some education spending has indeed been wasteful or misguided, and some has been used for reforms not based on research, or for initiatives based on research but implemented poorly, much of it has had a real and positive impact.[8] Average SAT scores have in fact been rising within each racial group even as more students—and therefore lower-achieving students—have chosen to take it. And a large percentage of increased expenditures on education have been for special education, including funds for aides and support staff whose assistance is far from administrative bloat.[9]

The evidence that money well spent improves educational outcomes is broad and clear. A comprehensive study of NAEP scores concluded that, "other things being equal, higher per pupil expenditures, lower pupil ratios in lower grades, higher reported adequacy of teacher reported resources, higher levels of participation in public prekindergarten, and lower teacher turnover all show positive, statistically significant effects on achievement." Investments in education also generate higher earnings.[10] A school district in Wisconsin, for example, that kept unusually careful records found that a small increase in teacher salaries was associated with an increase in student earnings decades later. The analysts calculated that the impact was over 80 times greater than would have occurred with a comparable increase in those students' family income.[11]

Investing in the education of poor children is especially likely to make a difference. This is hardly surprising; as one experienced analyst points out, "To reduce . . . inequalities [that students bring to the classroom] . . . requires the active intervention of the school; when the school lacks adequate funds, its ability to intervene is compromised." With those funds it can intervene. A district in eastern Kentucky, for example, used an influx of state money to reduce class size, improve reading programs, employ master teachers, hire art teachers and tutors, and simply feed the children who "show up on Monday mornings with voracious appetites" after a weekend of too little food at home. Their achievement gains were among the largest in the state. "If it could have been fixed by throwing money at it, we did that," says a school board member. "I think the success we've had is the result of having more resources now and perhaps having better strategies than we've had in the past." More generally, when concentrated in poor districts, increasing school spending is associated with higher test scores.[12]

Critics are mistaken when they assert that average test scores have remained flat during the several decades that expenditures on schools have risen. Results on not only NAEP but also commercial tests such as the California Achievement Test (CAT) improved during the 1980s, especially among black students.[13] But even test scores that simply stay the same may reflect real progress because more students are staying in school, including poor children and those with family problems, students at the bottom of the distribution of measured ability, and English learners—all of whom on average have lower test scores than better-off children.

Critics are also mistaken if they assume that rising test scores are the only valid measure of improved schooling: a substantial part of the increases in school funding have gone into needed expenditures that do not directly affect student achievement scores. Again, special education for children with disabilities has absorbed a large share, between a fifth and a half, of newly available funds. Public schools previously excluded those children or ignored and punished them; providing each with what he or she needs is required by federal law (as well as plain decency), but their inclusion does not boost average test scores. Rises in school spending also coincided with urgent needs for physical construction, abatement of environmental toxins, retrofitting schools to make them accessible to those with physical disabilities, new technology, and other changes often paid from operating expenses. Increased rates of immigration call for expenditures to improve students' proficiency in English. Schools have set up expensive programs to retain would-be dropouts and children of migrant workers, care for their students' babies, and otherwise help to alleviate dysfunctional family situations. In the 1990s, by one calculation, increasing enrollments combined with rising costs in special education, bilingual education, and nutritional programs absorbed almost all of the additional school spending.[14] And in any case, much of the increased funding in recent years has been spent outside of poor districts, where it could have had the most impact.

Parents of school-age children intuitively understand that money matters and have largely supported spending increases at the polls and with their feet. School boards and superintendents believe that money matters when they put their budgets together: "If money doesn't make any difference," asked the superintendent of one poor district, "how come the rich spend so much on their schools?" A superintendent of a rich district answered this way, after showing off his television production equipment: "Can you offer a student a good education without [such extraordinary facilities]? You can. Does this make it easier? Yes. Does this better prepare students for entering the world? We think it does." Governors and legislators also believe that money matters, or they would not spend so much on state education aid. The courts have largely accepted the proposition, whatever their final disposition of school finance cases. And almost two-thirds of Americans agree that "the amount of money spent on a public school student's education affect[s] the quality of his or her education."[15]

"Disparities not only look bad on paper, they feel bad in life."[16] Framing the crucial issue in terms of whether money matters, rather than whether funds are spent as effectively as possible and enough are provided, makes it too easy for schools and citizens to write off poor children before they have a chance to pursue success.

Rising above the noise about the effectiveness of funding is a basic question of justice. To quote the New Jersey supreme court:

> Poorer urban districts . . . are entitled to pass or fail with at least the same amount of money as their competitors. If the claim is that these students simply cannot make it, the constitutional answer is: give them a chance. The Constitution does not tell them that since more money will not help, we will give them less; that because their needs cannot be fully met, they will not be met at all.[17]

Poor children have many problems outside the arena of the schools, problems of nutrition, health and safety, inadequate care, and insufficient guidance that education alone can never overcome. But this only makes it more important for schools to do everything they can to give poor children a better chance. Unless they do, not everyone will have the opportunity to participate fully in the American dream.

The Politics of School Funding

The stakes on this issue are high, as are the costs. Americans spend about $390 billion a year on public primary and secondary education, up from about half that amount 30 years ago. Aside from social security, education is the highest budget priority for most people in the country. In every survey since 1980, a majority of Americans have reported willingness to spend more on education, even when told that their taxes would increase as a result or when the survey question set education against other possible priorities such as defense spending. In some surveys a plurality or majority of respondents endorse the view that "the best way to improve the local public schools" is "to give them more money," rather than doing such things as raising standards or tightening discipline.[18]

Sensibly, Americans prefer expenditures for specific programs over undifferentiated spending increases, and a majority—sometimes large majorities— of Americans report a sense of obligation to invest in them. When asked to set priorities, clear majorities support reductions in class size, improvements in school buildings, more preschools, increases in salaries for all or for meritorious teachers, and enhancements of technology. Blacks and whites, rich and poor, north and south, east and west, everyone agrees. A majority, sometimes large majorities, of Americans also agree that the nation should invest in preschool programs for the poor, programs for students with physical, emotional, or learning disabilities, or programs for English language learners. When asked to set priorities for reduced expenditures, majorities are unwilling even to consider actions to add more children to classes, freeze salaries, eliminate extracurricular activities, reduce special services, or do anything else except reduce the number of administrators and sometimes the support staff.[19]

Americans also consistently agree that students should be treated fairly, whoever they are and wherever they reside. Large majorities endorse an equal allocation of funds to all students "even if it means taking funding from some wealthy school districts and giving it to poor districts," as one question put it. As one resident of Vermont put it, "The point . . . is that all of us are responsible for educating all the students in the state. Not just for educating the students in Stowe or Manchester, but everywhere." Large majorities also endorse extra funding for poor or predominantly black schools; majorities even claim that they would pay more taxes to improve inner-city schools. Occasionally African Americans and Hispanics are more likely to favor redistribution, but most surveys find no variation across race, class, or region in this support. Residents of high-spending states are just as likely as those in low-spending states to endorse general increases in school funding or particular means of securing equity. Over half of American adults even claimed in the fall of 2000 that "how to reduce the gap between rich and poor school districts in a fair way" is a "very important" policy issue on which they would like to hear the views of presidential candidates.[20] They heard little, if anything, on this subject.

Despite this high level of apparent consensus, the underlying issues in school funding have proved to be too difficult politically for national candidates to touch, and the federal government has avoided them for years. State officials, who have the responsibility for providing education, also rarely take on equity issues unless forced to by the courts. None of this is surprising. On this issue, in the same way but not to the same extent as desegregation, Americans' powerful support for the principle of higher and more equal funding becomes weaker when it comes time to pay and other concerns take priority. In one survey half or more of the respondents identified uninvolved parents, drug use, and lack of discipline as "major problems" facing public schools; barely a third chose "inequality in school funding" (it came in just above last place, which was held by "inadequate academic standards"). In another survey only a quarter of respondents chose unequal opportunity as one of their deepest concerns about schooling, and only four in ten saw unequal opportunity as a serious problem at all.[21]

This discrepancy between principle and practice is not simply hypocrisy or confusion; it is evidence of the potential conflict between the individual and collective values implicit in the American dream. School finance policy raises two central political issues: the quality of education to which each student is entitled, and the level of obligation of each citizen to pay for it. At almost any acceptable standard of educational quality, students in poor districts require some support from taxpayers outside their district. If the collective goals are given priority, reformers succeed in getting more affluent citizens to use their resources for broader purposes than securing an advantage for their own children. "We have to talk about the rights of children in this state to equal access to educational opportunity instead of the claims of some towns to advantages to which they've become accustomed," insisted one Vermonter in the throes of that state's funding controversy. If, however, the individual goals of education swamp the collective goals, or if individual success is defined competitively, then citizens resist contributing more. Like the mother quoted at the beginning of this chapter, wealthier parents are tempted to focus on their own children, and that can submerge the promise of the American dream of equal opportunity from one generation to the next. And no parents, wealthy or not, want their children to lose ground so others may gain. Even a political activist who worked for Jesse Jackson's presidential campaigns finds that "when someone tells me, 'Now it's your turn to feel the pain'—these are my kids! . . . I *do* sympathize with parents of kids in other towns. But I don't think we should ruin the school system in the process."[22]

School finance reform has rarely been achieved by punishing one district in order to reward another. Because the problems of poor children are so deep, reform also does not really threaten the continued competitive advantage of the well-off, although it will narrow the gap. Nevertheless, this issue can easily be transformed into a fear that the progress of other children will come at the expense of one's own, and when it does, it becomes extremely volatile.

Issues of class in school finance are also not sharply distinguishable from those of race and ethnicity. As we have seen, African American and Latino students disproportionately reside in the poorest, mostly urban, school districts; in all of the school districts in which three-quarters of the students are poor, at least three-quarters of the students are African American, and many of the rest are Hispanic.[23] The resources, in contrast, are disproportionately available in the suburbs, where most residents are white. Thus for a community of interest to develop on matters of education funding, not only class and district lines, but often racial or ethnic lines as well, have to be crossed. Politically that can be hard to do.

But even without complications of race and class, arguments against increased taxation for schools, or any other purpose, can be politically powerful. Beyond general resistance to increased taxes, a majority of adults do not have children in the public schools and often do not share parents' urgency for increased funding. (As one supporter of reform put it, sharply and not alto-gether accurately, "The opponents are almost all rich people without kids who are upset because they face tax increases on seven-zillion-dollar houses.") Se-niors are also a growing share of the American population, they vote more than young people, and they can get angry. A 73-year-old Democratic Party chair in one community facing reform decided to vote Republican for the first time in his life because of his fear that "we're getting taxed out" of town.[24] With other factors held constant, the higher the proportion of elderly voters in a dis-trict, the less that district spends on public schools.[25] Young people support expenditures for schools more than senior citizens: on surveys the youngest re-spondents are most likely to endorse spending budgetary surpluses on educa-tion, whereas older respondents most support spending on Social Security. Similarly, parents of children in public schools are more likely, and parents of children in private or parochial schools less likely, than the median voter to support tax increases or bond issues for education.[26]

Raising property taxes to support schools within a district often proves very difficult, and raising state sales or income taxes to support schools across the state spurs even fiercer debates. These problems are compounded if a siz-able portion of the state funds is intended for poor urban districts; control-ling for a state's wealth and age structure, the greater the proportion of its population that lives in urban areas, the less it spends on public education per child.[27] Management and bureaucratic problems that have plagued urban districts, family and neighborhood problems that burden urban children, and public assertions that money will not matter for them, all make people in wealthier districts question the value of increased educational spending for others. When explicit or implicit messages about racial inferiority are added, they create a volatile mix. Although problems of bad or corrupt management have to be addressed at any level of funding (and are not limited to cities), despite the fact that theories of racial inferiority are nonsense, and even though poor children need and can benefit from the money, school finance reform remains a tough sell.

Raising state income or sales taxes and spending the new funds for poor or urban children has therefore proven to be politically very difficult. In the course of heated debate, redistribution of public revenues can sound like the loss of local control of the schools, an unpopular idea to say the least, and can lead otherwise sensible citizens to call school finance reform laws "horrendous" or "a great rape." Americans remain deeply committed to localism as a politi-cal principle. Even more than a citizen's race, class, or residence in a city or a suburb, the (often mistaken) belief that local control will be threatened is usu-ally the best predictor of opposition to school finance reform. As the governor of Maine pointed out, "We're the land of the town meeting and direct democ-racy. People in Brunswick don't want people in Topsham telling them how to run their schools."[28]

In short, debates over school finance reform are difficult. They involve class differentiation and racial or ethnic divisions; they become entangled with issues of local control and state prerogatives; they are concerned with tax burdens and effective use of resources; they raise the specter of generational conflict; and they revolve around ideological tensions between the pursuit of individual success and the collective goals of equal opportunity and social justice. It is not surprising, therefore, that in the middle of school funding controversies the governor of New Jersey was pictured on the cover of the *New York Times Magazine* as Robin Hood or that the state commissioner of education in Vermont was labeled a "Communist Dictator."[29] These debates involve all citizens and affect the distribution of billions of dollars. There are good reasons why they have dominated the political life of many state capitals for years.

The Educational Context for Reform

School finance, like most educational policy issues, is fundamentally a matter for states to decide. They are responsible for choosing the form of taxation, setting the process to determine budgets, and allocating responsibilities between the capital and the districts. More generally, states set most education policy, raise the necessary state revenue, determine the powers of school boards, draw district boundaries, create statewide standards, and do statewide assessments. They have, however, turned much of the authority for actually providing and administering education over to local districts and have given them the right and responsibility to raise property taxes to support their schools. Local districts therefore hire and fire, set budget figures, determine curricular details, and most importantly for school finance, secure local revenue.

There are almost 15,000 school districts in this country, with no consistent relationship between the size of a state and the number of its districts. California has almost a thousand districts, but the even larger state of Alaska has only 53. Some small states have 75 or fewer districts, and Hawaii has only one, but New Jersey, a small state, has 608. Nationwide, districts pay about 44 percent of the total cost of primary and secondary education, most commonly through property taxes. States currently pay another 48 percent, a share that has risen about ten percentage points over the past three decades. The federal government contributes most of the remaining 8 percent (down from a high of almost 12 percent two decades ago), with the largest amounts of federal money going for special education (almost nine billion dollars in 2002) and aid to low-income schools (over 12 billion dollars).[30] The mix between local and state taxes differs considerably from state to state, and surprisingly few states mirror the national percentage. State revenues pay 73 percent of the costs of education in New Mexico, 69 percent in North Carolina, and 64 percent in Delaware, but less than 10 percent in New Hampshire.[31]

Local districts, of course, vary greatly in their ability to pay their required share. In Connecticut, for example, the town with the most taxable property per student has nearly 15 times as much as the town with the least. As a result property-poor districts must tax themselves at a higher rate than property-rich districts to provide anything like a comparable level of per-pupil funding; in Connecticut the highest effective tax rate for education (in very poor towns) is three times greater than the lowest (in wealthy towns). Similarly, of the 238 municipalities in the Philadelphia metropolitan area, 25 (including Philadelphia) had a tax base per household of under $78,000 in 1995. But 39 enjoyed a household tax base of over $230,000; in three of them the base was $350,000 or more. (Not surprisingly the tax base map can be overlaid almost perfectly on a map showing the proportion of non-Anglo students in these districts.)[32]

The need for *non*educational services can also vary greatly across districts. Urban areas, in particular, face an especially high municipal overburden; that is, they have a high demand for police and fire services, sanitation, and emergency health facilities typically funded from the same insufficient property tax essential to fund the schools. The highest effective tax rate for noneducational services in poor Connecticut towns is almost 19 times greater than the lowest rate for the same kinds of services in wealthy towns. The level of municipal overburden is highly correlated with scores on the Connecticut Mastery Test and with dropout rates.[33]

Like the city and suburb described at the beginning of this chapter, districts within the same state can spend very different amounts on education. Variation around average-spending districts is sometimes low (less than 8 percent in Delaware, West Virginia, Florida, and North Carolina) but sometimes very high (close to 20 percent in Illinois, Missouri, and New York). The nation as a whole spent an average of $7,080 per student in 2001, controlling for regional cost differences, but some districts spent much more and some much less; between the highest-spending 5 percent of the districts and the lowest-spending 5 percent, there can be a variation of $5,000.[34]

These disparities occur within absolute funding levels that themselves can vary enormously from state to state. Again controlling for regional cost differences, the average amount spent on each child in 2001 ranged from $9,360 in New Jersey and $8,860 in New York to $4,580 in Utah and $5,600 in California.[35] These differences reflect variations in wealth and population, but also in local political traditions and policy decisions.

Many central city school districts have substantially lower expenditures per student than in most surrounding suburbs, although average expenditures across the nation are slightly higher in urban districts than in suburban ones, and much higher than in rural districts. These averages can present a misleading picture, however, for several reasons. Poor urban areas usually have a higher percentage of children with disabilities; their education is more costly. Operating costs are also higher in many cities, and not just for schools. Finally, poor urban districts have higher maintenance costs because their buildings are older and their equipment is replaced less frequently.[36] Thus spending for regular education programs in many poor cities ends up substantially lower than such spending in surrounding suburbs.

Districts with large poor populations have a great need for services to overcome educational disadvantage, social trauma, or health-related disabilities. Districts in California and New York, with huge populations of recent immigrants, must fund almost half of the English language instruction of the whole nation. Transportation costs can be very high in large rural districts, as one beleaguered school board member points out: "West Virginia allocates most resources based on the number of students. . . . [But] it costs more money . . . to bus students on mountain roads where the population density is one student per square mile."[37]

This great variation in the range of educational needs and resources to meet them provides the context for school funding reform. State and local policymakers are not responsible for differences in demography or wealth—but they do determine the amount and distribution of money to be spent on schooling. Citizens claim to support the public schools and to believe in equality of opportunity, but funding decisions take place within a structure of education based on residence and largely dependent on local taxation. This structure inhibits reform and makes it hard to create funding policies that fairly promote either the individual or collective goals of the American dream for all Americans.

School Funding in the Courts

With racial desegregation stalled and the worst educational problems concentrated in a minority of school districts unlikely to find relief in a legislature, advocates for reform went to court in the 1970s. In 1973 the Supreme Court decided a case on the issue of interdistrict financial equity. *San Antonio v. Rodriguez* was brought on behalf on Mexican American students seeking more funds for schools in their poor urban district in Texas. It sought to extend the equal protection clause of the Constitution to school funding and to build on the language in *Brown v. Board of Education* that established education as the most important function of state and local government.

The Court split acrimoniously in *Rodriguez*, with a 5-4 vote and five separate opinions. In the end the majority left it to states to deal with the issues of overall funding levels and interdistrict equity. The federal Constitution does not mention education at all; largely on these grounds, the Court ruled that school district boundaries and state financial policies were not a matter for federal intervention and funding standards were not a matter of federal constitutional concern, at least if the education provided was minimally adequate, as it was in Texas.

The funding method under review in *Rodriguez* relied on state money to support about half of all educational expenditures in Texas, and on property taxes for most of the rest. The Court did not dispute that the formula created substantial disparities between poor and wealthy districts in the state. Instead it articulated the tension at the heart of this book: "The Texas system of school finance is responsive to 'a continual struggle between two forces: the desire by members of society to have educational opportunity for all, and the desire of each family to provide the best education it can provide for its own children.'"[38]

Since *Rodriguez*, state policymakers have been entirely responsible for dealing with the issue of equity in school funding. The federal court had the discretion to decide not to act in this area, but states have no choice; the constitution of every state requires the legislature to educate its children. Although language differs somewhat in each document, the responsibility to provide education is clear in all. The obligation to provide an equal education, or an education adequate to meet different student needs, is much less clear. Variations in constitutional language are partly responsible for different outcomes in different states,[39] but legal and political traditions of the state and its policy environment matter a great deal. Courts are always sensitive to potential political reactions to their decisions and to problems that will be raised by nonenforcement; they know that reform can engender tremendous resistance from the legislature and executive. After a school finance decision in New Hampshire, for example, legislators introduced 20 bills as well as a few constitutional amendments to limit judicial independence; these were followed by impeachment proceedings against four of the five supreme court justices. The state bar association described the situation as a "classic confrontation between the branches of government over a difficult issue, namely the *Claremont* [school funding] lawsuit."[40] The situation there has not been resolved, several years after the decision. The *Weekly Standard* characterized the justices in another state as "career government lawyers who couldn't get elected dogcatcher at most town meetings. To get even, they issue arrogant decisions. . . . They emasculated town meeting and local control. Ruined public education, raised taxes, and created antagonisms and resentments all over the state. Not a bad day's work."[41]

School finance is, in short, political dynamite. Left on their own, elected officials will rarely touch it, or will handle it only in controlled and limited circumstances, such as good economic times when high revenues permit generally increased funding. Asked just how difficult it would be to build a consensus on school finance issues, the Speaker of Ohio's house of representatives responded, "On a scale of 1 to 10, I'd say it's a 12." Existing school funding formulas almost always developed over a long period of time and after considerable political bargaining; by definition a majority stands behind them. There is a great deal of money at stake in any reform and a high level of political risk; these formulas provide a lot of money to every locality represented by every legislator in every state. In the context of a school funding controversy in Massachusetts, the secretary for administration and finance pointed out that the state had "328 local and regional school districts operating, each with its own grievances over perceived historical inequities, spread over 351 towns and cities of varying wealth and demographics, represented by 160 representatives and 40 senators, courted by an array of organized interest groups, in an intensely political state. These are not the conditions for a smooth road to reform." School finance reform, said one educational consultant, "is always, everywhere, an extraordinarily powerful political issue. Not every legislator has a hospital or industry in his district, but everyone has a school district, and so everyone fights endlessly about how much of the pie they should get."[42] No wonder that courts are reluctant to order a substantial increase in funding or a dramatic redistribution among districts.

Nevertheless, real reform, when it has come, has almost always been initiated and sustained by the courts. Over the years there has been an enormous variation in the disposition of school funding cases. A few general trends emerge, although no clear patterns.[43] First, the equal protection clauses in most state constitutions provided the basis for the initial cases brought on behalf of poor students or poor districts during the 1970s; by the end of the 1990s, plaintiffs had largely shifted to constitutional provisions requiring the legislature to provide an adequate education for the state's children. Second, many cases in the 1970s sought mainly to equalize the impact of differential property value among the districts; later, in part because the increase in suburban property values during the 1980s made this strategy so difficult, lawsuits were instead designed to equalize spending in the districts. Since about 1990, plaintiffs have aimed for both financial and program adequacy in order to meet the educational needs of poor children. Finally, across the nation, plaintiffs won a higher percentage of cases in the second major wave during the 1990s than in the first wave of the 1970s.[44]

Throughout these decades, much of the testimony has remained consistent with the language of the American dream. As the former commissioner of education for New York State insisted, the claim to fair funding is a claim to the rights of all Americans:

> If you ask the children to attend school in conditions where plaster is crumbling, the roof is leaking and classes are being held in unlikely places because of overcrowded conditions, that says something to the child about how you diminish the value of the activity and of the child's participation in it and perhaps of the child himself. If, on the other hand, you send a child to a school in well-appointed or [adequate facilities] that sends the opposite message. That says, "This counts. You count. Do well."[45]

Some courts have found this kind of claim persuasive. In those cases they initially established either an adequacy standard that guaranteed a higher level of funding for poor students or poor districts, or an equality standard that required funding for them at the same level as that of wealthier districts. More recently some state courts have begun to require spending for poor children beyond adequacy or equality of this kind. They are demanding new legislation with specific programs to meet the needs of children who require more help.[46] The focus on individual student needs is a response to the fact that educational failure continues to be concentrated among the poorest students. "We've dragged out our focus on equity long enough and are now shifting to something more substantive," says Allen Odden, an expert on school finance reform. This is "part of a seismic shift of power," says attorney and journalist David Kirp, from local school boards that "zealously kept control over policy" to an "insist[ence] that states deliver an adequate education" to everyone.[47]

Forty-three states have had litigation on this issue; in 20 existing funding laws that permitted (or even created) unequal funding across districts have been declared unconstitutional. In the first state case on this issue, *Serrano v. Priest*, the California supreme court came down in favor of poor students and established an equality standard, but without setting any required level of funding. Its language was stirring:

> The California public school financing system . . . obviously touches upon a fundamental interest. . . . This system conditions the full entitlement to such interest on wealth, classifies its recipients on the basis of their collective affluence, and makes the quality of a child's education depend upon the resources of his school district and ultimately upon the pocketbook of his parents. We find that such financing system . . . denies to the plaintiffs and others similarly situated the equal protection of the laws.

But the decision was ineffective. Soon after the *Serrano* decision, tax-cutting fever spread across the state, culminating in a referendum that limited school revenue. It was followed by a recession and a huge influx of Latino students to whom many Anglos were hostile. The unintended combined effect of these developments was a leveling downward in funding for public schools.[48] The court decision, which had failed to set a spending level to accompany its equality standard, could not prevent it. In 1975 California ranked in the top twenty among states on spending; by 1995 it ranked in the bottom five. Spending per pupil declined over 15 percent during those two decades when compared with spending in other states.

Most other courts have avoided California's mistake. A recent case, *Campaign for Fiscal Equity v. New York*, illustrates the more usual issues raised in this kind of litigation. The trial court decided in favor of children—this time in the huge New York City district, which has 1.1 million students and 1,200 schools.[49] The plaintiffs claimed that New York State failed to provide sufficient funding to enable New York City to give the level of education required by the constitution. There were, they claimed, too many teachers of relatively low quality, especially in the lowest-performing schools, and too few certified teachers, especially in math and science, largely because salaries were too low to attract good new teachers. They also cited evidence from a state evaluation that school buildings in New York City were in "deplorable physical condition." (A commission in 1995, headed by the man who became chancellor of schools in New York City, found "collapsing building facades, thoroughly rusted structural beams, falling masonry, precariously hung windows, and roof gables held together with wire.")[50] Plaintiffs pointed out that the physical plant affects students' ability to learn; one cannot learn science in labs with obsolete equipment or none. Finally, they claimed that the state's funding mechanism violated the U.S. Civil Rights Act because it especially harmed the city's non-Anglo students, who constituted 73 percent of all the minority students in the state and 84 percent of the city's enrollment.[51]

The defendants "vigorously dispute[d] these claims," arguing that the state "spends more per student on education than all but three other states, that New York City spends more per student than any other large school district in the nation, and that this provision of funds is more than is necessary to provide a sound basic education." They pointed to agreements between the City board and the teachers' union that determined the distribution of teachers across schools, to the nationwide shortage in math and science teachers, and to "poor outreach [that] is in part to blame for any shortage of qualified teachers." They had their own board of education evaluations to show that "the vast majority of New York City public school buildings are in fair condition, requiring at most only preventive maintenance," and argued that in any case there is "no link between a school's disrepair and the test score performance of its students." They insisted, in short, that "any failure" in the schools is the fault of the city and the city's board of education. Finally, they denied any charges of racial or ethnic discrimination.

Both sides agreed that test scores are too low and dropout rates too high, but they differed on who was to blame for this sorry state and who was responsible for fixing it. Plaintiffs blamed the city's failures and inefficiencies on lack of state funding for everything from computers to classrooms. The state countered by claiming, as the judge's decision summarized, that it "is required only to provide the *opportunity* for a sound basic education, that it has done so, and that students' failure to seize this opportunity is a product of various socio-economic deficits experienced by the large number of at risk students in the New York City public schools." At one point the chancellor of the city schools left the courtroom in a fury.

Lawyers for each side, as is typical, made all possible arguments, consistent or not, in hope of finding something that would appeal to the judge. In addition to the civil rights argument, the plaintiffs asserted that the New York City school system was as efficient as it could be, that inefficiencies resulted from a lack of funds, and that regardless of how efficient it was, it had too little money to solve the severe problems of the system and its students. The state, in turn, insisted that money did not affect student outcomes because children brought such severe problems into the schools, that there would be enough money if it were used less corruptly and more wisely, and that any insufficiency in funding was the fault of the city, not the state.

The trial court found the plaintiffs' evidence more compelling, the school system so "abysmal" that something had to be done, and the racial impact of abysmal schooling completely unacceptable. In its words, "The education provided New York City students is so deficient that it falls below the constitutional floor set by the Education Article of the New York State Constitution. . . . In addition, the State's public school financing system has also had an unjustified disparate impact on minority students in violation of federal law." After all the dust settles, the trial court held, "The State Constitution reposes responsibility to provide a sound basic education with the State, and if the State's subdivisions act to impede the delivery of a sound basic education it is the State's responsibility under the constitution to remove such impediments."

The appeals court disagreed, overturning the decision of the trial court. It set the constitutional floor for a sound basic education at a much lower level than the trial court had, and found that the state had met its only obligation—to establish a funding system that "offer[s] all children the opportunity of a sound basic education, not [to] ensure that they actually receive it." In any case, "society needs workers in all levels of jobs, the majority of which may very well be low-level," wrote the appeals court. "The evidence at trial established that the skills required to enable a person to obtain employment, vote, and serve on a jury are imparted between grades 8 and 9."[52] They court also rejected the discrimination argument. It is impossible to know how the state's highest court will resolve the issues in this particular case.

The overall national impact of court decisions on school finance reform, however, has been very positive. In general, in states where courts have demanded action for greater equity or a higher level of adequacy, spending levels have increased and disparities between rich and poor districts have been reduced. In states without such decisions, the pattern in overall spending levels has varied, but disparities have stayed the same or gotten worse. Overall, when a court has declared a state's school finance system unconstitutional, there has been a 23 percent increase in school spending, and a decrease in inequality among districts of between 16 and 38 percent (depending on how it is measured). In most cases inequality declined because spending rose most in the poorest districts (11 percent on average), rose somewhat in the districts in the middle (7 percent on average), and did not change in the wealthiest districts. In general, without a court decision, little happens; the most systematic research finds that "legislative reforms that were not in response to successful litigation had no perceptible impact on the level of distribution of spending. Reform without successful litigation is typically ineffective."[53]

Median funding per pupil at least doubled in four of the five states where lawsuits succeeded during the 1990s (Texas, Kentucky, New Jersey, and

Connecticut) and almost doubled in the fifth state (Tennessee). Funding per pupil increased five times in Connecticut. In all five of these states, inequality in spending among districts declined, usually dramatically. Conversely, in two of the three states in which lawsuits failed during the decade, overall spending also rose, but in all three inequality in spending among districts did not change or even increased considerably.[54] Successful court action on school funding has clearly made a huge difference in promoting the collective goals of public schooling, but not without a struggle.

Responses to the Courts

When courts establish a new standard, governors and legislatures are obliged to respond. Their response has depended on the local political culture, the decisions of key policymakers, and the election cycle.[55] It has been influenced strongly by the state's school finance history, tax structure, and resources. In states where collective bargaining is permitted, teachers' unions have often had substantial impact; in states where economic development is seen as dependent on education reform, the business community has sometimes played an important role. The demographics of the state, its wealth structure, and its racial and ethnic composition can be crucial. The court decision requires a response, the context frames it, and elected officials (and sometimes the public through referendum) decide it.

Whether elected officials decide to redistribute or to raise entirely new revenue, they, like the court, face difficult choices between individual and collective goals. The first alternative can be viewed as helping some children at the direct expense of others, and the second can be seen as taking personal resources, otherwise available to the more privileged to use however they wish, and using them to educate other people's children. In reality children in wealthier districts have continued to receive the best available public schooling; there is no evidence that children in affluent districts in any state have been harmed educationally when the finance system has been reformed. But their parents nevertheless resist.

Because strong opposition can be expected whenever it is tried, only a few states have sought to redistribute local revenue to achieve reform. After 20 years of struggle over school finance, Texas in 1993 passed a law capping the amount of wealth that a district could tax for its own schools. Above that cap property tax receipts were to be transferred from one district to another. Residents of wealthy districts, many parents of children in public schools (even in receiving districts), ideological opponents of egalitarianism, and Anglos with hostility against African Americans have opposed this "Robin Hood" policy, making this part of the law difficult to implement, to put it mildly.[56] The courts extended the original three-year transition period for the transfer provision to seven years; poor districts have in return accused the state of finding loopholes for rich districts and claim that they have lost hundreds of millions of dollars in the meantime.[57]

Vermont's school finance reform law of 1997 is also an anomaly, by far the most dependent on redistribution and therefore extremely controversial. It substitutes a statewide property tax for local property taxes and distributes the funds to all students equally, regardless of district. If districts want to tax themselves to increase per-pupil spending, as most do, they must contribute a portion of those additional funds to a statewide "sharing pool." The wealthier the town, the more it must contribute to the pool—relabeled the "shark pool" by the disgruntled affluent. In the richest towns, therefore, property taxes have risen a lot, leading people like the author John Irving, who describes himself as a "notorious" liberal, to call the new law "Marxism, not democracy." A former state legislator similarly called it "the politics of envy. It's divisive. It's mean. The politics of going after other people is not what my state has ever been about." One teenager described the new law as "crazy. What's going on in this state? . . . My parents work hard to give me a good education. . . . Why are you punishing me?" On the other side were Vermonters from less wealthy districts, who would gain badly needed resources for their schools. From their perspective, what the wealthier districts are "going through now is what 90 percent of towns have gone through for years and years—having to make choices. They'll still have a quality education." Opposition to the new law in this view was just "bad behavior from good lookin' people." Opposition continues, but so far the legislature and governor have not budged; they continue to believe that the funding reform promotes the collective good of the state and the individual good of most of its children. As Governor Howard Dean put it, "The property-tax base, for the purposes of education, belongs to every child in the state, not just the children in special towns."[58]

Because shifting property tax revenues from rich to poor districts can be so divisive, because it raises the most volatile issues of local control and redistribution of wealth, it has been much more common for states to raise additional state revenues in response to court decisions. New revenues permit the distribution of funds so that poor districts can get substantially more funding, almost every district is better off, and no district is worse off. Raising taxes is never easy and it has sometimes taken a decade or more to be accomplished, but this has been the most successful approach over the long term to equalizing opportunities in several states. Two states, New Jersey and Kentucky, had court decisions that perhaps raised the fundamental issues most clearly and required the most substantial response.

New Jersey has all of the elements for high conflict. Residents of the state are deeply committed to localism; the state has over 600 school districts (some with no schools, or one school), and it depends heavily on local property taxes to fund them. Class and race sharply divide its localities. New Jersey is one of the richest states in per capita income, yet it has four of the ten poorest cities in the country as well as several others that would be the poorest cities in many states. Statewide it has one of the most segregated school systems in the country. Black and Hispanic students constitute a third of the public school population and are concentrated in cities with a history of poor school management. The suburban economy has boomed for most of the last 25 years, with many of the largest companies in the world drawn by an excellent transportation system, a highly educated workforce, and proximity to New York and Philadelphia. Its suburban property is among the most valuable anywhere, but in its cities the reverse is true. Although New Jersey spends a lot on education, it periodically has had spending in the largely white suburbs that was one and a half times that in the cities.[59] Political contests in New Jersey are unusually partisan since the two major parties are fairly evenly balanced, and the supreme court has been unusually activist for the past several decades.

A successful court challenge to New Jersey's funding formula came within a year of the decision in *Rodriguez*. The response to *Robinson v. Cahill* included the state's first income tax in 1976, intended to enhance the state's contribution to local school districts, and a wealth equalization formula designed to spread funding more evenly across districts. At first the formula significantly reduced the disparities between wealthy suburban districts and poor urban ones. The economic boom of the 1980s, however, greatly increased property values in the suburbs without doing much to help the cities; this permitted increasingly wealthy suburbs to use their property tax resources to easily outstrip the efforts that cities could make. The law was simply not powerful enough to overcome the enormous disparities, which by 1990 were greater than at the time of the court decision in *Robinson*. A second court case, *Abbott v. Burke*, was brought on behalf of children in the poorest districts, and the state supreme court decided in their favor in 1990. In the court's words, "Under the present system . . . the poorer the district and the greater its need, the less the money available, and the worse the education. . . . Education has failed there, for both the student and the State."[60] The court recognized, in our terms, that public schooling should satisfy both individual and collective goals of the American dream, and that drastically unequal funding violates both.

The decision in *Abbott* required the state to equalize spending on regular education between the cities and the rich suburbs, and to provide additional funding for programs to redress the educational disadvantages of poor children in urban districts, who constituted about a quarter of the state's students. It did not originally require any other specific programmatic changes, and it required no administrative or governance reforms. The legislature, controlled by Democrats, quickly passed a law establishing a very high foundation level of spending for everyone.[61] The great majority of districts, and 80 percent of the students in the state, would have received additional state funds, at least initially. Designated poor urban districts were slated to receive huge increases in state aid; the wealthiest districts did not initially receive less money, but over time would lose some forms of aid (although not others) and would become subject to caps on their annual budget growth. Overall, state aid to education would rise by about $1.1 billion, most of it going to middle-class districts whose representatives were essential to the passage of any new formula. All of this was to be paid for by an increase in the state income tax for high earners.

Debate on the bill and the accompanying tax increase was very partisan. The business community, relatively happy with the education of its top-end employees and resigned to some retraining for the rest, was barely involved, but not everyone else was so restrained. The powerful teachers' union opposed the bill because it included changes that undermined their previous bargaining-table advantage on pensions and Social Security benefits.[62] The fact that the state was immersed in a serious, sustained recession exacerbated the strong reaction against the proposal and tax increase. Much public debate revolved around the court case, which was concerned only with the 30 poorest districts, rather than the new formula, which was focused much more broadly.

Although middle-class districts were to receive most of the money and middle-class taxpayers were to pay little of the tax increase, supporters of the bill never delivered that message effectively. The message was overwhelmed, first by a powerful antitax campaign (substantially financed by the National Rifle Association, upset by the governor's ban on assault weapons), and second by the mistaken impression that poor districts were the sole beneficiaries of the new school formula and other districts its victims. Rhetoric in opposition was strident and included published concerns that "the money . . . will be shoveled hastily into the bottomless pit of New Jersey's disaster areas—that is, its cities. . . . Meanwhile," continued this writer, a long-term Democrat, "the state will have lost a priceless asset—its good public-school districts. . . . My wife and I believe in public schools. We scraped and borrowed to buy a home in a decent school district. We're relying on that for our kids, and now, evidently, it's going to be taken away from us." Superintendents from 25 wealthy districts formed a coalition to oppose the bill, arguing that it "goes beyond the mandate of the court . . . and includes provisions which will fundamentally weaken the most successful and highest-achieving public school districts in the state. . . . Weak schools should not be made strong by making strong schools weak."[63]

The law passed but was never implemented. Reaction to increased taxes led to a rapid rewriting that placated the teachers' union and provided for a smaller increase in aid to poor districts. Almost every nonurban legislator who voted for the initial tax increase was defeated in the next election. And the governor who championed the reform was narrowly defeated four years later. In addition to the usual ideological and party differences, race and class were significant predictors of voter reaction to school finance reform in New Jersey; three-quarters of white parents of school-age children opposed the reform law, whereas half of nonwhite parents endorsed it.[64] At that point the conflict was simply too sharp between action for the collective good and the (largely mistaken) perception of threat to the individual good of wealthier, whiter children. The genuine, but fragile, commitment to equal opportunity for all students could not stand up to this perception, concerted attack by interest groups, general anti-tax sentiment, and hostility to poor urban African Americans.

A new governor and legislature repealed part of the new income tax increase and enacted a series of temporary funding statutes during the mid-1990s. Although disparities between cities and suburbs narrowed somewhat, none of these laws met the court standard. The plaintiffs went back to court several times seeking a remedy. In 1997, under strong pressure from the judiciary, New Jersey finally provided sufficient funding to comply with the *Abbott* requirement for financial parity between rich and poor districts; the basic equity objectives behind the litigation have therefore been met.[65] In the face of executive and legislative recalcitrance, the court also began to define supplemental programs that would be required for poor districts, and in 1998 the state started to comply. As of 2002, plans are in place for universally available preschool programs for three- and four-year-olds in the poorest districts, comprehensive school reform programs in every school in the designated poor districts, and a massive school construction program costing billions of dollars, the largest in any state.[66] After ten years, despite serious conflict over taxation and distribution and continued low-level contention, schooling opportunities for the poorest students have improved, and more children have the chance to meet their goals through public education. The gap between ideology and practice in the American dream has narrowed in New Jersey.

Kentucky has also achieved a great deal but took a very different route. Unlike in New Jersey, all parties to the litigation and all branches of government cooperated in constructing a solution to problems in all schools in the state, a solution that included but went far beyond finance reform. This was possible for several reasons.

First, a very different pattern of wealth and race made reform easier than in New Jersey. Kentucky is a relatively poor state in which cities have the more valuable property and poverty is concentrated in the eastern, rural areas. Minorities, only 9 percent of the population, mostly live in the cities, but the state overall is much less segregated than New Jersey or most other states.[67] Second, the school system as it stood before reform had almost no defenders. By the 1980s Kentucky ranked near the bottom of the states on spending for education, and its state tax burden was proportionately low. It also ranked at or near the bottom on measures of literacy and college attendance, and residents of the state agreed that educational insufficiency was the main obstacle to state economic development. Virtually everyone saw the school system as corrupt.

Third, the politics of reform had a different, less contentious, dynamic. Because teachers cannot engage in collective bargaining in Kentucky, employee unions were not available to press their interests against what they perceived to be the costs of reform. Members of the business community did not seek to remain above the fray as in New Jersey, but rather participated directly in the Pritchard Committee for Academic Excellence, a broad-based, nonpartisan advocacy group that has operated throughout the reform effort. It includes representatives from a wide range of organizations and perspectives, runs local forums to involve citizens across the state, has helped to develop and implement reform proposals, and now monitors the reforms and proposes improvements in their implementation.[68]

In the late 1980s, in *Rose v. Council for Better Education*, 66 poor districts filed suit against the state; they won in 1989. "Lest there be any doubt, the result of our decision is that Kentucky's entire system of common schools is unconstitutional," wrote the court. "This decision applies to the entire sweep of the system—all its parts and parcels." The governor and legislature, despite being the nominal defendants in the case, seemed eager to accept the challenge. In the words of the governor, "The Supreme Court has given us an opportunity to start with a clean slate, and those of us in the executive and legislative branches are in agreement that we need to start from scratch."[69]

They did. The executive director of the Pritchard Committee describes the result of the legislature's ultimate response:

> The sweeping reforms require and measure high academic standards for all children, provide rewards and sanctions for school performance, push decision-making to the school level, control political hiring and nepotism, provide preschool for all four-year-olds, and much more. The tax increase that went with the reform has moved Kentucky toward the funding equity demanded in the initial court test. The gap in per-pupil expenditures between the poorest and the wealthiest districts has been cut by more than half.[70]

Although it required greater equality in spending across all districts, the court in *Rose* balanced the collective and individual goals of education by permitting the wealthiest to exceed the standard. The new law provided for a three-tiered funding system. It guaranteed a moderate foundation level of spending for all districts, provided matching state funds on a sliding scale to districts that taxed themselves up to 15 percent above the foundation level, and finally, permitted districts to raise their own property taxes another 15 percent. Permitting some disparities to remain between rich and poor districts reduced the level of equity, but also the amount of controversy. The tax structure only needed to be changed moderately, by New Jersey standards, to generate the necessary additional funds.

The combination of relatively low tax increases, less racial tension, more business support, and consensus on the need for school improvement to rescue the state's economy ensured that the revenue changes generated much less heat than in New Jersey. One legislator involved in drafting the bill noted with pride and relief that more lawmakers who voted against the bill than for it were defeated in the next election. In the words of a consultant involved in drafting the new law, "You're not seeing the demagogues coming out of the woodwork, trying to take advantage of people's disaffection for the law." Across the state there was a sense of accomplishment: a superintendent in one poor mountainous district reported proudly that his students finished their first year "in a school with a librarian, counselor, full-time art classes, aides assigned to assist potential dropouts, and watertight roofs. 'We just feel like we're on the move and feel like in a few years, we'll really be able to perform. We've had a good start.' "[71]

Not everything is perfect, of course, in Kentucky. Since its inception, educators and citizens have hotly debated some programmatic elements of the reform, particularly statewide assessments. The scope of change, however, eliminated questions about how money was to be used and made the momentum of reform hard to stop. Kentucky has been able to sustain most of its original reform through several changes in government; it now has a much higher level of funding equity as well as an overall increase in spending on schools. "Kentucky's School Reform Law," boasts Governor Combs, "is a classic example of how this democracy of ours can work for progress when the heads of the three coordinate branches of government lay aside their egos and pride of turf and work together. . . . The result was the enactment of a school reform measure that has been acclaimed as a model for other states."[72]

"The fight over equity never goes away," says the state superintendent of education in New Mexico, "and it never will." Contests over school finance reform can pit "gold towns" against poor cities, and set parents who believe that they have earned the right to pass on a competitive advantage against those who seek a fair chance for their own children. It can generate disputes between leaders who insist that "all we're asking is that we be allowed to preserve our schools" and reformers "invit[ing] people to think beyond the boundaries of their own communities, to think about all the children in the state."[73]

Providing poor districts with more money usually requires raising additional revenue and therefore some individual sacrifice. But it seldom requires the movement of local money, and it has rarely, if ever, hurt schools anywhere. Nevertheless, if not handled well politically, it can create a direct conflict between the individual and collective goals of the American dream. Political engagement can also ease these conflicts, and political coalitions, with the help of the courts, have moved states and school districts closer to achieving both collective and individual goals—to "equip students for their role as citizens and enable them to succeed economically and personally," in the words of the Wisconsin supreme court.[74]

Money matters, and a society as wealthy as ours has no excuse for depriving schools of the resources they need to help all children pursue success. Money, of course, is only the beginning.[75] For children to succeed, schools need not only to be financed well but also to spend well, to use their money honestly, fairly, and effectively. The issues of school finance are therefore not clearly separable from those of school reform, to which we now turn.

4

SCHOOL REFORM

Both left and right agree that there's something seriously wrong with our public education system. Our children are actually worse off when they leave the system than when they enter it.
—*Campaign for America's Children, 2000*

The evidence suggests that the perceived crisis in education has been greatly exaggerated, if indeed there is any crisis at all.
—*Alan Krueger, Princeton University, in a report to the Federal Reserve Bank, 1998*

Ultimately the battle over standards and accountability is a continuation of the civil rights struggle.... Standards and accountability expose the sham that passes for education in many heavily minority schools and provide measurements and pressure to prod schools to target resources where they are needed most.
—*Charles Taylor, vice chair of Leadership Conference of Civil Rights, 2000*[1]

A MERICANS GIVE A GRADE OF "B PLUS" to the schools attended by their own children, a "B minus" to the public schools in their community, and a "C" to the public schools nationally. Incumbent politicians extol the impact of the educational reforms they have sponsored while insurgents point to the problems that remain. Some analysts call for an "autopsy" on public education, others insist that such rhetoric represents a "manufactured crisis" comprised of "myths [and] fraud."[2]

The American public education system is not in crisis. Some public schools are impressive and many are doing a good job, although most are not as good as they should be. In a few places, chiefly in poor urban districts (and in some poor rural districts as well), schools are failing miserably; they provide the evidence for people who see a crisis.[3] Once again the most serious problems result from inequality.

In part because of home and community influences, poor children often come to school less ready to learn than others, and they face more obstacles to educational success as they grow up.[4] Parents and communities can and must contribute to alleviating this problem, just as social policies such as full employment, universal health insurance, and family allowances could help. As we have seen, however, it is the schools to which we have given the central responsibility to make the American dream work, to provide the structure and tools that all children need to pursue their dreams and maintain democracy. America has chosen to invest in schools rather than these other social policies[5] to try to equalize opportunity; if our nation allows public education to fail the children who most need its help, then the dream is merely a sham. We cannot simultaneously substitute schools for other policies to alleviate poverty *and* permit schools to shirk the tasks needed to do the job.[6]

School reform *can* help poor children, and others, improve their performance. The movement for high standards has created a mechanism that can help all students to learn more. Preschool, summer school, and small classes can help them. Better training and professional development can help their teachers. More generally, giving poor children the kind of schooling that middle-class children routinely receive would help them a lot. Americans, in short, know roughly how to enable all children to better pursue success, and they know how to promote more equality of opportunity through school reform; they are just not doing enough of it. As with school funding and desegregation, this is mostly a matter of political will.

The Quality and Distribution of Public Schooling

Over time various school reforms have helped improve the quality of public education. Americans get more years of schooling than do residents of many other nations, and more than at any previous point in our history. As we have pointed out, NAEP achievement scores have shown improvement and then stability in most subjects in most grades over the past 30 years; this is especially impressive since the students who generally do least well on tests are staying in school longer. Black students and younger Hispanic students have gained the most. SAT scores have gone up for both blacks and whites even though more people are taking the test. These results are due partly to the fact that students are enrolling in tougher courses in high school than they used to. Between 1987 and 1998, American students increased the number of courses they took in virtually all subjects—math, science, foreign languages, fine arts, social studies, and computer studies. Four times as many blacks and six times as many Hispanics now take a full curriculum (at least three credits in English, social studies, science, and math, along with computer science and foreign languages) as their predecessors did in the early 1980s. Many more students are finishing courses in advanced algebra and chemistry than used to, and here too African

Americans and Latinos are closing the gap with Anglos and Asians.[7] Only one-tenth of young adults now drop out of school without earning a high school credential; during the 1970s and 1980s, the dropout rate for whites declined and the comparable rate for blacks declined even farther. The gap in the dropout rate between children from high- and low-income families is also smaller, and college attendance is up in every racial or ethnic group.[8]

In short, more people are staying in school, and they are staying in school longer. They are not just attending but learning more, which puts most of them in a better position to attain absolute and relative success than their predecessors. Over the past 30 years, all of this has happened at a slightly faster rate in the most disadvantaged groups. This trajectory—better schooling outcomes across the board and a reduction in the gap between the best-off and worst-off—is clear evidence that Americans have a real commitment to reforming the public schools to ensure that everyone can pursue the American dream.

But by no means is everything fine in public schooling. Although the graduates of American colleges and universities compare favorably to those in other countries, high school students from the United States consistently rank lower than many of those from Western Europe on tests of science and mathematical knowledge; as the *New York Times* put it in a headline, "Students in U.S. Do Not Keep Up in Global Tests."[9] Students from poor families, residents of deeply poor inner cities, and recent immigrants are much less likely to graduate from high school than are others. Up to 30 percent of young Hispanics drop out of school, and the rise in the proportion of Latinos attending college is lower than that of other groups. And whether or not one goes to and finishes college is closely related to family income. Over three-quarters of well-off young adults go straight from high school to college, compared with fewer than half of poor youth. Well-off students are also more likely to go to a four-year rather than a two-year college, and much more likely to graduate.[10]

Even among those who stay in school, some students are not learning enough to attain relative or even absolute success, and by some measures outcomes are getting worse for the worst-off. On the NAEP the average reading score for fourth graders remained the same over the 1990s; however, scores of students in the bottom 10 percent declined significantly while scores in the top 25 percent improved. Results for blacks and Hispanics are much worse than those for whites and Asians. The average score in reading is 217, but the gap in reading scores between all African American and all Anglo children is 33 points, and the comparable gap between Hispanic and Anglo children is 29 points.[11] Even for fourth-grade children in families above the poverty line, the black-white test score gap is 22 points and the Hispanic-white gap is 19 points.[12] The children with the most severe achievement problems are both poor and non-Anglo. Almost half of young inner city students (compared with a third of others) and three-fifths of young poor students (compared with a quarter of the nonpoor) read at a level below basic.[13]

In mathematics overall scores rose substantially during the 1990s, but the racial and ethnic gaps remained steady, and African American and Latino students did considerably worse than Anglo and Asian American students in all grades. Across all NAEP tests, the achievement gap between students with well-educated and poorly educated parents (a good proxy for class status) grew or held steady throughout the 1990s. As the president of the Los Angeles' teachers' union puts it, "We have kids without teachers, teachers without classrooms, and a district without a clue. The system is broken. Students and teachers are a forgotten priority here in the poor city schools."[14]

For the majority of poor children, high quality preschool is unaffordable or unavailable, so they arrive in kindergarten or first grade less ready to learn. Their classes are larger and their teachers less qualified than those enjoyed by wealthier students. They are disproportionately placed in low-ability classes or in the general track; they therefore take fewer challenging courses and have less expected of them. In this environment many more poor than well-off students fail, become disaffected, and drop out. If they finish, they are less prepared for college; when they go to college, they frequently need remediation; if they need too much remediation, they never graduate. Poor urban students may have more family and community problems than other children, but their schools have also failed them.

The Context for School Reform

School reform is an extraordinarily messy process, for many reasons. The first is fragmented governance. Thousands of local districts do most of the work, 50 state governments set most of the policies, and the federal government can come in periodically and make influential demands on everyone.

In addition, most parents have experienced public schools themselves and hold stronger and more fully developed views about education than about most other policy arenas. They are generally satisfied with local schools, and their image of what a school should look like is often what a school did look like in their day; that makes change difficult. Because of the way they remember their own school and out of concern for their children, they focus on issues like discipline, safety, and the work ethic; school performance is often secondary. In a recent poll, a quarter of the respondents agreed that the biggest problem in schools today was "lack of discipline," and another quarter said it was violence, weapons, drugs, or gangs; only 8 percent chose "quality of education" as their major concern.[15] Until recently, in fact, Americans worried about too much innovation more than about too little. In 1970 and again in 1982, more parents thought the curriculum in local schools already met "today's needs" than thought it needed renovation. Only in 1997, after all the recent attention to school reform, did a bare majority agree that the curriculum needed to be updated; even then almost as many thought it was already adequate. In a 1999 poll, parents who were asked how they would improve local public schools again placed discipline first; only 5 percent focused on standards or curricular reform.[16] Twice as many Americans care that schools teach good work habits as care about advanced mathematics, and almost four times as many endorse teaching the value of hard work as compared with teaching Shakespeare or Hemingway.[17]

When they do attend to substantive reforms, most Americans want schools to use traditional pedagogies and focus mainly on teaching basic skills. "I think the basics is always a key thing in education," said one member of a focus group. "A lot of times you don't have the basics." Students "need to be able to read, they need to be able to write, they need to be able to do math," asserted another. Some add "computers" to that list, but many agree with a third person: "I tend to just go back to my own past and the people I grew up with. Most of us turned out pretty good and I think the way we did it back then must have been alright. To me, some of the modern thinking is not the way I'd like to see it go."[18]

Some, like a woman from Albuquerque, argue for a broader view based on both the collective and individual goals of education:

> If we don't teach our kids to think, then we would stop being a democracy. We would stop being a free society. If everybody was satisfied with their itty-bitty, very limited niche, then it would be the end of our way of life. . . . Those who can grow will grow, will invent, will write, will do whatever they can do because they've been taught not just the basics but also to think.[19]

"I would require [students] to take . . . higher level courses when they get through with the basics," echoed a man from Denver, "because . . . it challenges them, and they may exceed everybody's expectations and excel where nobody thought they would."[20] Some Americans clearly want critical thinking and higher-level courses; nevertheless, most focus first on school climate and basic skills, and this makes substantive school reform more difficult.

Teachers are arguably more important to successful reform than parents, but their attitudes can also create obstacles for some school reform efforts. Teachers have been sovereign within their own classrooms for a long time and many do not easily adopt new content or pedagogy; they become cynical when too many reforms are offered and tend to wait them out. As one teacher put it, "When you've been in the district 20 years or so, you just learn to go with the flow. It doesn't really matter who's doing what down there [at headquarters]. You just kind of go with it."[21] Others feel frustrated and powerless: as one told an interviewer, "In my school, teachers are dead last on the list of those who have influence over education. Custodians and secretaries have more influence on the administration than I do." Some blame the children: "The biggest change needed is that *students* need to take responsibility for their own education. . . . Right now, no matter how good a teacher is, at least 50 percent of the class doesn't learn anything. This is mainly because the students just don't bother to pay attention. I tell my students often: I can *teach* you something, but only *you* can *learn* it." Teachers consistently rank the absence of parental support or interest and low student motivation as their chief concerns.[22]

Like citizens in general, fewer than a tenth of all teachers rank poor curricula or low standards as the biggest problem facing their schools. They endorse higher standards in the abstract but are less urgent about their attainment than many policymakers.[23] A slight majority believes that the curriculum in their school "already meets today's needs" rather than needing improvement or updating. Over 80 percent agree that "reforms often have unanticipated consequences that people outside of education underestimate"; their caution exceeds that of superintendents, principals, school board members, and business leaders. When asked what would "improve the education you provide your students," their ambitions are sometimes low: they may ask only for "a large color TV and a VCR and cable with satellite access" in their classroom, or for "more money for classroom materials," or for a "change in the way that the community views education." A majority prefers traditional multiple choice tests to essay tests and portfolios, and a majority prefers current grouping practices to heterogeneous classrooms. Teachers consistently rate local schools much higher than do other Americans.[24] For good reasons or bad, many teachers are just not committed to reform efforts.

In addition, in those states where teachers are permitted to bargain collectively, teachers' unions are frequently part of the problem rather than the solution. Unions have been mostly focused on salaries and benefits rather than professional or educational concerns. Even Bob Chase, the former president of the National Education Association (NEA), recognized this:

> The National Education Association has been a traditional, somewhat narrowly focused, union. We have butted heads with management over bread-and-butter issues—to win better salaries, benefits, and working conditions for school employees. And we have succeeded. . . .
>
> While this narrow, traditional agenda remains important, it is *utterly inadequate* to the needs of the future. It will not serve our members' interest in greater professionalism. It will not serve the public's interest in better quality public schools. And it will not serve the interests of America's children. . . .
>
> Too often, NEA has sat on the sidelines of change, naysaying, quick to say what won't work and slow to say what will. It is time for our great association to lead the reform, to engineer change. . . .[25]

Unfortunately the national leadership of the unions is frequently out in front of its membership on issues of school reform. In 2000 NEA president Chase and other leaders endorsed what the *Washington Post* described as a "modest" proposal to link bonuses to teacher performance, as well as another to permit higher salaries for people with scarce skills in math and science. Delegates to the NEA's national convention rejected these proposals, leading the *Post* to conclude that "teachers' inflexibility damages their own claims to leadership in the reform debate." The statewide unions in Massachusetts threatened lawsuits against a proposal to test veteran math teachers even if most students in their schools fail to meet state standards, and called instead for additional funding. In reaction the *New Republic* wrote that "viewing additional funding and stricter standards as mutually exclusive is politically self-defeating and morally indefensible—in fact, it's precisely the reason teachers' unions have lost their moral authority in the American education debate."[26]

Collective bargaining agreements continue to structure relations between teachers' unions and educational management and can create serious obstacles to reform. These documents may set policy on everything from class size and teacher assignment to the scheduling of lunch breaks, and changing any part of them can mean a fight. One study of alternative schools in New York, for instance, found that

> attempts at innovation have met frequent resistance from the teachers' union. Although the UFT [United Federation of Teachers] offers rhetorical support for various educational reforms, the core interests of the organization lie elsewhere. Like most unions, the UFT's primary concerns relate to job conditions, pay scales, and protecting members from the arbitrary actions of administrators. . . . The top echelons of the UFT, generally regarded as more liberal than the rank and file, usually praise reforms. At the school level, however, union representatives routinely respond to innovations by characterizing changes as violations of the union contract and filing grievances that prevent reforms.[27]

Unions in a few states and localities have endorsed experiments in merit pay, charter schools, curriculum realignment, removal of incompetent teachers, and mentoring programs for new teachers. But they are the exceptions; teachers' unions will not go away, and their frequent resistance makes school reform much harder.

On the other side of contract negotiations are local school boards, but they too are often in the rear guard of reform. Although most school board members are hardworking and dedicated, board membership can instead be seen as a ticket to a higher political office, a route to illegal personal enrichment, or a platform for pursuing some goal other than children's education. In 1995, for example, most members of New York City's highly politicized community school boards could not say how many students were in their own community district, how well students were doing in reading or math, how many schools were overcrowded, or how much money was in their district's budget. There is little systematic research on school boards, but the little there is shows them to be relatively invisible or mistrusted within their community and typically uninvolved in or ineffective at setting broad policy agendas or changing the direction of a school system. One study, for example, found that boards spent only 3 percent of their time in developing and overseeing policy, compared with over half of their time on administration. As one ex–school board member recalls, "My board was ill equipped to deal with many crucial tasks. . . . Most of my time was spent in endless and unproductive meetings. . . . Staff members would ramble on, going over material already available in written form. . . . Hours were spent deciding what punishment should be meted out to a high school student caught with marijuana in his pocket. . . . After all this effort, the school system remained pretty much the same." He concludes that local school boards "can't begin to answer this country's education problems."[28]

Elected policymakers, who ultimately control the schools, also frequently belong on the list of obstacles to effective school reform. Many have been concerned mostly with short-term results, symbolic actions, and rhetorical advantage. They are overly responsive to shortsighted public demands, interest group pressure, the exigencies of the election cycle, and party advantage. One study found, for example, that

> Mayor Schaefer [of Baltimore] . . . preferred quick, decisive action aimed at visible problems and tended to eschew more complex policy issues. . . . In Mayor Schaefer's opinion, the school system was a political land mine, and heavy involvement in school affairs offered few rewards. Schaefer typically left school policy (other than the budget) to trusted associates on the school board and to African American administrators who owed their appointments to city hall.

As Adam Urbanski, the reforming president of the Rochester Teachers' Association, puts it, "Real reform is real hard . . . and takes a real long time."[29]

Reform in Cities

In addition to these problems, which can occur anywhere, and with a student body in much greater need of help, cities have to deal with special obstacles to reform. Urban mayors, who may be the only public officials with the clout and visibility needed to promote significant changes, often have little or no control over their school districts. Many urban districts are very big; changes made at the turn of the century to rationalize their administrations, professionalize their work forces, and prepare for huge waves of immigrants have ironically created large bureaucracies that are often unable or unwilling to respond to changing conditions. Local community groups in New York, for example, find themselves continually battling with even those school administrators designated to help them set up new and innovative schools. Malevolence or laziness need not be involved: what the groups define as necessary innovation and parental involvement is seen by the administrators as demands for favoritism and disruption of essential standard operating procedures.[30]

Many cities also have large schools in which it is harder to get to know and respond to the children, more complicated to get the staff to unify around a coherent educational approach, and much more difficult to manage or create a safe environment. Many urban children move frequently, which lessens their chances to make connections with their teachers, disrupts their ability to learn from ever-changing curricula, and creates obstacles to developing classroom communities with shared goals for learning. Poor parents have less bureaucratic and educational experience than parents in the suburbs; in increasing numbers urban residents do not have English as their native language, and many therefore feel unable to monitor the district or get involved in education issues at all.

A depressed urban economy in some places has created pressure to employ more people than necessary from the community, as well as a more intense temptation to use education funds for corrupt purposes. In the two decades after 1978, members of 18 of the 32 community school boards in New York City were suspended, involved in scandals, or indicted. In 1996 the *New York Times* described ten local districts with "histories of corruption" and drew a clear association between high levels of corruption and low levels of student achievement. At times school systems in poor cities such as Baltimore and Detroit have become job regimes; the school board of Atlanta became known as the "employment agency of last resort."[31]

Businesspeople in cities hesitate to get involved with schools because they find retraining students to be less trouble than urban school politics and more reliable than reform: as one business leader in St. Louis complained, "It would take an incredible amount of time to deal with that bureaucracy. Working in one election was enough of a commitment for me." Many live in suburbs or send their children to private schools so their personal commitment to public school reform is low; when they do become involved, their efforts tend to focus on making schools run more efficiently rather than on helping them educate students better.[32]

Racial politics has a profound, often unacknowledged, impact on school reform in cities. In Baltimore, for example, reform has for decades been inextricably entwined with issues of racial mistrust and hierarchy. In 1996 political leaders in Maryland appeared to have reached an agreement providing the city's schools with more resources in exchange for greater state oversight of their use in a school reform plan. But the African American mayor, Kurt Schmoke, backed off, contending in letters to the governor that "the idea that management is the primary problem [in the Baltimore City public schools] is insulting and paternalistic, and to my mind gains currency, in certain circles, because it is politically expedient and appeals to popular stereotypes."[33] He was responding to the teachers' union and a powerful alliance of African American clergy who opposed the partnership. As the analysts studying this controversy summed up, "The church community considered the proposal an 'outrageous' state 'takeover,' threatening the long tradition of black control of the Baltimore City Public Schools. According to the Reverend Roger Gench [cochair of one of the groups of clergy], 'racial prejudice and stereotypes [were] behind' the agreement."[34] The agreement that was eventually signed prompted further claims by ministers, union officials, and community leaders that it was "anti-democratic" and represented "racial paternalism." Opponents wrote an "open letter" asserting that

> We will not accept Baltimore becoming a colony of the state, with its citizens having no say in the education of their children. African-Americans, in particular, have fought a long, hard battle for equality. Over the years, too many paid the ultimate price for community empowerment. We will not stand and allow the gains those people sacrificed and died for to be given away. We have earned the dream of quality education for our children, and local autonomy in decision-making.

Since the politics in Baltimore are not very different from the politics of many other American cities,[35] the bitter fallout from America's long-standing racial hierarchy can present yet another major obstacle to school reform efforts.

Despite all of this, cities have recently made important reform efforts. As we will see, these are usually done in the context of the standards movement, are sometimes accomplished after changes in the governance structures of the district, and are often financed by successful lawsuits over school funding. Even in Hartford, with problems as bad as those anywhere, the state legislature instituted reforms, a new superintendent energetically pursued change, and the union took the lead to make things happen. The involvement of the union was particularly noteworthy because, as the *New York Times* pointed out, "For years the Hartford teachers' union relished its reputation as the most militant in the nation [and] . . . got its members the highest teacher salaries despite their students' having the lowest test scores in the state." As Sandra Feldman, president of the parent American Federation of Teachers (AFT), explained the turnaround, "I think there was a realization among teachers that unless we got involved in education reform, we would not get community support. Hartford is a place where there was so much conflict for so long, everybody was trying to blame everybody else. Now it's a model for how you can make this happen."[36]

Changing the direction of an urban school system, in Hartford or elsewhere, remains the most difficult educational challenge in the United States. Although the odds are still against the children in poor urban schools, all the necessary elements can be brought together, at least for a while. Although it is harder in cities than elsewhere, real reform is possible. Parents are willing to spend money for all kinds of initiatives, as we have seen; many teachers make a good-faith effort to implement change; some local unions have been progressive; some school boards have endorsed a wide range of reforms; and many elected officials are engaged in substantive school reform efforts. And because of what has been learned from the long history of school reform, the most likely time for it to make a difference is now.

The Stages of School Reform

The modern era of reform began in the late 1950s in response to the USSR's launching of the first satellite, Sputnik. Since then, the United States has gone through several stages of reform, successive periods in which one way of thinking has more or less dominated reform strategies. These strategies have been summarized by one set of researchers, with somewhat different meanings, as "fixing the parts," "fixing the people," "fixing the schools," and "fixing everything."[37] These remain useful generalizations.

During the cold war, Americans saw the first launching of Soviet satellites as not only a military threat but also a direct challenge to American education. The federal government responded with what the *New York Times* described as a "truly remarkable crash program to upgrade the nation's educational resources . . . [and] revolutionize the teaching of the sciences." Ernest Boyer, the best-known U. S. commissioner of education, recalled 15 years later that "there was an excitement in education at the time. The public seemed to turn to education for answers to a critical problem. Teachers and local schools were brought into the action."[38]

The effect of Sputnik lasted throughout the 1960s as experts and practitioners tried out a huge array of ideas in schools across the country. Their goal was to upgrade Americans' skills in math, science, and foreign languages, and to enhance the research capacities of the best students. Many reformers believed that a particular reform directed at individual problem areas in any district could by itself make a difference and could be replicated. Through experiment they thought they could find out how to "fix the pieces" and then spread successful programs through publishing their results or establishing organizations for that purpose. They experimented with curriculum design, building configuration, supervisory structure, or programs to help failing students. They developed language labs, open classrooms, and the "new math."

Many of these innovations, however, lacked rigor in design and evaluation, and the sheer number of targets and approaches assured confusion and many failures. (The new math even became the subject of one of Tom Lehrer's popular satires.)[39] Even programs with successful designs were rarely disseminated widely: simply informing educators about programs that worked elsewhere turned out to be insufficient to enable them to change their own curricula, pedagogical practices, and school climate.[40] A few well-designed programs made it past these hurdles, but here too some teachers did not have the capacity to fully understand and properly implement the changes. For all of these reasons, too many of the reforms did not produce the desired benefits for teaching or learning.

A justifiable next step, beginning in the 1960s, was to concentrate on the teachers, to try to "fix the people." This effort too involved a number of initiatives—attempting to attract better candidates, restructure teacher training programs, strengthen certification requirements, increase salaries, and create greater accountability for teacher performance.

Despite strong public support for improving the quality of teaching, most early initiatives did not succeed. Salaries increased with the greater overall investment in education, but efforts to create financial incentives for better performance proved hard to accomplish and sustain because of their cost, existing teacher incentive structures, union resistance, or the demands of politics and the labor market. Education programs at colleges also remained hard to change; even the AFT recently conceded that

> while some education programs at colleges . . . have taken significant and creative steps to reshape curricula and raise standards, many programs are still beset by serious problems that must be addressed. These include difficulty in recruiting the ablest students, . . . inadequate standards for entering and exiting teacher education programs, poor coordination between teacher education and liberal arts faculty, little consensus about what should comprise the pedagogy curriculum, . . . [and] lack of standards for clinical programs.[41]

School administrators also often paid little attention to teacher improvement efforts: they were focused on working with their local boards, setting budgets, or promoting programs in order to demonstrate their effectiveness. Both teachers and supervisors therefore contributed to the failure of the early attempts to "fix the people," at which point reformers shifted their focus to efforts to "fix the schools."

These initiatives, starting in the late 1980s, tried to go beyond improving school personnel in order to focus on their interactions. Reformers reasoned that a school, like other somewhat isolated institutions, develops a style and culture that becomes largely independent of the goals of any person in it. Thus adding a few new people or eliminating a few old ones, moving teachers around or giving them some additional workshops, even changing the principal, could make little headway against the school culture. Instead, everyone's understanding of the school's mission and identity, their pattern of relating to colleagues and students, their daily behavior within the classroom and outside of it, must change simultaneously for any particular reform to take root. As Robert Slavin, a proponent of school reform, put it, "We kind of do a heart- [and] lung transplant. . . . If you don't deal with both instruction and curriculum and school organization, things start to slide back."[42] In part this new wave of reforms was an attempt to improve the workplace and thereby attract, keep, and motivate teachers. But it also was an effort to create a school culture conducive to learning and reform, and to create a more coherent approach to education within each building. As the superintendent of schools in Memphis concluded, "We could no longer tinker around the edges of change. We . . . [had] to create a map that would guide whole systems of people to make the quantum leap necessary to turn all schools into student-centered, results-based learning environments where high achievement is the norm."[43]

School-level reform has taken many shapes. The most common form, with the broadest and sometimes most intense support, is site-based management. Teachers, administrators, and (often) parents come together in a more or less formal structure and obtain some authority over staffing patterns, scheduling, class size, and student assignment. They typically receive some control over budget and personnel decisions as well. Supporters hold out high hopes; in the words of the Minneapolis public schools:

> Site-based management . . . is a chosen strategy—to move decision-making closest to the students served. . . . Through site-based management, it is hoped that each school continuously renews itself, and its ability to improve the achievement of each of its students and eliminate gaps in learning. . . . Schools must be free to act in ways which help each of its students reach the learning standards, expecting and receiving support from the district.[44]

This devolution of power has sometimes given new motivation to the professional staff and parents and improved working conditions. But site-based management does not reliably change teaching practice, improve individual student performance, or ensure that collective educational goals are met. There is simply too much variation in the knowledge and ability of participants, as well as in their willingness to focus on shared educational goals rather than particular concerns. Site-based management also demands an enormous amount of time, effort, and resources that could otherwise be used to improve curriculum and instruction. When schools are left on their own without clear external standards, a strong commitment from the community, a lot of training for participating parents, and a great deal of technical support, this approach has not in itself been a sufficient agent of school change. In the end it is too far removed from what goes on in the classroom.[45]

Some efforts to "fix the schools" do seek to redesign what teachers do in class and to create support systems that will keep changes on track.[46] Some concentrate on early literacy, some on other aspects of the curriculum. With a few exceptions, each model is formed around a noted educator's vision and methodology and is shaped by that person's particular understanding of the overall process of learning. These models have correspondingly distinctive names, such as Modern Red Schoolhouse, Roots and Wings, or Voices of Love and Freedom.

At least 3,500 schools have tried one of the seven whole-school reform models sponsored by New American Schools (NAS), a privately funded nonprofit organization set up in 1991 for this purpose. Each well-developed model requires that substantially more than a majority of the teachers in that school vote to adopt it, that the school set aside sufficient financial and administrative resources, and that the whole school adopt all elements of the design. The developers of the model, in turn, typically send trained professionals to the school to start and help maintain the transformation, provide technical support and advice from a central location, design relevant forms of professional development and strategies for reorganizing the staff, and encourage participating schools to exchange ideas.

In addition to Memphis, cities such as Cincinnati, Los Angeles, Pittsburgh, and San Diego have experimented with NAS models. Schools were initially granted a substantial level of autonomy on budget and curriculum, were required to provide technological and other support services, and had to measure progress against agreed-upon standards. In each community there was an attempt to involve parents and secure support from the wider community for the school-level reforms.

Formal evaluations of NAS programs face the usual problems of self-selection among participants, protectiveness of program designers, and limitations of tests intended to measure success.[47] As so often occurs, however, the clearest conclusion is that "it's amazing how little evaluation there is," in the words of the dean of Harvard's Graduate School of Education.[48] The most recent and neutral evaluation found that about half of the schools using models from the NAS initiative have made gains in reading or math relative to their districts. The authors warn that reform is too new in most schools to warrant clear conclusions, since success depends mainly on how well the program is implemented, but they conclude with cautious optimism about whole-school reform.[49]

Federal funding (now over $300 million) encourages low-performing schools to adopt one of these models, and the supreme court of New Jersey has mandated whole-school reform in the 300 schools of the 30 poorest districts. But even the best-designed models can be difficult to implement. To quote the battle-scarred former superintendent in Memphis again, "The devil, as usual, is in the details. Guaranteeing that the system of beliefs, behaviors, policies, and practices that ensures . . . [that whole-] school reform is made and maintained is messy, difficult, and extremely complicated. . . . Whole-school reform is not a sprint. It is a marathon that requires the stamina and heart of the best long-distance runners." The new superintendent in Memphis, in fact, abandoned a citywide attempt to implement some of the well-known whole-school models, and other districts have had trouble with models that were badly designed, that could not function at a distance from the educational leader who developed them, or that could not be adjusted to fit an array of community and political contexts.[50]

Some attempts to reform individual schools fail because of a lack of support higher up. As the president of NAS put it, "States and districts have important and unavoidable roles to play in making . . . change happen."[51] No matter how hard people within a school seek to reform it, a lack of commitment by the district or the absence of policy coherence at the state level can create serious obstacles to their success. In retrospect, therefore, it is not surprising that reformers have now concluded that in order to fix the schools (and the people and the parts), it is necessary to take a more comprehensive approach, to try to "fix everything."

Systemic Reform

For advocates of the systemic approach, successful reform requires the whole educational system to function in a coherent and consistent way and move in a clear direction. Only then can schools give every student a chance to attain his or her dreams. In the late 1980s and early 1990s, therefore, reformers began to focus on the structural problems beneath the other approaches, seeing the essential issue as the "fragmented," "complex," and "multi-layered" education policy framework.[52] In their view each level and branch of government gave conflicting signals, politicians were afraid to confront stakeholders, and reform constituencies worked at cross-purposes. The New York State Board of Regents Advisory Council on Low-Performing Schools nicely summarized the "major obstacles to systemic improvement" this way:

- Far too much of the school improvement process is focused upon developing plans that are insufficiently coordinated, poorly implemented and inadequately evaluated.
- The technical assistance and support offered by the State . . . are often not commensurate with the enormity of the challenges faced by [consistently low performing schools]. . . . In turn, . . . [those] schools lack the capacity to ensure that students and their families have access to the comprehensive set of educational, health, and social services they need to succeed. . . .
- No one is held accountable for this failure and no one is given the authority to decisively intervene to change the situation.

The Council was "outraged that so many thousands of students are denied educational opportunity for year after year in schools that everyone knows are failing" and demanded "a significant overhaul of how we set priorities, make decisions, prepare and support school staff, involve parents, distribute and use resources, connect schools to communities, and design accountability systems."[53] The Council concluded its scathing indictment with 93 recommendations for change.

By focusing their attention on the system as a whole, reformers could see why the previous, partial methods of reform were ineffective. They issued a call to policymakers at the state or district level to articulate individual and collective goals, outline standards consistent with them, and then develop curricula for all schools based on those standards. They seek statewide or districtwide assessment systems to determine whether curricula have been mastered, standards reached, and goals met; they call for accountability for school progress and authoritative intervention when progress in a school is too slow. To support these reforms, they also endorse changes in the ways schools are governed and administered, ranging from abolishing state or local school boards to enhancing decision making at the school level.

The most thoughtful reformers insist that curricula be not merely systemic but also substantively rich and focused on learning beyond the basics. They want schools to be responsible for ensuring that students achieve at a high level, with depth of understanding, analytic skill, and the capacity to integrate knowledge; teachers and students alike should "prize exploration and the production of knowledge, rigor in thinking and sustained intellectual effort," as one pair of knowledgeable supporters put it. To achieve these goals, systemic reformers propose to change preservice and in-service training for teachers as well as teacher certification to ensure that teachers have sufficient knowledge of the subjects they are teaching and the methods appropriate to teach those subjects to all students.[54] Finally, they believe that preschool health and educational services are needed so that all children can come to school ready to learn, and so that support services for them and for their parents can help them concentrate on learning.

The logic of these reformers is compelling. By showing the way to improved instruction, systemic reform holds the promise of increased individual success; by applying the same high standards to everyone, it shows a way to greater equality of opportunity. By creating a set of curricular standards, it also enables schools to teach a common core of knowledge and inculcate the shared values and practices needed for democratic citizenship. It is hard to believe that educational goals, curricula, and tests were not aligned before, but it was true in many states. Correcting that and focusing teacher preparation on instructional content just makes sense to a lot of people. Even if it does not bring improvement by itself, this kind of coherence is surely the right framework to enable other reforms to work: the problems resulting from the lack of alignment during the long history of school reform cannot be denied.[55]

The political attractiveness of advocating coherence and high standards has proven irresistible to politicians, if only for the pleasure of challenging their opponents to favor incoherence and low standards. The political rhetoric of accountability is also powerful, as we will see below. Finally, systemic reform provides a way to respond to Americans' perceptions that the wider education system is in trouble even if the schools attended by their own children are not.

The political necessity to take dramatic steps resulted in part from a 1983 report by the National Commission on Excellence in Education. Reports from blue-ribbon commissions seldom rise above the visibility of a story on the inside pages of large city newspapers, but this one did despite the reluctance of the Reagan administration to release it. The Commission asserted baldly that our Nation is at risk. Our once unchallenged preeminence in commerce, industry, science, and technological innovation is being overtaken by competitors throughout the world. . . . The educational foundations of our society are presently being eroded by a rising tide of mediocrity that threatens our very future as a Nation and a people. . . . We have, in effect, been committing an act of unthinking, unilateral educational disarmament.[56]

Several prominent groups followed the Commission's report with their own, with similar conclusions. They echoed the Commission's call for "high expectations and disciplined effort" in order to regain "sight of the basic purposes of schooling." A prominent Harvard physicist spoke for other scientists in warning that post-Sputnik reforms had partially failed since they "turned out scientists, but the real challenge was to lay the foundation of scientific literacy in the nation as a whole." Ernest Boyer also worried publicly that "the problem today seems both more pervasive and more ominous" than in the days after Sputnik.[57] By the late 1980s, governors and business leaders had gotten involved, and elected leaders of both parties, including the president, were galvanized.

In 1989 Republican president George Bush convened, and Democratic governor Bill Clinton chaired, an education reform summit. It devised most of what became Goals 2000, federal legislation eventually passed during the Clinton administration in order to further eight educational objectives ranging from preschool health care to high levels of math and science achievement.[58] The legislation itself did not endorse any particular approach, but establishing goals was itself the first step in systemic reform and was followed by presidential proposals on standards, curricula, and testing. Trying to mandate systemic reform on the national level fell before the American commitment to a more local approach, but states took up the challenge.

School Reform in Kentucky

During the 1990s every state but two developed statewide standards for achievement in major curriculum areas such as math, reading and writing, and science. Kentucky was first and therefore has the most experience with systemic reform; it also has had the most success in putting it into practice.

Passed in response to the court order in their school funding case, the Kentucky Education Reform Act of 1990 (KERA) substantially increased and equalized funding across districts. It also included all of the basic elements of coherent, systemic change: broad statewide goals for schooling, specific substantive standards for math and reading, curriculum frameworks oriented around those standards, performance-based assessments to determine how close students come to reaching the standards, a major investment in technology for classrooms, recertification and professional development for teachers, preschool programs, and resource centers to involve and help families in the educational effort. KERA also established a new governance system for schools and radically changed the state department of education to focus it on facilitating reform.

The courts jump-started reform in Kentucky, but state legislators have been mainly responsible for its breadth, depth, and persistence. They interviewed 60 national experts in education policy to identify the most promising strategies for reform, brought legal and educational consultants to the state to write the law, enlisted prominent businesspeople to promote reform among employees and customers, joined forces with the Pritchard Committee to build support among parents and community leaders, and fended off opponents.

KERA and the tax increase that accompanied it enjoyed widespread support. At the time of its passage, Kentucky ranked at the bottom in nationwide achievement tests and high school dropout rates, and over half of adult Kentuckians were functionally illiterate. The state's economy was suffering from the poor quality of its workforce. There was a broad consensus that something had to be done.

Some opposition did develop after the passage of KERA, first from teachers worn out by the pace and scope of the changes and from the unions that represented them. (The initials were said to stand for "Kentucky Early Retirement Act" or "Keep Everyone Running Around.") "It's really hard," said one teacher. "Am I scared? Yes. I have to keep enough of the old way to know it will work, and then add to it and build in the new way. . . . I can't throw away what I have learned in 19 years." Some school board members also opposed KERA, in several cases because the state department of education began to crack down on the use of school systems as employment regimes. As *Education Week* reported,

> In response to charges of cronyism, nepotism, and abuse throughout the state, lawmakers in 1990 banned school boards from hiring anyone below the level of superintendent, required that they institute competitive bidding and other commonly accepted business practices, and made it easier for the state to remove administrators for malfeasance or failure to comply with the law. . . . As a result, many board members and their chief executive officers perceive KERA as a distinct loss of power.[59]

Residents of poor rural communities who looked on the school system as a source of jobs, prestige, contracts, and power opposed the change; some parents protested the ouster of local school board members even though the KERA reforms were designed to end what one former legislator called "out-and-out thievery."[60] Nevertheless, the boards' loss of power was real, and despite protests the system was cleaned up.

Adjustments have been made to KERA along the way, but not to the basic systemic approach. A few parents and advocacy groups attacked two of the six Learning Goals—enabling students to become "self-sufficient individuals" and "responsible members of a family, work group, or community"—on the grounds that they led to interference in the domains of family and religion. It was "a classic case of cultural warfare,"[61] but a poll showed that 80 percent of the public did not agree with the protesters. The goals were maintained, although any attempt to measure them was suspended. A requirement to have the youngest students mixed in ungraded classrooms was similarly changed into a suggestion, and few remain in mixed-age classes. More importantly, the portfolio component of the statewide assessment has also been scaled back because of difficulties in administration and in response to demands for greater objectivity; there is also greater focus in the test on more basic mathematical computation and grammar. Sanctions for poorly performing schools have largely been eliminated.

Nevertheless, the core of KERA remains in place. With the help of a broad constituency, including vigorous vocal and financial support from the business community, it has been sustained through several governors, legislatures, and commissioners of education. Some supplementary reforms have been enacted, in particular to improve high schools and professional development programs for teachers. Family resource centers and preschools have developed committed constituencies and performed demonstrable services. There are more school-based councils, they are becoming more adept at making decisions, and they too have become a vocal constituency on behalf of more reform. A majority or plurality of citizens in Kentucky, depending on the survey, approve of the changes KERA has wrought. By 1999 large majorities even of teachers and school board members reported that schools in their district had improved over the previous five years or that particular features of KERA were working well. Even students agree: "The work is a little bit harder, but it's more interesting and it sticks with you longer," reports one 14-year-old. "There's more writing, but you've just got to tough it out," concurs a student a few years older. "When you have to write something, it makes it penetrate your mind. I am thinking as I'm writing."[62]

In short, the systemic approach is working in Kentucky. During the 1990s the state moved from the lowest ranks in NAEP assessments of states to the middle of the pack, and in 1999 the National Education Goals Panel cited Kentucky as one of the most improved states in three of the Goals 2000 most directly focused on K-12 education. Teachers in the best schools in Kentucky have learned how to align curricula and tests, develop their knowledge and skills where necessary, incorporate writing into more student activities, respond to initiatives from the principal, and work to help all students. The state also appears to have developed a strategy to help less successful schools emulate some of the aspects of the award winners.[63]

Although schools with the highest proportions of students in poverty usually continue to show the lowest test scores, many are doing better. "We are no longer satisfied saying your mom and dad didn't amount to much, and you won't either," as one administrator from eastern Kentucky put it. Two-thirds of the schools that did best in the science and writing tests in 1999 had an enrollment that was half poor children. Even the normally skeptical *Business Week* concluded that "by dumping an inadequate system and starting from scratch, by investing more and tying funding to performance, Kentucky has boosted its children's academic prospects. Arguably, that has lifted its economic prospects as well. Those are important lessons from an unlikely place."[64]

Other states may not do as well as Kentucky in securing and sustaining all the elements of systemic reform. But Connecticut, Colorado, Maryland, and Texas have also put into place fairly stringent and widespread programs of systemic reform, and all have made unusually strong gains in elementary school reading levels. Although teachers everywhere remain concerned about implementing new tests, they generally believe that higher standards have helped to improve curricula, teaching quality, professional development, teacher motivation, and student achievement.[65] Achievement gains have been registered on national as well as state indicators: to quote a headline in *Education Week*, "States Committed to Standards Reforms Reap NAEP Gains." Evidence increasingly shows that most students do in fact achieve more when more is expected of them individually and of their schools.[66]

The systemic approach has real strengths in fostering the core goals of education. It can give coherence to administrators, teachers, parents, and students. Its transparency in developing standards, curriculum, and assessments permits greater public accountability. Its scope can mobilize the entire reform community, all those interested in fixing the parts, and the people, and the schools. Finally, its focus on high standards and a challenging curriculum provides a direct response to those who fear mediocrity. To be sure, the political structure in any state will have elements that sometimes work at cross-purposes, the changes in policy will be sporadic, the electorate will waver, and the vested interests will not. Nevertheless, as we have seen in Kentucky, systemic reform provides a way to keep educational policymakers focused on both individual and collective goals of education without provoking a major political backlash.

Standards and Accountability

In the fall of 2000, Democratic presidential candidate Al Gore told voters that our country should "invest more in our schools while demanding more from all of our teachers, students, schools, and states . . . , use state accountability systems to reward successful schools and identify failing schools to ensure they are turned around quickly . . . , encourage states to create rigorous high-school exit requirements and . . . help parents measure their children's progress using . . . tests." We must, he said, "demand . . . high standards from our schools, teachers, and students while investing in the tools they need to succeed." A few months later, Republican President George W. Bush sounded as though he was reading from the same speech when he promised to "leave no child behind" and proposed legislation to "increase accountability for student performance: states, districts and schools that improve achievement will be rewarded. Failure will be sanctioned. Parents will know how well their child is learning, and that schools are held accountable for their effectiveness with . . . assessments. . . . Funds will be targeted to improve schools and enhance teacher quality."[67]

This surprising bipartisan agreement on the outlines of reform results partly from the fact that politicians are reading the same public opinion poll results. Most Americans support setting standards, testing students, and rewarding or punishing students and staff based on the test results. Enthusiasm is even higher among parents in large cities with many unsuccessful schools, such as Los Angeles, New York, and Cleveland, and it is higher among nonwhites than whites. Solid, and sometimes huge, majorities agree that students should have to "meet higher academic standards in order to be promoted or graduated," as long as summer school is available to give them a second chance. Parents also claim to endorse the policy even when asked to contemplate the idea of their own children being held back. Majorities would require teachers to retrain if students in their classroom consistently fail standardized tests, and endorse financial rewards for teachers whose students consistently do well. Two-thirds or more endorse "requir[ing] teachers to pass a competency test each year," think government funds should support training for school staff, and believe that schools should be able to remove poorly performing teachers. Majorities agree that publicizing test scores is "a good way to hold schools accountable," are willing to fire principals "if their schools failed to reach specific goals," and, eventually, would "shut down schools that do not meet the minimum standards."[68]

While increased accountability is popular and testing can provide leverage for educational improvement, they raise difficult issues, particularly about equity. The most crucial question is whether all students really have the opportunity to learn. If all students are not given a fair chance to meet the new standards but are held to account if they fail, then systemic reform will just provide a new way for disadvantaged children to fail. As the director of the American Association of School Administrators put it, "Our problem isn't that American students can't meet higher standards. The problem is that we lack the will as a people to do what we have to do to see that all students have the same opportunities that some of our children have." By revealing the effects of disparity in educational quality on some students and some districts, systemic reform provides another powerful argument for equity in school finance, and perhaps for state funding of additional programs to overcome educational disadvantage. It may even create a new legal standard in court challenges demanding finance reform; it has already provided a new way to look at funding in states such as New Jersey, Kentucky, and New Hampshire.[69]

Second, systemic reform focuses attention on the capacity of teachers to meet new instructional demands, and therefore also on the distribution of knowledgeable, successful teachers. Good teaching matters perhaps more than anything else, and many teachers may have sufficient knowledge, training, and experience to do what is required of them by the higher standards. But many do not. Too many of those who do not can be found in poor districts or poor schools, despite the fact that low-achieving students benefit first from better teaching. No matter how one measures good teaching,[70] poor schools and districts consistently have less of it. They have the most inexperienced teachers, the largest proportion not certified or licensed, the largest proportion teaching outside their fields of expertise (especially in math and science, where it matters the most), the greatest turnover among teachers, and the largest proportion of teachers who themselves test poorly.[71] In California the number of unqualified teachers rose dramatically in recent years, mainly in classrooms with Hispanic and disadvantaged students; in the late 1990s, third-grade students with the poorest reading skills were five times more likely to have an underqualified teacher than third graders with the best reading skills. On the other side of the country, Harold Levy, the former chancellor of schools in New York, admitted that the city had "so many teachers teaching higher-level math who are not math teachers that it borders on being irresponsible."[72]

The evidence is strong on the positive effects of good teachers and the serious, cumulative harm that can be done by bad ones. One study, for example, shows that elementary students taught for three years in a row by particularly good teachers ended up in the eighty-fifth percentile or higher on state math tests, while those taught by very ineffective teachers over the same period ended up in the forty-fifth percentile or below.[73] Systemic reform therefore creates a tremendous obligation to make sure that teachers are educated properly, meet substantively meaningful certification standards, get proper mentoring when they first come to school, and receive helpful, curriculum-based professional development once they are there. States, districts, and education schools have started to act to ensure that these changes occur. Some mentoring and support systems for new teachers have begun to increase retention, and professional development programs tied to curricula have had a noticeable impact on teacher effectiveness.[74]

But there is a long way to go. Recruitment of new teachers and the quality of those recruited to teaching depend partly on labor market concerns beyond the control of school districts, and payment of teachers is subject to larger local and state budget considerations. Recruitment also depends on the nature of teachers' work environments; attracting good new teachers to cities will clearly cost a lot of money as well as require changes in school culture. Many education schools also must be subject to stricter standards and accreditation, but that change too gets caught up in other issues such as political support for individual schools and the internal politics of higher education. There are no standards for schools of education, and fewer than half of the 1,200 colleges that prepare teachers are endorsed by the National Council for Accreditation of Teacher Education. "States pay more attention to the qualifications of veterinarians treating the nation's cats and dogs than to those of teachers educating the nation's children," declared the privately funded National Commission on Teaching and America's Future.[75]

Equity issues raised by the unfair distribution of resources and qualified teachers become most stark when students are held accountable for test results. By 2008 students in 28 states will have to pass a state exam to graduate from high school; in several cities such as Chicago, some students are already being held back if they do not perform well enough. Other jurisdictions feel considerable pressure to give more tests and attach higher stakes to them. The recently passed federal education law, supported by President Bush and members of Congress from both parties, requires state-administered tests every year from grades three to eight. Tests can be helpful tools for diagnosing the problems of individual students, they can reveal the poor performance of a teacher or school, and they can provide proper motivation if strongly tied to a demanding curriculum.[76] But they always spark disputes over their validity and objectivity, and if the stakes are high, they can do real damage to students who have not been given a fair chance to learn the material being tested.

When educational opportunities are distributed as unequally as they are in this country, policymakers are therefore left with difficult choices. Systemic reformers rightly want high standards and teaching directed beyond the basics to a deeper understanding of the curriculum. Without a fair opportunity to learn, however, poor children can seldom reach those goals. Tests that measure them against high standards will yield a correspondingly high failure rate in poor districts or poor schools (where the students are disproportionately black and Latino). Alternatively, tests pegged to lower standards or basic knowledge may produce fewer failures but can lead to "drill and kill" instruction focused only on test preparation.

Many tests still focus only on basic skills such as grammar, spelling, or arithmetic computation; when they do, teachers in poor districts often end up spending an inordinate amount of time just drilling students. Particularly among teachers who are not very creative, this takes time away from learning such things as how to conduct a scientific experiment, how to analyze a novel, how to find information through the Internet, or how to write well—things that will help the students achieve their dreams and compete for success later in life. Teachers in Virginia, for example, tell reporters that in order to make sure their fifth graders pass the state tests, they "need to rely heavily on drill and practice techniques—as opposed to literature discussion groups, journal entries, and research projects." They point out that "hands-on projects" are the best way to learn "critical thinking, problem solving and how to work together," but such projects grind to a halt when the tests approach since "we can't do all of this well between 9 A.M. and 3 P.M."[77]

At the same time, students and educators in the most affluent districts see tests of basic skills as a waste of time. Superintendents in Westchester County, New York, report that "tests only distracted their districts from teaching what is already a high-quality curriculum. 'I don't want to sound arrogant,' [said one,] 'but I'm blessed with a student population that's exceptional, with supportive parents and excellent teachers. So standards weren't created for us.'" The superintendent in Wellesley, Massachusetts, was even more blunt about high-stakes testing: "If the urban schools like it, let them have it. But from our perspective, it's too long and it's not worth the time. We're already teaching well beyond the MCAS [test] level."[78]

Parents in Scarsdale, New York, among other places, have organized boycotts among their children of statewide tests on the grounds that the tests were diluting and distorting what education should be. "These kind of tests reduce content, they reduce imagination, they limit complex curriculum, they add stress and cost money," explained one mother. Parents in an affluent district in Michigan similarly refused to allow their children to take the high school's exit test, arguing that it would not benefit them but might hurt their chances to attend a selective college.[79]

But focusing instead on higher-order skills and more sophisticated knowledge generates problems for students not lucky enough to live in Wellesley or Scarsdale. "There are probably a fair number of students out there who will fail to pass these exams because of poor instruction," says Richard Elmore of the Harvard Graduate School of Education. "And under the current structure, it's the students who are going to be bearing the consequences of the failure of the adults to adjust. . . . High schools have been very irresponsible about the lowest-performing students for a very long time."[80]

When tests are hard and stakes high for students, those who fail can be denied a high school diploma, which will affect their ability to get a job and earn decent wages. They can be held back and may drop out, as may their demoralized peers.[81] Teachers in failing schools can be stigmatized, whether they individually did a good job or not. If tests are hard and jobs, salaries, or assignments of teachers are threatened by poor performance, teachers have an incentive to cheat. Teachers have been accused, for example, of giving students extra time, extra instructions, advice to change answers, "practice" sessions with actual test questions, or instructions not to take the test at all. If stakes are high for administrators, they may be tempted to exclude from the test categories of students with special needs and others likely to fail, thereby denying them benefits of inclusion in the effort to attain high scores. When stakes are high and the failure rate politically unacceptable, legislators may feel pressure to dilute the content of tests or lower the passing grade, which defeats the purpose of the test.[82]

As always in the United States, issues of poverty and inequality of opportunity are intertwined with issues of race and ethnicity. Parents from Johnston County (North Carolina), Chicago, and the states of Arizona and Texas have filed official complaints or sued educational policymakers, arguing that high-stakes tests are discriminatory because African American and Hispanic children disproportionately fail them. They cite such evidence as the fact that African Americans comprise just over half of Chicago's students but more than 70 percent of those whose test scores fall below the graduation point for eighth grade. Testing of this sort, as plaintiffs in these suits see it, "has proven to be an educational disaster for children in minority and poor schools." Gary Delgado, director of the Applied Research Center in Oakland, California, is even more pointed: "We have the data and we know the potential negative consequences of the exit exam proposal. At this stage, advocating a policy that has been shown to enhance patterns of institutional racism is, in itself, a racist act."[83]

While one side in the debate sees discrimination in high-stakes testing, the other sees unfairness in anything else. The judge in Texas ruled against the plaintiffs claiming discrimination on the grounds that they "failed to prove that . . . the adverse impact [of high-stakes testing] is . . . more significant than the concomitant *positive* impact." "What would be discriminatory," said Paul Vallas, former chief executive officer of the Chicago schools, "would be promoting students to the next grade who are not academically prepared." Richard Mills, the commissioner of education in New York, echoes him: "It's not fair to graduate children without the knowledge and skills to make it in the world. We are setting them up for failure." As Dr. Mills points out, even in affluent Westchester County, at least one in ten students fails the state tests—and they deserve as much attention as the successful students who scorn the tests.[84]

In the end, as long as children have unequal opportunities to learn, there is no good response either to the charges or the countercharges. To deal with the consequences of this choice between high standards with sophisticated tests that many will fail, at least initially, and low expectations with stultifying tests that can be passed without real learning, five states have chosen a different route. They focus on student progress rather than their absolute level of performance in order to ensure that everyone is learning more, the best students as well as the worst.[85] Kentucky and Tennessee are at the forefront of this effort. This approach recognizes the different starting points of poor and affluent students and acknowledges that some teachers begin with low-performing students and teach in difficult conditions, including high student mobility. It also draws attention to the quality of teaching and provides a measure of teachers' ability that moves beyond debates over certification and appropriate training. This approach, however, risks the possibility that poor students will be held to a different, lower standard of absolute achievement than others, a situation that is unacceptable to many of those seeking equal educational opportunity.

A recent federal law, the No Child Left Behind Act of 2001, adopts the progress approach. In order to avoid lower standards for poor children, it also requires each state to develop objectives so that "all groups of students reach proficiency within 12 years." Based on a method used in Texas, the law requires reporting by "poverty, race, ethnicity, disability and limited English proficiency." An expert on testing from Texas makes clear the virtues of this approach: "Prior to . . . the accountability system, for many groups of kids no teaching had been going on. . . . [Now there are] fewer kids who fall through the cracks, fewer kids who are ignored, and fewer kids whose education is considered irrelevant."[86] This approach makes sense to keep the failure of particular groups from being submerged in unfocused averages, that is, to keep worse results from poor children from getting lost in better results from others. At their best, however, tests are only a way to measure reform; they do not by themselves produce better results. And objectives are a way to express aspirations, not fulfill them.

High standards, challenging tests, and demanding scores for passing are essential if the systemic approach is going to work and if all children are going to have a chance to share in the American dream. Commissioner Mills of New York makes it clear why: "We have adopted high standards because we want every student to be prepared for citizenship, for work, for a rewarding life. The tests bring the standards to life."[87] By avoiding testing, he concludes, "you simply decide in advance that some students don't have access to the good life."

The National Academy of Sciences has provided guidelines to ensure that poor children and low achievers get tests that enhance opportunities, not impede them. The recommendations include these:

- Tests should be used for high-stakes decisions about individual mastery only after implementing changes in teaching and curriculum that ensure that students have been taught the knowledge and skills on which they will be tested;
- Neither social promotion nor retention alone is an effective treatment for low achievement . . . . [Schools should] use a number of other possible strategies to reduce the need for these either-or choices, for example, by coupling early identification of such students with effective remedial education;
- High-stakes educational decisions should not be made solely or automatically on the basis of a single test score;
- [U]sers [should] respect the distinction between genuine remedial education and teaching narrowly to the specific content of a test;
- [All] students [should participate] in large-scale assessment, in part so that school systems can be held accountable for their educational progress.[88]

Most importantly, high-stakes tests are not a substitute for substantive changes in teaching and learning; they provide a reason, and hopefully a motivation, to make such changes. As Professor Elmore points out, helping the lowest-performing students to learn "is going to require learning to teach these kids in different ways. . . . You have not taught the content unless the students have learned it. It's you ["school people"] who are first accountable for producing the results."[89] The National Academy of Sciences concurs: "Accountability for educational outcomes should be a shared responsibility of states, school districts, public officials, educators, parents, and students. High standards cannot be established and maintained merely by imposing them on students." Federal testing requirements will provide information, but that is all. Federal aid, even with recent increases, will remain a small percentage of all funds spent on students; it will not put a qualified teacher in every classroom or ensure that no child is left behind. For high-stakes testing to be fair, for standards to be met, state-level finance reform will be necessary, and strong action will have to be taken to improve the quality of teaching for students who are now not learning enough to pursue their dreams.[90]

Reform for Poor Children

"The ideas embodied in standards-based reform are exceedingly difficult to realize in urban districts," say the authors of a comprehensive study of systemic change. Few districts have made "systemic efforts to strengthen instructional practices directly," and they fear that "the current heavy emphasis on external testing and accountability and correspondingly less attention to curriculum, instruction, and professional development will prevent the ultimate goals from being realized." For standards to apply fairly to everyone, effective instruction is essential everywhere, and poor urban districts have the longest way to go. They can do it, but only by focusing attention where it is needed and keeping it there.

The comprehensive study found that several urban districts had made clear achievement gains; they taught the lesson that "clear expectations for instruction are critical" and resources have to be "dedicated to building the knowledge and skills of educators and providing additional instructional time for low-performing students."[91] To be effective, teachers must know their material and stay on the job long enough to learn how to teach it. City districts in particular must therefore make a concentrated effort to provide professional development for their existing teachers and mentoring and support for new teachers.

Within the framework of systemic reform, some other programs have made a real difference to poor children, even though the number of proven reforms is small compared to the thousands that have been proposed or tried. Without underestimating the complicated and difficult process of development and implementation, we can conclude that most successful reforms stem from a few commonsense themes that have taken much too long to be heard: early is better than late in dealing with educational disadvantage; more schooling is more effective than less; and smaller educational settings can be better than big ones.

Excellent preschool programs provide the most promising results. Generally, the best programs run all day and almost all year, with well-educated personnel, small classes, and good supervision. A few such programs have been extensively evaluated, including the Carolina Abecedarian Project in Chapel Hill, North Carolina, and the High/Scope Perry Preschool Project in Ypsilanti, Michigan; their effects were dramatic and lasted through adolescence and adulthood. Some half-day programs, such as the Chicago Child-Parent Centers, have also had success. For over 30 years, these Centers have provided training for early literacy, and health and social services, for predominantly poor African American children, as well as opportunities for their parents to be involved. Graduates are more likely to complete high school, less likely to be retained in school or to require special education, and less likely to be arrested for crimes than otherwise similar children who attended a weaker preschool program or none at all.[92] One expert who has testified extensively on the issue of preschool concluded that "the weight of the evidence establishes that early care and education can produce . . . sizable persistent effects on achievement, grade retention, special education, high school graduation and socialization." Prekindergarten appears to have an especially large impact on later achievement scores for children from poor families and is especially cost-effective in raising test scores. Not surprisingly the positive effects of preschool last longer and run deeper if high quality compensatory education continues into the early grades of school.[93]

Head Start is the biggest public preschool program. Begun in 1965 as part of the federal antipoverty program, its budget is currently about 6.5 billion dollars, and it enrolls about 860,000 preschoolers. It provides poor children with education, nutrition, health care, and social services at community centers and schools. Most evaluations over the years have found that Head Start succeeds reasonably well in its health and nutritional goals but does too little to enhance children's ability to learn once they begin primary school.[94] A recent law added specific learning guidelines for children and strengthened requirements for teacher training; President George W. Bush, like President Jimmy Carter before him, also proposes to move it to the Department of Education so that its educational goals will receive an even greater push. More importantly, Head Start needs resources to train teachers and pay them better, design curricular materials appropriate for very young children, and buy the materials needed in the classrooms.[95] Those resources have never been sufficient, and Head Start has never been funded to serve anywhere near all of the children who are eligible.

Although the number of children in preschool programs has increased steadily over the past several decades (reaching about 40 percent in 2000), a much higher percentage of well-off children are enrolled in them. Several states such as Georgia and South Carolina have therefore substantially expanded their preschool programs for all children, are training the necessary teachers, and are finding ways to build or renovate facilities to house them.[96] In New Jersey the court has mandated universal, free, high quality preschool for all three- and four-year-olds in the poorest districts.

In addition to preschool, substantive summer school and afterschool programs for older children can help overcome disadvantage. Without summer school, poor students with little access to reading materials or enrichment programs can lose over the summer a lot of what they learned during the school year. Similarly, afterschool programs can increase attendance and thereby achievement, as well as decrease crime during the afternoon, when there is otherwise a spike in vandalism and victimization.[97]

Persuasive evidence shows that small classes in the early grades help poor students, especially minorities. A study in Tennessee, which ran a multiyear, unusually well-controlled experiment to determine the effect of small classes, showed that when students, particularly African American students, were enrolled in small classes in elementary school, they had higher middle school test scores and a greater likelihood of taking the SAT or ACT. The black-white gap in college test taking was reduced by more than half.[98] In addition, smaller schools in urban districts, roughly the size of schools in most suburban districts, enable the staffs to know and respond to their students better.[99] They too show some promising achievement effects, but most of them have been established too recently for the results to be conclusive.

The costs of some of these programs are fairly modest, although quality preschool is very expensive and afterschool programs, summer school, and small classes also have substantial costs attached. The necessary expenditures thus raise all the issues associated with school finance reform. Nevertheless, these programs in conjunction with broader systemic reform provide real hope for poor students to achieve their dreams, and for the nation to make opportunities more equal for all its children.

A scholar who has closely examined the links between schooling and democracy summarized things this way: "There is a strong basis in democratic theory for arguing that student assessment policies should be linked to capacity-building strategies that fulfill the public's side of the social contract between political communities and their schools." Student motivation is a necessary element in educational achievement,[100] but so is institutional capacity; the individual pursuit of success is part of the American dream, but so is the role of government to make the pursuit possible for everyone. In the context of systemic reform, along with greater equity in education resources, necessary (though difficult) improvements in the quality of teaching, and proven programs for poor children, the government can meet its responsibilities. Each part of this approach can work; each part has worked. Together they can help public education bring the dream to everyone.

The process of school reform will be messy because democracy is messy. But most Americans believe in public education, endorse systemic reform, and say they are willing to spend money on new initiatives. Based on what educators have learned, this approach is the best way to forward both individual and collective goals of the American dream. It is political leadership and political will that are required.

For some, however, this approach is not enough. They believe the system of public education is fundamentally flawed and in crisis, that it endangers individual achievement and will not create equal opportunity. With conviction but without convincing evidence, they believe that hope for improvement lies mainly in solutions based on the market, and the way to the American dream lies largely through choice. Disagreement between market advocates and reformers has been central to the education policy debate in this country for several years, and to that dispute we now turn.

5

CHOICE

In modern times, the diligence of public teachers is more or less corrupted by the circumstances, which render them more or less independent of their success and reputation.

—Adam Smith, 1776

I support school choice. If the neighborhood school is failing in its basic mission, parents and teachers don't need more excuses. They need answers. . . . A parent with options is a parent with influence.

—Presidential candidate George W. Bush, 2000

Americans like the public school system. While they may not be ecstatic about its performance, most are reasonably satisfied with what they are getting overall. . . . For the voucher movement, then, the problem is obvious but fundamental: it must attract support from a public that is actually quite sympathetic to the existing system.

—Terry Moe, Stanford University political scientist
and voucher proponent, 2001[1]

ALL OF THE REFORMS DISCUSSED SO FAR seek to promote the individual and collective goals of education by improving *public* schooling—making schools and classrooms more racially integrated, more equitably funded, more academically challenging, more focused on student learning. The most vehement critics of public education, however, look at the forty-year history of reform in this country and conclude that pursuit of the American dream through public schooling is bound to fail. They believe that the current system of public education exists for the adults who work in it and eats money, that the public has invested more than enough time and resources in trying to make the system work and should try another approach. In the words of a mother and choice advocate from New Hampshire, the public system is about "Power and money! The public school system is a powerful monopoly. The people running this monopoly fear change. They fear the resulting demise of their power." To her mind, only by fighting this "chokehold" can we promote collective as well as individual goals of schooling:

If the school system doesn't live up to our standards, we should have the right to "save" our children. . . . Any child not educated to be the best that he can be is heartbreaking to most parents. Any child not educated to be the best that he can be is of less value to the community he lives in. . . . This is where the concept of "school choice" becomes so important as a civil right.[2]

Advocates of choice believe that public schooling cannot work and dooms poor children. "The combination of monopoly in the public sector, significant profitability for those who serve the monopoly and the unique ability for the wealthy to choose the best schools has translated into a nightmare of predictable results for 'haves' and 'have-nots,'" says Lisa Keegan, the former superintendent of public instruction in Arizona:

Public education in the United States should be that in which the money necessary for an education follows a child to the school his or her parent determines is best. . . . The nation cannot abide a system that is blatantly unfair in the access it provides its students to excellent education. This battle for the right of all children to access a quality education is the civil rights movement of our time, and it will succeed.[3]

As these people do, proponents of choice sometimes invoke the language of civil rights and the collective goals of education. At other times they speak in terms of individual achievement alone. But either way their message is clear: there is only one path to securing the American dream through education, and taking that path will change everything. "Reformers would do well to entertain the notion that choice *is* a panacea," wrote John Chubb and Terry Moe, the advocates who jump-started the choice movement in the 1990s. "It has the capacity *all by itself* to bring about the kind of transformation that, for years, reformers have been seeking to engineer in myriad other ways."[4]

Chubb and Moe were talking about a very broad kind of choice plan, involving private religious and secular schools as well as the public system, but "choice" has almost as many meanings as "reform." In its mildest form, choice allows parents to choose their child's public school from an array designated by the school district or state. This type of choice originated in the magnet school movement of the 1960s. Magnet schools were originally tools of desegregation; the goal was to create a school of high quality and distinctive profile, with an emphasis on such things as the health professions or the arts, "back to basics" or "open classrooms." Such schools, it was hoped, would attract middle-class blacks and whites who might otherwise move to the suburbs or enroll their children in private schools. Thus one strand of choice was developed and continues to function in more than 1,000 schools across the nation to promote the collective goals of equalizing opportunity and providing experience with racial and class diversity.[5]

In a few districts, magnet schools have broadened into a "controlled choice plan." In these places parents identify their preferred public schools, and their children are assigned to them subject to limits designed to maintain a racial or ethnic balance in each school. The most fully developed and best-known cases are in Montclair, New Jersey, and Cambridge, Massachusetts.[6] A few school districts are moving toward controlled choice plans that focus on family income in addition to or instead of race and ethnicity. Here too choice is seen as an instrument of collective as well as individual goals of schooling.

Charter schools represent another type of choice with a very different history and purpose. These are schools that receive public funding but are often established independent of any regular school district. In the roughly two-thirds of states that recognize them, any individual or group can propose a charter school; the charter is granted by a university, state department of education, school district, chamber of commerce, or other entity designated by the law of that state. Charter schools are freed from many, though not all, regulations governing public schools, and they have more leeway to choose students, pick staff, design curricula, and create a particular atmosphere than do regular schools. In turn they must meet the specified achievement goals or other conditions of their charter in a few years or go out of business. Charter schools are thus something of a hybrid between public and private schools; their proponents see them as a way of "breaking the mold" of rigidified public schools. Depending on their sponsors' vision, they may focus solely on promoting individual success or they may pursue collective goals of opportunity, diversity, and democratic participation as well.

The most controversial and publicly visible form of school choice moves out of the public arena into private and sometimes parochial schools. Some proponents seek laws to grant public funds to children in order to pay some or all of their tuition at private or religious schools. They may focus on poor children, children of color, children in a particular location, or simply any child whose family wants to participate. Other proponents of choice are even more ambitious: they would like to see, eventually, the elimination of all "government-run schools" so that all schools become what we now term "private" and all children can use their public funds to help them attend any school they choose. As former superintendent Keegan puts it, "The nation's education profession should supply an array of schools from which parents may choose, and the state should limit its role to ensuring fair access and reporting on academic quality at each school."[7] As with charter schools, the reasons for endorsing private school choice vary. Most focus solely or primarily on promoting individual success. But others incorporate or even insist on the pursuit of collective goals, particularly equal opportunity for children of color, or group-oriented objectives for children in particular religious or cultural communities.

Public school choice is increasingly widespread and widely supported from presidents down to educators and parents. It sometimes reduces racial and class separation, it usually increases parents' satisfaction with public schools, and with fair guidelines, it is consistent with both individual and collective goals of education. Charter schools are growing rapidly but still involve a small fraction of public school children. They can bring excitement and commitment into the public school system. But they also have a substantial potential to increase racial and class separation, and there is no good evidence yet on whether they actually improve or equalize achievement. They make sense as an educational experiment, at least in poor districts, but so far that is all.

Private school choice financed by public funds involves only a tiny fraction of public school students—fewer than a tenth of one percent. There is no persuasive evidence that it improves the quality of schooling for the children who use it, and there is some reason to fear that it may harm the quality of schooling of the many who remain behind. It also challenges the very *publicness* of education, which is deeply troubling in a country with almost no institutions other than public schools that reach across all citizens for a large fraction of their lives, and no other institutions that play such a central role in promoting the American dream. At this point there is also no reason to think that private school choice has a chance of succeeding politically except in a few idiosyncratic cases. While plenty must be done to improve the public schools, vouchers are therefore not a feasible solution to the inequities and inadequacies of public education. The American dream requires an American institution to teach it, sustain it, and provide the tools children need to pursue it; public schools are still the best lever we have for improving the quality of individuals' lives and the quality of democratic governance in the United States. Even if vouchers would create desirable alternatives in a few places that need them, a huge array of fragmented, privatized, inward-looking schools simply cannot create the atmosphere in which the ideology of the American dream will thrive.

The History of School Choice

At various points in the past half century, school choice has been associated with reformers from both the right and the left of the political spectrum. And although the majority of current choice advocates are politically conservative, some alliances have recently developed across political lines. Nobel laureate economist Milton Friedman initially broached publicly funded vouchers for private schools in the mid-1950s as a way for parents to escape the stultifying effects of governmentally imposed uniformity. He predicted that "if present public expenditures on schooling were made available to parents regardless of where they send their children, a wide variety of schools would spring up to meet the demand. Parents could express their views about schools directly by withdrawing their children from one school and sending them to another, to a much greater extent than is now possible." According to this theory, being able to choose between schools would benefit everyone, just as being able to choose where one works or lives increases everyone's well-being. As Friedman put it, "Here, as in other fields, competitive enterprise is likely to be far more efficient in meeting consumer demand than either nationalized enterprises [i.e. public schools] or enterprises run to serve other purposes. . . . A market permits each to satisfy his own taste . . . , whereas the political process imposes conformity."[8] He was echoing insights of Adam Smith two centuries earlier, with little more expectation than Smith had that they would ever be put into practice.

Libertarians and people who supported market-based reforms were indeed intrigued by Friedman's idea, but the first real effort to create "freedom of choice" took place in the late 1950s within public schools, as part by the attempt of southern whites to resist substantial desegregation. In principle black parents were permitted to transfer their children to better, predominantly white schools; in practice they were strongly discouraged from applying to these schools and excluded if they did. In addition, many southern school districts authorized transfers upon parental request to make sure that "no child shall be compelled to attend any school in which the races are commingled," to quote the Alabama statute.[9] The language of these laws was neutral, the practice not at all so: encouraging one set of choices and discouraging another set was generally enough to keep schools firmly segregated while pretending to comply with the ruling in *Brown v. Board of Education*.

The first serious educational effort to create choice between public and private schools came from people with a very different political orientation from Friedman or the segregationists. Members of the countercultural left in the 1960s promoted alternative schools, sometimes known as independent or free schools. Their goal, explained in 1973 by a professor active in the alternative schools movement, was to respond to what they heard as children's "cries for freedom from the manipulation of adults in order to explore self, interpersonal relations, and cognitive curiosities, whether these lead to status mobility or not."[10] In cities such as Boston, Washington, Chicago, St. Louis, and San Francisco, opponents of "the Establishment" set up private schools mainly for poor and non-Anglo children, with an educational program intended to empower and liberate them. Some were desegregated and focused on diversity; others were all black and focused on "blackology"—a predecessor of what we now describe as emancipatory multiculturalism or Afrocentrism. In a few cases, well-off white members of alternative communities created rural free schools to protect their children from mainstream political and social influences.[11] By 1970 the New Schools Exchange, an information clearinghouse for free schools, listed over 1,000 alternative schools nationwide, mostly private and independent.

Proponents of alternative schools shared with Friedman the view that public schools were the enemy, despite the fact that they had very different visions of what schooling should do. Also like Friedman they came to see that without public funding their vision could not solidify and grow. By 1970 alternative educators were calling for governmental tuition vouchers for private independent schools, and the *New Republic*, then a magazine far left of center, promoted the cause. Leftists were thus the only reformers willing to take up the standing offer from President Lyndon Johnson's Office of Economic Opportunity (OEO) to provide federal funding to school districts willing to conduct a voucher experiment.

The first instance of school choice with public funding was in the small working-class district of Alum Rock, California. The experiment was inconclusive and not very encouraging. It was intended to last five years, but after two years of innovation the program fell apart. Even at its height it was subject to so many restrictions that market forces had little chance to operate; although the (liberal) OEO wanted to include private schools, for example, the California legislature refused. Schools that were supposedly organized around different themes did not appear very distinct from one another; that mattered little, in any case, because parents chose schools based on location and other features that had little to do with thematic content. In the end few families participated in the experiment, and it failed.[12]

During the 1970s, in small part as a response to alternative schools but mostly as a reaction to desegregation efforts, conservatives focused on the importance of neighborhood schools, which permitted children to be near their homes, community members to work together to improve local schools, and parents to have easy access to teachers and principals. But by the 1980s, as part of a more general argument about the virtues of markets, conservatives began to support school choice; their position gained strength as Americans' overall faith in government appeared to decline. In the 1990s market conservatives were joined by groups favoring separate education for specific racial or religious groups, enthusiasts for particular pedagogical techniques, and some reformers who despaired of eliminating racial and class segregation in large urban schools.

By now a fascinating mix of people argues that choice among schools is the best, or only, way to promote the American dream through schooling. Most, like President George W. Bush, quoted at the beginning of this chapter, focus on the individual goals of education, on ways to improve children's chances to pursue their private dreams. Some also believe that parents ought to have a greater say in the way their children are educated, asserting that schooling decisions cannot be left to the state without an unacceptable loss of liberty. "Educational choice," says the mission statement of the Milton and Rose D. Friedman Foundation, "means that parents are given back a basic American ideal of freedom to choose as it applies to the education of their children." The Institute for Justice, a libertarian think tank and law firm, similarly promises to engage in litigation in order to "transfer power over basic educational decisions—including choice of schools—from bureaucrats to parents. . . . Only with such fundamental change can our nation deliver on its promise of educational freedom and opportunity."[13]

Some voucher supporters address the collective goals of schooling, seeking choice because they believe it will enhance opportunities for the worst-off children in the worst schools to achieve the American dream. A few in this group are white liberals such as Robert Reich, former secretary of labor in President Clinton's administration. In 2000 he argued for "giving kids 'progressive' vouchers that are inversely tied to the size of their family's income. . . . There is a powerful case for giving every possible advantage to better-behaved poor kids who are fortunate enough to have caring parents. School vouchers offer them an escape route."[14]

Others are concerned less with class and more with race or other distinct characteristics that put some children at an educational disadvantage. The Black Alliance for Educational Options (BAEO) argues that "Without a good education" African American children

> will have no real chance to engage in the practice of freedom: the process of engaging in the fight to transform their world. . . . We need systems that truly empower parents, that allow dollars to follow students, that hold adults as well as students accountable for academic achievement, and that alter the power arrangements that are the foundation for existing systems.

Other prominent African Americans, such as former Democratic member of Congress Floyd Flake and former Baltimore mayor Kurt Schmoke, also endorse vouchers, using similar language. The Hispanic Council for Reform and Educational Options joined an amicus brief to the Supreme Court urging it to sustain a voucher program in Cleveland that provides public funding for poor children to attend private or parochial schools. The National Council of La Raza (the nation's largest constituency-based Hispanic organization) is sponsoring 50 new Latino charter schools, with a budget of $25 million, on the simple grounds that "the public school system has failed Latino children."[15]

Libertarians generally have little in common with those seeking racial transformation or economic equality. But occasionally market-oriented conservatives and progressive advocates for particular groups ally, and in a few cases they have succeeded. Milwaukee's voucher program is the best-known case of a state law permitting public funds to be used for private school choice. Its progenitors were state representative Polly Williams, a former welfare recipient, Black Panther, and state chair of Jesse Jackson's presidential campaign; Clint Bolick, cofounder of the Institute for Justice; and Republican governor Tommy Thompson.[16] A mix of leftist (often racially nationalist) local activists and right-wing (often libertarian) choice advocates made possible the voucher plan in Cleveland and the statewide public choice plans of Minnesota and Massachusetts. Nevertheless, it has been conservative politicians and policy advocates who have largely framed the debate on school choice over the past decade and provided the greatest rhetorical support for private choice programs.

Choice in Practice: Public Schools

Public school choice plays a much greater role in the educational system than private school choice. A few school systems have run public choice programs for years, ranging from magnet schools and controlled choice plans to programs promoting academic specialization at various sites, most notably in East Harlem, a densely populated, heavily minority district in New York City. Public school choice has also been used occasionally to create ethnically or culturally based schools serving an entire district, as in the case of Milwaukee's experiment with Afrocentric schools during the early 1990s.[17]

By 1999 about 15 percent of children in the United States were attending public schools within their own districts that their parents had selected. As of 1999, public school choice was more available in urban areas than elsewhere. As a result, poor children were more than twice as likely as well-off children to attend choice schools. The number of African American students in choice schools was double the number of Anglos; Latinos were somewhere in the middle. Forty percent of districts in the west and almost 30 percent in the midwest, many relatively homogeneous, offer some sort of intradistrict public school choice program. The proportion declines in the South and especially in the Northeast.[18]

Students move within a district for a variety of reasons. One unusually detailed study found that kindergarten parents in Minneapolis typically did not choose schools that produced high test scores or showed strong evidence of improving children's achievement. Instead they chose schools near their homes, schools mostly populated by students of the same race or ethnicity as their own child, or schools whose students appeared to have an ability level similar to that of their own child. Central-city parents are best characterized as having very low levels of information about schools even when they are required by the district to choose among them.[19]

There is little evidence on how intradistrict choice plans affect participants with regard to either individual or collective goals of schooling, and even less evidence on their effects for all students in a district. The best study focused on Chicago, where about half of high school students opt out of their neighborhood schools. It found that choice had little impact on the degree of racial segregation within the district (even though the choice program began as an effort to desegregate Chicago's public schools). Choice did, however, lead to "dramatically increased sorting by ability; high ability students are much more likely to opt out of their neighborhood schools and virtually all travel involves attending a school with higher-ability peers." Students who chose to move graduated at a higher rate than students who did not, but this was probably the result of their self-selection rather than the move itself. That is, these students are typically among the most able and have unusually high motivation—qualities that would make them more likely to graduate in any case. The researchers concluded that intradistrict choice by itself neither harmed those who remained in neighborhood schools nor demonstrably helped those who moved. Career academies showed a slightly different pattern: students in the middle of the ability distribution were most likely to attend them, and those students were more likely to graduate than similar students who did not move into such academies. Again, however, it is not possible to fully sort out the separate effects of the move itself and the students' motivation and self-selection, so the researchers were reluctant to come to any conclusions about the effects of choice on student outcomes.[20]

Intradistrict public school choice programs do not usually raise serious funding issues, change the accountability structure for teachers, or alter the governance structure of the district. Thus they are not nearly as controversial as other forms of choice, and they receive strong public support—about 70 percent in recent surveys.[21] Almost all politicians of both parties endorse them, and parents of students in intradistrict choice plans are generally satisfied. Their educational impact is probably minimal, but the high level of satisfaction with them strengthens parental attachment to the public schools as the central institution for realizing the American dream. Where they do not result in increased segregation or stratification, where the movement of students does not hurt those left behind, these plans make sense.

Seventeen states also have mandated interdistrict public choice plans, and another 14 have plans in which districts may choose to participate. These plans are more complicated than intradistrict ones: transportation problems can create substantial obstacles and funding issues across district lines can be difficult. In particular, where property taxes account for a high share of school resources or where spending disparities among districts are large, substantial political controversy has developed on the issue of how much local money follows a child to another district.

The greatest restriction on interdistrict choice, however, is the strong preference of parents to send their children to schools in their own neighborhoods or towns. In the 1990s an average of 5 percent of eligible students participated in choice plans across districts. Some parents or students select a school for its more convenient location or for idiosyncratic personal reasons: one urban student chose a suburban school because "I'd always wanted to go to Westridge. I just like the name." In other cases transfers demonstrate "upward filtering," in which students enroll in districts or schools with higher test scores or wealthier families. Some African American students who traveled from St. Louis to its whiter suburbs every day, for example, particularly appreciated "classes that will help you with college," or "good teachers and good counselors," or the fact that "they give you the freedom to be grown up, young adults." In still other cases, students for some reason transfer away from districts with higher test scores, honors courses, or graduation rates than the ones they choose to go to.[22] In Wisconsin almost no low-income students apply for transfers even though they could receive free transportation to another, sometimes better, district. In Michigan and Wisconsin, affluent or growing districts typically do not participate in interdistrict choice plans: their students do not need to filter upwards and the districts do not want new students from other districts. Whatever their reason, parents appreciate having the choice: "You have some options," says a mother in Wisconsin. "It's not necessarily that one school system is better or worse than another. . . . One system may meet the needs of a certain child but not necessarily another child. And so, what works for one doesn't always work for the other."[23]

As with intradistrict choice, there is very little evidence on the effects of interdistrict choice on various goals of education; what evidence we have suggests little measurable impact. A comparison with other nations that have longer and more extensive experience with school choice helps to fill that evidentiary gap, though lessons from such comparisons must be taken cautiously. The British educational system, for example, permits parents to choose any public school in England or Wales, subject to space constraints; funding to schools follows the students. The number of students choosing their schools has increased considerably since the program began in 1989 and now reaches over 1,200,000 in England, about 15 percent of public school students. Segregation of poor children in secondary schools declined for the first eight years of the program, after which it started to rise, although it has not reached the original level. Schools that control their own admissions are much less likely to have a proportional share of low-income students than other schools. Average student achievement scores have increased steadily and substantially; achievement gaps have diminished by gender, ethnicity, and region, and between the highest- and lowest-achieving students, although not by socioeconomic class. The authors of this comprehensive study conclude that "education in the U.K. would appear to be moving in the right direction."[24]

Like intradistrict public school choice, interdistrict choice seems on balance to be a good policy. It provides some students with the chance for a better educational alternative or just a new start; it can thus help a few students pursue their dreams. As we will see, however, the politics of race and class mean that too few students can participate for public school choice to be a major solution to the problems of unequal opportunity and declining diversity within student bodies.

Choice in Practice: Charter Schools

More controversy and harder judgment calls arise with charter schools. They provoke passionate reactions, for and against. A former assistant secretary of education characterized them as "schooling based on freedom, innovation, choice, and accountability, . . . a new model for public education"; the head of a state teachers' union, in contrast, called them an "idea . . . hijacked by profiteers and ideologues, . . . an abandonment of public education."[25] Charter schools typically have a contract that sets eligibility criteria for attending the school, achievement targets and deadlines, and relevant regulations. The charter may include waivers that permit the school to hire teachers who are not licensed or not members of unions, to give salaries and pension rights that differ from those in public schools, to offer curricula and set graduation standards unlike those of public schools, and to provide fewer and less frequent reports to state authorities.

Depending on their nature and extent, these regulatory waivers can provide a limited or broad challenge to aspects of the public system and its vested interests, such as teachers' unions. If waivers are extensive and achievement goals clear, charter schools can respond to many of the criticisms raised by critics of reform; they can, for example, more easily innovate in teaching methods or develop curricula more tailored to particular student needs than conventional public schools. In sufficient numbers they could theoretically provide a high level of competition with each other and with conventional public schools. However, they could also further fragment and stratify public education and draw resources and support from the public schools.

Charter schools vary enormously from one another. One was founded in 1997 in Princeton, New Jersey, a wealthy school district with both a very well educated set of (mostly white) residents and a substantial and poorer non-Anglo enrollment. By almost any standards, its public schools are near the top. But some parents believe that the schools have succumbed to fads and too many progressive shibboleths. The charter school prides itself on "drill and skill," using textbooks from a series called "The Classics"; its mission statement calls for "a rigorous curriculum that requires mastery of core knowledge and skills." So far the Princeton Charter School offers education only in elementary grades. A quarter of the eligible students in the public school system have applied for admission, which is by lottery (some of the founders' children were not admitted the first year it opened). The school is small and has small classes, which may be part of its attraction. Whatever the reason, this is a place concerned entirely with the individual goals of education rather than the needs of the wider community, and focused only on its direct participants.

Barely 50 miles south of Princeton is Nueva Esperanza, whose students are Latinos from a poor north Philadelphia neighborhood. In his old high school, says 18-year-old freshman Mark Cruz, "The door was always wide open, you could do anything you wanted to, there were always fires in the school." Perhaps not surprisingly, "I was not learning in there"; were it not for this new school, "I'd be dropped out." The force behind Nueva Esperanza and a group of other new charter schools for Hispanic students is Anthony Colón from the National Council of La Raza. Latinos, he says, are "not getting what they need from the public schools for a whole host of reasons." In a charter school, however, "we're able to provide . . . a sense of mission. You own it." Danny Cortés, the chief administrative officer of Nueva Esperanza, echoes him: "I want a private-school feel in a public institution. We want to create the traditions, . . . the ethos and culture" of a school committed to its students. He also wants the school to reflect the students' ethnic heritage; although all classes are taught in English, everyone must study Spanish. "I don't want to be a ghetto," says Mr. Cortés, "but we want the place to express who they are, culturally. We want that to be affirmed." The school is far from scorning individual achievement—"I really want those kids to be competing with you for your job," says Mr. Colón—but it is committed to the collective goal of equalizing opportunity and the group-based goal of cultural affirmation. This distinguishes it sharply from the Princeton Charter School.[26]

The profiles and goals of charter schools differ, but they all carry the weight of their founders' high hopes. So far this enthusiasm rests more on faith than on facts. Nueva Esperanza includes only two grades so far, and like the Princeton Charter School, is very new. In general, charter schools are too new and too diffuse for there to be systematic evidence on whether they improve students' achievement more than regular public schools. One prominent supporter, Paul Hill of the University of Washington, is unusually blunt: "As for are students doing better or worse, they [states or chartering agencies] haven't got a clue. We haven't figured out the difference between success and failure." A recent analysis by the Rand Corporation of charter schools, based largely on evaluations of charters in Texas and Arizona, nevertheless calls for "cautious optimism" about their effects on students' learning.[27]

So far two-thirds of the states have authorized charter schools. Since they began a decade ago, their numbers have grown fast, and there are now about 2,500; most are concentrated in Arizona, California, Michigan, Texas, and Florida. They are usually very small schools, and together they enroll roughly 1 percent of all public school students in the nation.[28] They are clearly not yet an alternative to a national public system, and no one can predict with confidence whether they will continue to grow at the same pace.

Although a majority of Americans admit to knowing nothing about charter schools, a majority consistently supports their creation when asked for an opinion.[29] Surveys of parents and their children in charter schools can be misleading, since many of those who are dissatisfied or disappointed have presumably left. Nevertheless, their overall tone is positive. In a poll taken by one advocate, three-fifths of charter students say their teachers are better than in the old schools (only 5 percent say they are worse), and half say they are more interested in their school work (compared with 8 percent who report less interest). In the same poll, substantial majorities of participating parents report that charters are better than their children's former schools in everything from class size and quality of teaching to curriculum, academic standards, and discipline. More neutral surveys also provide evidence of parents' and students' enthusiasm as well as greater parental involvement with the schools and more services from the schools. Even the NEA (hardly a group of enthusiastic proponents) found that three-fourths of charter teachers would choose to teach in a charter school if they were to decide again despite the fact that salaries are no higher and job security is lower; only one-tenth would not.[30] Greater options do provide higher satisfaction for all kinds of participants in charter schools; it is just not clear that they provide any better results.

In a majority of the 21 states with a relatively large number of charter school students, they enroll a higher proportion of nonwhite students than do regular public schools. About half of these states also have a disproportionate number of poor children enrolled in charter schools. In Illinois and Ohio, in fact, almost 70 percent of charter school students, but only 30 per cent of regular school students, are poor. If charter schools can help these poor children to catch up to others, they will promote the American dream; to quote an advocate, "We have a deeply inequitable public school system in which the wealthy already have school choice. . . . The charter approach expands options for families who have the fewest options now."[31]

A serious problem remains. Except in relatively homogeneous districts, charter schools that focus on poor or non-Anglo children, like those that appeal to wealthier or white children, will reduce diversity and make it harder for students to engage comfortably with those different from themselves. Right now, overall, there is a higher proportion of nonwhite students in charter schools than in regular schools, roughly even proportions of poor students and English language learners, and a much lower proportion of students with disabilities. But compared with other schools in their own districts, charter schools sometimes have many more, or many fewer, nonwhite students.[32]

This pattern is consistent with a variety of studies showing that when public school choice is available, parents (especially white parents) typically choose schools in which their children will not be in a racial or socioeconomic minority. Washington, D.C., for example, has a Web site with a variety of information on all District schools so that parents can choose among them. Since it was made available, almost a third of parents—more than looked at any other single piece of information—checked information on students' race and class very early in their search process. They look next at school location; very few examine information on teacher quality. Highly educated parents are especially likely to focus on student demographics (and then on test scores).[33] Similarly, a study of 1,006 charter school households in Texas found that even though no parents claimed to care about shared race or ethnicity when choosing a charter school, each group (blacks, Anglos, and Hispanics) ended up in schools that had considerably more members of their own race or ethnicity than the schools that they had left. These results held even when the analyst controlled for a variety of parental and school characteristics.[34] As with other experiences with parental choice, then, the early evidence on charter schools suggests that they are more likely than not to increase the overall level of racial and ethnic isolation in the school system.[35]

Charter (or other public) schools run by profit-making companies, rather than by nonprofits or individual reformers, can raise additional difficult issues. In general these schools look like most other charters: the company agrees to run the school for the same per-pupil cost to the district as a similarly situated public or charter school, and in exchange promises to reach a predetermined set of student achievement levels or other academic objectives. At the same time, the company hopes to make a profit if it can run the school for less. This approach can produce efficiencies, particularly in the delivery of custodial, cafeteria, and other support services. But since most of a school's budget goes into salaries for staff, the greatest potential savings comes from replacing union with nonunion teaching personnel or from replacing some teachers entirely with computer-based instruction. Substantial savings can also come from receiving waivers from special education regulations of various kinds. This was the basic approach when Education Alternatives, Inc., (EAI) tried to run the Hartford schools in the mid-1990s; it is not an approach that has been shown to enhance student achievement.

All charter schools are unstable because they can be closed if they do not meet their mandates, and some have been closed because of financial or educational malfeasance.[36] But for-profit schools face an additional level of instability. Profit-making companies are subject to the vagaries of financial markets, takeover or bankruptcy, or problems in the company's other corporate divisions that drain financial and personnel resources. In addition, at present only a few companies are in this business; school districts can therefore face a real dilemma when a company's initial contract expires and the company seeks to set more expensive or less responsive terms. Most importantly, when the company appears to protect profits and eliminate services at the expense of children, trust between parents and schools can be broken; this situation greatly contributed to the termination of the EAI contract in Hartford. While none of these problems necessarily follow for-profit charter schools, few school districts have been willing to take the risk. Most parents are just as reluctant, as demonstrated in New York City by the overwhelming rejection of a plan to allow a for-profit charter company to take over even five very troubled public schools.[37]

Charter enthusiasts promise that they will enhance the education not only of their own students but also of those in conventional public schools. Joseph

Lieberman, the Democratic senator from Connecticut, argues, for example, that "competition from charter schools is the best way to motivate the ossified bureaucracies governing too many public schools. This grass-roots revolution seeks to reconnect public education with our most basic values: ingenuity, responsibility, and accountability." The evidence is mixed on whether charter schools do, or do not, induce constructive reforms in noncharter schools. Some public schools in districts with charters have become more energetic themselves, advertising in the local media, trying to reduce costs by outsourcing noneducational services, or enhancing preschool programs. In other places school leaders ignore or know little about nearby charters. In a few cases, schools may even be pleased that a charter is easing pressure by removing disaffected parents or unhappy children.[38] So far, in fact, charter schools' main impact has been in the political arena; despite some hostility from both public school educators and voucher proponents, they have provided a compromise between those who would focus on reform within the public system and those who would replace it with a broad private choice program.

The evidence is similarly mixed on whether charter schools are themselves very innovative. Advocates see them as "seedbeds of innovation and educational diversity," but reliable academic studies find that "when compared with traditional public schools, many charter schools seem unremarkable." Founders of charters most often describe their goals as "realiz[ing] an alternative vision" focused on curricular or instructional innovations intended to improve individual achievement, in the words of the most extensive survey. In contrast, about a quarter seek mainly to "serve a special population of students."[39] Advantage Schools, a for-profit charter school company, sees the core "customer base" as one that "crave[s] a school setting that is orderly and safe and focused and on task. And that's the brand we endeavor to provide them with."[40] It is too soon to tell whether any consistent pattern of educational innovation will actually result from these various goals.

In sum, many states promote charter schools (for different reasons), and most citizens endorse them; they have some unrealized potential to bring energy and innovation into the education system, and they may spur on the public schools. They can, however, also further separate the student body along racial, ethnic, or class lines and can draw funds and support from the public schools; for these reasons they do not make nearly as much sense in districts with schools that are good or have problems that can be rectified with some concentrated effort. In those places potential charter school parents can provide a strong force for reform; in those places it is best to keep the money and parental attention focused on schools for all children.

In contrast, in overwhelmingly poor, minority districts where schools are failing, problems are widespread, and reform will take many years, an experiment with charter schools is hard to oppose. "In a community where there are high dropout rates, very low literacy rates, overcrowded classrooms, and a myriad of obstacles in the acquisition of education for our kids," says Rev. Luis Cortés, who heads an organization in Philadelphia beginning a charter school, "anything that is innovative, that is different, that tries [to do better] is being welcomed."[41] Charter schools in districts like this can hardly increase the existing high level of segregation, and they may help to equalize opportunity as well as give some students a better chance to pursue their dreams. This is a situation in which experimentation makes real sense.

It is "as yet unclear," in the words of a careful researcher, whether charter schools will "prove to be a public alternative that encourages greater performance in the system as a whole . . . or to be a minor passing fad."[42] They are too new, too few, too diverse, too mutable, and too bereft of careful evaluation to allow any strong conclusion about their impact on the realization of the American dream.

New Zealand, which created a national system of charter schools a decade ago, may offer a perspective on what a more extensive system of charters might mean in the United States over the long term. It devolved authority to local public schools with elected boards of trustees, eliminated most central governmental regulations, and allowed students to choose among schools, a change that won the approval of most New Zealanders. Edward Fiske, the former education reporter for the *New York Times*, and Helen Ladd, an educational economist at Duke University, have evaluated this reform with an eye toward its implications for choice programs in the United States. They found that most parents in New Zealand evaluate a school by the class and race of its students. As a result, schools with the highest-status students are oversubscribed, so they can choose among applicants. Average performance in these popular schools has improved; some minority and poor white children have been admitted to them, and evidence shows that those students receive a better education than they would have under the old system. However, New Zealand's schools overall are more polarized by race, ethnicity, and class than a decade ago, and average performance in less popular (that is, mostly poor and predominantly nonwhite) schools has declined. The least popular schools are caught in a spiral of failure where "rolls decline, which leads to a reduction in staff, which affects the quality of the academic program, which makes it even more difficult to attract skilled staff," which further reduces rolls. These schools have stumbled along for a decade, and only recently has the government recognized that they need many more resources and much more help than simply advice on how better to manage budgets and personnel. Few schools, even the most successful, are very innovative or seek to appeal to students outside the mainstream; they are too dependent on attracting parents who turn out to be quite conservative in their curricular and pedagogical choices.[43]

All this is consistent with the evidence so far on charter schools here and with our knowledge of parental preferences in the United States. The authors "highlight the fact that the competitive system increased the disparities among schools not only in terms of the ethnic and SES [socioeconomic] level of the students but also in terms of student performance." They conclude that "other countries . . . would have to be extremely vigilant . . . to avoid similar outcomes."[44]

Private and Parochial School Choice

A broad choice program, one that provided public funds to help pay the tuition of students at any parochial or private school in the state, would obviously present the greatest challenge to the current system of public schooling. The system would no longer be public in the same sense and it would no longer be subject to democratic control in the same way. The public schools would no longer be the central institution chosen by Americans to put into practice the various values of the American dream. Some voucher proponents endorse both individual and collective goals of the dream, and some add group-specific goals as well, but many focus mainly on individual achievement and are willing to take substantial risks with the other goals in its name. All believe that public schools have failed to incorporate all children into the dream because they are deeply, perhaps irremediably, flawed. Moderate supporters make this claim about troubled inner city schools; the strongest proponents make it about the whole system, which should in their view be abandoned. In the first category is the angry mother in Cleveland who is tired "of being told to stick it out and wait because they [public schools] will eventually improve. But my children and all children cannot wait. Their lives cannot be put on hold until the public schools improve." The *Wall Street Journal* sometimes provides the rhetoric for those less moderate: test scores, it says, show "not simply failure. This is mass fraud. And in an economy that increasingly puts a premium on skills, this is a system condemning too many . . . children to second-class citizenship in the American Dream. What these kids need is not more money thrown in but more back doors opened up."[45]

Voucher proponents are right about the dismal state of some public schools, particularly those attended by poor children in poor neighborhoods. But they are not right in claiming that a system of market-based schools will solve the educational problems of those children. There is little evidence on the effects of private and parochial school choice through vouchers, and what we have is inconclusive. There is overwhelming evidence, however, on the ability of better-off parents to insulate their children from poor (and often non-Anglo) classmates. Vouchers will be not be politically acceptable to the majority of Americans if they are designed to move more than small numbers of poor children into middle-class schools, and they will not be educationally effective if they just move poor children from public to private schools with almost the same proportion of poor children. Markets cannot solve, and could even exacerbate, the educational problems created by the preference of parents for class (and racial) separation.

The idea of vouchers has a more general, deeper, flaw as well. Public schools are the only institution in which, in principle, all American children have equal standing and are expected to interact on the same footing. They are also the only institution in which, in principle, American children are taught to become good citizens through learning a common core of knowledge, acquiring a common set of democratic values and practices, and developing a common commitment to their nation and its people. That some public schools fail to achieve these goals is a deep problem, but the collective goals of the American dream are too important for failure to mean that we should give up on the public system.

This does not mean that all public schools deserve to be protected or that private and parochial schools do not benefit their students. It does not imply that educators bear no blame for children's failure or that incentives for improved performance would not help. It certainly does not mean that experiments in private choice should not be carefully evaluated to see if we can learn lessons to help children in the worst schools. But broad claims on behalf of publicly funded, systemwide, private or parochial school choice are empirically unwarranted and ideologically destructive.

Despite all the talk about vouchers, the United States has had very few broad choice plans involving public funding of private or parochial school tuition. The only ones have been in Milwaukee, where an initially small program recently expanded and now includes parochial schools, a similar program in Cleveland, a new statewide program for failing schools in Florida that quickly ran into trouble in state courts, and small programs in Vermont and Maine. In total they involve about 15,000 children—less than a tenth of 1 percent of all K-12 students. (There are also privately funded experiments in roughly 90 districts around the nation, including Indianapolis, San Antonio, and New York City, involving about 60,000 low-income students. They remain private and usually operate on a small scale in any one location, so up to this point they have raised few challenges to public schools.)[46]

The Supreme Court recently decided, in *Zelman v. Simmons-Harris*, that it is constitutional for public funds to be used to pay tuition to religious schools. Since over three-quarters of private school students now attend such schools, this decision could permit a substantial expansion of broad choice plans. It will certainly make it easier for groups of parents united by ideology, religion, or values to assert their right to control the education of their children and have their tax money support the schools that their groups favor.[47] States have until recently accommodated these parents' desires mainly by permitting home schooling[48] or by providing limited support for services to some students enrolled in private or parochial schools. Using public funds on a wider scale to support schools sponsored by churches or other religious groups will clearly enhance the legitimacy of group values in education.

Most advocates of broad choice programs, however, probably care less about group-based goals than about enabling individual students to pursue success. As the mission statement of the pro-voucher Institute for Justice puts it, "Our vision is one of individual initiative and opportunity, not group rights and entitlements."[49] Advocates also argue that families pursuing success for their own children will enhance the possibility that others will also find success. That is, regardless of income, all parents with vouchers and sufficient information about school quality would be able to patronize successful schools and thereby provide motivation for other schools to improve or go out of business. Schools seeking students would specialize enough for parents to find one that matches their goals, and some would experiment enough to find the right mechanisms for promoting success. These would attract more parents and imitators—thereby improving the quality of yet other schools. This system requires a high level of school autonomy and therefore a minimum of district-level management or direct democratic control by the public at large.

Finally, some advocates believe that vouchers promote fairness, participatory democracy, and engagement with public debate as well as improved quality of education. Subsidies in their view would enhance fairness by giving poor parents the same freedom to choose a private or parochial school that wealthier parents have always had. The very fact of choosing, they continue, will encourage parents and their children to care more about their schools and to become more involved in decision making within the schools.[50] As political scientists Paul Peterson and David Campbell put it, "Students who attend non-government schools . . . are . . . not being taught to withdraw from civic life but to practice it in a certain way. . . . In fact, many parents who have removed their children from government schools have done so to re-attach them to a civic idea." Thus in this view a properly managed voucher program would promote individual *and* group-based educational goals, *and* it would strengthen the community in ways consistent with the collective goals of the American dream. They believe, in short, that "teachers will be more effective, parents more engaged, students increasingly challenged, and minority learning problems better addressed."[51]

Opponents of broad choice programs worry, however, that market-based incentives will result in low-cost, low-quality schools. They fear that without careful monitoring schools will hire unqualified teachers and cut corners on safety, financial safeguards, and facilities. They are skeptical about the quality and extent of information about teaching likely to be available to and used by parents, especially those with little education, thin social networks, or poor English language skills. They are concerned about what will happen to students when schools close or move or when public schools, especially in poor districts, lose essential funds, innovative teachers, and engaged parents to the private sector.

Voucher opponents, perhaps ironically, anticipate that choice plans could actually lead to *less* parental control over their children's schooling. Successful private schools may be unresponsive to parents who are unhappy with something in the school but who do not want to remove their children. "The legitimate response of school officials to parents who protest a policy or a curriculum in a choice system," says democratic theorist Iris Young, "is 'so take your voucher someplace else.' In a public school system there are more grounds for claiming some democratic input into what the schools do."[52]

These concerns revolve around individual achievement; others focus on implications of a broad-scale voucher program for the collective goals of education. Opponents' chief fear is that desirable schools will select children of privileged parents and vice versa, so that students of different races or ethnicities, classes, religions, ideology, and levels of ability or disability will mingle even less than they do now. Differences in educational quality across schools are similarly likely to be exacerbated if the privileged or preferred are chosen and the difficult or disfavored are left to the strained public schools. Furthermore, critics fear that market incentives will lead schools to choose curricula too narrowly tailored to particular group norms or actually hostile to broad democratic values; even the eminent pro-choice sociologist Nathan Glazer points out that vouchers would probably produce "a number [of schools] that will outrage even the most fervent advocates of the freedom to choose one's school and one's education."[53] With the *Zelman* decision, some critics fear that public funds will end up supporting religious schools that teach values incommensurate with American liberal democratic practices.[54]

It may be possible to design a system that deals with programmatic concerns about promoting achievement and equal opportunity, especially if vouchers were limited to those who were poor and voucher schools were well regulated.[55] But no design for a broad choice system is likely to overcome the desire of better-off parents to ensure that their children attend school with others just as well off, and a voucher system would by definition discount the importance of the public schools, thereby undermining almost two centuries of commitment to them as the vehicle to turn the American dream into reality. A full choice plan would shift the way Americans think about their government, relating to it less as citizens and more as consumers or members of identity groups. A system of public schools now framed by citizens with one vote each who must come to some agreement about education would be replaced by a marketplace framed by consumers with very different resources and no need to reach consensus on educational issues. To the extent that debates about schooling have functioned as a forum for setting social priorities, that debate could be seriously curtailed or distorted by a fragmenting market. Most importantly, the loss of public schooling would mean the end of the only institution that affects just about all Americans, teaching them what it means to be an American and how to reconcile their own dreams with those of very different others.

If vouchers substantially enhanced individual achievement, they would raise legitimate questions about priorities among the individual, group-based, and collective goals of education. But there is no solid evidence that they do. The first voucher program, in Milwaukee, has had three sets of evaluators. John Witte and his colleagues at the University of Wisconsin found over its first five years "no consistent difference" in test scores for students who used the vouchers and a matched set of students who remained in the Milwaukee public schools. Paul Peterson and his colleagues at Harvard University used a different comparison group and found statistically significant improvements in the scores of voucher students. Finally, Cecelia Rouse at Princeton University used yet another set of techniques and split the difference—finding improvements in math but not in reading. She also identified a set of Milwaukee public schools with small classes that outperformed both the choice schools and the other public schools.[56]

This was not a polite squabble among scholars who view the world through slightly different lenses; the disagreement was public, nasty, and consequential. Professor Peterson and his colleagues wrote in the *Wall Street Journal* that Professor Witte's study was "so methodologically flawed as to be worthless," and that it "isn't just bad science—it's actually harmful to the underprivileged children who most need the opportunities vouchers would provide." Witte replied that the Peterson group's work was a "confusing, tortured effort to try to find any evidence" that students in a voucher plan would benefit. Their methods, in his view, were "theoretically inappropriate" and "very biased"; the data "are woefully inadequate and inconsistent"; and "the paper is so poorly presented that many of the tables are incomprehensible."[57] Senator Robert Dole used Peterson's results as part of his justification for supporting voucher plans in the 1996 presidential race; President Clinton used Witte's results as part of his justification for opposing such plans in that race.

This exchange reveals much about the intensity of views about vouchers but little about their effects. In the end none of the results from Milwaukee provide much useful information (Witte, Peterson, and Rouse all concur); only a few hundred students and seven or fewer schools were involved, and both students and participating schools came and went during the years that the program was being evaluated.[58] A study of the somewhat larger program in Cleveland is equally uninformative, both because some schools that were involved have left the voucher program (to become charter schools) and because the evaluation has substantial methodological problems.[59] The results of evaluations of voucher programs funded by private donors in several cities such as New York, Dayton, and Washington show that African American students with vouchers gained from attending private and parochial schools. But these results too are not clear-cut. The evaluators themselves have disagreed on how meaningful the results are; the changes in test scores vary in puzzling ways across grade levels, cities, and racial or ethnic groups; and there is insufficient evidence on whether the private and parochial schools chose vouchered students in a nonrandom way.[60] Publications like the *Economist* of London cite these latter studies in defense of its claim that "the biggest reason why the center of gravity [in the debate over school choice] is shifting is simple: vouchers seem to work,"[61] but that conclusion is not warranted.

Three results do consistently appear in evaluations of voucher programs. Parents are generally more satisfied than they were with their child's previous school, and children frequently, though not always, behave better when they move to a private school with a voucher; not surprisingly, the more satisfied they are, the more likely they are to stay in the new school. Second, in relatively large programs, a substantial number of eligible students choose not to participate. In Milwaukee the program now permits about 15,000 students to participate, but fewer than 11,000 have enrolled. In Edgewood, Texas, where the entire student population of over 13,000 were offered privately funded vouchers, only 1,655 accepted the offer in 2001. In the second year of a program in Florida, about 8,900 children in 10 schools were made eligible to receive vouchers to transfer; parents of only 659 had applied for vouchers by the beginning of the school year in 2002. Finally, where they have the option, most voucher students end up in religious schools; as the pro-voucher Friedman Foundation puts it, "No current school choice program of significant size can exist without the inclusion of parochial schools."[62]

Analysts do not agree on whether voucher programs affect the quality of the public school system at all, never mind whether the effects are beneficial or harmful. And even choice advocates agree that small-scale experiments tell us little, if anything, about the likely impact of vouchers if their scale were to be dramatically increased within a single district or across many districts. In the words of the most recent study of vouchers by the Rand Corporation, "Even if the experimental findings are methodologically sound, they may be imperfect predictors of the achievement effects of more generous, publicly funded voucher and charter programs that would bring in a larger segment of the population" and a different set of schools.[63]

Voucher proponents naturally want a big experiment to settle the question of the impact of a large-scale program, but they are unlikely to get one, for political and substantive reasons. Opponents are likely to block or distort a major experiment, as they did in Alum Rock, California; voters are likely to reject it, as they have every time they have been asked in a referendum. And school districts are likely to refuse to cooperate with it, as would any organization asked to undermine itself. Evaluations are also intrusive: educators in Edgewood and the three comparison districts threw the evaluators out after one year. Finally, the substantive evidence on large-scale voucher systems in other nations will not impress anyone who cares about the role of schools in promoting the American dream.

In 1980, for example, Chile implemented a voucher plan similar to that now advocated by American proponents. Private schools were deregulated and fully subsidized if they chose to participate in the system, and they now com-

pete for students with deregulated locally run public schools in most metropolitan areas. Private schools were allowed to charge fees and screen students;
teachers' unions were essentially eliminated after 1990, as were national curricula and national standards.

By 1990 three-quarters of the poorest 40 percent of the children attended
municipal public schools, and three-quarters of the richest 20 percent attended
subsidized or elite private schools. During this first decade, achievement test
scores overall remained about the same, with slight gains for middle-income
students and slight losses for poor students. In the second decade, under a new
governmental regime, the schools received much more funding, overall achievement rates rose, and the gap between highest- and lowest-scoring schools declined somewhat. Since 1996, however, improvements have stalled and debate
over the effectiveness of the 1990s reforms has risen. Two careful evaluators
of this experiment have found that "non-religious and profit maximizing
voucher schools . . . [were] marginally less effective than public schools in producing Spanish and mathematics achievement in the fourth grade. . . . [They]
are even less effective than public schools when they are located outside of the
capital. . . . Catholic voucher schools . . . [were] able to achieve higher test
scores for similar students but only by spending more." Even the pro-choice
Economist points out that "poorer parents lack information and cannot afford
the bus fare to more distant schools in better-off areas. Neither can bad teachers or heads be easily sacked."[64] As in New Zealand's extensive charter school
system, parents like having more choices, but overall, achievement scores
changed in different directions for different sets of children, and schools became more separated by socioeconomic class. Neither those who put a priority on individual goals of schooling nor those who care most about group-based
or collective goals should want to emulate this experience in the United States.

A broad voucher program in the United States would represent the kind
of fundamental change in schooling that has historically been justified only by
a present or imminent crisis. But most people do not perceive the schools in
their districts to be in crisis. Typically 40 to 50 percent of survey respondents
rank their local public schools as excellent or good, and about 30 percent rank
them as fair; the majority of parents are reasonably satisfied with their own
child's school.[65] After all, students in most schools have held steady or made
gains in achievement and attainment over time.

If asked, citizens usually endorse the idea of more choice, especially for
children in "underperforming" schools; frequently a majority of African Americans, Latinos, the poor, the young, urban residents, and the poorly educated
support the idea of vouchers on public opinion surveys.[66] But confronted with
a direct choice, a larger majority prefers investment in school reform to spending on vouchers for private schools. When asked in 1999, for example, what
the next president should do to improve education in this country, almost two-
fifths of respondents endorsed increases in public school funding, one-fifth

proposed better teachers, and only 2 percent chose vouchers and competition.[67] Even general support for "choice" should not be taken too seriously: when asked directly if they understood what vouchers entailed, 80 percent of Americans said that they knew too little to have an opinion on them. Substantial majorities of parents even in Cleveland and Milwaukee know nothing about them and have no opinion on their merits.[68] Most generally, two-thirds of Americans agree that "the public schools deserve our support even if they are performing poorly," and two-fifths agree that "the more children attend public schools, rather than private or parochial schools, the better it is for American society." As staunch voucher supporter Terry Moe said in one of the comments heading this chapter, "Americans like the public school system . . . [and most] are reasonably satisfied with what they are getting overall."[69] That attitude is unlikely to provide the support needed to make the huge changes inherent in a big choice program.

The public's actions, for once, accord with their sentiments as expressed in surveys: despite much expressed interest in the idea of vouchers, there is little commitment to their actual implementation. Private voucher programs in large cities with bad schools often receive many more initial applications than there are spaces, but many of those families selected (usually by lottery) do not take up the voucher or withdraw their children from their new schools after a year or so. And voucher proposals have suffered definitive losses whenever put to a popular vote. A proposition in California in 2000 received the support of only 30 percent of the voters; the result was the same in Michigan in the same year despite the fact that proponents of vouchers spent more than twice as much as opponents. No demographic group came close to giving vouchers majority support in either state; even a majority of self-identified Republicans or conservatives voted against them.[70] Congress has consistently refused to pass a voucher proposal, even one coming from President George W. Bush as part of an enormously popular education reform bill, and private choice programs have similarly failed to gain sufficient support in most state legislatures. Even the vehemently pro-voucher Heritage Foundation counts only 12 governors as supporting vouchers, and only four of them enjoy unified Republican rule in their legislatures; without Republican majorities, and sometimes even with them, these proposals have little chance. *New York Times* reporter Richard Rothstein summarized the situation this way: "Yes," he said in a headline, "Vouchers Are Dead."[71]

The Political Conundrum of Vouchers

In principle the broadest choice program would permit students to attend, at public expense, any public, private, or parochial school in a state. If poor urban children could attend schools in wealthier (and whiter) districts, it would increase racial and class integration for all students as well as the chances for individual success of predominantly nonwhite children. The most compelling arguments for choice have been made on behalf of poor children trapped in failing schools; this approach would provide them with a way out. But when it comes to broad programs involving urban children, especially programs that include suburban public schools, the politics of choice begin to resemble the politics of desegregation; most middle-class whites profess belief but few are willing to participate in anything more than token numbers. The new federal education reform law ostensibly gives children in failing schools the option to transfer out, but public schools in various districts have already announced that they will have no room for them. "I don't see the choice thing as a big change," said the deputy commissioner of education for Massachusetts. "Good schools that are doing well are pretty much at capacity already."[72] It does not take a high level of suspicion to assume that if they have any excess capacity at all, good schools will add other students before turning to poor inner-city children who have already suffered through several years of atrocious schooling.

In addition, since the number of private and parochial schools is small, their capacity to accommodate additional students from the public schools is very limited. So is their willingness to participate in such a program, in at least some cases. As the author of a letter to the editor of *Education Week* observed,

> Most private schools . . . do not need the money badly enough to take on the challenges of teaching at-risk voucher kids. Neither do they care to personally save the ghetto with their own schools' reputations. If they did, they would be leaders in the pro-voucher movement, which they most assuredly are not. . . . When middle and upper-middle-class parents asked themselves the what's-in-it-for-me question, they quickly realized the answer was nothing. . . . [W]idespread voucher support disappeared.

President Bush apparently recognizes this fact: in January 2001 he inadvertently broadcast a whispered observation that "there are a lot of Republicans who don't like vouchers. They come from wealthy suburban districts who are scared to death of irritating the public school movement, and their schools are good."[73]

For broad choice programs to really help many children, a substantial number of schools outside the cities would have to participate. Few nonurban politicians, however, can risk supporting a program that permits a large number of poor non-Anglo children from the city to attend public schools (and sometimes even private schools) in the suburbs. That political dynamic in good part explains why the two major private choice programs in this country were authorized only within the city limits of Milwaukee and Cleveland, and why no public schools in suburban districts adjoining Cleveland accepted either the state's invitation or the federal judge's plea to participate.[74]

Like liberal proponents of desegregation, therefore, conservative advocates of market-based solutions are caught between ideology and reality: they endorse the idea of the broadest possible choice but they cannot find a way to do it that is acceptable to them or their constituents. And as in the case of desegregation, poor urban children, who could gain access to better schools and increase diversity within them if such a choice program were implemented, are unlikely ever to benefit from it. Once again a majority of Americans outside the cities will not accept a proposal for change—this time from the right rather than the left—in part because they fear its impact on the achievement of their own children and on their own associational preferences.

On vouchers, then, both politics and substance lead to the same conclusion: large-scale privatization of public schooling would not necessarily promote individual success, and would undermine the public's long-standing commitment to put the American dream into practice through the shared institution of the schools. Americans believe strongly in what Terry Moe describes as the public school ideology:

> Many Americans simply like the idea of a public school system. They see it as an expression of local democracy and a pillar of the local community; they admire the egalitarian principles on which it is based, they think it deserves our commitment and support, and they tend to regard as subversive any notion that private schools should play a larger role in educating the nation's children.[75]

In our terms, Americans believe that schools should not only promote the ability of individuals to pursue their dreams but should be the vehicle for Americans to learn to engage in a common enterprise of shared citizenship. Voucher programs for private and parochial schools violate this ideology. Americans love the idea of choices. But school choice is too weak a lever to provide the answer to the problems of American education. Help can only come on the difficult roads of finance equity, school reform, and inclusion.

6

SEPARATION AND INCLUSION

We don't humbly ask for fairness. We demand educational equity and justice for all children and their families.
—*Member of Padres Unidos, an organization of Spanish-speaking parents of children in Denver public schools*

[Education] has a fundamental role in maintaining the fabric of our society. We cannot ignore the significant costs borne by our Nation when select groups are denied the means to absorb the values and skills upon which our social order rests.
—*U.S. Supreme Court, Plyler v. Doe, 1982*

Do we evaluate the long-term effects of our grouping practices with open minds, or do we see only what we want to see. . . . [T]o what extent [do we] . . . automatically offer some youngsters more than their share of the American dream while deferring that dream for others?
—*Corkin Cherubini, superintendent, Calhoun County, Georgia*[1]

IN LOS ANGELES HISPANIC PARENTS PICKET A SCHOOL, demanding that their children be taken out of bilingual education classes and put into regular, English-speaking classes; in Florida the state department of education officially chastises the schools in Orange County for not providing bilingual education classes. A mother hires attorneys and spends two years fighting to have her developmentally disabled teenage daughter placed in a full-time residential facility at public expense; another set of parents pays for neuropsychological testing for their five-year-old son with cerebral palsy so that they can do battle if the Wellesley, Massachusetts, school district tries to move him out of a regular kindergarten class. In Montclair, New Jersey, one parent opposes a plan to eliminate ability grouping in ninth-grade English because he "doesn't want his daughter jeopardized by the possibility that the new plan isn't going to work"; another supports the plan because "an end should be put to a [grouping] system that intentionally or unintentionally privileges a small minority and fails to do justice to the rest of the children."[2]

It is extremely hard to figure out how best to educate children who are in some way distinctive in their physical, emotional, or academic capacity, or in their English language proficiency. These children may differ not only from the majority of students but also from those perceived to have the same characteristics. Their advocates sometimes disagree passionately about how the inclusion of students with distinctive characteristics affects their achievement and that of their peers. In addition, the placement of these students is often affected unfairly by the usual racial and class hierarchies. Everyone concurs that whether we help children with distinctive characteristics to achieve their dreams is an important test of our nation's commitment to the American dream. But deep disagreements remain about how to do it.

Most Americans believe, in principle, that interaction in the classroom and playground is the best way for children to learn to appreciate, or at least deal with, people different from themselves. Mixing in this way may even lead students to find new dreams, see new possibilities, invent new futures. This is the premise behind the view that the collective goals of education are best achieved when students are educated together regardless of variations in ethnicity or race, gender or religion, ability or disability, background or beliefs. This is the basic idea behind the traditional American "common school" and the chief reason why students are generally assigned to public schools based on where they live rather than who they are.[3]

However, some of those who place priority on individual goals of schooling seek separate instruction for particular kinds of students—especially children with physical, mental, or emotional disabilities, children who are not fluent in English, or children with very high or very low perceived academic abilities. Parents, educators, advocates, or elected officials sometimes support separation but often for different reasons. Some fear that students with distinct needs will not be taught well or will be ostracized in a regular classroom; others believe that the education of other children will suffer if those with distinct needs are in the same classroom and require too much attention or otherwise change the dynamics. The decision of whether to give priority to collective goals and therefore educate students together as much as possible, or to individual goals and therefore perhaps educate more students separately, creates another variant of the educational dilemma inherent in the American dream.

Policy decisions become even more complicated when students with these distinct educational needs are also African American, Hispanic, poor, or otherwise at a social disadvantage. Advocates may claim that these students can achieve their dreams only if schools pay more attention to the special needs of their groups, which might imply lower priority for both the individual and the broader collective goals of schooling. Advocates in such a case may pressure schools to promote a new curriculum, use particular teaching techniques, hire staff from the same group, or create a separate instructional program for members of that group in deference to its needs or values. Out of a belief that this may be the most appropriate education for these children, or to provide opportunity and recognition to a group treated badly in the past, schools sometimes concur.

For one or several of these reasons, schools often do separate students with emotional problems and some kinds of learning or physical disabilities, or give students separate classes focused on English language education for a transitional or extended period. They also usually divide students into ability groups or career tracks. But each of these policies is controversial: other parents, educators, and activists oppose this kind of separation. They believe that greater inclusion, sometimes full inclusion (with appropriate changes in the process of schooling for all students), would be best for individuals, groups, and the collective goals of education. Thus they seek mainstreaming for almost all children with disabilities, English-only instruction as soon as possible, or heterogeneous classrooms across ability groupings.

Both those who advocate separation and those who want inclusion believe that their strategy is the best way to promote the American dream. Nevertheless, disputes can be fierce and involve complicated crosscurrents of goals and tactics, cultures and demography, practice and pedagogy. To some, inclusion of children with distinctive needs in mainstream classes is "a trek across a vast wasteland, . . . where . . . parents have been duped"; to others separate placements are themselves the moral equivalent of slavery or apartheid.[4]

Special education, bilingual education, and ability grouping are three arenas in which issues of separation and inclusion confront the goals of the American dream in public schooling. Policies in each area raise the same two underlying questions: What is educationally best for the students? How far should we push the premise that children should be educated in the same classrooms, separated only by age and grade, once they are assigned to a district and school according to where they live? Disputes on all of these policies involve all three goals of education, group-based as well as individual and collective; advocates for children are on all sides of the issue; and educators over time have changed their views about the best things to do for children with distinct needs or characteristics. Despite these similarities the political dynamics on the three issues differ significantly. The vast majority of parents remain uninvolved in disputes over special education or bilingual education; in contrast, many parents, especially elites, become involved if districts try to change their policies with regard to ability grouping—which is why they mostly do not.

About a tenth of parents and educators in all districts are deeply engaged with the issue of special education. Physical disabilities can appear in any family at any time, as can learning disabilities and severe emotional problems, although racial and class differences complicate the identification of children in the latter cases. Parents of children with disabilities are often deeply engaged (as are their lawyers, since they have an extensive set of rights under statutory and case law), but other parents usually are not.

The proportion of students who do not speak English varies enormously across the country; in some places all are fluent in English, and in a few places almost none are. Unlike with special education, the number of people involved with bilingual education therefore differs considerably across districts, communities, and states. Also unlike special education, the distribution is not random: immigrants or the children of immigrants live disproportionately in a few cities and states (although that is rapidly changing), and it is reasonable to assume that their numbers will grow where they already have a presence. Parents usually do not get involved with this issue unless their children know little English or until the proportion of students with limited English proficiency (LEP) in their district is high and rising. Parents in Los Angeles or San Antonio are likely to have strong views on bilingual education; parents in Missoula, Montana, may not. The issue of bilingual education has seen some litigation, but it does not involve legal rights in anything like the manner of special education.

Finally, children everywhere vary in their academic ability, at least as measured by classroom performance and test scores, and almost all schools above the elementary level (and many of those as well) group students according to their measured ability. This is not a salient political issue until someone tries to change the terms of separation or abolish ability grouping altogether. At that point it quickly becomes an intense controversy. There has been little judicial involvement on this issue except when it has become entangled in broader desegregation cases.

If we take these issues together and consider the evidence across all three, it is clear that separating students usually does more harm than good in light of the tenets of the American dream. Separate education sets up barriers among students and labels them; by definition it reduces diversity in the classroom and makes learning respect and mutual engagement more difficult. Separate education also too easily turns into second-class education for some, as it did in the case of racial segregation; by definition this results in unequal opportunity, and it reduces the chances for individual students to achieve their dreams. The burden of proof should therefore be on those who advocate separating children. As we will see, the evidence on all of these issues is not clear enough to make the case for separation as a general policy.

The most recent federal law on special education is consistent with our view: it strongly encourages mainstreaming even among those with substantial physical, emotional, or learning disabilities. There is no clear federal policy with regard to bilingual education; various state policies are unsettled or vague, but the trend here too is toward greater inclusion in regular classrooms of children with limited English proficiency. Ability grouping is different: there are no federal or state laws on it and it remains almost universal, though less rigid than it used to be.

Increasing inclusiveness almost always requires difficult adjustments in teaching practices and support structures and sometimes engenders opposition from concerned parents and established educators for that reason alone. The deeper problem is that inclusion can cause strong reactions when parents in the majority begin to fear that their children's achievement will suffer if they are taught alongside others deemed less able, or when parents in the minority fear that their children's needs are being ignored in the name of the good of the whole. This kind of reaction occurs to some extent with special and bilingual education and is usually very strong whenever ability grouping is discussed, as we will see.

Special Education

Over the past few decades, students requiring special education have made a great deal of progress toward inclusion in mainstream schools and classes. About 6.2 million students (about 13 percent of children) are currently designated as having disabilities that qualify for special education services. That represents an increase of 68 percent since the mid-1970s, and the numbers continue to increase. This expansion has occurred for several reasons, including improved medical methods for diagnoses and diagnoses at ever-younger ages. But the major factor has probably been broadening definitions of disability, in particular the increased classification as learning disabled of children who in earlier years would have been ignored or regarded as merely slow or difficult. Twenty-five years ago about a quarter of special education students were classified as suffering from retardation and about a fifth as learning disabled. At present, learning disabilities that affect students' capacity to read or write account for fully half of the students in special education, and only about 11 percent are classified as retarded. Nineteen percent fall into categories of speech or language impairment, and 8 percent are classified as seriously emotionally disturbed. Most of the others have physical disabilities, including visual or hearing impairments, and about 113,000 students are classified as severely or multiply handicapped.[5]

Special education is on average more than twice as expensive as regular education, although the range of costs is very large. Programs for some students, such as those with most speech impairments, require only a modest additional cost, but some cases of severe or multiple disabilities require enormous sums. Special education now costs more than $40 billion a year[6] and accounts for up to 40 percent of recent increases in education funding. Despite its statutory commitment to pay 40 percent of special education costs, the federal government pays much less than half of that, and states and local districts cover the rest.

Although the high cost of special education is a serious problem for school budgets, spending for this purpose represents a triumph for Americans committed to equal opportunity and the goal of individual achievement for all children. Special education "is the biggest success story in American education in my lifetime," says the superintendent of a small district in Arkansas.[7] Before 1975 separation of most children with disabilities was absolute: a million disabled children were kept completely outside the public school system, 90,000 of them in institutions. A law in North Carolina still on the books in 1969 permitted the state to declare a child "uneducable," a decision that parents could not legally appeal. These children were clearly not considered part of the community to which the ideology of the American dream applied; any chance for personal success depended entirely on private resources and commitments.

That exclusion ended with successful litigation and the passage of laws in the 1960s and 1970s. Using *Brown v. Board of Education* and its successors as models, advocates such as the various state Associations for Retarded Children and civil rights groups pushed the federal and state governments to respond to the needs of these children.[8] In 1975 the federal government passed legislation, now known as the Individuals with Disabilities Education Act (IDEA), that gave disabled children the right to receive a "free appropriate public education" in the "least restrictive environment." Unlike all other students, they became entitled to an individually appropriate program; unlike all others the parents of disabled students were given the right under federal law to appeal to school officials and then to the courts if they believed their children were improperly classified or inappropriately placed. Since IDEA was passed, schools have been obligated to provide the education that a panel of experts approves as necessary for each identified student and to prepare them for independent living as adults. Over the past few decades, Congress has expanded the scope of IDEA by including preschool and even infant children, adding new types of disability, such as severe attention deficit disorder, to those already covered, and increasing the "related services" that schools must provide.

Children with disabilities require a range of instructional settings. At present over 95 percent of children with disabilities attend the same schools as other children. About 47 percent are in regular classrooms most or all of the day with an aide or other assistance, almost 30 percent spend part of the day in regular classes and part in small group instruction or "resource rooms," and about 25 percent are in fully separate classes or separate public or private schools. Only 26,000 children, usually those with severe or multiple disabilities, remain in institutions.[9]

As soon as public schools were required to educate children with disabilities, controversies began about how to do it effectively. Initially many supporters thought it a mistake to educate them in classes or schools with students who did not have similar types of disability. As Brent Staples, a member of the editorial board of the *New York Times*, put it, parents fear that "disabled children tend to do poorly in public schools, and often their problems go undiagnosed. Ashamed of failure, they act out in class, become truant and eventually drop out. The luckiest children are those whose disabilities are detected early and who are sent to special . . . schools."[10] Supporters of separation also worried that fears of stigmatization in a mainstream setting would undermine a student's or parent's resolve to obtain needed services, or that educators in regular classrooms already held low expectations for poor, rural, or nonwhite students and therefore would be especially inclined to ignore poor performance among disadvantaged children with disabilities.

Some educators of students with unusual problems remain committed to education in separate settings. Jeanne Angus, the director of a special education school in New York City, points out, for example, that children with Asperger's syndrome (a neurological disorder that roughly resembles a highly articulate autism) are "normal in so many ways. They're often very sweet. And they're often amazingly precocious, with sky-high IQ's. But look closer and you'll see cracks. Many of them have had appalling difficulties in the regular school system." Inclusion "doesn't work," she says. "We teach them the facial expression charts here [pictures showing what a face looks like when it is happy or angry]. . . . We make them focus and maintain eye contact, they all have to do it. It doesn't make them feel abnormal."[11] From this perspective inclusion is what makes children with special needs feel isolated; in their own place they can feel part of a group that is valued and understood on its own terms.

The broadest argument for separation of children with disabilities is the claim that they are a distinctive group with a distinctive culture deserving of respect and protection, best obtained in their own unique setting. Supporters of the Deaf articulate that view most clearly. Roslyn Rosen, former president of the National Association of the Deaf, insists that she is "happy with who I am, and I don't want to be 'fixed.' Would an Italian-American rather be a WASP? In our society everyone agrees that whites have an easier time than blacks. But do you think a black person would undergo operations to become white?" In this view Deaf children should attend schools with others like themselves and run by Deaf adults; they should also learn in their own language, American Sign Language (ASL). Otherwise, according to the National Association of the Deaf, " 'full inclusion' creates language and communication barriers that are potentially harmful, and consequently deny many of these children an education in the Least Restrictive Environment." As the well-known Deaf educator Leo Jacobs puts it, "Mainstreaming deaf children in regular public-school programs" will yield only "a new generation of educational failures," who will become "frustrated and unfulfilled adults."[12]

A few years after the passage of IDEA, however, another set of advocates began to express a different set of concerns, leading to the opposite demand for greater or even full inclusion in regular classrooms. They became concerned about the new tendency of schools to identify too many children as needing special education—the opposite problem from the earlier concern that schools identified too few. Overidentification can occur for several reasons. If disabled children are to be removed from regular classrooms, for example, teachers can have an incentive to label as emotionally disturbed those children who are unusually active or occasionally defiant, and thereby to eliminate the problem without necessarily helping the child. Schools in some cases have an incentive to overidentify failing students who then become exempt from tests used to measure the school's academic progress; when that happens, these students can be safely ignored by teachers struggling to meet their testing goals.

For slightly different reasons, white, middle-class parents may seek to have their underachieving children classified as learning disabled (but not retarded or emotionally disturbed) in order to obtain extra aid and a legal boost against potential competitors in the arena of high-stakes testing. "Indeed," points out Wade Horn, the assistant secretary of the U.S. Department of Health and Human Services (HHS), "while children from families with more than $100,000 annual income account for just thirteen percent of the SAT test-taking population, they make up 27 percent of those who receive special accommodations when taking the SAT." This phenomenon runs the risk of depriving children (often poor and nonwhite) who have legitimate claims on public resources in order to give extra benefits to children (often white and well off) who may well have a real problem but not one that is generally conceived to be a public concern. And districts in some states have been inadvertently rewarded for classifying students under funding formulas designed to make sure that education for the disabled was adequately financed.[13] Critics came to believe, in short, that the cumulative effect of removing special-needs students from the classroom were substantial, harmful, and costly, and many began to advocate greater inclusion.

Proponents of more inclusive policies also have ideological and pedagogical reasons for rejecting separation. They believe that students with disabilities can only attain success later in life if they begin in a regular classroom, and they believe that all children, disabled or not, will benefit when more students are educated in regular classrooms. These arguments were well stated by the principal of an elementary school in Virginia and two teachers in his school when they pointed out that "classrooms reflect real life with its challenges and distractions. . . . This is the 'normal' world that they will be required to live and work in, so their education ought to take place in classrooms that reflect that world. To be truly prepared to take part in the real world as adults, children with disabilities need to be educated in language-rich classrooms and to interact daily with peers who are appropriate role models."[14]

In addition, argue the principal and his coauthors, children without disabilities will acquire skills in an inclusive classroom that will also help *them* attain success later in life even if a classmate is prone to "challenging behaviors." After all, "Peers need to understand why the behaviors are occurring and to brainstorm and plan for ways to help their classmate. . . . Children learn to work together, to plan, and to put their plans into action. Such skills are valuable throughout a lifetime and cannot be learned from any textbook." Thus all students can pursue individual success in classrooms where "teachers . . . believe that students with disabilities can learn successfully," where teachers "do not lower their expectations," where "effective discipline strategies are in place," and where "each student . . . feel[s] valued." This is all the more true because many changes made to help the mainstreamed children with disabilities, such as individualized instruction, cooperative learning, and smaller classes, will benefit all students.[15]

Finally, proponents believe that an inclusive classroom promotes the collective good by teaching children and adults essential lessons in democratic values and practice. Although students in an inclusive classroom "may learn different things at different times," says one scholar of education, "their learning is enhanced by contact and interaction. . . . Individual and group diversity contributes positively to classroom climate, learning outcomes, and community quality." More dramatically, the Virginia principal and his teachers insist that "every society has had to face the question of how to treat individuals who differ from the norm, and the vision of building strong communities based on peace, unity, and acceptance for all is an appealing one. We can begin to make this vision a reality in our public schools by accepting and valuing children with disabilities exactly as they are."[16]

Battle is thus joined between proponents of inclusion and advocates for separation, even though both sides had worked hard to get children with disabilities into the public school system in the first place, and both share the core goal of promoting individual success through public education. And the battle sometimes goes beyond these disagreements to bring in contrasting views of the legitimacy of group-based goals. Proponents of separation frequently value and seek to maintain the distinctive features of an unusual group; proponents of inclusion, in contrast, downplay support for a distinctive group in favor of arguments based on the commonality of all students, diversity within a classroom, or the good of the individual.

Although separatists predominated in the early debates on special education, proponents of inclusion have had more impact in recent years. Concerns about overidentification, especially when linked with issues of race and class, and the persuasiveness of arguments about the value of inclusion, have led policymakers and educators to scrutinize classification and its consequences more closely.

What they have found is often disheartening. Guidelines for classification and placement still vary greatly from state to state and district to district. As the National Academy of Sciences tactfully put it, "Whether the current technology for student identification is sufficient . . . is an issue worthy of further inquiry. . . . There is a great deal of variability from place to place in the criteria used to define disability, the financial incentives and disincentives for classification, and in the local implementing conditions for deciding who qualifies as having a disability." About 18 percent of students in Massachusetts and Rhode

Island, for example, but roughly 11 percent in Arizona and California, are identified as having disabilities. Rates of identification for specific disabilities vary even more. The proportion of children receiving special education services increased during the 1990s by 5 percent or less in Mississippi, Alaska, and Pennsylvania, but by over 60 percent in Arizona, Georgia, Hawaii, and Nevada.[17] Some poor urban districts identify many more children, and some many fewer, than the average of the state in which they are located; in Connecticut, for example, over 13 percent of the students were classified as needing special education in 1995—but fully 18 percent in Hartford and only 10 percent in Bridgeport.[18] Disabled children in inner cities are on average twice as likely as those outside inner cities to be in full-time special education classes. This disparity holds for all types of disability, although the degree of disparity varies with specific diagnoses.[19]

Separating students with special needs varies not just by location but also, even more troublingly, by student characteristics. Higher proportions of black than white students are typically placed in special education classes, especially those for children with retardation or emotional disturbances. Proportionally few Asian American students are placed in special education at all; some fear that teachers mistake problems of these children for cultural differences or lack of facility in English. Boys are about twice as likely to be in special education as are girls and are especially likely to be identified as having a serious emotional disturbance. Poor children are more likely than affluent children to be classified as disabled.[20] Nonwhite children may be especially likely to be placed in special education when most of their classmates are white.[21]

Although disadvantaged children clearly have more problems, including disabilities, than other children, analysts differ on how much of these various discrepancies in placement result from real need rather than from the racial, class, or gender biases of the educators and other professionals involved. Advocates are convinced that assignment is discriminatory, and experts are sufficiently concerned that they tend more and more toward support for inclusion.[22] The high level of variability in classification from place to place and from one kind of student to another suggests a randomness in application or in criteria for placement that are irrelevant to the child's real needs, and thus provides a more general and powerful argument for inclusion as a general approach.

Some students clearly need to be placed in separate schools throughout their education, but we have no firm evidence that placing less-disabled students in separate classes actually helps them. Evidence on the long-term impact of separation for most students is contradictory or ambiguous. Even though it is more than a decade old, the National Longitudinal Transitional Study (NLTS) is the best, and almost the only, survey with national-level results about the effects of various educational choices on disabled children. It found that students with disabilities did worse overall than others on all measures of attainment and achievement (which is not very surprising), but that children with disabilities who participated in regular education, with supplementary services as needed, found greater success as adults than disabled students who remained in special education. They were also more likely to live independently, obtain a job, and earn higher wages.[23]

More recent analyses have contradicted one another on the value of special education. Economist Eric Hanushek and his colleagues found that in Texas, "special education programs on average boost the achievement of students provided this special treatment, and it appears that schools target services toward students who derive larger benefits." The authors also found, to their surprise, that the more students classified as both physically and learning disabled in a school, the greater the achievement gains made by students in regular classrooms. An equally sophisticated study by equally respected economists, however, examined students who were reclassified from low achieving to learning disabled as a result of fiscal incentives and found that for them "special education is negatively and significantly related to student mathematics and reading test scores." In fact the "estimated effects are implausibly large"; the reading and math scores of the newly classified students fell by 40 percent. Even the authors question the magnitude of the harmful impact, but they have confidence in the basic conclusion.[24] In part because of confusing and conflicting findings like these, the largest influence on policymaking remains the earlier, widely accepted NLTS study and its finding that disabled children in mainstream classes did better as adults.

Based on both the NLTS findings and a more general ideological move toward openness, federal law now makes it clear that "to the maximum extent appropriate, children with disabilities are [to be] educated with children who are nondisabled" and that they are to be separated "only when the nature or severity of the disability of a child is such that education in regular classes with the use of . . . supplementary aids and services cannot be achieved satisfactorily."[25] Special education students must now—in principle though not always in practice—be included in state assessments, with the same standard setting, testing, and reporting as all other students in the context of necessary accommodations or modifications. Their curriculum must, again in principle, be aligned with the general curriculum regardless of whether they are in separate or regular classes. Some states, such as Vermont, have responded to these changes by moving close to full inclusion.

Courts usually respond favorably to parental demands for greater inclusion of children with disabilities. In doing so they have begun to provide guidelines that may be widely applicable to other issues of separation and inclusion. School districts have a clear burden to prove that a child needs to be separated; within that statutory framework, courts have required districts to consider "the educational benefits of placement full-time in a regular class, the non-academic benefits of such placement, the effect . . . on the teacher and children in the regular class, and the costs of mainstreaming."[26] The central legal decisions in the early 1990s required reluctant schools to put even children with substantial disabilities into regular classrooms. The right setting for each student necessarily remains a balancing act, but there is a judicial as well as legislative weight on the scale that works against separation.

As a consequence of increased emphasis on inclusion, the number of disabled children taught in regular school buildings and spending most of their day in regular classrooms steadily increased during the 1990s, even as the number of children diagnosed as needing special education also grew. Some advocates and a few schools went all the way to argue for full inclusion of all students in mainstream classes. Authors Dorothy Lipsky and Alan Gartner assert that "the education of students with disabilities should occur with their age peers in the general education classroom, with the necessary supplemental aids and support services. Anything other than full inclusion denies the students' rights to an appropriate education." They are supported by several substantial advocacy groups such as The Arc (formerly the Association for Retarded Citizens), which claims that "each student with mental retardation should be educated with appropriate supports and services in an age-appropriate classroom with peers who are not disabled." The United Cerebral Palsy Association shares this view as does the Council for Exceptional Children and others.[27]

This movement toward extensive or even full inclusion has generated a reaction from those who continue to endorse separation of a larger number of students with special needs. Reaction focuses most vehemently on the demand for full inclusion. The Learning Disabilities Association of America, for example, opposes policies that "mandate the same placement, instruction, or treatment for *all* students." It argues that "the regular education classroom is not the appropriate placement for a number of students with learning disabilities who may need alternative instructional environments, teaching strategies, and/or materials that cannot or will not be provided within the context of a regular classroom environment. . . . The placement of all children with disabilities in the regular classroom is as great a violation of IDEA as the placement of all children in separate classrooms on the basis of their type of disability."[28]

Some educators concur. Over 70 percent of elementary school principals in one poll agreed that "the concept of inclusion has been pushed to such extremes that it's robbing non-handicapped children of their right to learn, while depriving handicapped children of the specialized teaching they need to achieve their highest potential." The AFT has called for a halt to the movement for full inclusion, claiming that

> it's not just teachers who are paying the price. Inappropriate inclusion lowers expectations that any student in that classroom can get the education they deserve, and the student who needs the most help invariably suffers the most. As inclusion is increasingly practiced, it bears no resemblance to what most well-

wishing people think of as mainstreaming children with disabilities into regular classrooms. It places children who cannot function into an environment which doesn't help them and often detracts from the education process for all students.[29]

Those who endorse full inclusion and their most forceful opponents are at the extremes of this debate. To the former only full inclusion will prevent students' being "relegated to the fringes of the school by placement in segregated wings." To the latter, in the words of the losing attorney in one of the key cases, "Full inclusion is the latest egalitarian fad to be imposed upon the nation's schools. . . . It represents a triumph of liberal ideology over education under the guise of civil rights. This is an educational nightmare in which all the children emerge as losers."[30] Closer to the center are proponents of greater but not full inclusion, or general but not complete separation. The former believe that individual success is usually best achieved in a regular classroom, and they are equally concerned about teaching all students to respect diverse others. The latter believe that individual success is often best achieved outside the regular classroom and are more concerned about the distinctive needs of their group than about the good of the whole. A dispute that is apparently about pedagogy is at least as much about the tensions embedded in the ideology of the American dream.

Americans in general are conflicted on the questions of how to educate children with disabilities and how much to spend on their schooling. In the abstract most endorse special efforts to help children with disabilities attain individual success, and at least two-thirds of the public believes that local school districts should be required to provide special education. Almost half of Americans agree that schools are spending too little, compared with only 5 percent who think they are spending too much, on students with special needs. Nevertheless, most survey respondents dramatically underestimate the actual costs of special education, and almost none choose special education when asked to set priorities for possible additional educational funds.[31]

Elected officials and others sense this ambivalence, especially in the context of general opposition to tax increases, and have reacted to the high cost of programs for students with disabilities. Former mayor Rudolph Giuliani of New York openly criticized the differential in spending per pupil between special and regular education, which according to him was more than four to one. Dennis Pollard, an attorney who represents school districts in special education court cases, argues that "school districts can only absorb these costs for so long, and then they don't have any choice but to start cutting off general programs." As the journalist Tyce Palmaffy puts it, the growth of requirements for special education have "elicited a wave of fear and anger over the exploding costs of special education." The Minneapolis *Star Tribune* ran a series with headlines such as, "Average kids are losing; soaring special education costs squeeze Minnesota school budgets."[32]

Elected officials have responded by trying to remove the financial incentives for overidentification and unnecessary separate placement. Some seek a system that is more accurate in paying only for actual costs; others try to make districts that identify students share more of the costs of educating them. Most recently, despite parental pressure, elected officials have tried to separate the funding from the education. New Jersey, for example, caps the percentage of students for whom it will pay but requires districts to provide services to anyone who is classified. Pennsylvania has moved toward creating census-based funding that assumes a certain percentage of all students will need services and provides money to the districts regardless of the actual count and the distribution of specific disabilities. The last approach, although not subtle or responsive to the needs of the districts, has had real impact on classification and cost. All these actions are evidence of the desperation of elected officials in dealing with the huge growth in special education expenditures with no clear end in sight.

Controlling overidentification saves money, but inclusion generally does not. It is usually as expensive to educate disabled children in a regular classroom with proper support as it is to educate them separately. Successful inclusion of children with disabilities requires not only additional aides and specially trained teachers in the regular classroom, but also training for the regular classroom teacher and sometimes for the students and their parents. It may require substantial technological adjustments as well. The costs of special education therefore remain high.

Americans are as uncertain about the appropriate extent of inclusion, independent of questions of cost, as they are ambivalent about the costs of special education. Two-thirds agree that physically handicapped children should be in the same classrooms as other students. But at least three-fifths think the learning disabled and "mentally handicapped children" should be in separate rather than mainstream classes, and over half of Californians with an opinion oppose full inclusion of students with behavioral or learning disabilities.[33] In this survey, teachers in California were even more opposed to full inclusion, with about two-thirds of those with an opinion opposing it, and most of them disapproving "strongly." Seventy percent of students in one small survey said they did not think they would benefit from having disabled students in their classes, and 67 percent did not want to be in the same class as students with disabilities.[34]

Much of the argument against greater inclusion focuses on the most disruptive children. In a 1994 *Phi Delta Kappan* poll, a majority of Americans agreed that a "very important" cause of increased violence in the nation's schools was "trying to deal with . . . emotionally disturbed students in the regular classroom instead of in special classes or schools." And more adults think it is better for *other* students in a school if emotionally disturbed children are taught separately than think it is good for the disturbed children themselves.[35]

Most believe that children with chronic behavioral problems should be removed from regular classes; two-thirds prefer an alternative school, even though only half expect such a setting actually to help the troubled students. Over half claim that they would pay an additional $100 a year in taxes to set up an alternative school in their community. As one state legislator put it, "We can't pay attention to only those children we designate as special. All children are special. We've got to be concerned about all their education."[36]

According to the polls, most Americans believe in equal opportunity and respect for those who are different, they sympathize with the disabled and want to include them in their society, but they are not sure it can be done through regular classrooms in public schools. They endorse the general approach of proponents of inclusion but share the concerns of opponents about its most extreme forms. Americans have worried for decades about insufficient discipline in classrooms, about class sizes that are too large, and about teachers who cannot devote enough attention to individual students.[37] They have now added fears that increased inclusion of students needing special education will exacerbate these problems, harming their own children and perhaps the educational system as a whole.

Despite the rhetoric federal law does not in fact permit a blanket policy of full inclusion: it requires an individually appropriate education for every disabled child, and that is unlikely to change. Some children will always require placement outside the regular classroom. The placement of each child is by law a matter of pedagogy and expert evaluation. The policy can only be about the presumptive placement, about the burden of proof, and research evidence is not clear enough to settle the issue.

But for reasons beyond research, the federal mandate for the least restrictive environment, combined with the judicial guidelines placing the burden on those who would separate children, is the right approach. Separate education too easily becomes inferior education. A report by the District of Columbia City Council, for example, shows that the during much of the 1990s, the D.C. special education system was marked by "institutional inattention; poor record-keeping; sizable backlogs in assessments, placements, and reassessments; and due-process hearings." The district, said the report, "has only vague plans for building special education programs within its schools and has failed to demonstrate that the system has made local school programming a priority." During this period the division of special education expended one-third of the school district's budget, although it involved about a tenth of the district's students. Administrators could not say how many special education students graduated in 1999, and the Office of Special Education advises people to ignore earlier graduation reports as unreliable. Even the state of Massachusetts, a leader in the movement to properly identify and educate children with disabilities, found itself in the embarrassing position in September 2001 of having 500 teachers without appropriate certification in its special education classes. "We're getting a whole lot of baby sitters," worried the mother of a son with bipolar disorder and learning disabilities.[38]

In addition to the dangers of a lower-quality education, judgments about students with disabilities can by themselves be self-fulfilling: students are separated because school officials do not think they can do as well as the majority, and then they do not do as well because they are separated. Labels of "normal" or "abnormal" have real power and can affect the way students think about themselves and the way others think about them for a long time. Unless there is clear reason for an individual exception, inclusion wherever possible will do the most to promote the first, individual, goal of the American dream.

Finally, separation can cause serious harm to the democratic objectives of education because it works directly against learning to deal with diverse others. Talking about mutual accommodation and shared values beneath visible differences is one thing; figuring out how to accommodate and jointly pursue a shared goal with someone very different from oneself is quite another. Interaction done badly can generate anger and frustration as much as understanding and appreciation, but contact in a supportive setting can lead to engagement and respect. Where there is no contact, schools cannot even try to achieve the collective goals of the American dream; inclusion whenever possible is necessary, though not sufficient, to promote it. The cautious but steady move in the United States toward inclusion of most students with special needs is one of the best examples of how Americans can, when they choose, manage the conflicts built into the American dream.

Bilingual Education

The debate over including or separating children with distinctive linguistic characteristics in part mirrors the debate over how to educate children with distinctive physical, emotional, or neurological characteristics. Americans generally agree that English-speaking children need to be taught to respect and appreciate immigrant classmates if public education is to help our nation promote the collective goals of the American dream. They also believe that children who are not fluent in English need help to learn it so that they can pursue their individual dreams. But Americans disagree strongly about how best to accomplish these goals. Here too proponents of extended separation worry that a drive toward inclusiveness will not permit the children with the greatest or most unusual needs to achieve their dreams: they believe such children will be lost in the mass. They also fear that distinctive group values and outlooks will be overrun in a move toward inclusion, to the detriment of the children in that group and the nation as a whole.

Opponents of extended separation, in turn, worry that some children are separated for the wrong reasons or for too long, that many are stigmatized by labeling, and that most are receiving a second-class education. They believe that American democratic practices and values can incorporate differences without submerging them and that the nation as a whole is stronger if all participate jointly. In our terms, opponents do not believe that linguistically based separation promotes individual success or produces equality of opportunity, experience with diversity, or training in democratic citizenship for all students.

While most of those who promote civil rights for special education students call for more or complete inclusion, most who seek civil rights for English learners endorse longer or more complete separation from mainstream classes. Nevertheless, because the underlying conflicts are the same, they can and should be managed in the same way. The burden of proof should be on those who would separate students, and here too the evidence is not clear that separation is better for learning English, at least not after a brief initial period. In the absence of evidence to the contrary in individual cases, children with distinctive linguistic needs should be included as soon as possible in regular classrooms so that they are not treated as second-class citizens, so that all children benefit from the diversity of their classmates, and so that classrooms become training grounds for democratic citizenship.

The number of LEP children in public schools has risen steadily over the past few decades. Roughly 5 million children in public schools speak English poorly or not at all; that represents more than 9 percent of all students and an increase of almost 300 percent since the mid-1980s.[39] Put another way, in the 15 years after 1980 the proportion of K-12 students who spoke a language other than English at home increased by about half, from almost 9 percent of students to over 13 percent. Only some of them also speak English fluently.[40] About three-quarters of English learners speak Spanish, followed by Vietnamese, Hmong, and up to 150 other languages, many spoken by no more than a few percent of LEP children.

In the early 1990s, a substantial majority of language-minority individuals lived in just six states (California, Texas, New York, Florida, Illinois, and New Jersey in descending order in the number of LEP students) and were concentrated in a few school districts within them. Since then, the immigrant population has spread to many more states and districts, although it remains the case that 40 percent of English learners live in California—comprising roughly a quarter of the students in that state. Districts vary enormously; among the 15 largest school districts, 44 percent of the students in Los Angeles but only 3 percent in Fairfax County, Virginia, are served in programs for English learners.[41] Over half of language-minority children are in early elementary grades.

The students who qualify for special and bilingual education overlap somewhat,[42] and LEP students are also disproportionately poor.[43] Over three-quarters of English learners are eligible for free school lunches (compared with just over a third of students overall), and they are concentrated in urban schools where the other students are also likely to be poor. In fact, in the early 1990s the federal program to aid poor children (now known as Title I) aided more LEP students than did the federal bilingual education program targeted specifically at them. About two-thirds of English learners now receive support from these federal programs.[44]

LEP students with different native languages are often in school with each other and are with African American students more than with Anglo or Asian students. Almost half of English learners attend a school where at least three in ten of their peers are also English learners. In California there are twice as many LEP students in the average black student's school or district as in those of the average Anglo. An increase in the proportion of English learners is more likely to occur in an elementary school with mostly black students than in a school with mostly Anglo or Asian students. The proportion of LEP students differs more across district lines than among schools in the same district, in the same pattern as school separation between blacks and whites. In short, the "pattern of *segregation*" is "the separation of majority non-Hispanic whites from both LEP students and African Americans, not the separation of LEP students and African Americans from each other." Given the difficulties that schools and students encounter when there is a high concentration of English learners, this segregation, says the author, "may . . . becom[e] a *new source* of racial inequality in educational opportunity."[45]

There is no consensus about the cost of programs for English learners beyond the expenses of their regular schooling. The federal government allocated $665 million a year to bilingual education in 2002, but that is surely a small share of the total expenditures. Schools, districts, and states do not add up the marginal costs of extra teachers and classrooms in any systematic way, and even that would not account for the additional expenditures in materials, time, and attention. The American Legislative Council estimated a nationwide expenditure of two to three billion dollars per year in the early 1990s, and analysts in New York City estimated an extra $900 to $1,000 a year per child a few years later.[46]

Throughout the nineteenth and early twentieth centuries, local communities of immigrants sought and sometimes obtained public funding for schools or classes taught in languages other than English. The arguments for and against these efforts were remarkably similar then to those heard today. By World War I, however, bilingual education had been swamped by the drive to Americanize immigrants, and by the early 1920s about half of the states passed laws that forbade public, and sometimes private, schools to teach substantive courses in languages other than English. Even many young immigrants themselves preferred to learn English than to retain the language of their ancestors.[47]

As with special education, civil rights protests in the 1960s on behalf of a distinctive group of children revived the issue of language of instruction. The

Bilingual Education Act of 1968 permitted federal funds to be used to help educate children who were both poor and "educationally disadvantaged because of their inability to speak English," but it did not require schooling in any particular language. The Supreme Court in *Lau v. Nichols* (1974) supported help for these children, holding that "there is no equality of treatment merely by providing students with the same facilities, textbooks, teachers, and curriculum, for students who do not understand English are effectively foreclosed from any meaningful education."[48] The Court, like Congress, did not require any particular form of education for LEP students.

Financial support was slow to come and meager when it did. Nevertheless, by the end of the 1990s, 9 states mandated bilingual education (that is, programs that included teaching the students substantive courses in their native language), 25 states required help for English learners but did not specify programmatic content, 5 states forbade all but short-term transitional programs, and 11 had no laws.[49]

Before these laws and rulings, poor migrant children, who often spoke only Spanish, frequently received almost no public schooling at all. Other non-English speakers were simply left on their own in regular classrooms—the teaching method now described as "sink or swim." So in ways similar to the drive for special education, advocates sought to bring all children into schools *and*, simultaneously to separate students who spoke English poorly into classes specifically designed for them.

Classes and methods for teaching English learners proliferated dramatically in the 1970s and 1980s. English as a second language (ESL), in which instruction focuses on English-language skills, was most prevalent. Transitional bilingual education, in which students receive some academic instruction in their native language, accounts for most of the remaining programs; its goal is to move students into English-only teaching as soon as the student is ready, although the transitional period can be brief or extend over several years. (A third approach, cultural maintenance, is discussed in chapter 7).

Just like students with disabilities, English learners sometimes suffer from overidentification and sometimes from underidentification, and many do not receive high-quality services. On the one hand, anecdotes and a little systematic evidence suggest that some students are shunted into classes for non-English speakers simply because their last name is Hispanic, their parents are immigrants, or they do not read well in any language.[50] The government reported in 1994 that only 43 percent of students identified as limited-English-proficient were immigrants, but it did not explain why so many native-born students were classified as LEPs. Rosalie Porter, an avowed opponent of bilingual education, suggests that many of these nonimmigrant LEP students are "children who speak English but may not read and write it well enough for schoolwork. In that case, there surely are a large number of students who are wrongly enrolled in programs where they are being taught in another language when what they urgently need is remedial help in reading and writing in English." Anecdotes and some systematic evidence similarly suggest that students are too seldom moved into regular classes even when they are able to learn in an English-only classroom.[51]

On the other hand, non-English speakers who are a small minority in their district may receive no bilingual services at all. And most districts find it difficult or even impossible to find bilingual or ESL teachers. In 1992 only 10 percent of teachers with LEP students were certified in bilingual education, and another 8 percent in ESL; by 1999, 40 percent of teachers had English learners in their classrooms, but only 12 percent had received recent training in how to teach LEP students. Even now fewer than a fifth of teachers with English learners in their classrooms are certified in bilingual education or ESL. In California two-fifths of the adults providing bilingual instruction are teachers' aides lacking *any* of the standard credentials for effective teaching.[52] Thus many students eligible for bilingual education receive no services or poor ones.

English learners do worse in school and are more likely to drop out than proficient English speakers, even controlling for economic class.[53] Everyone deplores that state of affairs, but few agree on how to improve it. Unlike special education there is little call for "full inclusion": even most advocates of inclusion concur that some temporary separate education is necessary to help English learners get started in their schooling. But advocates, politicians, educators, taxpayers, and parents are engaged in a deep and bitter controversy about how best and how long to provide separate education.

Through most of the 1990s, the Department of Education's Office of Bilingual Education and Minority Languages Affairs (OBEMLA) argued for extended programs on the grounds that "years of linguistic research have shown that it takes five to seven years to master 'academic' English. Academic English, which allows a student to succeed in school, should be distinguished from conversational or 'playground' English, which can be learned in a year or two." But other experts deny the distinction between conversational and academic English and argue that children learn academic English, and other subjects, more quickly and effectively in a predominantly English-speaking setting.[54]

Once again academic evaluations provide no resolution to this debate. The reasons are familiar: different programs fall under the vague rubric of bilingual education; the quality of programs and teachers is mixed; characteristics of English learners are extremely variable; testing has often been unfair, inappropriate, or limited; and program evaluations have been badly done or too politicized to permit reliable conclusions. Ronald Unz, a millionaire physicist and software developer who sponsored the successful proposition in 1998 in California to end bilingual education, calls the research on bilingual education "an academic field that's utter and complete garbage." Even the National Academy of Sciences used uncharacteristically blunt language in 1997 to conclude that "the past 20 years has [sic] not been a heyday for research on this topic":

> Often . . . policy has been driven by the kinds of stereotypes, political prefer-ences, and misconceptions that informed debates on bilingualism in the nine-teenth century. Nor did the research systematically contribute to improvements in practice, partly because of problems with the research methodology. . . . [Research] suffer[s] from design limitations; lack of docu-mentation of study objectives, conceptual details, and procedures followed; poorly articulated goals; lack of fit between goals and research design; and ex-cessive use of elaborate statistical designs to overcome shortcomings in re-search designs.

Although the Academy concluded that the best programs did ensure "some use of native language and culture in the instruction of language-minority stu-dents," it provided little guidance for a policy choice among programs. "The beneficial effects of native-language instruction are clearly evident in programs that are labeled 'bilingual education,' but they also appear in some pro-grams that are labeled 'immersion.' There [also] appear to be benefits of programs that are labeled 'structured immersion.'"[55] That does not provide much help in choosing among programs.

Academics have conducted careful analyses of the effectiveness of bilingual education, but their studies, taken together, are also inconclusive. Jay Greene, a political scientist then at the University of Texas, examined all the previous work on this subject and found that "children with limited English proficiency who are taught using at least some of their native language perform signifi-cantly better on standardized tests than similar children who are taught only in English." He concluded, however, that "the evidence for bilingual educa-tion is not of a very high quality and there isn't enough of it." As if in response, the economist Mark Lopez found "no evidence of positive effects for bilingual education" on the likelihood of completing high school. "In fact," said his study, "most effects are negative." He and a coauthor also found that, controlling for other factors, adult Hispanics who participated in bilingual education programs as children "appear to earn significantly less than otherwise similar English-immersed peers."[56]

California has provided something of a natural experiment on the effects of switching from bilingual programs to structured immersion. In the years since the change, standardized test results show that English learners in struc-tured immersion classes have made substantial gains, in some cases outdoing the gains of LEP students who earlier had been in bilingual programs. Ken Noonan, cofounder of the California Association of Bilingual Educators (CABE), concluded as a result that he had "believed that bilingual education was best . . . until the kids proved me wrong." But even his new conclusions are subject to challenge because California instituted other school reforms, such as smaller classes and changes in reading instruction in elementary schools, at the same time—and they too may have affected test scores.[57] The essential point, once again, is that research-based evidence does not give clear answers to the question of whether separate or more inclusive education is best for individual achievement. The policy choice must be made on other grounds.

In contrast most analysts agree that a relatively new kind of program, dual immersion, does benefit students. In this alternative classes are divided evenly between English-speaking students who want to learn another language and students who speak that language seeking to improve their English; teachers are bilingual and students are taught in both languages. The small amount of research shows that these programs improve the achievement levels of all participants and do more to promote diversity and mutual respect than any program taught in a single language. Advocates for dual immersion argue that speaking a language other than English is a resource for the individual, for other students, and for the nation as a whole, rather than a problem to be overcome as quickly as possible through some conventional method of bilingual education. "It's the marriage of the best bilingual program and the best foreign language program," says the principal of two elementary schools in Bryan, Texas. A director of the bilingual education program at Texas A & M University, Rafael Lara, agrees and points to the collective values that underlie such a program. "The kids, regardless of their background, have the opportunity to learn a new language as well as a new culture. Both languages have value. Both cultures have value. In terms of bilingual education, dual-language programs are having tremendous acceptance by the whole community." Proponents as well as opponents of bilingual education endorse dual immersion programs.[58]

While this may be the ideal solution, it is very difficult to extend the program to a large number of schools and students. There are several hundred dual immersion programs across the nation, involving perhaps 50,000 children, disproportionately in California and New York. But they are only viable in a district with a sufficient number of students moving in both directions and appropriately trained teachers. Most participants are in the middle class, but most of the need is in poor, overwhelmingly immigrant districts. The choice for most English learners therefore realistically remains between substantive instruction at some level in English immersion programs and the separate, bilingual approach.

Research does consistently show that any of these approaches to the education of LEP students can produce good results if they are well taught. Measurable outcomes depend more on the quality of teaching in any given program, or on the fit between the details of the program and the particular children in it, than on its form or duration. Programs help students if they are carefully designed, enthusiastically and knowledgeably supported by parents and teachers, based on high expectations for achievement, balanced in curriculum, open to student participation, and appropriately assessed and revised. In other words, good programs work and bad programs do not.[59]

But except for dual immersion, good programs are not the norm. Even while defending the integrity of bilingual instruction, CABE conceded that "perhaps 10 percent or fewer of the state's bilingual programs are well implemented." In CABE's view, the problem was insufficient funding and political support; others are not so sure and do not want to wait to find out. In the words of Wilfredo Laboy, the Puerto Rican superintendent of the Lawrence, Massachusetts, school district, "What we know from the evidence is that even though there are pockets of success, children in bilingual education fall further and further behind. That painful experience has moved me to say that after 29 years [of supporting such programs], we have to change it."[60]

Questions of bilingual education, of course, are tied up with immigration and therefore get caught up in identity politics and disputes about illegal immigrants. Immigrants themselves are split on this issue. In Los Angeles, one journalist reports, "Irate Hispanics . . . have taken to the streets here to launch a boycott . . . demanding instruction in English." Bilingual programs "'have had much negative effect,' said . . . an immigrant from Mexico City . . . 'They have to speak, read and write English to have success in this country. In the bilingual program, they don't learn either language well.'" A Spanish-speaking mother of four in Denver, Colorado, echoes this point (in Spanish, through a translator): "English is the language of this country and it is the language of my kids. How is it that kids who are in bilingual education and receive their instructions in Spanish will be successful?" But other immigrants recall "having to sit through English-only sessions and being pinched by teachers for speaking Spanish," and fear that mainstreaming today will produce the same insults, humiliation, and bewilderment. As one father says, "It's difficult for the children. Sometimes, it's almost like a blank day, because they don't understand the language."[61] Others worry that without separate classes for bilingual education, resource-starved urban schools will be even more deprived of funding and class sizes will grow larger. Some older immigrant children are not only without English proficiency, but have had virtually no schooling; without separate bilingual programs, they would be placed in mainstream classes dramatically below their age level. These children "sold trinkets by the highway when they should have been learning to read," said one teacher, and it is "unreasonable to expect children who had never been in school before to learn English." Finally, there are bilingual teachers, who have a huge financial as well as emotional stake in the continued existence of substantial bilingual programs; even a report from the state library of California "wonder[ed] whether teachers themselves have a negative incentive to move English learners out of their classes if teachers' salaries are connected to the number of English learners being instructed in their classes."[62]

Those outside of the immigrant and bilingual teaching community are less divided on the issue, more in favor of a rapid transition and an inclusive approach. Ronald Unz, the sponsor of Proposition 227 (which proposed to restrict special programs for most LEP students in California to one year), has talked both about the individual goals of education and some of his own broader community-oriented purposes for sponsorship. He included in the proposition the claim that "the government and the public schools in California have a moral obligation and a constitutional duty to provide all of California's children, regardless of their ethnicity or national origins, with the skills necessary to become productive members of our society." But he became involved in this issue, he explained, mainly in order to give "the assimilationist approach to American ethnic diversity the . . . opportunity to demonstrate its appeal and popular support." He hoped that "a campaign to eliminate these programs [of bilingual education] could attract substantial, perhaps overwhelming, support from immigrants themselves, thereby helping to puncture the mistaken anxieties of California's white middle class." A teacher in Pleasanton, California, where first graders speak six languages, concurs: "As a school we've become aware that our population is changing. We need to make these kids feel included."[63]

Other reasons for opposing bilingual education are narrower and less generous in spirit. Ten percent of respondents in a survey about Proposition 227 thought that bilingual education hurt California's schools, cost too much, or harmed English-speaking children. Children of illegal immigrants, according to some residents of Orange County, "are the kinds of students who tend to be disruptive, who tend to drop out. This is why our schools in California aren't as good as they should be." Bilingual education, said another Californian, is "the biggest factor in the downfall of education in this state." In the same California survey, a tenth of parents (though none of the students) believed that Latinos were treated better than other groups in public schools.[64] A resident of Denver, which is also changing its bilingual program, argues that if immigrants "want this opportunity . . . to settle in America. . . , make them learn our language, it is a sign of respect." Although Ronald Unz worked very hard to ensure that his referendum would not take on a racist cast, he had to admit that "lots of people who support the initiative are anti-immigrant."[65]

The identity politics and anti-immigrant connotations of the bilingual issue, along with the inconclusive evidence about what is best for children and arguments on both sides invoking the American dream, have together produced some surprising political shifts and coalitions. At the national level, the Democratic and Republican parties have been on both sides. A Texas Democrat, Senator Ralph Yarborough, sponsored the original federal bill on bilingual education, but President Lyndon Johnson, himself a Democrat from Texas, opposed it. President Nixon supported federal funding for bilingual education, but a later Republican presidential candidate, Bob Dole, opposed the whole idea as an invention of the "embarrassed-to-be-American crowd." Governor Ronald Reagan of California backed his state's bilingual education bill, but President Reagan did not support funding at the federal level. A few years later,

Richard Riley, then secretary of education in the Clinton administration, endorsed bilingual education programs as "the wave of the future." President George W. Bush opposed California's Proposition 227 as "divisive," and in 2000 he endorsed "bilingual programs that work," but a year later he supported an education bill intended to move LEP children into English-speaking classes relatively quickly.[66]

The politics are just as confused at state and local levels of government. The Republican party of California remained neutral on Proposition 227 in order to avoid any more accusations of immigrant bashing after Proposition 187 (which sought to deny state services to illegal immigrants). Latino leaders in Los Angeles also stayed on the sidelines during the campaign: according to a 1997 survey quoted in the *Nation*, they did "not consider defending bilingual education to be among the top five cutting-edge issues facing Latinos."[67] Latino political activists mostly but not uniformly opposed Proposition 227. Despite active opposition by the California Teachers Association and local union leaders, about half of the teachers in Los Angeles public schools supported it. Over 60 percent of Hispanic voters opposed Proposition 227, but it was favored by two-thirds of white and almost 60 percent of Asian American voters (black voters were almost evenly split). The sponsors of a similar proposition in Arizona in 2000, as well as many of its most vehement opponents, were Hispanic; the staunchly Republican superintendent of public instruction did not support it.

Although at a slower pace than in the case of special education, the movement toward greater inclusion seems to be gathering momentum. California's proposition, like the one in Arizona two years later, carried with over 60 percent of the votes; moves to present a similar proposition to voters of Colorado and Massachusetts are active. The Chicago and Denver school systems recently required schools to mainstream children with limited English proficiency within three years (in the former case it was after "heated, tearful, and even nasty debate," according to one local reporter). Other districts such as Houston, and states such as Connecticut, are moving in the same direction. Out of dissatisfaction with the quality of teaching and length of participation in its bilingual program, New York City plans to implement a new policy to enable parents to decide whether their children will participate in a (shortened) bilingual program or an (enhanced) program of English immersion; the clear expectation is that many will make the latter choice.[68]

Finally, the federal education law of 2001 gives parents greater power over their children's assignment to bilingual classes, requires schools to give parents more information in order to make such a decision, and eliminates the directive that most federal bilingual funds be used to teach substantive subjects in the student's native language. It also mandates that schools test English learners for proficiency in English after three years of attending schools in the United States and permits penalties to schools whose students do not increase in English fluency.

Americans as a whole almost always report more support for ESL or English-immersion programs than for bilingual education. A 1997 survey of Californians was probably the most extensive investigation of attitudes toward bilingual education by a neutral party. After receiving an explanation of various programs, 55 percent of respondents supported bilingual education, but fully 69 percent supported English language immersion programs.[69] Latino and Asian American parents endorsed English immersion even more strongly than did white and African American parents. In a major national survey, about half of Americans supported short-term transitional bilingual classes; the rest were split among the other alternatives or uncertain.[70] In another, the same proportion of Hispanic parents—two-thirds—as African American and all other parents endorsed the very strong proposal to teach new immigrants to speak English "as quickly as possible, even if this means they fall behind in other subjects." Fully 75 percent of foreign-born parents concurred. By a two-to-one ratio, teachers across the nation also believe that the government should mandate that "substantive subjects should be taught in English" rather than in the student's native language.[71]

Bilingual education as generally practiced creates too many obstacles to the achievement of the American dream to be acceptable. Students in bilingual programs too often suffer from overidentification and stigmatization as well as adjustment problems when they move into conventional classes. They are too often victims of poor teaching, in part because there are simply not enough well-trained teachers and high-quality classrooms to make the pursuit of excellent bilingual education a realistic goal in the foreseeable future. There are no grounds for believing that the federal government will provide funds to generate the additional training and higher salaries needed, among other things, to improve teaching in the field. And states show no inclination to fill the gap: if they did not do so during the booming 1990s, they are unlikely to do so in more stringent times. For example, one bemused journalist points out that although a federal judge held that "Arizona doesn't spend enough money on programs for children learning English," in the same year "the Arizona Senate Education Committee killed a proposal . . . that would have tripled state funding for English as a Second Language programs."[72]

Thus most language-minority students will remain in overcrowded classes with teachers who are expert neither in their language nor in the specialized techniques needed to reproduce the successes of exemplary bilingual classrooms. In this situation, according to a teacher of ESL for 15 years in Texas, bilingual classes have too often "become holding pens for poorly performing students," with students treated "as members of a social caste, a group of helpless individuals in need of a warm, fuzzy environment created by caring but undemanding teachers."[73] This is not the way to achieve the individual goals of the American dream.

Extended bilingual programs do equally little to promote training for democratic citizenship or to achieve any of the other collective goals of the American dream. Most white and African American students attend schools in which fewer than 5 percent of their peers are English learners; conversely, nearly half of LEP students are in schools in which a third or more of their schoolmates also do not speak English fluently. And as researchers from the Urban Institute point out, "LEP segregation is compounded by the practice of pooling LEP/bilingual services and personnel in specific schools within districts to concentrate scarce resources in a few places."[74] Separating students with limited English proficiency in this way reduces diversity in classrooms and creates yet another obstacle to the acquisition by all students of democratic values through direct, daily contact. Native-born students do not learn to interact with peers from a different cultural (and often religious) background and to understand how American culture is changing; young immigrants find it harder to learn to think of American government and society as their own. Mixing students from different backgrounds does not always lead to real integration—but not mixing students absolutely guarantees that it will not occur, as the history of school desegregation shows. On the issue of bilingual education, therefore, with no clear evidence on the best approach (except where two-way immersion is possible), but with evidence of a second-class education pervasive, separation is once again hard to defend in terms of the American dream. Our nation is moving slowly and fitfully toward greater inclusion, and that is the right direction (even if it sometimes occurs for the wrong reasons).[75]

Finally, focusing on bilingual education diverts attention from the deeper structural problems faced by English learners. As the chair of the National Educational Research Policy and Priorities Board puts it, "Limited-English-proficient kids go to high-poverty schools that have more than just a language difference going on. Just looking at the language of instruction is going to remove us from considering other important factors, such as organizational climate, professional development, standards, and curricula."[76] That points us directly toward ability grouping, the third and most troubling form of separation among students with different characteristics.

Ability Grouping

Ability grouping is the issue that brings together most of the themes discussed in this chapter and throughout the book. Children who are white or come from well-off or professional families have traditionally dominated high tracks and college prep programs. In many places, therefore, grouping is a race issue like desegregation or a class issue like funding. By definition grouping is also about the separation of students and therefore involves all the complex calculations about distinctive needs and legitimate claims on the society, about the benefits to individuals and to the collectivity, that we have seen so far in this chapter. But grouping is unlike special education and bilingual education in that it affects virtually all students, and its opponents have made less headway in the past few years.

Whether grouping by ability is good or bad remains deeply in dispute. Some reformers argue that it helps almost no one and harms many, so it should be eliminated for the sake of equity and to bring students together. Others argue that ability grouping, when properly done, produces the best educational outcomes for individual students, groups defined by ability or motivation, and the society as a whole. Still others see an inevitable trade-off between benefiting some and harming others, or between what is good for individuals and what is good for the collectivity, whether schools separate students by measured ability or not. Thus ability grouping brings into the sharpest possible relief the tensions embedded within the American dream as applied to schools.

Ability grouping has been almost universal since the Sputnik era, although it began long before that. Its presence depends considerably on the size of the class or the school. It can start as early as first grade, although it usually begins in middle school or high school. After elementary school it typically affects math and science courses, but it can be applied to English and other subjects as well. As usual in education policy, we lack consensus on even simple descriptive data about the amount and types of ability grouping. Estimates of how many high school students are in grouped math classes, for example, range from less than two-thirds to 90 percent.[77]

Full-scale tracking is usually intended to be voluntary, although direct or indirect pressure may be applied. Placement can depend on some combination of test scores, previous academic performance, teacher recommendations, and assessment by guidance counselors of student potential; thus the process can be either rational or biased. Like special education it is often affected by parental and sometimes by student preferences. Tracking used to be rigidly fixed across most subjects and all years of secondary education; at least in principle, it is increasingly fluid across subjects within a given year of schooling and across years of school.[78]

Career tracks are decades old. Students can be placed in a college-preparatory track, a general track, or a vocational track in which students combine academic courses with hands-on classes designed to enable them to move into a craft job or service job right after high school. The general track is often more a residual category than a real program or curriculum: it involves academic courses that are not intended to prepare students for college and courses in "life skills" or "general knowledge" that are not focused on preparing students for a career. Its use grew quickly in the North at the time of migration of black students from the South.[79]

Up to 45 percent of high school students still remain in the general track. Another 5 to 15 percent are in vocational programs, many of which are out of date; attempts to modernize them to make them a viable option for students in the general track have been fitful and limited. Students in the vocational and general tracks earn less as adults than do students in the academic track, even controlling for other factors that affect incomes.[80]

In part as a result of these tracks, but also because of ability grouping, American teens in the mid-1980s "received very uneven exposure to a range of curriculum topics" compared to students in other countries, according to the National Center for Education Statistics. For example, most American students "were in schools offering two or more differently titled mathematics classes. In contrast, many of the countries that scored high on the SIMS mathematics tests [the Second International Mathematics Study of 1982, a test comparing students across nineteen nations] . . . offered the same mathematics courses to *all* students."[81]

A disproportionate number of poor, African American, and Hispanic children are located in the lower ability groups or the general track, and well-off, white, and Asian American students are at the opposite end of the grouping spectrum. As of 1992 about a third of Latino and African American students were in a college-preparatory track, compared with close to half of Anglos and just over half of Asian Americans. In the eyes of critics such as law professor Angelia Dickens, these data show that "the tracking system has had racial and ethnic overtones since its inception."[82]

But this evidence is insufficient to determine racial bias. While the fact of disproportionate placement is clear, there remains a serious dispute about whether blacks and Hispanics are still placed in the low ability groups too often if one controls for achievement and measured ability. The declining overt prejudice of most Americans (presumably including teachers) over the past 40 years, the nation's increased focus over the past 20 years on helping all students achieve, the growing importance of reform movements, and the increasing prominence of minority administrators led a researcher at the College Board to conclude that "prejudice is playing a less substantial role in shaping teacher expectations and grouping/tracking practices than was the case several decades ago." In another study, when teachers' recommendations for grouping their students were compared with the students' test scores, the same proportion of blacks and whites were overplaced or underplaced. Others find that African Americans are even slightly likely to be *over*placed in actual classrooms according to test scores. Tracking therefore has problems of overidentification and underidentification similar to special education and bilingual education. In the words of Ronald Ferguson, an educational economist at Harvard University, "The claim of racial discrimination in group placement by teachers is not supported by research, once conventional indicators of merit or economic standing are accounted for."[83]

However, analysts almost universally agree that ability grouping discriminates on the basis of *class*, even controlling for achievement and other factors.

The raw facts are startling enough—almost three times as many students from high-income as from low-income families are enrolled in college preparatory tracks. Although achievement and ability—typically measured by test scores, prior placements, and teachers' judgments—almost always show up in careful studies as the chief determinants of student placement, class-based factors usually come in second.[84] And since poor (especially poor black and Hispanic) children consistently learn in the worst conditions and receive the worst teaching, prior measured achievement itself probably partly reflects class and racial bias. It is clear that ability grouping has discriminatory elements that, in direct violation of the tenets of the American dream, keep schools from helping all students to pursue individual success; it is clear, as well, that it reduces diversity in the classroom and makes training for democratic citizenship less effective.

The impact of ability grouping on overall educational achievement is less clear, which makes consensus on the right policy response more difficult. The empirical literature on the effects of ability-based separation, in fact, does frustratingly little to help determine its achievement effects; some researchers believe that methodological problems make any conclusions from the studies impossible.[85] Efforts to overcome these problems, as well as other difficulties in measuring students, classrooms, and achievement, have not yielded consistent results.

In the first careful analysis of controlled comparative studies of ability grouping across classes in primary and secondary schools, sociologist Robert Slavin showed no difference in achievement between tracked and untracked classes. A more recent study similarly found that heterogeneous grouping in English, although not in math, "does not disadvantage" students at any level of ability; others found that schools with more flexibility in their grouping generate higher math scores as well as less disparity between the scores of high and low groups in both math and verbal skills.[86] These studies imply that grouping, on balance, helps no one.

Many more studies, however, show that ability grouping benefits those in the high groups; the impact on those in the low-ability groups varies from none to serious harm. In some studies gifted students gained from programs designed for them, and the remaining students did not lose as a consequence of grouping. In other studies students in enriched and accelerated classes benefited considerably from their participation, but these classes increased the gap between high and low scorers in their schools. Similarly, a study that controlled for other characteristics of the classroom found that high school students in lower-level mathematics courses would gain in a heterogeneous class and students in honors courses would lose.[87] The authors of a recent National Academy of Sciences study concluded that they "do know that some specific . . . gifted and talented interventions have been demonstrated to have positive outcomes for students," so they endorse the continuance of these programs despite deep concern about racial and ethnic bias in assignment to them. Another scholar worries similarly that school reforms sometimes lead to "a lack of stretch in curriculum and instruction to accommodate the highest achievers and insufficient availability of higher level course offerings in all schools."[88]

Experimental studies that hold constant most factors affecting student outcomes show that when the curriculum and instructional methods are similar for all students, grouping by itself neither consistently helps nor harms students. But studies of actual settings usually find that students in the low-ability groups do worse than they should, even given their presumedly lower ability. They show, in other words, that students in low groups are treated unfairly compared with those in high groups. The debate among scholars, then, is whether educators should focus on abolishing ability grouping or should concentrate on ensuring a challenging curriculum, equal instructional quality, and a fair allocation of resources across groups.[89]

But even this portrayal is incomplete. There is, finally, evidence showing that grouping that avoids discriminatory placements and provides all students with a good curriculum could widely enhance individual achievement. Ronald Ferguson shows that ability grouping in elementary school involving "more tailoring of curriculum and instruction to students in the group, . . . [is associated with] higher scores for students who are grouped than for those who are not." Students in low-ability as well as in high-ability groups benefit. Another researcher found that eighth-grade students at all levels benefit from taking algebra and that all learned more in tracked than in heterogeneous algebra classes. Some schools have demonstrated that with motivated teachers and high-quality curricula, students in low tracks can thrive.[90] Thus the broadest sensible conclusion is that of the sociologist Adam Gamoran: "Decisions about grouping are preliminary and what matters most comes next: decisions about what to do with students *after* they are assigned to classes. Given poor instruction, neither heterogeneous nor homogeneous grouping can be effective; with excellent instruction, either may succeed."[91]

As with many school-related issues, the deepest problem is that too many students are poorly taught, and students in low-ability groups usually end up with the lowest quality of teaching. Virtually all analysts agree that the worst teachers, poorest curriculum, and fewest resources disproportionately afflict students in the lowest levels of courses. For example, about a tenth of students in high- and medium-level English classes, but fully a quarter of students in low-level English classes, are taught by teachers out of their main fields. This is not a consequence of grouping *per se*, but the presence of grouping makes it much more likely that schooling resources will be distributed unfairly. In addition, teachers typically treat students whom they perceive to be low achievers very differently from presumed high achievers. They are given less attention and less chance to reason and debate.[92] Ability grouping, like other forms of separation, has consistently provided the mechanism to give many students a second-class education.

The huge differences in educational opportunity across school districts also mean that schools and districts vary in the kind of course offerings and the quality of teaching that would permit any student to achieve at very high levels. More high school seniors of all races and ethnicities are taking advanced math and science courses than a decade ago, and there is less overall racial and class disparity in the number of high school students who take high-level mathematics and science than there used to be. But inequalities across schools and districts persist.[93] Middle schools in poor or non-Asian minority communities frequently do not offer algebra in eighth grade, which is essential for doing high-level mathematics in high school. High schools in poor areas are less likely to offer Advanced Placement (AP) courses, other advanced courses in math and science, or honors English and history courses than schools in wealthier and predominantly white communities. Sometimes only the "best" students are permitted to take those that are offered. Children of parents who have not attended college, who are disproportionately poor and nonwhite, are twice as likely to attend schools that do not offer algebra in eighth grade as children whose parents completed college.[94]

In response to evidence of this type, one of the heroes of the civil rights movement, Robert Moses, recently turned his attention to racial biases in education and developed the Algebra Project. It is a curriculum and teaching method designed to encourage all middle schools to offer high-quality math courses in a way that engages even poor and badly trained non-Anglo students. He now calls the knowledge of mathematics "a civil rights issue[,] . . . something that's necessary in order to have viable participation as a citizen in the country." In his view "the absence of math literacy in urban and rural communities . . . is an issue as urgent as the lack of Black voters in Mississippi was in 1961."[95]

Others increasingly concur on the need for high-quality instruction for all students. Although the number of students who are candidates for AP exams has increased over sixfold in the last 20 years, still only 4 percent of AP exams are taken by black students and only 9 percent by Hispanics.[96] In 1999, the ACLU filed suit against the state of California, claiming that "129 California public high schools with 80,000 students do not offer any AP courses; and 333 schools offer four or fewer. In contrast, . . . 144 public high schools in California offer more than 14 AP courses." Small rural schools and schools in poor urban districts in California are least likely to offer AP courses, thus disadvantaging African Americans, recent Latino and other immigrants, and poor whites. The availability of such courses has a crucial impact on a student's future, since the University of California at Berkeley and UCLA weight AP courses and their test scores heavily in admissions decisions. The general counsel for the California department of education agreed that "this is a genuine equity issue and I think it will have enough political push to bring about a solution." Prodded by the lawsuit in California, the College Board set up a program to encourage all public high schools to offer AP courses (currently 40 percent do not), and some schools are enabling more students to take them.[97]

Public opinion shows deep ambivalence about ability grouping. On survey questions over the last 45 years, a majority of Americans have endorsed spending more on and giving more attention to "gifted" children, including separate classes—perhaps because up to half agree that they "have a gifted child." African Americans support ability grouping as much as Anglos do.[98] On other questions, however, Americans report that they do not believe that gifted children should receive special consideration compared with other children. On one survey twice as many blacks agree that tracking "causes unequal treatment and should be eliminated" as believe that it is fair and should be continued. A recent direct query about ability grouping showed the public split almost in half, with a slight preference for separation even in elementary school. Focus groups demonstrate the same ambivalence. On the one hand, a participant in Cincinnati argued, "Most kids want a challenge. . . . Sometimes the more difficult it is, the higher they want to go." But a participant in Sacramento, as if in response, said "I don't think you need to push them into something that is just going to frustrate them. . . . If they can't get the math and they are not going to be heading in that kind of career to use that math, they should be shown into another direction that they could better use."[99]

The variety in these results fits the pattern we have found so often before. Citizens seek to ensure that their children have all of the resources they need to succeed, *and* they want all other individuals to be able to pursue their own dreams, *and* they endorse equality of opportunity for all students. But they do not know how to reconcile these sometimes-conflicting goals.

Neither do professional educators. A majority of professors of education, but not of teachers, endorse mixed ability grouping. The National Governors' Association, the ACLU, the Children's Defense Fund, the Carnegie Corporation, the College Board, and the NAACP Legal Defense Fund are all on record in opposition to strict tracking, though not to all forms of ability grouping. The states of California and Massachusetts have issued reports urging middle schools to detrack, and some have done so.[100] New York City, conversely, is creating a college-level program for students who have already surpassed the requirements for the state's standardized test. The NEA officially opposes discriminatory tracking—no surprise there—but it also urges funding for special programs for the gifted and talented; the AFT has no official position on the subject, but has expressed sympathy for parents who endorse ability grouping. The National Council for the Social Studies, "motivated by a commitment to equal opportunity and the fostering of democratic ideals, . . . opposes ability grouping in social studies." But the authors of the National Science Education Standards note that "there are science activities for which grouping is appropriate. . . . Decisions about grouping are made by considering the purpose and demands of the activity and the needs, abilities, and interests of students. A standards-based science program ensures that all students participate in challenging activities adapted to diverse needs."[101]

Some teachers speak passionately about the dangers of heterogeneous classrooms for students with low as well as high ability. As a math teacher in California observes,

> They have attempted some of this heterogeneous grouping. And they are finding that it is a disaster. . . . The fast students in the class are the ones that are controlling the class, in that they have all the answers. And the really slow students in the class are absolutely lost. They have no idea what's going on. And they are causing mayhem in the classrooms. . . . Teachers who have had good control in the classroom in the past are finding that they are ineffective in working with these heterogeneous groupings.

Others strongly endorse its virtues. A middle school English teacher argues that

> Cooperative learning works better with heterogeneous classes. There's more to draw from. But, more importantly, we have not just that technique but a number of other techniques and things that we should have been doing for years but kind of gave up when we gave up one-room schoolhouses—peer tutoring, different grouping practices, flexible grouping practices, kids working in pairs.

To be able to have more heterogeneous classes, schools have to "undertake changes in curriculum or instruction likely to improve actual teaching."[102] That observation, of course, returns us to the issues of school reform.

Rigid tracking is less prevalent, racial bias has diminished, and advanced courses are more widely available, but districts that have tried to eliminate ability grouping have faced powerful opposition. Opposition comes from teachers who either believe that eliminating grouping is a pedagogical mistake or do not want to give up the way they do things, and from wealthier parents who either agree with them or do not want to give up the advantage it secures for their children. In Montclair, New Jersey, for example, detracking just one ninth-grade English class became deeply controversial, resulting in confrontational board meetings, extended newspaper coverage, and the threatened departure of some families from the district.[103] That class remained heterogeneous, with some real educational benefits, but the experience discouraged further attempts to eliminate ability grouping in the district.

Educating children together is the best way to teach democratic values such as mutual respect, as well as to equalize access to resources and teaching quality. Ability grouping is particularly hard to defend for the early grades. Assumptions about the ability to learn should not be fixed at the beginning of the quest for success, and barriers should not be placed between children on that basis without very good cause. Poor children do not start with less ability, just less money, but once again they have been the principal victims of American educational practices. On these grounds, as well as for all the reasons that encourage greater inclusion in special and bilingual education, ability grouping is a questionable general policy for a society based on the American dream.

Unlike special education, however, the trend toward inclusion on this issue is not very strong; unlike bilingual education the politics here are not muddled. Given intense opposition to the elimination of ability grouping (made stronger by some of the research), it makes sense in the upper grades to insist first on a high-quality curriculum for everyone, as well as the unbiased assignment of students, the most effective allocation of resources, and the most equitable distribution of good teachers among groups. As we saw in the discussion of adequacy in school finance, this may mean more resources for classes with a lot of poor children and more of the best teachers as well. In this context, as the famed sociologist Christopher Jencks and his coauthor have said, "Eliminating demanding courses seems ridiculous. We should be trying to get more black [and Latino and poor] students to take challenging courses, not trying to eliminate them as an option" for others.[104] If these changes occur, we will get a much better idea of what works and the pattern of support and opposition to ability grouping may also change. As it is done now in most places, grouping is not acceptable. In part because of it, educational stratification at the end of schooling too closely replicates social stratification at the beginning. Ability grouping exemplifies the serious challenges we face, as well as the benefits we can imagine, in putting the American dream into practice in public schools.

7

CHALLENGING THE AMERICAN DREAM

Excessive promotion of allegiance to groups, instead of to ideals such as democracy, human rights, and justice, encourages the breakdown of civil society.
—*Albert Shanker, late president of the American Federation of Teachers, 1995*

[A] society is not truly democratic if it imposes on some of its members, as a price of admission to equal protection and status, the requirement that they deny or hide a deeply felt identity.
—*Elizabeth Kiss, political philosopher at Duke University, 1999*

This is a multilayered debate. It's about politics. It's about culture. It's about power. It's about disfranchisement. And it's about . . . the purpose and responsibility of the school system.
—*Member of the Santa Barbara, California, Board of Education, 1998*

If we teach kids they were descended from monkeys, don't you think they'll act like monkeys?
—*Representative, Arkansas General Assembly, 2001*[1]

MULTICULTURAL EDUCATION, whether as a curricular reform or as a general goal for education, swept the nation's schools during the 1990s. As generally understood and practiced, it does not challenge the American dream; it is a central way of teaching respect for difference and part of the continuing process of redefining the common American culture. Similarly, bilingual education is usually intended to help students pursue success within the mainstream, not to remain outside it. But some Americans go beyond claims for respect and incorporation. They seek to use multicultural or bilingual education to enable members of their group to attain distinctive treatment within public schools, or they promote changes in school curricula or methods of teaching that reflect their racial identity or religious beliefs in ways that challenge the American dream. They promote "allegiance to groups," in Albert Shanker's terms, or they insist on the value of difference.

Some of these advocates do not believe that fostering individual success should be a central value of public schooling, or they reject the usual formulation of democratic citizenship, or they believe that the whole ideology of the American dream is an exercise in power thinly disguised as a formula for fair treatment. When they couch alternatives in the language of discrimination or make proposals in the context of school failure, their impact can be politically volatile.

These issues of religion and culture show the acute difficulty of balancing the claims of one, some, and all in American public schooling, as well as the virtues and defects of using the American dream as the framework for that balancing act. To the degree that proponents—of multicultural education, cultural maintenance, African-centered pedagogy, or religious values—appeal to fairness, challenge discrimination, or demand respect for diverse viewpoints, they can and should gain broad support. But when advocates of particular groups seek to use public schools to help them maintain their separate identity, try to separate themselves within schools, or propose to have an entirely separate education within the public school system, support appropriately drops. If they try to transform all the schools in accordance with their particular cultural views or religious beliefs in rejection of the American dream, support in the wider community melts away, as it should.

Nevertheless, those who challenge the dream can have a disproportionate influence on debates over educational policy, partly because they sometimes disrupt accepted political categories. Claims based on religious belief come from the political right as it is conventionally defined, and claims based on race, language, or culture come from the left. But commitments and alliances may be unpredictable, and the politics of challenge can be so unusual that policymakers may have to deal with it one group or one school at a time.

In addition, the trajectory of these challenges is very unstable. A number of people well beyond the core advocates can sometimes be mobilized to support distinctive treatment for some students, whether because they are frustrated with the failure of a school to promote individual success or the collective good, or because they have some sympathy with the goals or identity-based claims of particular groups. Even when schools accommodate the demands of those who challenge the dream in this way, however, accommodations typically do not last. Identity groups themselves are often divided—there is at times no love lost, for example, between advocates for African Americans and advocates for immigrant groups. Those outside the groups often object to the special treatment or the cost, and courts reject the approach when it crosses the remaining line between church and state. Finally, schools decide, correctly, that they cannot cope with a situation in which people from dozens of nationalities, language groups, or religious denominations each make a claim for special treatment, separation, or transformation of the curriculum.

As a result, initiatives that promote the goals of some, instead of the goals of one or all, may generate a great deal of activity in schools, districts, and state capitals but only occasionally affect many children in classrooms. The activity itself is one of the best indications of how passionately Americans care about public schooling; the limited impact of the challenges also marks the boundaries of the ideology of the American dream. The ideology is flexible enough to encompass the aspirations of most Americans and is consistent with most understandings of democratic citizenship. But not all: some people want to remain outside the bounds of the dream. That is their right, but they cannot expect the public schools to accommodate them when they challenge the American dream in this way.

Multiculturalism

Multiculturalism has been dismissed by one educator as a "slogan, any specific definition of which lacks consensus." While this dismissal is unfair, multiculturalism does have close to as many meanings as users. The first Commission on Multicultural Education tried to provide a definition as early as 1972: "Multicultural education," they said, "recognizes cultural diversity as a fact of life in American society, and it affirms that this cultural diversity is a valuable resource that should be preserved and extended. It affirms that major education institutions should strive to preserve and enhance cultural pluralism."[2] In its broadest meaning, multicultural education endeavors to enrich the understandings of American students by incorporating a variety of cultural perspectives into the dominant Anglo-Saxon Protestant framework of schooling, and thereby to change it into something new and more inclusive.

Understood this way, multiculturalism fits perfectly within the two basic goals of the American dream in public schooling. First, it seeks to promote individual success by ensuring that all students see members of their own culture taken seriously by the schools. When they see people like themselves represented in the curriculum, so the theory goes, they can relate to the material in a way that will improve their ability or willingness to learn. As Carlos Jimenez, a history teacher at Garfield High School in East Los Angeles, puts it, "It enhances the students' self-image to see that their ancestors were not savages, that they were very advanced civilizations. When the school validates a person's culture by making it part of the curriculum, the student feels value in what and who they are." Multicultural education simultaneously seeks to promote the collective good by exposing all students to the array of cultural heritages represented in the school, district, state, or nation. Teaching students about each other's traditions and values, when properly done, enhances a sense of inclusion, creates mutual respect, promotes a common core of knowledge and shared values, and enables citizens to deal better with each other in the public realm. One typical list of goals for multicultural education, for example, includes some focused on individual success—"providing . . . powerful ideas for how to live successfully in the general American society, [and] useful skills for succeeding in the world of work"—and three focused on the collective good— "understanding various culture groups, gaining identity and strength from participating in one's own culture group, and learning ways to contribute to greater equity and opportunity for all individuals and groups."[3]

Most Americans came to endorse this understanding of multiculturalism during the 1990s. More than seven in ten respondents to a 1992 survey agreed, for example, that schools should "increase the amount of coursework, counseling, and school activities . . . to promote understanding and tolerance among students of different races and ethnic backgrounds." Three-quarters endorsed teaching "the diverse cultural traditions of the different population groups in America" along with the "common, predominant cultural tradition," rather than the common tradition alone.[4] Almost half even reported themselves willing to support reductions in "the amount of information [taught] on traditional subjects in U.S. . . . history" in favor of increasing "information on non-Western cultures and on women and minorities in the U.S." (Blacks felt much more strongly than whites about this, as well as about whether the schools are doing enough to promote intergroup "understanding and tolerance.")[5] This is a rather new conviction for most Americans; the rapidity of its acceptance is testament to how strongly Americans believe in the need for mutual respect in order to promote democratic citizenship.[6]

As with so many of the other issues discussed in this book, there is very little systematic evidence on how schools engage in multicultural education, and virtually none on its effects. By the early 1990s, over 70 percent of large school districts, according to one sample, had implemented multicultural curricula of some kind; the proportion has presumably risen since then, and smaller districts also have become more involved in this new approach. Most described their programs in terms of " 'an emphasis on behaviors, values, and institutions existing in all cultures,' 'appreciation of and respect for diversity,' [or] 'a cross-cultural process focusing on all cultures.' "[7]

Multicultural education is easy to endorse but difficult to implement well. At a minimum schools do not have time to do everything: if they teach the history of African Americans and Hispanics as well as that of European immigrants, they risk leaving out Asian Americans and Native Americans (not to speak of the manifold variations within each racial or ethnic group). The more inclusive school curricula and activities become, the sharper the exclusion of those remaining outside the fold. And absent a lot of thorny intellectual work, the more inclusive the curriculum becomes, the more superficially it treats all subjects. Finally, the more inclusive it becomes, in the usual sense of adding another cultural dimension to those already taught, the more difficult it is for teachers and students to retain any focus on the culture and values that have traditionally been considered American, or any other common core. These problems are real, but they can be mitigated by curricular innovations and focused teacher training; multiculturalism is hard to teach well and inevitably competes for attention with other school reforms but it does not challenge the American dream.

Challenges to the dream begin when advocates of multiculturalism change their emphasis from respect to separate treatment, when claims shift from "commonality politics" to "identity politics" and eventually to "emancipatory narratives," described below. As social critic Todd Gitlin of New York University defines these terms, commonality politics is "a frame of understanding and action that understands 'difference' against a background of what is *not* different, what is shared among groups." It is what most Americans have in mind when they endorse multicultural education; 85 percent of parents (including almost as many foreign-born as native-born) agree that it is "absolutely essential" for public schools to teach children "that whatever their ethnic or racial background, they are all part of one nation." Identity politics, conversely, "began as an assertion of dignity, a recovery from exclusion and denigration, and a demand for representation," but moved beyond that to become "a form of self-understanding, an orientation toward the world, and a structure of feeling" framed around the assumption that Americans' differences outweigh their commonalities.[8]

Multicultural education began, to quote one curriculum expert, as a "hopeful and idealistic response to the Civil Rights Movement," but this harder-edged form developed largely out of disappointment with the conservative reaction to the reforms of the 1960s. In response to continued discrimination against students of color, its advocates shifted their focus by the 1980s to "redress of racial inequities in a society built on and maintained by White privilege" and to affirmation of "the democratic right of each ethnic group to retain its own heritage." Advocates of identity-based multicultural education gained momentum and attention—both supportive and critical—with the rise of a movement for national standards in the late 1980s. Both Republican president George Bush and Democratic president Bill Clinton endorsed national standards, but when experts actually began to draft them, especially in U.S. history, they became embroiled in intense politics. On one side supporters, including advocates of identity-based multiculturalism, demanded that their perspectives be acknowledged and the contributions of their group recognized; on the other side were those, like the scholar and former assistant secretary of education Diane Ravitch, who sought to protect the schools from "an adversarial culture, a treatment of American history that emphasizes the nation's warts and failings and diminishes its genuine accomplishments." How can "a common culture even [be] possible," she asked, "if the public schools were charged with celebrating every culture that might be represented in the student body (but certainly not celebrating our common American culture)?"[9]

These public battles over curriculum reform are mostly over, and most combatants have moved on to other concerns. But identity politics continues to generate controversy among educators over how best to teach children with different cultural backgrounds. Asa Hilliard, an educational psychologist at Georgia State University, begins with "the assumption . . . that two groups of students with the same intellectual potential would, because of diversity in cultural socialization, develop habits and preferences that would cause them to manifest their mental powers in somewhat different ways." In his view that assumption is supported by "abundant and overwhelming data . . . show[ing] that cultural groups vary with respect to behavioral style." Lisa Delpit, who won a MacArthur Foundation "genius grant" for her research on education, concurs and concludes from her own research that teachers must "learn about the brilliance the students bring with them 'in their blood,'" because once "we know the intellectual legacies of our students, we will gain insight into how to teach them."[10] From this view point, identity politics implies that students from different cultures should be taught differently; others take the point further to imply that conventional pedagogies and measures of achievement are racially and ethnically suspect or even invalid.

Identity politics has implications for the central questions of who should teach, how to teach, and what should be taught. Proponents argue that students need high self-esteem in order to learn well, and that self-esteem results in part from having teachers who resemble the students. Professor Delpit continues the observations quoted above by concluding, "I am not suggesting that excellent teachers of diverse students *must* be of their students' ethnicity. . . . [H]owever, . . . we should strive to make our teaching force diverse, for teachers who share the ethnic and cultural backgrounds of our increasingly diverse student bodies may serve . . . to provide insights that might otherwise remain hidden." A chapter in the *Handbook of Research on Multicultural Education*, the central text in this field, argues similarly that "when students and teachers share a common cultural background and are able to engage in productive interactions, it is possible that they might develop attachments to education that they otherwise might not."[11]

Advocates of identity-based multiculturalism also believe that students' motivation to learn is increased when their group figures prominently and distinctively in the material they are learning. For students who are not European Americans, argues Molefi Asante, the most vigorous exponent of Afrocentricity, "*centricity* . . . locat[es] students within the context of their own cultural references so that they can relate socially and psychologically to other cultural perspectives." Most education in American classrooms, he says, is "approached from the standpoint of White perspectives and history." But only an African-centered curriculum will enable a 13-year-old student in Milwaukee, for example, to be able to say, "When I hear something in school about my black ancestors, I'm like, 'Wow! I can be like them.'"[12] In this view conventional education, even liberal multicultural education, neither enables individual children of color to succeed in attaining their dreams nor promotes a truly collective set of values and democratic practices, and must be changed.

When identity politics is at its strongest, multiculturalism moves far away from the goals for public schools envisioned by the American dream. Proponents seldom reject the concept of individual success (although they may define it differently from most Americans): their animus is chiefly against the collective goals. They usually reject tolerance as weak and patronizing, see efforts to incorporate new cultural perspectives into the dominant American value system as superficial or imperialistic, and suspect democratic politics of being a vehicle for majority domination of minority interests and values. In this view a good school will resist rather than reinforce many elements of the standard ideology of the American dream. As the noted black theologian Vincent Harding puts it, "Our emphasis is on exposure, disclosure, on reinterpretation of the entire American past," rather than on broadening it to include those left out so far. "Education in this country," says Asante, has been "based on White supremicist notions whose purposes are to protect White privilege and advantage in education, economics, politics, and so forth."[13]

In this way multiculturalism can slide from an earnest effort to put into practice the values of the American dream into critique and rejection of many of its central tenets. At that point it moves into an emancipatory narrative, which, in the words of reformer Ellen Swartz, seeks to "expose and contest the use of school curriculum as a pipeline of dominant ideology. As such it has the political potential and agenda of unmasking and unraveling the supremacies upon which this ideology is based."[14] These narratives focus on inequalities of power and resources more than on cultural differences or group-based pride—and they are very far from the liberal celebration of diversity and democracy. Their advocates reject the ideology of the American dream as a hypocritical cover for a system of white, male, bourgeois domination; not surprisingly, they also reject the idea of either promoting individual success or pursuing the collective good within the framework of that ideology.

Advocates of emancipatory education are few in number but ambitious in their agenda; they see the main mission of educators to be teaching students how to overturn structural inequalities. For them curricular materials should highlight injustices in American society and identify ways to correct them. Students should be guided to actions outside the school that help to alleviate inequality and powerlessness; adults should ensure that students who are not white, male, or well off have positions of leadership in the schools.[15] These advocates concur with Benjamin Franklin and Thomas Jefferson when they claimed that schools educate students morally and politically as well as teaching them the "3R's," but beyond that there is almost no agreement at all.

"Children's biographies of Christopher Columbus function as primers on racism and colonialism," says an article in the magazine *Rethinking Schools*, edited by teachers in Milwaukee. "They teach youngsters to accept the right of white people to rule over people of color, of powerful nations to dominate weaker nations. And because the Columbus myth is so pervasive . . . it inhibits children from developing democratic, multiracial, and anti-racist attitudes." In such a context, the article concludes, "a multicultural curriculum should be a rainbow of resistance. . . . Students should be allowed to learn about and feel connected to this legacy of defiance." This is far from the traditional multiculturalism that most Americans support, far from teaching "respect [for] others who are from different ethnic, racial, or religious backgrounds," as one public opinion survey puts it.[16]

Few Americans espouse identity politics as a framework for organizing schools; even fewer endorse emancipatory narratives. Most proponents are leaders of political advocacy groups or scholars of racial and ethnic politics or of education;[17] some are teachers in mostly minority school districts. Their direct impact on the school population is limited. But like advocates of vouchers, those who challenge the American dream on the basis of culture matter beyond their numbers. Because they use the language of identity, because they can tap into the dissatisfaction of many people with the unfairness or inequity in the larger society and in the schools, they can have a disproportionate influence. State education leaders and district officials must therefore pay close attention to their insistent calls for changes in curriculum, teaching staff, or methods of teaching.

Multicultural education is an essential component of, and need not be a threat to, a common American culture and shared American values. In their study of American history, literature, and government, students should see people who are like, and unlike, themselves; well-off whites who live in racially and economically isolated suburbs probably need diversity training the most. Similarly, all students need to understand how American society changes as its population changes, so that they come to see inevitable transformation as a possible gain rather than a likely loss. Again, native-born American children probably need this education in historical change more than immigrant children do. Since the composition of the American population is shifting at a very rapid rate and will probably continue to do so over the next few decades, learning about the many different ways to be American, and the ways that "being American" is itself changing, will become increasingly important. Students from all backgrounds also need to learn how to jointly create a shared culture with common values, and how to mutually construct a democratic political system; as the philosopher Joseph Raz puts it, "Multiculturalism, while endorsing the perpetuation of several cultural groups in a single political society, also requires the existence of a common culture."[18] If they do not learn in public schools to develop shared commitments as well as appreciation for differences, children are unlikely to learn it anywhere else in American society.

Multicultural education fits well within the goals of the American dream in public schools so long as it teaches mutuality rather than rejection, inclusion rather than assimilation, engagement with rather than rejection of the dream's collective goals. There is probably too little high-quality multicultural education in America's public schools, but there is no place in them for undemocratic approaches to these issues, whether taken in the name of emancipation or not.

Cultural Maintenance

Identity politics, and occasionally emancipatory politics, get a boost when combined with the politics of language. Proponents of cultural maintenance programs usually occupy the same roles as proponents of hard-edged multiculturalism—they are professors of education, leaders of racial or ethnic advocacy groups, teachers in non-Anglo communities. They oppose inclusion in mainstream schools because they see it merely as assimilation into what educational reformer Donaldo Macedo calls an "Anglo-conformist" culture, in which membership in a non-Anglo ethnic or racial group triggers mainly cultural denigration and personal discrimination. The effort to move children quickly into English-only classes is "designed primarily to maintain the status quo . . . , which systematically does not allow other cultural subjects, who are considered outside of the mainstream, to be present in history." As sociologist Michael Olneck sees it, transitional bilingual programs that are intended to be as brief as possible "reproduce a symbolic universe that subordinates and obscures ethnic culture, identity, and values."[19]

To avoid this subordination, advocates of cultural maintenance believe that, in the words of one Puerto Rican educator,

> [The] definition of cultural pluralism must include the concept that our language and culture will be given equal status to that of the majority population. It is not enough simply to say that we should be given the opportunity to share in the positive benefits of modern American life. Instead, we must insist that this sharing will not be accomplished at the sacrifice of all those traits which make us what we are.

Nathan Glazer, the scholar of American ethnic relations, makes the same point in more neutral language: "The demand for bilingual-bicultural education is not purely linguistic or pragmatic. It is a demand not only for educational achievement and jobs; it is also a demand made out of an alternate loyalty, loyalty to a culture and language that must inevitably be linked to foreign countries."[20]

Fostering assimilation by limiting or eliminating bilingual education is unacceptable to proponents of cultural maintenance for several reasons. The first focuses on the individual goals of schooling. It begins with the assertion that a person can formulate and pursue a dream only when rooted in a cohesive group with a distinctive culture. Teaching a second language before fully developing an identity in the first may cause "cultural trauma" to the child, according to education professor Enriqué Trueba of the University of Texas. He goes on to argue that "at the heart of academic failure may be a profound cultural conflict," leading to children's depression and "a cumulative sense of impotence, isolation, and low self-esteem." Teaching such students in culturally insensitive English classes ensures that "minorities are set up for failure." Scholars at the University of California's Linguistic Minority Research Institute spell out how such a cultural trauma can occur. A "too-rapid shift to English-only for limited English proficient students (and their families) typically results in the loss of the first language and breakdown in communication between children and parents, with sometimes disastrous consequences:

- Parents cannot teach their children about things like ethical values, responsibility, and morality;
- Parents cannot provide emotional and social support children need to make the adjustments to life in a society that does not much value diversity or tolerate differences; . . .
- Parents lose moral authority and control over their children."

Most simply, as a high school student in San Jose, put it, "When you force children to learn English, and they only speak Spanish or another language, you make them give up a part of themselves. . . . It's not just a language that you give up. It's a way of communication with your parents, of keeping your heritage alive."[21]

Even more seriously, according to proponents of cultural maintenance programs, language-minority children may learn the wrong values and pursue the wrong dreams if isolated from their native culture. Cornel Pewewardy, an educator and member of the Comanche tribe of Oklahoma, warns that "the loss of language . . . causes [children] to be cut off from their past and their heritage" and become too immersed in the culture of "today's American schools which are mainly Eurocentric, competitive, individualistic, and materialistic." Advocates, instead, want to emphasize the values of their traditions, like the Mexican American who asserts that immigrants from Mexico believe in "respect for elders and concern for collectivity, which promote interdependence and family unity." Mainstream American schools, in this view, undermine the desirable values of the home culture and replace them with undesirable American ones.[22]

Some arguments for cultural maintenance programs also challenge the American dream on the grounds that it fosters the wrong kind of democratic citizenship. In this view democracy is to be achieved through mutually respectful interaction among distinct groups—each with its own resources, members, visions, values, and political bases—rather than through interaction among individuals who themselves negotiate cultural and ideological boundaries. A professor at the Southwest Hispanic Research Institute at the University of New Mexico makes the point this way: "The full and equal participation of language minorities in American society requires not that these groups try to become indistinguishable from the white majority, but rather that they strengthen themselves from within—culturally, socially, politically, and economically."[23] Although she rejects it in the name of shared liberal values, the Boston public school teacher and political philosopher Meira Levinson summarizes the advocates' view well:

> Children from minority communities may . . . be at risk of cultural disenfranchisement, as they try unsuccessfully to mediate between the conflicting assumptions, values, and ways of life represented by their families and home community on the one hand, and by the school on the other. . . . Liberal political education should not be forced upon all students, because human beings' need for cultural coherence takes priority over their inculcation into the habits, knowledge, skills, and dispositions needed for full exercise of citizenship in the liberal state.

Some proponents of cultural maintenance also make constitutional claims. They assert, in the words of one political scientist, that "the right to retain and develop one's native language and culture . . . [is] a fundamental civil and political right."[24] The legal foundation of this claim is an expansive interpretation of the Supreme Court decision in the 1974 case of *Lau v. Nichols*. Its broader provenance is the claim that the rights to self-determination and autonomy that underlie the American dream apply to groups as well as to individuals.

The final argument for cultural maintenance moves beyond critiques of schooling to directly reject the dream itself: it is an ideological challenge to the ideology. In this view the American dream hides a structure of deep hierarchy under a cover of proclaimed equality. The political philosopher Charles Taylor articulated this view when he wrote that a "group of people can suffer real damage, real distortion, if the people or society around them mirror back to them a confining or demeaning or contemptible picture of themselves. Nonrecognition or misrecognition can inflict harm, can be a form of oppression, imprisoning someone in a false, distorted, and reduced mode of being." In this view the history of American ethnic relations, at least for Native Americans and immigrants from places other than Europe, is precisely a history of confinement, contempt, and discrimination. The effects are material as well as symbolic, since immigrants of disfavored ethnicities, speaking languages other than English, are consistently kept poorer and farther from the centers of power than are other Americans. This is in part the view, summarized by a former teacher who now directs the program in bilingual teacher education at a California university, that "the forms of inequality, from neglect to ugly racism, are structured and implemented through language."[25] To reject assimilation is to challenge a society that promises equal opportunity and respect for diversity but delivers neither. In this way of thinking, a separate education designed to reinforce a child's native culture and language is the only path to equal status, power, and resources.[26]

There is no inventory of cultural maintenance programs around the nation and no systematic evaluation of their effects on individual or collective goals of schooling. Only a few such programs have been implemented at the school district or state level, although many teachers in communities with a large proportion of Spanish-speaking immigrants have sympathies with this approach. Until recently the school district of Tucson, Arizona, ran a maintenance bilingual education program with the explicit goal of helping students to retain their native language while learning English. That program, however, was cut by more than half in 2001, after Arizonans passed a proposition requiring English-immersion instruction for all students who do not request a waiver for bilingual training. New Mexico still permits students to remain in bilingual education programs through high school so that they can retain their native language or become fully bilingual. Many Native Americans now work hard to enable students to retain (or learn) their tribal languages. Like proposals for emancipatory multicultural politics, claims for cultural maintenance programs matter not because of their impact on a large number of children but because of the substantial political effects they sometimes generate in particular districts or states. These views, as well as the reactions to them, also reveal the boundaries of the American dream.

Although surveys show that most Americans oppose bilingual education after a child has adequately learned English, some groups express more than average sympathy for its use in cultural and linguistic maintenance. In 1994 only 14 percent of Anglos, but 20 percent of blacks and Hispanics, agreed that "students who want to keep up with their native languages and cultures should be able to take many of their classes in Spanish or other languages all the way through high school." A year later 22 percent of whites compared with 32 percent of "minorities" agreed that public schools' primary goal should be to "help new immigrants maintain their own language and culture, even if it takes them longer to absorb America's language and culture as a result." On other surveys fewer than a tenth of Anglos, but more blacks and roughly a third of Hispanics, agreed that "public schools should teach children of immigrants in their native language as long as it helps the children learn or improves their self-esteem." Over a third of Texans agree that students should be taught in both English and their native language, rather than being taught in English only or in their native language for a brief time.[27] Those results were not reported by race or ethnicity, but they are higher than national averages in any poll and surely higher than one would find in states with few immigrants or non-Anglos.

Hispanics, not surprisingly, are the most sympathetic to claims about cultural and linguistic maintenance. A fifth do not think that being able to read and speak English is a very important obligation for Americans. They are more likely than Anglos (though less likely than African Americans) to agree that "people of other races can't really understand the way my race sees things."[28] Their views on this issue, however, reflect competing cultural loyalties and aspirations, and perhaps political volatility: in the most recent survey of Hispanics, fully nine out ten thought it important for Latinos to "maintain their distinct culture," but 85 percent also agreed that Latinos should "change so that they blend into the larger society as in the idea of the melting pot."[29] Like other nonnative English speakers, most Latino families seek to become incorporated into mainstream American society. But immigrants can be mobilized in particular communities to support distinctive and even oppositional treatment for their group in the public schools if they believe that inclusion in the educational mainstream will require abandoning their heritage.

American society has many arenas in which groups can appropriately work to maintain their language, culture, values, and distinctive perspectives. Americans have always done that in their homes, churches, and community organizations; a liberal democracy permits and even encourages group self-definition, and our nation is richer for it. Private and parochial schools can help fulfill this function as well. But public schools cannot have a mission to enable groups to define themselves separately from the rest of American society.

Public schools do have an obligation to increase students' knowledge of cultures outside the United States as well as to promote engagement with and respect for them. Given the influx of immigrants to the United States and the increasing importance of global trade and communications, it makes more sense than ever for schools also to teach other languages and to see bilingual individuals as assets rather than drains on the resources of society. Public schools, in addition, have an obligation to teach critical thinking, so that students can help American society adjust to new conditions (including a changing population), preserve what is best about our traditional institutions, and attend to what must be improved; that must include questioning the ideology and practice of the American dream. But public schools cannot have the responsibility of maintaining the culture of any particular group; the schools simply would not be able to deal with the hundreds of nationalities, ethnicities, and language groups that could legitimately make the same claim on them. As a matter of practicality as well as purpose in a country this diverse, public schools have to focus most on what we have in common.

Similarly, the strongest forms of cultural maintenance, those in opposition to core American values, have no place in the public schools. First, such programs can hurt the chances of many students to achieve their dreams: if they have the same kind of career goals as most other Americans, or simply seek to connect with them, students will not be able to succeed unless they are fluent in English and comfortable in mainstream culture. As the political philosopher Alan Patten points out, "A policy promoting the integration of members of smaller language communities into a larger language community could, in the long run, . . . expand the choices and opportunities available to members of the minority community."[30] Furthermore, if non-Anglo children are taught that they have no power or opportunity in America, that the structure and values of the society in which they live are stacked against them, they are likely to lose hope and limit their dreams.

Second, oppositional cultural maintenance programs can undermine the collective goals of the American dream. The United States will not be better off with culturally and linguistically isolated communities that interact only in the formal governmental arena. If non-Anglos remain linguistically and culturally separate, they will lose most political battles in the wider society: refusing to participate in conventional democratic politics will hurt them even more than current hierarchies of power and status do. And non-immigrant communities need to be encouraged to integrate *more* across ethnic and racial lines, not given an excuse for remaining aloof from the great demographic, political, and social changes facing our nation.

Democratic debate to produce national decisions requires participants who can talk to each other, and that communication will be in English. Democratic debate also requires some level of identification with others in the conversation: "Fellow citizens must be willing to tolerate and trust, defer to the requirements of public reason, and accept certain burdens and sacrifices for the sake of the common good," as Alan Patten puts it.[31] Identification of this kind can only happen if well-off Anglos abandon their complacency and their sense of entitlement, *and* if new immigrants accept the challenges of moving away from an oppositional group identity. Both groups must change, and each will do so in part because the other does. For better or for worse, we are all in this together.

Afrocentric Education

Afrocentrists are typically more hostile to the American dream than are immigrants and their allies; most directly challenge the goals of the dream both within and outside of schools. As scholar of African American studies Manning Marable observes, "We are in the West but not of it; our status . . . yields critical insights into another world which is not our own. We employ the language and technical tools of the West for the purpose of dismantling structures of inequality and domination which Europe deliberately imposed upon us." Although Marable is not an Afrocentrist, this comment captures the sense of distance and opposition felt by many black Americans.[32]

Afrocentrists can oppose the individual goals of education or its collective goals, or both. Walter Gill of Morgan State University objects to the focus on personal success: "Eurocentric models," he says, "house several 'hidden' ideologies within their frameworks: individualism, subjugation of the environment, competitiveness, achievement motivation, aggressiveness, and a futuristic orientation." These models suffer from "inapplicability for non-White groups," and they are "malfunctioning for students of color and females." Ellen Swartz of the University of Rochester adds the argument that the collective good as usually understood is "Eurocentrically bound." The pursuit of common values, a common core of knowledge, mutual engagement, training for democratic citizenship—all such ideals "are grounded in Eurocentric and White supremacist ideologies" which "legitimiz[e] dominant, White, upper-class, male voicings as the 'standard' knowledge students need to know."[33] Finally, Afrocentrists deny that schools promote equal opportunity; instead, they reinforce Western, white domination under its guise. Afrocentric texts usually begin with an account of decades or centuries of racial hierarchy and control, catalogue its horrendous effects, and conclude with evidence on the persistence of white success and black failure as conventionally measured. Public schooling, in their view, is deeply implicated in this system of domination.

Afrocentric curricula and pedagogy emerge from these critiques. According to Asa Hilliard, one of the founders of Afrocentric schooling, their core is "the deep structural cultural unity that can be found among many African populations all over the world." Wade Nobles of San Francisco State University similarly argues that an Afrocentric curriculum "should (1) refer to the life experiences . . . and traditions of African peoples as the center of analyses; (2) utilize African and African-American experience as the core paradigm for human liberation and higher-level human functioning; . . . (3) assist African American students in the self-conscious act of creating history; [and] (4) reinforce a quality of thought and practice which is rooted in the cultural image and interest of African people." Ramona Edelin, former president of the National Urban Coalition, is more combative: "The point of making the paradigm shift we seek . . . , overturning European cultural hegemony by crafting African-centered curricula, . . . is not simply to train African people to do the same things that Europeans are now doing. The point is . . . *a change in the way we think, and teach students to think.*" After all, concludes yet another advocate, "a particular community" has the "prerogatives . . . to reject as socially, politically, and therefore epistemologically irrelevant a system of ideology, theory, and method that fails to advance that community's interests. Such a critical position has been integral to the Africentric conception."[34]

In short, Afrocentric theory as described by these and other advocates represents a direct attack on the American dream. It is difficult to tell, however, how much the schools or districts that claim to use Afrocentric curricula actually engage in such an attack. Once again, there is no systematic listing of Afrocentric districts, schools, or classrooms for any state or for the nation. There are, however, some well-known examples. The Portland, Oregon, public schools have used the *African-American Baseline Essays*, a set of Afrocentric essays and readings by Asa Hilliard, for over a decade. The *Essays* have also been used in Milwaukee, Detroit, and Prince Georges County, Maryland. The Atlanta City School District instructed its teachers to include the *Essays* among their teaching resources and has spent several million dollars training teachers and developing Afrocentric curricular materials. In 1991 Baltimore schools decided to include Afrocentric material in all elementary school classrooms. Diane Ravitch describes a visit to a school in Brooklyn, New York, in which "every classroom I entered, every lesson I observed, every hall display, every library exhibit, was Africa-centered."[35] Most large school districts with considerable black populations have probably at least experimented with and may still use some kind of Afrocentric curricular materials or teaching approaches.

However, it is not clear whether these districts and schools have adopted these materials in order to further a more conventional multicultural approach, perhaps understood as identity politics, or to challenge in a fundamental way the American dream. Nor is it clear how much Afrocentric materials are actually used in daily teaching. There is little in the record to tell us and almost no systematic research, in this case partly because the presence of reporters or researchers is likely to affect what goes on in the classroom while they are there.[36]

Many black Americans (like most white, Asian, or Hispanic Americans) know nothing of Afrocentrism or would be skeptical about it if they did. But in some polls between a fifth and a half agree with its underlying premise, that the solution to the inadequacies of public schooling for many black children includes cultural nationalism and possibly a separate education. In 1998 almost a third of black parents agreed that schools in heavily minority inner-city neighborhoods should design courses around minority writers and heroes. Four in ten concurred that an American history course for black students should focus mainly on African American experiences and struggles. Ten to 20 percent of African Americans nationwide say that being black is more important to them than being American; roughly the same proportion endorse the idea of a separate black nation; and many more endorse milder expressions of racial nationalism.[37] About two-fifths of blacks would prefer that "different racial and ethnic groups maintain their distinct cultures" rather than "adapt and blend into the larger society." Up to half of black respondents in several surveys endorse the idea of separate public schools for black boys. Up to half of whites concur, although perhaps from different motives.[38]

As survey data suggest, Afrocentrism generates a political dynamic similar to cultural maintenance programs and emancipatory versions of multiculturalism. A few educators and citizens passionately believe that schools should promulgate a racially based alternative to the ideology of the American dream. A larger number of educators and citizens are not fully convinced by the proposed alternative but are dismayed and angered by failures of the public school system, particularly in inner cities. Many are available to be mobilized around an ideology and pedagogy that promises to do better, and in their view could hardly do worse. When all of this occurs in a school district whose children are already isolated from the racial and economic mainstreams, separatism can take an institutional hold. As educational consultant Jawanza Kunjufu asks, "So long as the class is already segregated, why not turn it into a class for winners?" There was a "rationale behind starting with African and African-American history and culture here," says the curriculum director for the Atlanta public schools, and "that was the population. The school district was at least 92 percent black, and it still is today. . . . For me, it's primarily right now about Afrocentric because we have so much catching up to do."[39] Following this logic, despite the controversy that it always arouses, many urban school systems have therefore accommodated at least some form of Afrocentric education.

Critics are right when they point out the terrible quality of education in many inner-city schools and when they insist that all Americans should know that everyone did not share the experience of European immigrants and does not now share their viewpoints. But Afrocentrism is not an effective solution to the problems of racial and class hierarchy in the United States: the answer to the limitations of earlier textbooks is not to limit them in a new and different way. Acknowledging the impact of slavery and persistence of racial bias will make all children better citizens. But like hard-edged forms of emancipatory politics or cultural maintenance, Afrocentrism goes too far in opposition to the American dream to be a legitimate component of public schooling. It sharpens racial anger without providing a viable alternative vision.

An Afrocentric curriculum risks harming the children and communities that its proponents want to help. To have a chance to succeed in mainstream society, African American children need to know an array of shared information; they need to learn history, math, science, and other subjects like other Americans in ways that are commonly recognized as legitimate. They also need to be taught from texts that open new horizons: it will not liberate their dreams or secure their futures to be taught that separation in a small minority community is the only answer to racial bias or that whites are an all-powerful enemy.[40]

In the same way, hard-edged Afrocentrism will do little to help African American communities. Isolation within a relatively small group is a losing proposition in a political system based on majority rule. And blacks' rejection of mainstream society makes it too easy for whites to escape both the fact of diversity and recognition of inequality in our schools and communities. Whites need to pay *more* attention to racial and class hierarchy, not be handed an excuse to turn their backs. Once again those concerned about public schooling in America should work to make the American dream live up to its promises, not abandon it in favor of an alternative ideology that can not and should not succeed.

Religious Fundamentalism

Although their ideology is in crucial ways antithetical to the other proponents of oppositional politics, some religious fundamentalists share their rejection of conventional understandings of the American dream. As Paul Weyrich, president of the Free Congress Foundation, mourned a few years ago, "The culture we are living in becomes an ever-wider sewer. . . . We are caught up in a cultural collapse of historic proportions. . . . I do not believe that a majority of Americans actually shares our values." Conservative Christians should therefore "look for ways to separate ourselves from the institutions that have been captured by . . . enemies of our traditional culture. . . . We need some sort of quarantine."[41]

Religious conservatives responded to Weyrich's call in several ways. Many transferred their children to religiously based private schools or decided to educate them at home, removing them from the arena of public education altogether. Others keep their children in the public school setting but, like advocates of various forms of identity politics, seek to insulate their children from some of its values and have alternative values taught to them. Still others work to transform their local school, their district, or the entire public system of education because they believe it to be their religious and civic duty to ensure that public schools teach true Christian values.[42]

Although conflict has swirled around classes ranging from science and literature to health and sex education, the teaching of evolution has been a central focus of controversy.[43] In legal cases, school board election campaigns, and protests to educators, Christian fundamentalists argue that public schools are indoctrinating students in a particular religious and epistemological view often labeled "secular humanism." They argue that such indoctrination violates the first amendment to the Constitution, parents' rights, and the good of the nation as a whole. Contests over these issues, in particular the debate between evolution and creationism, have in part been conflicts of constitutional interpretation and in part debates about the meaning of science and truth. But they have also been disagreements about the validity of separation within public schools and the values taught to all public school students, which directly implicate the goals of the American dream in schooling.

Unlike other challenges to the American dream discussed in this chapter, creationism as a belief has wide and deep public support. Roughly half of Americans agree with a strong creationist explanation of human origins, while fewer than a quarter accept secular evolutionary theory.[44] Half or more respondents in some surveys agree that teaching the theory of creationism should be mandated along with the theory of evolution; even more agree with proposals that it be offered as an elective. (Roughly the same proportions agree that the theory of evolution should be required or available.) Appealing to this majority, George W. Bush, while a candidate for the presidency, argued that "children ought to be exposed to different theories about how the world started." Vice President Gore read the same polls and came up with almost the same answer: as his spokesperson initially put it, "The vice president favors the teaching of evolution in public schools. Obviously, that decision should and will be made at the local level, and localities should be free to decide to teach creationism as well."[45] Up to 40 percent take a more extreme position than candidate Bush, saying that evolution should not be offered at all (no more than 30 percent say the same about creationism). Almost 40 percent of Floridians agreed in 1987 that schools should provide alternative textbooks if parents have religious objections to teaching evolution.[46]

Fundamentalists believe that teaching evolutionary theory in public schools legitimizes the way some people view the world at the expense of the religious and epistemological convictions of others. Law professor Phillip Johnson argues that "the effect of the education system is to instill belief . . . that you were created by this purposeless, material, mechanical process, and that's all there is. . . . So, what we are getting is a tremendous propaganda barrage which is really aimed not at educating, but at instilling belief." As a federal judge described these beliefs, they include "the religions of atheism, materialism, agnosticism, communism, and socialism. . . . Make no mistake: these are to the believers religions; they are ardently adhered to and quantitatively advanced in the teachings and literature that is presented to the fertile minds of the students in the various school systems." According to the Institute for Creation Research, evolutionary theory is dangerous precisely because it promotes the kind of individualism implied by the American dream: it "leads to the notion that each person owns himself, and is the master of his own destiny. This is contrary to the Bible teaching that mankind is in rebellion against God."[47]

To supporters of creationism, these are not merely theological problems: teaching evolution has had serious negative consequences in the schools and other public arenas. U.S. House majority whip Tom DeLay, for example, claimed that the murders in Littleton, Colorado, and other violent acts in schools have occurred "because our school systems teach the children that they are nothing but glorified apes who have evolutionized out of some primordial soup of mud. . . . We teach our children that there are no laws of morality that transcend us, that everything is relative and that actions don't have consequences." Ken Cumming of the Institute for Creation Research linked evolutionary curricula to the beliefs behind the terrorist attacks of September 11, 2001: "While the public now understands from President Bush that 'We're at War' with militant Islamics around the world, they don't have a clue that America is being attacked from within through its public schools by a militant religious movement of philosophical naturalists (i.e., atheists) under the guise of secular Darwinism. Both desire to alter the life and thinking of our nation."[48]

These advocates are therefore infuriated by the idea that the religious views of their opponents are permitted to masquerade as empirical science and their own views get dismissed as inappropriate for public schools. A letter to the editor of the Omaha *World-Herald* captures this view: "What an illustration of bigoted, prejudiced, intolerant education. When creationism was the prevailing viewpoint, liberals asked for tolerance, for consideration of all viewpoints, for unbiased teaching. Now that evolution is the prevailing viewpoint, there is no tolerance, no freedom to express an opposing viewpoint, no open-mindedness to examine all theories regarding origins."[49]

Creationists have tried several routes toward solving this problem of secular intransigence. They initially proposed state laws to forbid the teaching of evolution, a move that the Supreme Court declared unconstitutional in 1968. The Court found that the passage of such a law in Arkansas had no purpose but a religious one, so that it violated the first and fourteenth amendments to the Constitution by establishing one religious view above others, or none. Creationists then urged that schools teach the Christian view of origins as well as the evolutionary view. That too was blocked by a Supreme Court decision in 1987 on the same grounds.[50] In response to these legal rulings, creationists have sought to have schools abjure from teaching any group's beliefs about creation or evolution. In 1999, for example, the state board of education in Kansas removed from state science standards any reference to evolution, the Big Bang, geologic time, or other evidence of long-term cumulative change. That move invited, although it did not require, local districts to delete the study of evolution from their curricula. (A year later voters endorsed a new board majority that reversed the policy.)

Finally, since the early 1990s some creationists have sought to shift the framing of the argument from a debate over religion versus science to a debate over evidence available through science. Scientific creationism encompasses an array of views in which the six-day Genesis narrative is taken to be a metaphor for a much longer—even eons-long—period of creation. Its supporters distinguish themselves from secular Darwinists by identifying evidence showing that evolution is a product of intentional design and that humans were created by a Maker, not accidentally evolved from a different or lower species of being. Many also assert that there are "irreducible complexities," certain features such as the human eye that are too complicated to have evolved from simpler or different life forms. They therefore argue that biology classes should include both evolution and creation science so that students can study both, evaluate the competing theories and evidence, determine their beliefs, and make their choices.[51] For them this is the way to promote the collective goals of democratic deliberation, free speech, and mutual respect for alternative viewpoints.

Creationists continue to win at least temporary victories with school boards and superintendents and to have some success at the state level as well. During the 1990s state education departments in Kentucky and Illinois replaced the word "evolution" with "change over time" in the science curriculum. From 1996 to 2002 biology textbooks in Alabama contained a disclaimer describing evolution as "a controversial theory that some scientists present as a scientific explanation for the origin of living things. . . . Any statement about life's origins should be considered as theory, not fact"; Oklahoma has had a similar disclaimer. According to an evaluation by the Fordham Foundation, 19 states ignore evolution completely, handle it poorly, or skip over it lightly.[52]

Virtually all professional scientists and scientific associations deplore the concept of creation science and insist that students exposed to it will be harmed educationally: as the executive director of the Center for Theology and the Natural Sciences puts it, "We can't have an informed generation if they don't know basic science. It's their right, it's their inheritance." The British biologist and Nobel prizewinner Sir Peter Medewar is more blunt: "The alternative to thinking in evolutionary terms is not to think at all."[53] The fight over what constitutes good science in the curriculum has to be fought mainly on the battlefields of that discipline; what matters for our purposes are the challenges that religious fundamentalism presents to the American dream in public schooling. There are several, aimed at both collective and individual goals of schooling.

On the collective side, supporters of creationism and creation science in the schools reject the general goal of a neutral, secular, civic education whose purpose is to teach all Americans a common set of public values. They also reject the separation of the public and private spheres, as well as many of the values that they associate with evolutionary science, such as individualism and tolerance for dissent and ambiguity. Some similarly reject the general goal of providing citizens with a common core of factual knowledge—in this case of evolutionary theory and its biological underpinnings[54]—that is necessary to participate intelligently in the resolution of important public issues such as genetic engineering or cloning. On the individual side, fundamentalist parents often care less about enabling their children to succeed in conventional ways than about protecting them from exposure to material offensive to their beliefs. More generally, creationists implicitly argue that schools should promote certain values even at the cost of harming the chances for students to do well in conventional terms, in this case on conventional science tests that could affect graduation or admission to college. In all of these ways, they defy the usual understandings of the ideology of the American dream.

In 1987 fundamentalist parents in Tennessee brought a case in federal court, *Mozert v. Hawkins County*, in order to enable their children to "opt out" of reading classes that contained "offending materials." They feared that after reading the texts chosen by the school district, "a child might adopt the views of a feminist, a humanist, a pacifist, an anti-Christian, a vegetarian, or an advocate of a 'one-world government.'" As Vicki Frost, one of the parents involved in the lawsuit, wrote to her son's school principal, "[When I read the textbooks] I could not help but cry. How could we have come so far from basic truths, and love for God, country, and fellow men, to such reading materials as we have today?" In letters to the local newspaper, she described the texts as full of "lessons in rebellion, self-authority, situation ethics, distorted realism, magic, occult symbols, and scary artwork." Additional plaintiffs objected to teaching the students about "evolution and secular humanism," even though the text used by the schools identified evolution as a theory rather than a fact; others objected to items such as "biographical material about women who have been recognized for achievements outside their homes."[55]

The court declared that the parents "sincerely believed that the repetitive affirmation of these viewpoints was repulsive to the Christian faith—so repulsive that they must not allow their children to be exposed to the [reading] series" that included them. The school board, however, argued that the reading curriculum was advancing the general good because it taught understanding and tolerance of a variety of viewpoints and promoted critical thinking and discussion. Although the parents won at the district court level, the federal appeals court agreed with the school board in language upholding the tenets of the American dream. It ruled that "public schools serve the purpose of teaching fundamental values 'essential to a democratic society,' . . . 'includ[ing] tolerance of divergent political and religious views' while taking into account 'consideration of the sensibilities of others.'" Because the schools required only a "civil tolerance"—that is, "a recognition that in a pluralistic society we must 'live and let live'"—and did not require students to endorse religious tolerance, the school board policy entailed no "compulsion to affirm or deny a religious belief."[56] The schools, the court went on, have an affirmative obligation to teach children "to think critically about complex and controversial subjects and to develop their own ideas and make judgments about these subjects." They have a similar responsibility to "'promot[e] cohesion among a heterogeneous democratic people' . . . [and] avoid religious divisiveness."[57] They cannot achieve these goals if students are permitted to "opt out" of classes on topics that are not included within their faith, so long as the students are not required to agree with any viewpoint on those topics. The Supreme Court declined to hear an appeal.

Fundamentalist parents have also occasionally sought separate public schools in order to protect their children's religious beliefs from the dominant ideology. Federal and state courts have, for example, overridden three attempts of the New York legislature to create a separate school district for disabled children of the Satmar Hasidim (a tightly linked community of orthodox Jews who hold very strict standards of religious observance, moral action, and rejection of secular modernity). Public pressure has halted efforts to maintain schools, or programs within schools, attended only by members of the

Plymouth Brethren of Minnesota and Michigan. The Brethren, a deeply fundamentalist group of Christians who reject almost all features of society not articulated in the Bible, sought separate classrooms or schools "for the instruction and well-being of our children in the face of the continuing decline in moral judgment and values."[58] In both cases, the claim on public resources and the case for separation were too weak and too far removed from the core goals of public schooling to be acceptable to courts or the public.

Schools must demonstrate respect for alternative ways of seeing the world, including different evaluations of the dream itself and different definitions of success, but that does not require anyone to reject their faith, forget their heritage, or abandon their people. Public schools must also give all children—regardless of their race, ethnicity, language, class, or religion—the academic knowledge they need to pursue their dreams. Schools have the further job of transmitting the culture we have in common, even while that culture changes as the population of the nation changes. Finally, it is the job of the schools to teach the values that define us now and will continue to define us as Americans, such as faith in democracy and the rule of law and respect for those who differ from the mainstream. As professor of law Alexander Aleinikoff puts it, "What the *unum* has a right to ask of the *pluribus*, . . . is that groups identify themselves as American. To be sure, there may be significant disagreement over what it means to see oneself as an 'American.' But the central idea is that a person be committed to this country's continued flourishing and see himself or herself as part of that ongoing project."[59] Despite the deep passion and moral commitment demonstrated by those who oppose the American dream on behalf of their particular group, the public school system of the United States cannot be expected to, and should not, contribute to the fragmentation of the society it is trying to unite, subvert the liberal democracy it supports, or undermine the collective goals of the American dream.

8

PUBLIC SCHOOLS IN THE NEW AMERICA

The American Dream will succeed or fail in the 21st century in direct proportion to our commitment to educate every person in the United States of America.

—President Bill Clinton, 1995

Both parties have been talking about education for quite a while. It's time to come together to get it done, so that we can truthfully say in America: No child will be left behind.

—President George W. Bush, 2001

There has probably been no era in history in which access to knowledge has been more indispensable. . . . And there may also have been no time, in our recent history at least, in which the quality and availability of education has been less equally dispersed. . . . The differences between the best American schools and the worst are now not just differences in degree but also, increasingly, differences in kind.

—Alan Brinkley, historian at Columbia University, 2000

I see no point in pretending that . . . [democratic schooling] will not entail significant changes especially in the various . . . cultures. . . . [E]ven the dominant groups are unlikely to emerge unchanged . . . . Democracy itself . . . will appear in new versions. . . . Democracy is still, always, a politics of strain.

—Michael Walzer, political philosopher at the Institute for Advanced Studies, Princeton, 1995[1]

THE LANDSCAPE OF PUBLIC SCHOOLING in the United States has changed dramatically over the past 40 years, in part because of substantial movement toward the collective goals of education. Schools are more racially integrated than before *Brown v. Board of Education*; desegregation continues to contribute to the growth of the black middle class. Levels of school funding are higher than a generation ago, and in many states funding is more equitable across districts. Children with severe disabilities spend more of their days in the mainstream; children with subtle learning problems are increasingly identified and helped; parents have the legal right either to challenge the separation of children with disabilities or to demand special services for them. Most English language learners get at least some help in making the transition to English-speaking classes. Dropout rates have declined for whites and for blacks (although not for Hispanics). NAEP scores are higher in many subjects in most grades, with the greatest gains being made by black students. Most states have adopted standards and are developing curricula and professional development programs to bring those standards into the classroom; some states have shown demonstrable improvement in student learning as a consequence. Schools are increasingly sensitive to students from varied religious and ethnic backgrounds, and curricula are more multicultural. Ability grouping is more flexible than it used to be, more students have access to Advanced Placement classes, more take a reasonably demanding curricula, and more attend college. Through it all, despite concerns and disagreements, Americans have sustained their commitment to public schooling. While conflicts over education policy remain serious and policy irrationality persists, policy and practice have changed in ways that bring the ideology of the American dream closer to reality.

These developments took place mostly in a context of economic stability (or even great prosperity) that made it relatively easy to dedicate more resources to public education. Broader political, social, and demographic developments, beginning with civil rights protests, also strongly affected them. Yet schools would not have moved toward greater quality, equality, and inclusiveness unless enough Americans believed deeply in the American dream and expected public education to foster the institutions and practices needed both to promote the pursuit of individual dreams and to keep democracy vital.

Progress has nevertheless been limited, and may become harder as national priorities shift after September 11, 2001. Many Americans have not attained either absolute or relative success: they have not met their schooling goals or surpassed their parents' level of education. Progress was limited in the 1990s, especially among the very poor, recent immigrants, or African Americans. The structure of nested inequalities—from states through districts, schools, and classrooms—and the concentration of problems in the poorest schools make it very difficult for the worst-off to achieve competitive success through schooling.

Schools *have* over time increased the quality of schooling for students formerly victimized by the system and have done more to incorporate difference, but their progress is constrained by the same ideology that enables it. Class separation in schools is growing, by some measures differences in outcomes by class are growing, and racial and ethnic discrimination persists in a form more subtle than Jim Crow. Class and race hierarchies continue to overlap and to affect decisions about racial separation, funding, reform, choice, disability, language, ability grouping, and the treatment of distinct groups. The cumulative impact of these pressures is to sort students, in particular to determine who has the best chance to complete college and move on to a rewarding career, in ways that are not legitimate according to the ideology itself. Educational stratification at the end of the process still too closely replicates economic and racial stratification at the beginning.

It still matters which state you come from, in which district you reside, which school you attend, and which classes you take. The wealth of your classmates and your neighbors still affects the quality of your education, perhaps more than the wealth of your own parents. This structure is very hard to change. The disadvantaged population has always been defined as a minority (by setting the poverty level low enough or through some other such means). In a society whose political choices are determined by majority rule, this means that the poor and the "minority" races are too small a group to improve their chances on their own. Similarly, the somewhat overlapping black and Latino populations were relatively small for most of the twentieth century, were marginalized by their definition as "minorities," and were often unwilling to ally with one another. Correctly or not, they frequently perceive that they have different, even competitive, interests with regard to language training, jobs, the drawing of school and district boundaries, and the allocation of public resources to schools.

Poor people and people of color secured initial help from the courts, and in the cases of desegregation and school funding, a majority of the population now publicly endorse the goals of equal treatment, incorporation, and respect. The means to achieve those goals, however, have been limited because too many Americans are unwilling to take the required risk, pay the necessary price, or surrender their initial advantage. The American dream promises equality of opportunity to poor people and to people of color *and* provides legitimacy to those who prefer to keep most of their resources to help their own children. The remaining question for this book is whether Americans can and will take the steps needed to move the tension between collective and individual goals of schooling any closer toward resolution. As the makeup of American society changes, and with it the social order, can we make the American dream more of a reality, less of a fantasy, for *all* Americans?

The New Demography

The profile of Americans is changing, and the change is reflected strongly in the public schools. The outstanding demographic impact for the next few decades will come from the aging of baby boomers and, absent a major change in immigration laws, from increased racial and ethnic diversity in the population, especially the school-age population.

The first of the baby boomers will reach age 65 shortly after 2010. About 13 percent of the American population is now over 65; by 2030 the aged will comprise roughly 20 percent, nearly 70 million people. Only Florida now has an elderly population of almost 20 percent, but a majority of states are expected to exceed that figure by then.[2] At the same time, the Anglo population of the country will become a smaller proportion of the total, decreasing from 70 percent in 2000 to about 60 percent in 2025 and close to 50 percent in 2050. Forecasters expect the black population, about 13 percent of the total in 2000, to grow slowly, but the percentages of Hispanics (also 13 percent) and Asian Americans (4 percent) are both projected to almost double by 2025.[3] These trends will be felt most powerfully in California where non-Anglos are already more than half of that state's population, and the number of Latinos could exceed the number of Anglos by 2020. Other states will see major changes as well: in at least 15 states, more than 40 percent of the school-age population will be non-Anglo by 2015. Latino children already outnumber black children by several million. Large cities will be especially affected: about 40 percent of the residents of New York City were born outside of the United States, and over half of its children are immigrants or children of immigrants. They come from close to 200 countries, and there are no indications that the influx is slowing.[4]

Because of the growth in the elderly population and the size of the school-age population, the dependency ratio—the ratio of those of working age to the young and old—is likely to become much higher.[5] In addition children will be more racially and ethnically diverse, while the aged will be disproportionately Anglo. In Los Angeles County, as demographer William Frey has noted, the "elderly population is still majority white, its working-aged population is only about one-third white, and its child population is predominantly Hispanic and other racial and ethnic groups." As these changes spread across the country, continues Frey, they "are going to have enormous implications. We're looking down the road at a huge racial generation gap between the old, white baby boomers and these young, multiracial people."[6]

This racial generation gap could create some real policy dilemmas. The need for schooling for the young will be great at the same time that the demand for health care and social services for the elderly will peak; at the least we can expect severe competition for public resources.[7] As school finance expert James Poterba points out, even now, before these population shifts have fully materialized, "An increase in the fraction of a jurisdiction's population over the age of 65 tends to reduce per-child school spending, and . . . the effect is especially pronounced when the elderly residents are from a different ethnic group than the school-age population."[8]

The potential for social division will be very high. In addition to polarization between young and old, we might see increased divisions between wealthy and poor, Anglo and non-Anglo populations, immigrants and native-born Americans, cities and suburbs, among ethnic or racial communities, and between supporters and opponents of the ideology of the American dream. All of these divisions could affect schools: polarization could, for example, make funding reform more contentious, testing more divisive and punitive, and multicultural or inclusive policies more controversial. It could increase the frustration of groups who feel excluded from the American dream and make them more likely to reject it rather than seek to participate in it; it could make the privileged even more protective of their resources and their insulation.

The central question is whether political leaders will inflame these divisions or seek to ameliorate them, practice the politics of educational exclusion or inclusion, try to preserve the old social order of the schools or ease the entry of the new one. Of course many policymakers, particularly elected officials, think little about the long run: the horizon until the next election is too short and rewards for small symbolic actions too great. In the face of the new demography, some will no doubt yield to the temptation for demagoguery, especially in situations of volatile transition.[9] Other political activists will concentrate on securing benefits for their group rather than on broader policy considerations.

But others might take a different stance. As the situation changes, some ethnic group leaders will be able to seek coalitions rather than focus on competition. And most importantly some candidates for public office might decide it is best to try to lead all Americans by placing a priority on the democratic, collective values of participation, respect, inclusion, and opportunity. With the potential for political and social chaos so great, it is possible that more Americans will want their leaders on the high road rather than in the swamp.[10]

Recent political developments in California provide evidence that this is more than wishful thinking. Early in the 1990s, political debate there revolved around the conflict between native-born residents and undocumented immigrants, which blurred into a conflict between white and nonwhite Americans. In 1994 Governor Pete Wilson and the Republican Party sponsored Proposition 187 (initially known as "Save Our State"). It held that illegal immigrants could not use public services such as schools and hospitals, and it required public employees to report service-seekers presumed to be illegal.[11] The proposition distinguished legal from illegal immigrants, but supporters and opponents alike frequently saw it as a signal of general opposition to immigration: one of its coauthors claimed that "those who care at all about our country will support this [proposition] to save our country from the immigration invasion." It passed overwhelmingly, supported by more than 60 percent of Anglo voters and almost 60 percent of black and Asian American voters. Latino voters opposed it two to one.[12]

Proposition 187 was followed two years later by Proposition 209, which abolished affirmative action programs in public institutions in California. Opponents interpreted this proposition also as an effort to protect white domination. It too passed, by a narrower but still persuasive margin of eight points. European Americans again were most favorable (over 60 percent support), followed by Asian Americans (over 40 percent); again, few Latinos (about 30 percent) concurred. Three-quarters of African Americans opposed it.[13]

In short, racial and ethnic tensions worsened during the early 1990s as the proportion of non-Anglos in California rose. In 1993 a third of Anglos in southern California agreed that Hispanics had a "negative impact" on life in their region. A year later a quarter of whites in Los Angeles County thought the influx of nonwhites had made their quality of life worse, and over a third agreed that the government "paid too much attention" to minority groups.[14]

By the end of the decade, however, the politics of division no longer worked so well in California. By 1999 the proportion of Anglos agreeing that Hispanics had a negative impact on life in Los Angeles declined by a third, and the proportion saying the same about African Americans declined by over half. Only half as many whites in 1999 as in 1994 felt that the influx of non-Anglos had harmed their quality of life; one and a half times as many whites in 1999 as in 1994 felt that the new groups had improved it. By 1998 a solid majority supported "outreach programs" and "special educational programs" to help minorities get jobs and a college education. In 1999 almost three-fourths of non-Latino Californians agreed that illegal immigrants should not "be prevented from attending public schools."[15] In the three years ending in December 2001, the proportion of Californians who perceived immigrants to be a "benefit" to their state increased substantially while the proportion who saw them as a "burden" decreased.[16] There remains plenty of prejudice in California—in 1999 almost half of Anglos and almost three-fifths of African Americans living in Los Angeles still saw "too many immigrants in Los Angeles today."[17] And more than two-fifths of Anglos, more than one-third of blacks, and even a quarter of Latinos in the same survey agreed that immigrants have had a negative impact on the public schools of their city. Nevertheless, public opinion has moved toward greater accommodation of diversity.[18]

Electoral politics moved in the same direction during this period. A 1998 *Los Angeles Times* headline proclaimed that "In Contests Big and Small, Latinos Take [a] Historic Leap." Hispanic candidates won the positions of lieutenant governor and sheriff of Los Angeles County, additional seats in the legislature, and the first major city mayoralty since statehood. The Democratic candidate for governor in 1998 ran on a platform of tolerance and accommodation, and won. "Four years ago," said a Latino assemblyman, "we were scapegoated and used as political fodder. Now that era is over. Thank God."[19]

Many factors led to this change, but what matters most over the long run is that demographic transition eventually led to political recalibration. In 1994 non-Anglos comprised about a seventh of California's registered voters; by 2001 that percentage had increased to almost a third.[20] And their proportions will continue to increase dramatically as more immigrants become naturalized citizens and then registered and participating voters.[21] As the director of the National Immigration Forum points out, "How they [the immigrants] break to one party or another may well determine which party dominates in the next few decades. It's a high-stakes battle. Republicans have realized they can't win by relying on a declining number of angry white men."[22]

The same demographic transition and political recalculation are having a direct impact on public schooling in California. In the early 1990s, the major education debates focused on whether proposed new standards and textbooks exaggerated the flaws of white Americans and underestimated the contributions of non-Anglos. Arguments were sharp and polarizing. By the end of the 1990s, attention had largely shifted to issues of class size, teacher quality, overcrowding, and test scores. These issues are not easy to resolve, but they do not inherently divide Americans by identity group.

By the beginning of the twenty-first century, even disputes over bilingual education were muted, focusing more on the best pedagogy than on identity politics, hostility to immigrants, or emancipatory narratives. The presidential candidates set the tone by pursuing a bland middle ground in the 2000 electoral campaign: as candidate Bush put it, "If a good immersion program works, I say fine. If a good bilingual program works to teach children English, we should applaud it." In the words of Harry Pachon, president of the Tomás Rivera Policy Institute, there is now a widespread perception that "the politics of immigrant bashing has backfired."[23]

As in the early decades of the twentieth century, a large group of immigrants combine an experience of exclusion with a strong desire to become American. For them the collective goals of education can be as much a matter of personal interest as the individual goals always have been for most Americans: they seek not only success but incorporation, respect for their culture and values, and a voice in decision making. As in the New Deal era, a large and growing group of new Americans may think of themselves as disadvantaged or feel sympathy for the problems of disadvantage because of their own recent experiences. Hispanics in California, for example, are much more likely than others there to place themselves among the "have-nots," much more likely to agree that "the government should do more to make sure that all Californians have an equal opportunity to succeed," and especially likely to identify public education as a high priority for state spending.[24]

The huge demographic and political changes shaping our nation, the commitment of Americans to public education for all children, and the fact that some reforms have been shown to work make this a propitious time to begin to build a new consensus on education policy. If leaders really believe that no child should or need be left behind, or even if they think that it is in their best interests to act as though they believed it, we have an opportunity to create enduring education policies that can make the American dream work for more people.

Education and the New America

In this new, multicultural America, mutual accommodation will be more important than ever. To make that happen, students should as much as possible be educated with one another. In addition, schools will need to begin the hard work of developing a meaningful curriculum that teaches students to understand and respect the history and perspectives of a broad spectrum of groups. Students will have to learn that members of different cultures have different norms, that differences are legitimate, and that most occur within a common framework of values. It will also be increasingly important for teachers and administrators to transmit the message that the best way to settle disputes is through democratic decision making, not violence or subordination, and they will need to act in a manner consistent with what they teach.

There will be plenty of problems, but teaching has already begun to change the way Americans understand themselves and their nation. Even in Iowa, one of the most homogeneous states, non-Anglo groups are the most rapidly growing segment of the population and classrooms are beginning to reflect it. Initially, says the state's consultant on equity and school improvement, it was "hard to get [Iowans] to think of diversity as a strength, and their sameness as a problem rather than an asset." But the president of the state board of education insists that districts are increasingly engaged in an effort "to maximize the capacity of each student to be able to get along with others and respect others as part of the learning experience." Districts, she said, want "equity to be inseparable from the school improvement process."[25]

At the same time, public schools will need to transmit a common American culture, rooted in the history of this nation and based on English. English will remain the shared language of public discourse in the United States as well as the language required for individual economic success. But it need not be the only language children learn, or learn to respect. *How well* children are taught English and other languages, not *how* they are taught it, should be the focus of attention for parents and educators; various methods may be appropriate so long as they aim to bring children together and not separate them into first- and second-class citizens. Most immigrant children are eager to become Americans (however they define it), and immigrant parents, like all others, want the best for their children. In the long run, this kind of motivation should help schools overcome inevitable disagreements about the best means to a shared end and should help reduce the volatility of these issues.

These recommendations, like the arguments made in the last chapter, will displease members of racial, ethnic, or religious groups who want a longer or different exposure in the schools to their particular views, values, or cultures. Opposition to these preferences can sound like discrimination or at least insensitivity, so it can become political dynamite. But opposition need not imply failure to recognize persistent discrimination; instead, it will be increasingly important in the new America to ensure that separatist or oppositional demands do not undermine either individual or collective goals of public schooling. There is too much at stake.

States and districts will continue to decide most important issues in education policy. As the population changes, federal efforts are likely to be directed more and more to the needs of senior citizens in programs such as Medicare and Social Security. Despite presidential rhetoric over the last 15 years that has overemphasized the federal role in education, no more than a tiny part of the federal budget has ever been devoted to education and only a small percentage of support for schools comes from Washington. That is unlikely to change much. Most federal aid has been and continues to be assistance for disabled and poor children. Out of commitment to the American dream, and in order to reduce the number of dependent people of working age when there will be so many old and young people unavailable to pay taxes, these programs should be protected. That is especially the case for programs for poor children, who do not have the legal or political protections available to others.

To really help disadvantaged children, and to offset opposition to increased spending for them, it will be essential to invest education funds wisely, on initiatives for preschool, early literacy programs, small classes in the early grades, summer school, and afterschool programs. These initiatives are particularly cost-effective where there are a lot of poor and non-Anglo children; they also require qualified, knowledgeable teachers. Investments in increasing the capacity of teachers by providing better training and curriculum-based professional development will be essential to help disadvantaged children.

Standards will continue to make sense as a basis for improved education for all students, a mechanism for increased accountability in schools, and a way to create incentives for better teacher preparation, recruitment, and assignment. With standards in place, schools can create meaningful professional development and effective induction programs to help new teachers perform better and stay in teaching longer. The supply and distribution of good teachers will always be partly determined by workforce issues out of the control of the education system, and salary increases big enough to make teaching competitive with other professions will remain difficult to secure. But investments in helping new teachers, and serious professional education for all teachers, will make even more sense in the coming decades when teacher shortages, especially in schools that most badly need excellent teaching, could be chronic.

Standards are not a panacea, and testing is not a reform in itself but rather a way to measure the impact of reform. Because their costs are limited and the rhetoric of achievement so attractive, it is always tempting to try to use tests to drive reform. No matter how well students are motivated, however, they cannot learn without adequate resources, sufficient time, appropriate curricula, and good instructors. Once these things are available, students can justifiably be punished or rewarded on the merits. Until then high-stakes testing will punish poverty too much of the time and reward privilege as if it were earned.

To permit the achievement we expect and for reasons of social justice, to make the American dream work as it should and to avoid wasting human resources that the country will need more than ever, communities with a lot of poor children will need extra help. They should, at a minimum, receive as much financial support as districts with a lot of affluent families. For both political and substantive reasons, this is best done through state-financed increases to poor districts rather than decreases in wealthy ones. Beyond equality of resources and for the same reasons, all students should be funded well enough to receive an adequate education, in the new and expansive sense of that word. This new understanding of adequacy provides more flexibility than does financial equity alone, and it keeps the focus where it ought to be, on the quality of the education that is provided.

If investments are adequate to give all children a real opportunity to learn, if teaching is improved and good teachers are distributed fairly to all kinds of students, if standards are high and everyone has a challenging curriculum, then we can justifiably hold students, teachers, and schools accountable for results. Accountability is a worthy goal: as the education policy expert Lorraine McDonnell and her coauthors point out, "Democratic control assumes that as a governmental institution, schools derive their legitimacy from the consent of the electorate and that they should be held publicly accountable."[26]

As we have seen, Americans endorse all of these programs and have provided substantial increases in funding for them over the last several decades. People claim to be willing to provide funds for even more reforms. Support may actually increase as the population changes. Californians, for example, agree by a wide margin that the highest priority for "the state's limited funds" should be K-12 education and they approve reducing class sizes for elementary students—and Latinos endorse these positions slightly more strongly than everyone else.[27]

It will be hard to pay for all needed reforms and to promote wise use of the funds, but it can be done. The votes of younger Americans, especially parents of public school children, can help offset the votes of increasing numbers of senior citizens. Advocates can continue to push the courts to maintain pressure on state legislatures for financial equity and adequacy.

For all the difficulties involved in school finance reform, it will remain necessary to equalize educational opportunities and give poor children a chance to achieve their dreams. It is easier to move money than state borders, district boundaries, or people. The structure of nested inequalities among states, districts, schools, and classrooms will not disappear. States will continue to be responsible for education, and some will invest more energy in public schooling than others; the walls between school districts will remain high; and people will continue to sort themselves by race and class. Racial desegregation has met its limits, and privileged parents have shown that they are no more enthusiastic about bringing low-income children of any race into their schools than white parents have been about mixing races. This reluctance means that public/private choice programs, which now affect less than a tenth of 1 percent of the population, will do little to break down racial and class barriers, and could make them worse. The United States will have to rely on more funding and its more effective use, if poor Americans are to have a better chance of participating in the American dream.

Even with greater and more wisely used resources, however, first-class schooling will always be more available on the right side of the tracks. Because the education of children depends so much on the social or economic class of their peers, it remains important to do what we can to educate poor children *with* middle-class children, not just *like* them. Even though such programs are likely to remain too limited to have a dramatic impact on the class structure of education, public officials should do what they can to promote magnet schools and interdistrict choice plans that permit poor children to leave their neighborhoods to find a better education. This action will not solve the problems of the worst urban schools, but it will give some children a greater chance for success.[28]

Ethnic and racial issues will not go away, but class issues will remain the most difficult. Americans will continue to believe that every child should have an equal chance to succeed, and they will continue to try to use the fruits of their labor to secure an advantage for their own children. This paradox, embedded in the ideology of the American dream, will keep on shaping public education in the United States. But so will the ennobling vision the dream sometimes represents. For all its flaws, public schooling remains our most accessible and democratic national political institution.[29] Public action on schools will therefore provide the best chance for the liberating side of the American dream to take effect. Schools can help us meet the challenges of a new economy and realize the opportunities in the new demography but we have to get it right. If poor and non-Anglo children continue to lack sufficient resources, good teachers, decent facilities, and real connections with other Americans, the ideology of the American dream will be just a cover for systematic injustice, and the promise of "no child left behind" will be just another lie. Public education *can* help make the American dream work for everyone, and that will be more important than ever in our new America.

Notes

Notes to Chapter 1

1. Franklin 1962 (1749): 52–53; "Learning: PBS Studies . . ." 2001.

2. Hochschild 1995 develops the meaning and history of the American dream more fully.

3. Clinton 1993; Steger and Bowermaster 1993: 288–89.

4. With slightly fewer blacks and Hispanics than whites or Asians, slightly fewer high school dropouts and postgraduates than those with high school or college degrees, and just as many poor as wealthy (*Wash. Post* et al. 1995).

5. Shearson Lehman Brothers 1992.

6. In this case blacks and Hispanics agree even more than do whites; those with less education agree more than do those with more education, and the poor agree more than the rich (Pew Research Ctr. 1997b). See also Public Agenda 1998a; Pew Research Ctr. 1997a, 1999a. These citations also support the next two sentences in the text.

7. Quotation from Bush 2000; survey data are in Shearson Lehman Brothers 1992; Phi Delta Kappa 2000.

8. Rizk 1995.

9. Other writers share our view that disputes over educational pedagogy and policy are really disputes over the content and priority of core values. Recent works include Labaree 1997; Levin 1987; Paris 1995; and Levinson 1999a and b.

10. Public Agenda 1998d; Phi Delta Kappa 1998. See Hochschild 1995: 16–17 on meanings of success.

11. Miller-Kahn and Smith 2001.

12. Miller 1954: 66; Franklin 1987 (1749). Survey data are from Phi Delta Kappa 1996. Women, African Americans and Hispanics, those with little education, the poor, and those under age 50 were especially likely to agree with the "Puritan" view. The same groups, except for Hispanics and the young, also were especially likely to endorse the "Franklin" view.

13. Economic functions of education are beyond our scope, partly because the connection between the quality and amount of schooling in a nation and that nation's economic standing is surprisingly unclear, at least over a short period

(Krueger and Lindahl 2001). We do briefly examine the effect of years of schooling on income, but we mainly assume that more schooling is better than less and a high-quality education is better than a low-quality education, for reasons that include but are not limited to future income.

14. Milligan 2001; Ackerman 2001.

15. Sharpes 1987: 27–28.

16. On schooling for citizenship, see citations in note 9, and Gutmann 1987; Galston 1989; Barber 1992; Westbrook 1996; McDonnell et al. 2000; Macedo and Tamir 2002; Ravitch and Viteritti 2001.

17. Columnist is Kersten 2001. Surveys are Public Agenda 1998d; Democratic Leadership Council 1999b. In two other surveys, preparation for citizenship ranked higher than all other proffered purposes of schooling (Phi Delta Kappa 1996, 2000; see also ibid., 1998).

18. Public Agenda 1998a.

19. Flathman 1996: 13; surveys are Phi Delta Kappa 1996, 2000. Wagner 1996 analyzes community meetings.

20. There is always tension between maintaining educators' authority and teaching democratic practices through actually permitting students to make decisions. Schools and teachers negotiate this tension differently, depending mostly on the age and social class of their students.

Many Americans want schools to pursue even more objectives, such as health care and hot lunches. We do not address these objectives because they are not a central part of the American dream. The desire to promote self-esteem is on the borderline, however, since many argue that students need high self-regard in order to achieve success and respect others different from themselves. But no empirical evidence shows self-esteem to be either necessary or sufficient for attaining the core goals of schooling; in fact, some suggests that it is the consequence of success or unrelated to it in any systematic way (Ross and Broh 2000; Schmader et al. 2001). Thus we consider it as an element of what some Americans want schools to do (see especially chapters 6 and 7), but not as a basic goal of schooling.

21. Jefferson 1856 (1818): 434.

22. *Plyler v. Doe* 1982, quoting two earlier cases; see also Stolzenberg 1993: 641–46. The recent case is *Abbott v. Burke II* 1990.

23. "The emphasis on education and social security programs are . . . the cores of alternative strategies pursued by emerging welfare states" (Heidenheimer 1981; see also Castles 1989; Hokenmaier 1998).

24. Enrollment rates are in Easterlin 1981: app. table 1. The economists are Goldin and Katz 1997: 10–13; see also Dewhurst et al. 1961: 315.

25. National Center for Education Statistics (NCES), *Condition of Ed. 2001*: table 32-1; see also Barro and Lee 2001.

26. Spending data are in Hokenmaier 1998; comparisons are in OECD, *Education at a Glance 2001*: table B1.2; spending preferences are in Shapiro and Young 1990: 166–67.

27. OECD, *Education at a Glance 1995*: 48.

28. Bureau of the Census 2002: table 450. Those figures compare with, for example, about 162,000 employed in providing social insurance and just under three million civilians and military personnel in the armed forces (ibid., tables 450, 499).

29. "Immigrant Integration," *Migration News* 1998, http://migration.ucdavis.edu/mn/pastissues/aug1998mn_past.html; Rich 1996: 16; Orr 1998: 103.

30. *Fortune* magazine comparisons are in Picus and Bryan 1997: 442; data on enrollment and budget are in NCES, *Digest of Ed. Statistics 2001*: tables 1, 30. The United States spent $299 billion for defense and $434 billion for Social Security in the same year (Bureau of the Census 2002: table 458).

31. Natl. Assn. of State Budget Officers 1999: 12. Until about 1960 states spent as much on highways as on education; since then educational spending (including higher education) has risen at a much faster rate until it now takes up over a third of state budgets (Ringquist and Garand 1999: 283–85).

32. *Hazelwood School District* . . . 1988. Goldin and Katz 1999 describe the intensely localist origins of American public schools.

33. OECD survey, 1993, in Wirt and Kirst 1997: 341; see also Hochschild and Scott 1998.

34. Olson 1998a: 1.

35. Reinhard 1998.

36. Hodgkinson 1999: figures 2, 3. See Natl. Ctr. for Public Policy and Higher Education 2000: 166–68 for reports on states' preparation of their students for college.

37. Data on expenditures and dropouts are in NCES, *Digest of Ed. Statistics 2001*: tables 168, 105. Data on the influence of state residence is in NCES 2000d: 40–42; Murray et al. 1998.

38. Connecticut Conference of Municipalities 1997: vii–ix, 5.

39. Ibid.: 10–12.

40. Hertert 1995; Iatarola and Stiefel forthcoming 2002. See also Rothstein 2000a.

41. Hout forthcoming 2003; Karen 2002. Whites still have an advantage in completing college once they have enrolled. Hout and others find growing racial as well as class disparities in college-going for the youngest cohort (Cameron and Heckman 2001; Biblarz and Raftery 1999; and Biblarz, personal communication with the authors, July 2001).

42. Ellwood and Kane 2000. They find that even controlling for race, state college costs, measured achievement (itself strongly affected by parents' income), and parents' education, well-off children are still considerably more likely to attend college than poor children. See also Beattie 2002.

Widening inequality in family incomes over the past few decades has further worsened inequalities in schooling by *increasing* the likelihood that well-off children would graduate from college while *decreasing* the likelihood that poor children would graduate from high school. These results obtain even after controlling for parents' income (Mayer 2001. See also Card and Lemieux 2001; Acemoglu and Pischke 2001; Fry et al. 2000).

43. Devroye and Freeman 2001; Blau and Kahn 2001: 12–13; see also NCES 2001d for similar results among 15-year-olds across 32 nations in 2000. The presence in the United States of immigrants who speak and read English poorly explains only part of the dismal reading scores of the bottom fifth.

44. Danziger and Reed 1999: 16; Ashenfelter and Rouse 2000; OECD, *Ed. at a Glance 2001*: table E5.1.

45. Betts 2000. Figures are in 1996 dollars.

46. Quotation is from Verba 2001: 47. Political understanding is in Nie et al. 1996: 31–32. On political knowledge see Delli Carpini and Keeter 1996: ch. 3; on tolerance see Davis et al. 2001 and Nunn et al. 1978. On voting see NCES, *Condition of Ed. 1996*: indicator 37, charts 1 and 2.

47. Verba 2001.

48. NCES 2001b: 4–5. "Poor" and "near-poor" are defined as eligible for free- or reduced-price lunches.

49. *Ed. Week* 1998: 9–23, 56–72; NCES, *Condition of Ed. 1998*: supp. table 58–5; General Accounting Office (GAO) 1995a: table III.4; Dept. of Housing and Urban Development 1998: 16–17.

50. Furstenberg and Kmec 2002; *Campaign for Fiscal Equity . . .* 2001.

51. On the gap between inner city and other schools, see Cook and Evans 2000. On NAEP, see Zernike 2001b.

52. Massey 1996: 396–399; Madden 2000: 3–7. By the end of the 1990s, the poorest were even more concentrated in the 100 largest cities (Allen and Kirby 2000).

53. On disparities see Ho 1999; M. Orfield 2002: 50–53. On separation by income, see Abramson et al. 1995; Rusk 2002.

54. Coleman et al. 1966: quotation on p. 22; documentation is in Kahlenberg 2001: chs. 3 and 4; Hoxby 2000; Hanushek et al. 2003a. The example is in Orr et al. 2000: figure 1.

55. Districts that have considered or attempted class-based integration include LaCrosse (WI), Cambridge (MA), Wake County (NC), Jefferson County (KY), Montgomery County (MD), St. Petersburg (FL), and San Francisco. See Richard 2002 on the difficulty of maintaining such a program.

56. Jargowsky 1997: 31.

Notes to Chapter 2

1. Lemay 1991: 210; Malcolm X and Haley 1965: 203.

2. Morgan 1975. Quotation is from Lemay 1991: 217.

3. Hotakainen 1995.

4. *Brown v. Board of Education I* 1954; Maraniss 1990: A22.

5. Quotations in, respectively, Applebome 1995; Hendrie 1998c; "Charlotte Contemplates . . ." 1999.

6. Public Agenda 1999a: 26; Armor 1995: 112.

7. Both quotations in Holmes 1999. That this mother is black and participated as a child in Boston's desegregation effort suggests the complexities of school desegregation.

8. Williams 1995: C4.

9. Jacoby 1999; Fuerst and Petty 1992: 65.

10. Kennedy 1963: 469; Jencks et al. 1972: 106.

11. *Brown v. Board . . . II* 1955.

12. "Editorial Excerpts . . ." 1954; "NAACP Sets . . ."1954.

13. O'Reilly 1995: 179, 186.

14. *Green v. Board . . .* 1968; *Swann v. Charlotte-Mecklenburg . . .* 1971.

15. *Keyes v. School District . . .* 1973. *Keyes* for the first time included Latinos as subjects for desegregation, but we do not consider Latinos in this chapter for

two reasons. Their relationship with school desegregation is complicated and ambivalent (e.g. Moran 1996a, 1996b), and they have generally cared more about such issues as bilingual education than about desegregation. In California, for example, organized political pressure from Hispanics early in the period of desegregative activity was associated with a *reduction* in racial and ethnic balance (Wegner and Mercer 1975). In addition, most policy efforts and political debates about school desegregation have focused on bringing together African Americans and European Americans.

16. Jacoby 1999; Orfield 1978: 244–47. On Nixon see also O'Reilly 1995: ch. 7.

17. *Milliken v. Bradley I* 1974.

18. In St. Louis, Missouri, a settlement out of court mandated a desegregation plan that crossed the city-suburban boundaries once it seemed likely that the court would order such a plan.

19. The three relevant cases are *Board of Education of Oklahoma . . .* 1991; *Freeman v. Pitts* 1992; and *Missouri v. Jenkins* 1995.

20. Governor Fife Symington of Arizona even declared that he would "seek legislation to *make* all school districts seek release from their desegregation agreements with the courts" (Sidener 1995; emphasis added). The proposal was not enacted. On released districts see Orfield et al. 1996.

21. Rusk 2002: 64.

22. On courts' inactivity see Parker 2000. Quotations are from *Wessmann v. Gittens* 1998; and Hendrie 1998b.

23. Orfield and Gordon 2001: 31–33. U.S. Commission on Civil Rights 1967: table 2 shows the situation in other parts of the nation before the big push to desegregate.

24. Moody and Ross 1980; Gendron 1972.

25. Orfield and Gordon 2001: 31–33. David Rusk's analysis of 100 large metropolitan areas during the 1990s shows that black segregation in schools was stable in 32, declined in 23, and worsened in 44 (Rusk 2002: 64); for similar results see M. Orfield 2002:52.

Gary Orfield disagrees with Rusk somewhat on the trajectory of Hispanic segregation. According to Orfield 55 percent of Latinos attended schools with at least half minority enrollment in 1968; that figure rose steadily until it reached 76 percent in 1999. According to Rusk, "Elementary school segregation for Hispanics was . . . stable [during the 1990s]. . . . The average masks contrasting trends (stable 14 [large metropolitan areas]; down 36; up 49) (ibid., 65)."

26. On large cities see NCES 2001b: table 9. On smaller communities see Reardon et al. 2000; Orfield and Gordon 2001: 26–27; Oliver 2001: 100.

27. Clotfelter 1999, 2001; Cutler et al. 1999; Reardon and Yun 2001; Reardon and Eitle 1998.

28. *Swann v. Charlotte-Mecklenburg . . .* 1971.

29. Sugrue 1996; Delaney 1994; and Farley and Frey 1994 all analyze the relationship between public policy and housing patterns.

30. There is surprisingly little agreement about long-term effects of school desegregation, for several reasons. Scholars share the strong feelings of other citizens, so evaluations have usually been biased in one direction or another. Fears that assumptions would prove unfounded have led to resistance to any evaluation; and researchers, like policymakers, are often too impatient to wait for slow changes to

mature over many years. Finally, some view desegregation or "forced busing" as moral issues that should not be addressed in terms of their end results at all.

31. On Boston see Van Arsdell 1976. On whites' achievement see St. John 1975; Schofield 1995b: 603. However, Jencks and Mayer 1990; Pogue 2000; Phillips 2001: ch. 4; and Bankston and Caldas 2002 have evidence suggesting that, even with socioeconomic and other controls, white students, like black and Latino students, typically gain more from attending school with mostly white peers. Bankston and Caldas, however, find that "school racial composition has no relation to school achievement after we take the percentage of students from single-parent families into consideration" (2002: 202).

Most white parents, like all others, will resist a policy that holds the possibility that their children will not be able to attend a school that maximizes their chances for success. But few desegregation plans proposed to send white children into predominantly black schools, so these concerns were exaggerated.

32. NCES, *Digest of Ed. Statistics 2001*: tables 8, 108, 112, 124.

33. Ibid.: table 133; Rothstein 2000b; Koretz 1997. The proportion of white 17- and 18-year-olds taking the SAT rose from 18.5 to 22 percent between 1977 and 2000, and the average white's SAT score (combining verbal and math scores) rose over the same period from 1036 to 1060 (calculations by authors from census data and data provided by the Educational Testing Service [ETS]).

34. On degrees, dropouts, and college attendance, see NCES, *Digest of Ed. Statistics 2001*: tables 8, 108, 184, 268. On less segregated cities, see Cutler and Glaeser 1997.

35. On test scores see NCES, *Digest of Ed. Statistics 2001*: tables 112, 124, 130; Rothstein 2000b. The proportion of African American 17- and 18-year-olds taking the SAT rose from 12 to 19 percent from 1977 to 2000, while blacks' average SAT score also rose over the same period, from 789 to 859 (calculations by authors from census data and data provided by ETS).

36. David Armor found 15 studies showing that desegregated students learn more, in some cases substantially more, 12 showing virtually no effects, and 8 showing that desegregated black students learn to read less well than their segregated peers. Roughly the same pattern held for mathematics achievement (Armor 1995: 87–89). The psychologist Thomas Cook focused on only the most sound studies and found that desegregation had no effect on black students' math scores but did improve their reading scores somewhat (Cook 1984). See also Jencks and Mayer 1990.

37. Entwistle and Alexander 1992; Trent 1997; Grissmer et al. 1998; Pride 2000; and Guryan 2001a all find some evidence that, even controlling for socioeconomic status, desegregation helps to improve blacks' achievement scores or increase their schooling attainment.

38. Phillips 1998.

39. Hochschild 1984: ch. 4. On St. Louis see Lissitz 1994; Clough and Uchitelle 1995: 38; Freivogel 2002. On other cities see Buckman 1995; Orfield et al. 1992; Rubinowitz and Rosenbaum 2000 (quotations on pp. 134, 168–69). The *Gautreaux* program grew out of the remedy in *Hills v. Gautreaux* 1976; see also Ludwig et al. 2001.

40. Viadero 2000a; National Ed. Goals Panel 2001; GAO 2001a.

41. Quotation in Maraniss 1990: A22. In addition to the works cited above,

see Meier et al. 1989; Schofield 1995b; Wells and Crain 1997; Yu and Taylor 1997: 19–21.

42. For this and the preceding paragraph, see Braddock et al. 1994; Wells and Crain 1994; Wells 1995; Schofield 1995b.

43. Payne et al. 1978; Leland and Smith 1997. On effects of contact in desegregated schools, see Forbes 1997: 48–59.

44. In addition to citations above, see Schofield 1995a; Sigelman et al. 1996; Dutton et al. 1998.

45. Quotations are in Blanding 2001; Eaton 2001: 128–29. Survey data are in Schuman et al. 1997: ch. 9.

46. On Wilmington, see Pappas 1997; on Charlotte, see Smith forthcoming 2003 (quotation on p. 8 of ms.). On residential integration, see Pearce 1981; Denton 1996; Kentucky Commission on Human Rights 1983.

47. Johnson 1965.

48. Kettering Foundation 1971 (results not available by race); Phi Delta Kappa 1988, 1996; CNN/*USA Today* 1994, 1999.

49. See citations in previous note. Both questions show no clear patterns by region; people with less education were more likely to see gains for whites than were those with more education. One would not have predicted either result in 1975.

50. Quotation is in Daniels 1983: 37. Survey data are in Kettering Foundation 1971; Elam 1989: 30; CNN/*USA Today* 1994. In the 1994 poll, better-educated respondents were more likely to see improvement than were less-educated ones.

51. Survey data in Schuman et al. 1997: 103–10, 240–41; Gallup Organization 1997; Davis et al. 2001: q. 133A-B. Quotation is in Burrows 1972. For more on whites' increasing support for desegregation after it occurred, see Hochschild 1984: 179–87.

52. Schuman et al. 1997: 123–30, and updates at http://tigger.cc.uic.edu/~krysan/t32.htm; Davis 1997; Harris 1970; NAACP Legal Defense and Education Fund 1989: 24–25.

53. Sullivan 1995.

54. Among 16 districts that had recently desegregated, the U.S. Civil Rights Commission found that transportation costs remained the same or declined in five, increased less than 1 percent in seven and increased 1 to 2 percent in four (Van Fleet 1977: 75–77). See also Hochschild 1984: 58–62; Fuerst and Petty 1992.

55. "School bus services account for 25 percent of trips and 28 percent of student-miles traveled during normal school travel hours. . . . School buses account for less than 4 percent of the injuries [to students] and 2 percent of the fatalities." Conversely, cars with teen drivers represent about 15 percent of student-miles and trips, but over half of the injuries and fatalities. Students walking or riding a bicycle to school account for 14 percent of trips, about 2 percent of student-miles, 11 percent of injuries, and 22 percent of fatalities (Transportation Research Board 2002: ES3-ES6).

56. On busing times and mileage, see Hochschild 1984: 219, note 67. On consolidation see Bureau of the Census 1975: Part I, Series H412–432, Series H531–534; Benjamin and Nathan 2001: 168–77. Survey data are from Harris 1972.

57. Gallup Organization 1973; see also ibid. 1975; Harris 1978.

58. Kahlenberg 2001: 42.

59. Saporito and Lareau 1999; Henig 1996; Clotfelter 2001; Lankford and Wyckoff 1999; Cutler et al. 1999.

60. Maraniss 1990.

61. Focus groups are in Public Agenda 1999a: 26, 27; Finn is quoted in Bronner 1999.

62. Poverty ratios are in Madden 2000: 6. Test scores are in Abernathy 1996.

63. Traub 1994; Libov 1988.

64. On regional planning groups, see Lennon 2000; McDermott 1999: ch. 3; Judson 1994a. Glastonbury quotation is in Judson 1994b; poll results are in *Hartford Courant* 1993.

65. *Sheff v. O'Neill* 1996.

66. Frahm 1996a, 1996b.

67. Darryl McMiller, message to Race-Politics listserv, Nov. 13, 1996; Lennon 2000.

A member of the West Hartford Board of Education demonstrates nicely the slide away from a focus on racial inequality: "The *Sheff v. O'Neill* challenge is a magnificent opportunity to design education for the 21st century. . . . Solving the issue of local integration must be a side effect, but not the sole objective. . . . As critical a question is how the current systems are also segregating all students from participation in the global economy of the new century" (Sloane 1996).

68. Green 2000; *Sheff v. O'Neill II* 1999.

69. Keedle 2000; McDermott et al. 2002.

70. Lee 1999: 520–528 criticizes the legislature's response to *Sheff*. Elizabeth Horton-Sheff, mother of the original plaintiff and now majority leader of the Hartford City Council, recently again asked the court to intervene to mandate more desegregation (Weizel 2002).

71. Schuman et al. 1997: 240–252; *Newsweek* 1988; CNN/*USA Today* 1994, 1999.

72. See citations in previous note, and *Wash. Post* et al. 1995: app., p. 80.

73. CNN/*USA Today*/Gallup Organization 1999; Public Agenda 1998d: 38–41. On transfers, 87 percent of whites prefer local schools to desegregative transfers.

74. Hernandez 1995: B1; Ahearn 1995; Hallow 1997.

75. Joiner 1994; see also Orr 1999; Rich 1996; Henig et al. 1999.

76. Mother is quoted in Hendrie 1998a; Carter 1996: 21; Denver official is in McQuillan and Englert 2001: 5.

77. Justice Thomas is in *Missouri v. Jenkins*; New Yorker in Williams and Crew 1994: 703; attorney quoted in Haynes 1995.

78. Ruffins 1999: 18.

Notes to Chapter 3

1. *Seattle v. State of Washington* 1978 (internal citations omitted); *Abbott v. Burke II* 1990; Goodman 1999.

2. Information and quotations on these schools is from Hayward 2000, and personal communication from Clarissa Hayward to the authors, Sept. 5, 2001.

3. Students with family incomes below $10,000 averaged 864 (out of a possible 1600) on the SAT in 2000–2001; students from families with incomes of $40,000–$50,000 averaged 1004; and students from families enjoying over $100,000 received 1126 on average. Scores exactly tracked family incomes in every intervening income bracket, as has always been the case since SATs were widely prom-

ulgated (NCES, *Digest of Ed. Statistics 2001*: table 136; see also Camara and Schmidt 1999).

SAT scores also exactly track parents' education, which is a good indicator of socioeconomic status ("2001 College Bound Seniors . . .": graph 10).

Even after enrollment in college, wealthy students are more than twice as likely to attain a bachelor's degree as poor students (NCES, *Digest of Ed. Statistics 2001*: table 314).

4. Burkett 1998: 42.

5. Quotations from Hanushek 1998: 12, 18; see also Betts 1995; Hanushek and Somers 2001. Survey data are in Hochschild and Scott 1998: 113–14; Phi Delta Kappa 2001.

6. Preston 1998: B6; "Reading Without Money" 2001.

7. These and other examples are from Center for Education Reform, "Back to School Bulletin #2," Sept. 4, 2001, http://edreform.com/update/2001/010904.html.

8. We discuss corruption in schools and ways in which school systems can become job regimes in chapter 4.

9. Opponents of increased or equalized funding for public schools also frequently observe that even though California spent millions of dollars reducing class sizes in recent years, test scores continued to drop. California, however, spent much of the money earmarked for reductions in class size in suburban districts where few poor or non-English-speaking students lived. This turned out to be not just inefficient but counterproductive, since it enabled suburbs to hire away the best city teachers, creating a shortage where the poor students lived (CSR Research Consortium 2002; Jepsen and Rivkin 2002).

10. On NAEP see Grissmer et al. 2000: 98. On earnings see Card 1999; Krueger 1999; Angrist and Lavy 1999.

11. Olson and Ackerman 2000: 26. These results control for parents' education and income.

12. Quotations in Wenglinsky 1998: 279; Viadero 2000b: 38; on test scores see Ferguson 1991.

Burtless 1996; Ludwig and Bassi 1999; and Ladd and Hansen 1999: ch. 5 are excellent recent compendia on whether, when, and how money matters. Ferguson and Ladd 1996; Mosteller et al. 1996; Grissmer et al. 1997; Card and Payne 1998; Krueger 1999; and Guryan 2001b provide more evidence that greater expenditures on at least some resources improve students' educational or labor-market outcomes. These results hold especially for poor students.

13. Loeb and Bound 1996; Card and Payne 1998; Wenglinsky 1998; Pogue 2000; Payne and Biddle 1999; Verstegen and King 1998. On commercial tests see Berliner and Biddle 1995: 32.

14. On reasons for increased spending, see Hanushek and Rivkin 1997; Lankford and Wyckoff 1995; Rothstein and Miles 1995. "One calculation" is in Rothstein 1997.

15. Quotations are in Burkett 1998: 43; Ferdinand 1998. Analysis of courts is in Dayton 1993. Survey data are in Hochschild and Scott 1998: 113–14; Phi Delta Kappa 2001.

16. Minow 1991.

17. *Abbott v. Burke II* 1990: 375.

18. Hochschild and Scott 1998: 103–10; NPR et al. 1999; Public Agenda 1998c; Program on International Policy Attitudes . . . 2000; CNN/*USA Today* 2000: 17; Joint Ctr. for Political and Economic Studies 1997: table 6; 1998: table 3; 1999: table 4.

19. On spending priorities see Miller Brewing Company 1983; Phi Delta Kappa 1993, 1994, 1995, 1998; *Los Angeles Times* Poll 1995, 1997; Am. Assn. of University Women 1998; Milken Foundation 1997; CNN/*USA Today* 1998; Public Agenda 2000a; Public Education Network and *Ed. Week* 2002. On reduced expenditures see Hochschild and Scott 1998: 111–12.

20. Quotation is in Goodman 1999: 72. On equalization see Hochschild and Scott 1998: 112–113; NPR et al. 1999; Joint Ctr. for Political and Economic Studies 1992; Advisory Commission on Intergovernmental Relations 1993; Reed 2001: ch. 6; Public Education Network and *Ed. Week* 2002.

On support for spending, see Davis and Smith 1999; Phi Delta Kappa 1993, 1998. We used data from the on-line collection of the Institute for Research in the Social Sciences, University of North Carolina, and the paper archives of RPOLL at the University of Connecticut to analyze funding preferences across states; the analysis is on file with the authors.

On the 2000 presidential election, see Institute for Policy Studies and *The Nation* 2000.

21. AFT and NEA 1998; Public Agenda 2000a: 3.

22. Goldberg 1997; Goodman 1999: 74–75.

23. *Ed. Week* 1998: 62–65.

24. Burkett 1998: 43; Ferdinand 1998.

25. For voting by the elderly, see MacManus and Turner 1996: 161–81; Binstock and Day 1996; Rhodebeck 1998; Gerber et al. 2000.

Although the United States spends less in absolute terms on social welfare policies than do most other comparable nations, it spends relatively more on its elderly compared with its nonelderly. The ratio of public spending on those over age 65 to those under age 65 ranges from 2.3 in Japan and Sweden to 3.8 in Italy and the United States (Poterba 1997; see also Lynch 2001).

26. On comparisons by age, see NBC News/*Wall Street Journal* 1998; CNN/*USA Today* 1998. On comparisons of parents using public or private schools, see Rubinfeld and Thomas 1980; Hamilton and Cohen 1974; Bergstrom et al. 1982.

27. Poterba 1997: 57–59.

28. First two quotations in Goodman 1999: 73; Burkett 1998: 43. Data on localism are in Reed 2001: ch. 6; governor quoted in Ferdinand 1998; see also Briffault 1992.

29. Sack 1998: 23.

30. "Fiscal 2002 Education Appropriations . . ." (2002). The federal budget for health care rose $290 billion dollars (in 1999 dollars) from 1980 to 1999, and for social security it rose $70 billion. For education, however, it increased only $23 billion (Orfield 2002: 70).

31. NCES, *Digest of Ed. Statistics 2001*: table 158.

32. Orfield 1998: 16–17.

33. Property tax rates for education, however, are not correlated with these two outcome measures (Connecticut Conference of Municipalities 1997: 5). Data on overburden and tax rates are in ibid.: vii, 112, 116; see also Orfield 2002: 25–28.

34. *Ed. Week* 2002: 86–88. Rothstein 2000a: 37–63 has the best discussion of this discrepancy.

35. Five states (Alaska, Arizona, Connecticut, Maryland, and Florida) spent the same or less per pupil in constant dollars in 2000 than a decade earlier; eight states (Alabama, West Virginia, Idaho, Indiana, Kentucky, North Dakota, Oklahoma, and Mississippi) increased their public school per capita spending by 25 percent or more. Nationally, per-pupil spending increased 10 percent from 1990 to 2000 (*Ed. Week* 2002: 86).

36. NCES, *Condition of Education* 2002: indicator 56; see also NCES 2001b: iii, 6. The appeals court in New York State, for example, notes that in New York City, "343 schools were heated by inefficient coal-burning boilers in 1995, whereas *only* 125 still had such boilers by 1999" (*Campaign for Fiscal Equity* 2002; emphasis added).

37. McKean 2000.

38. *San Antonio Independent School District . . .* 1973, quoting James Coleman. Coleman goes on to observe that "neither of these desires is to be despised; they both lead to investment by the older generation in the younger. But they can lead to quite different concrete actions" (in Margolis and Moses 1992: 7). This book is in many ways an explication of that observation.

39. For example, Kansas' constitution speaks only of "establishing and maintaining public schools," and Utah's speaks only of "a public education system, which shall be open to all children of the state." Conversely, the constitution in New Jersey requires a "thorough and efficient education" and that of Washington claims that "it is the paramount duty of the state to make ample provision for the education of all children residing within its borders . . . . The legislature shall provide for a general and uniform system of public schools." New Jersey and Washington are under judicial mandate to reform their provisions for financing schools; Kansas and Utah are not.

Roch and Howard 2001: 11, 14, 18 show how the language of the state constitution matters in whether funding equalization cases are brought and how courts decide them.

40. Quoted in Laura Jensen, on Law and Courts discussion list, lawcourts-l@usc.edu, Apr. 5, 2000. One state legislator refused to support the impeachment investigation, for example, on the grounds that "it is a political hack job. . . . This is payback for *Claremont*" ("Reactions to House Vote . . ." 2000).

41. Norman 2000: 23. This article is entitled "The New Vermont: Give It to Canada."

42. Archer 2000: 25; Crosby 2001: 7; Lewin 1998.

43. Scholars disagree on which factors explain courts' decisions in school finance cases, but they concur that variables that usually explain outcomes of state courts' rulings do a poor job on this topic (Lundberg 2000; Swenson 2000; Roch and Howard 2001).

44. Verstegen and Whitney 1997; Minorini and Sugarman 1999a; 1999b: 41–46; Corcoran and Scovronick 1998: 70–83; and Rothstein 2000a: 65–70 all offer characterizations of patterns in school finance litigation.

45. *Campaign for Fiscal Equity . . .* 2001.

46. The move to require specific programs to help poor children began in Kentucky in 1989 and has since moved to about 15 other states. Courts' decisions have provoked more real change in some places than in others, ranging from an over-

haul of the entire educational system in Kentucky to essentially nothing in a few (Schrag 2001; Rothstein 2000a: 74–79). Recently Maryland became the first state to tie school finance reform to explicit promises of adequacy for all students through legislative action, without a court case behind it. "People *chose* to do this. This is a sea change," said one expert who had worked on the legislation (Montgomery 2002).

47. Lewin 1998; Kirp 1998. See also Reed 2001; Berne and Stiefel 1999.

48. The court's words are in *Serrano v. Priest I* 1971. On California's funding levels, see Silva and Sonstelie 1995; Gerber et al. 2000; Sonstelie and Richardson 2001.

49. *Campaign for Fiscal Equity . . .* 2001; unless otherwise noted, all citations in this and the next four paragraphs are from this decision.

50. "Report of the Commission on School Facilities and Maintenance Reform" of New York City, 1995, quoted in *Campaign for Fiscal Equity . . .* 2001.

51. Like those in New York, plaintiffs in Los Angeles, Philadelphia, Hartford, and Minneapolis have tied charges of racial bias to claims for greater equity in school funding. The link is the claim of "racially disproportionate misfortune" (Morgan 2001; see also Roos 1998; McDermott 1999; Brittain 1993; Ryan 1999). It remains to be seen how courts, elected officials, and citizens respond to this new claim to racial and class equity.

52. *Campaign for Fiscal Equity . . .* 2002.

53. Quotation is in Evans et al. 2001: 224; evidence is in Evans et al. 1997; 1999; and Murray et al. 1998.

54. Reed 1998.

55. Gittell 1998.

56. Tedin 1994. These results come from a survey about a slightly earlier version of the funding equalization policy. Notably, although almost all respondents in the losing district knew that their district would lose school funds, fully half of the respondents in the *winning* district *also* thought their district would lose funds (pp. 640–644); see also Cortez 1998.

57. Johnston 1998; see also Bosworth 2001: ch. 3; Reed 2001.

58. Quotations from the wealthy are in Burkett 1998: 43; quotations from the poor are in Sack 1998: 23; Goodman 1999: 70. The governor is quoted in Goldberg 1997.

59. On segregation see Orfield and Gordon 2001: 44; on spending disparities see Newman 1999.

60. *Robinson v. Cahill* 1973; *Abbott v. Burke II* 1990.

61. Nathan Scovronick was a senior member of Governor James Florio's administration, and as executive director of the New Jersey State Treasury Department was a member of the working group that designed the new school-aid formula.

62. It seems surprising that teachers' unions would oppose efforts to equalize funding, especially when the effort would also have increased the amount of funds going to public schools by over a billion dollars. But such opposition is common; in Ohio, according to one journalist, a proposed sales tax increase to aid schools and property owners "made for some unlikely political bedfellows, . . . aligning some school leaders and labor organizations for the first time with conservative, anti-tax groups. The Ohio Federation of Teachers . . . was among the program's loudest detractors" (White 1998: 21). In Texas "We don't support either one [of two bills to restructure school funding] because neither one supports teachers'

salaries," reported the president of the Texas State Teachers Association (Johnston 1997: 8).

63. First quotation is Sacks 1990; second is *Position Paper*, quoted in Goertz 1998: 107.

64. Reed 2001: ch. 6; Reed 1997, table 5. The politics in Texas were similar; residents of high-income districts were more likely to oppose a proposition to allow the state to redistribute property taxes, whereas residents of districts with higher proportions of non-Hispanic blacks and Hispanics were more likely to support it (ibid., tables 5 and 6).

65. The funding statutes are described in Corcoran and Scovronick 1998, Firestone et al. 1997 describe uses of the newly appropriated funds in poor districts.

66. Gewirtz 2002.

67. Orfield and Yun 1999: 19–20.

68. The Pritchard Committee is chaired by the former governor of Kentucky who was also lead counsel for the plaintiffs in *Rose v. Council*; although privately funded, it has a quasi-official status as a spokesperson for citizens and monitor of the reforms.

69. *Rose v. Council* . . . 1989; governor is quoted in Walker 1989.

70. Sexton 1998: 201.

71. Legislator is in Harp 1990; quotations are from Harp 1991.

72. Adams 1997; and Bosworth 2001: ch. 4 describe the Kentucky plan. Petrosko et al. 2000 (and others in the same volume) evaluate the plan's impact. The governor's statement is in Combs 1991: 376. Hochschild 1984 provides additional evidence that broad-scale reform may be easier to implement than narrow changes.

73. Lewin 1998; Burkett 1998: 45, 44.

74. Walters 2000.

75. Most school districts also face problems with long-term support for capital needs. Many buildings, especially in poor urban or rural areas, are very old and in poor repair, overcrowded, or inadequate for modern demands. In 1999 63 percent of schools with high proportions of poor students reported at least one feature in inadequate condition, compared to 45 percent of schools with few poor students. Once again race and class coincide: in the same survey, three-fifths of schools with more than half minority enrollment reported such features, compared to half of all-white schools (NCES 2000a). In 1995 New York City reported a need for $8 billion in repair and construction; Chicago for $3 billion, and Washington, D.C., and New Orleans for half a billion dollars each. GAO estimated the cost to bring all schools "to a good overall condition" to be $112 billion (GAO 1995b; see also Ladd and Hansen 1999: 199–202).

Notes for Chapter 4

1. Campaign for America's Children 2000; Krueger 1998: 30; Taylor 2000: 41, 56.

2. Survey data are in Hochschild and Scott 1998: tables A4, A5, and Phi Delta Kappa polls since 1998. Quotations are from Lieberman 1993; Berliner and Biddle 1995.

3. In a math and science test given throughout the world in 1999, eighth graders from a few affluent districts in the United States matched the highest scorers, who were from Singapore, Hong Kong, and Korea. But students in Miami-Dade County, Rochester, and Chicago scored only as well as the low-scoring residents of Thailand, Tunisia, and Iran (Loveless 2001: 32).

4. In 1990 fully 73 percent of Americans blamed "the effect of societal problems" for the "problems currently facing public education in this community"; only 16 percent blamed the schools themselves (Phi Delta Kappa 1990).

5. These social policies are important and relevant, as are the potential contributions of parents and the community. A discussion of them, however, is beyond the scope of this book. For a start see Garfinkel et al. 1996; Anyon 1997; Finance Project 2000.

6. A majority of Americans concur: 55 percent agree that it is the responsibility of the public schools to close the achievement gap between white students and black or Hispanic students (Phi Delta Kappa 2001).

7. Data from OECD, *Ed. at a Glance 2001*: chart C1.1; NCES 2001a: 1–8; Ctr. on Education Policy and American Youth Policy Forum 2000: 6–8. In particular, NAEP math scores continued to rise in the 1990s, except among poorly achieving high school seniors (NCES 2001e).

Students who take advanced math courses in high school are more likely than other students to graduate from college and to earn more a decade later. Those results hold even controlling for race or ethnicity, gender, family income and parents' education, motivation and ability, and an array of characteristics of the school. In short, "math matters" in the title of the book reporting this study (Rose and Betts 2001).

8. NCES, *Digest of Ed. Statistics 2001*: tables 108, 109, 187; "Dropout Rates in the U.S. 2001."

9. NCES, *Digest of Ed. Statistics 2001*: tables 407, 408; OECD, *Ed. at a Glance 2001*: 308–319; Schemo 2000.

International comparisons of test scores are complicated because different groups of students may be tested at different stages of their schooling. Nevertheless, such comparisons play a large role in the rhetoric on education reform because American students frequently do not come out well in them. They also provide a general indicator of what American schools and students do well and poorly. Schmidt et al. 2001 provide the most comprehensive analysis to date of these tests.

10. In addition to previous citations, on dropouts, see also Driscoll 1999; Civil Rights Project and Achieve Inc. 2001; Hauser et al. 2001. On college attendance see also Card and Lemieux 2001; and Ellwood and Kane 2000.

Students whose parents did not attend college are much less likely to attain higher education, and they take longer to enter and complete college, than students whose parents were well educated. These results hold even after controlling for family income, academic preparation, and other factors that affect college attendance (NCES, *Condition of Ed. 2001*: xviii–xliii).

11. NCES 2001c. Almost 30 percent of white fourth graders read "below basic," a result that has not changed since 1992, when first measured. Fully 63 percent of blacks scored "below basic" (a slight improvement over the 1990s), and almost 60 percent of Hispanics did the same (a slight decline). Only 22 percent of

Asian Americans read "below basic"; that figure was cut in half over the 1990s. See also Barton 2001 on the growing gap between proficient readers and nonreaders, as evidenced by state-level NAEP scores.

12. Loveless 2001: 31–32.

13. There are no comparable scores from years earlier than 1998, so we cannot compare changes over time (NCES 2001c).

14. White 1999b.

15. On parental conservatism see Tyack and Cuban 1995. For poll results see CBS News 1999, as well as every Phi Delta Kappa poll and virtually all others by other survey organizations.

16. Phi Delta Kappa 1970, 1982, 1997, 1999. In 1974 over a quarter of public school parents thought local schools were "too ready to try new ideas," whereas only a fifth saw them as "not interested enough." Their children disagreed; about half of high school juniors and seniors thought schools were insufficiently innovative, and only a tenth thought they were too ready to change (Phi Delta Kappa 1974).

17. Public Agenda 1995a: 43.

18. Public Agenda 1995b. See also Public Agenda 1994; Metropolitan Life Survey 2000: 22. For analysis see Tyack and Cuban 1995; Finn 1997.

19. Public Agenda 1995b: 10.

20. Public Agenda 1995b: 7.

21. On teacher conservatism or cynicism, see McLaughlin and Talbert 1993; Hess 1999b; Elmore 2000; McDermott 2000; Payne 2001; Stone et al. 2001: ch. 2. Quotation in Public Agenda 1996: 21. On the value of trust in a school community, conversely, see Bryk & Schneider 2002.

22. Quotations in Metropolitan Life Survey 2000: 108 (emphases in original). Teacher concerns are in Phi Delta Kappa surveys of teachers, conducted in 1984, 1989, 1996, 1997, and 1998.

Teachers, like parents, also worry about discipline; twice as many would enhance school discipline and increase academic requirements when asked how to improve schooling (Metropolitan Life Survey 1995: 37).

23. Phi Delta Kappa teacher surveys; Public Agenda 1996: 22–25. When asked to rank groups by their lack of enthusiasm for "proficiency testing," for example, almost twice as many (43 percent) superintendents in Ohio identified teachers as parents, the next highest group (Sutton 2001).

24. Unlike other citizens most teachers also claim that local public schools outperform private schools. For these various views, see Phi Delta Kappa 1997 (teachers); Public Agenda 1992: 14; 1996: 19–20; Metropolitan Life Survey 2000: 112.

25. Loveless 2000; "Identity Crisis . . ." 2001. Quotation is in Chase 1997–98: 13–14.

26. "Teachers Against Reform" 2000; "Union Dues" 2000.

27. Ross 1998: 127.

28. On New York see Sugarman 1995; more generally see DC Appleseed Public School Governance Project 1999; Natl. School Boards Foundation 1999; Natl. Commission on Governing America's Schools 1999. On time use see Olson and Bradley 1992. Quotations are from Silver 1997.

29. Orr 1998: 102; Kerchner et al. 1998.

30. On mayors see Stone 1998a; Hess 1999a; Hill et al. 2000; Stone et al. 2001. On New York see Ross 1998.

31. On New York see ibid.: 129; Purdy and Newman 1996; Purdy 1996. On other cities see Tucker 1993; Rich 1996; Orr 1999.

32. Business leader in Stone 1998b: 259; Shipps 1998.

33. Letter from Mayor Kurt Schmoke to the Hon. Parris Glendening, June 20, 1996, cited in Orr et al. 2000.

34. Orr et al. 2000, quoting Maybank 1996; Shen and Babington 1996.

35. Quotation from "Open Letter" 1997; on other cities see Henig et al. 1999; Stone et al. 2001.

36. Zernike 2001c.

37. Sashkin and Egermeier 1993.

38. Boyer added wistfully, "What we need is another Sputnik! Maybe what we should do is get the Japanese to put a Toyota into orbit" (quotations in Fiske 1982).

39. "You take away seven, And that leaves five. Well, six actually. But the idea is the important thing. . . . Hooray for New Math, New-hoo-hoo Math, It won't do you a bit of good to review math. It's so simple, so very simple, That only a child can do it!" www.wiw.org/~drz/tom.lehrer/the_year.html#math.

40. See Elmore 1996 on "getting to scale."

41. On financial incentives see Asimov 2000; Solmon and Podgursky c. 1999; Olson 1999a. Quotation is from AFT 2000: 6. Debates over improving the quality of teachers are in Am. Council on Education 1999; Humphrey et al. 1999; Darling-Hammond and Sykes 1999; Gallagher and Bailey 2000; Fordham Foundation 1999.

42. Olson 1998b: 43.

43. As New American Schools (NAS—described below) puts it, "Whole-school designs . . . [are] based on the premise that high-quality schools each possess a 'design' that guides the school's mission and instructional program and that establishes common expectations for accountability and performance among students, teachers, and parents" (Rand Research Brief: Education 1998). Superintendent is in House 2000: 38.

44. "Site-Based Management. . ." 1994 (amended 1995, 1997); see also Anderson 1999; Malen 1999; Keith 1999.

45. Summers and Johnson 1996; Office of Educational Research and Improvement 1996; Herr 1999; Vincent and Martin 2000.

46. The roots of whole-school reform lie in the effective schools movement (Edmunds 1979; Puma and Drury 2000: 18–19; Downs 2000).

47. Evaluations produce intense controversy of their own; analysts of one model, for example, have accused each other of conflict of interest, ad hominem attacks, hypocrisy, "radical relativism," being "misleading in the extreme," and having "a callous disregard for the achievement of students" (Walberg and Greenberg 1998, and letters to the editor of *Ed. Week* on Apr. 29, May 5, and May 20, 1998).

48. Olson 1999b: 14, quoting Ellen Lagemann, then president of the Natl. Academy of Education; see also Puma and Drury 2000: 19–21.

49. Berends et al. 2002; see also Datnow et al. 2002; Mirel 2001; Viadero 2001b.

50. On New Jersey see Erlichson and Goertz 2001; quotation is from House 2000: 38. Memphis was the marquee district for whole-school reform in the late 1990s, since all schools were required to participate and it was the earliest district to involve more than a few schools. The new superintendent, however, withdrew the district from the program in 2001, citing students' failure to improve on state achievement tests and teachers' lack of enthusiasm for the reforms.

51. Anderson 1998: 52.

52. Smith and O'Day 1991; Fuhrman 1993, 1999; Knapp 1997; Elmore 2000. Portz 1999 usefully distinguishes among civic, market, and professional strategies for reform. Here we focus on the latter; in chapter 5 we address market-oriented strategies. See, similarly, Cochran-Smith and Fries 2001.

53. Advisory Council . . . 1994: Letter of Transmittal, ix–x.

54. Smith and O'Day 1991: 246. Puma and Drury 2000: 12 summarize evidence on the "association between consistent higher-order classroom instruction and greater student achievement."

55. Newmann et al. 2001a; Cogan et al. 2001; Cohen and Hill 2001.

56. Terrel Bell, secretary of education in the Reagan administration, remembers President Reagan telling him that education reports do nothing but "weigh 40 pounds and draw dust" (Jordon 1993). Quotation in Natl. Commission on Excellence in Education 1983.

57. Groups included Task Force on Federal. . . 1983; Education Commission of the States 1983; Natl. Science Foundation 1983. Quotations from Fiske 1982.

58. Natl. Education Goals Panel 1994; Stedman 1994.

59. Jordon 1993; Olson 1993.

60. Harrison 1992.

61. Harp 1994.

62. On reforms see Petrosko et al. 2000; on teachers' views see Petrosko and Pankratz 2000. Students are in Jordon 1993; Harp 1997.

63. Corcoran 1995; Kelley 1998; Pankratz and Petrosko 2000.

64. Viadero 2000b: 38; White 1999a; Galuszka 1997: 94.

65. Business Roundtable 2001; Belden, Russonello, & Stewart 2000; Albert Shanker Institute 1999; Swanson and Stevenson 2002.

Chicago has also made notable, though incomplete, gains in student achievement largely as a consequence of systemic reforms and accountability (Roderick et al. 1999; Roderick et al. 2000; Hess, G. 2002). Around the world students have higher achievement scores in nations with curriculum-based exams for promotion and graduation than do students in comparable nations without such exams, even controlling for differences among school systems (Bishop 1997).

66. Headline is in Hoff and Manzo 1999; on expectations see Betts and Costrell 2001; Newmann et al. 1999.

67. www.education-world.com/a_issues/issues129a.shtml; www.whitehouse.gov/news/reports/no-child-left-behind.html.

68. NBC News/*Wall Street Journal* 1997; Hochschild and Scott 1998: 110–11; Penn 1999; NPR et al. 1999; Public Agenda 2000b, 2002a; Phi Delta Kappa 1999, 2000; Business Roundtable 2001; Gallup Organization 2001a; Public Education Network and *Ed. Week* 2002. For some public skepticism, see "Improving Our Schools" 2001.

Even though 40 percent of Latinos in Texas believe the TAAS to be biased against minority students, only 30 percent oppose the use of TAAS as a graduation requirement (Dyer 2000).

69. Quotation is in Houston 1997; see Viadero 2002 on new standards of accountability in New Hampshire.

70. On low-achieving students see Education Trust 1998b. For disputes over measuring good teaching, see, for example, Goldhaber and Brewer 2000 and re-

sponse by Darling-Hammond et al. 2001; Abell Foundation 2001 and response by Darling-Hammond 2001; Archer 2002 summarizes the dispute well.

71. The importance of good teachers and the disparity in their distribution is one of the very few issues in the field of education for which the evidence is consistent and overwhelming (Education Trust 1998a, 2000; Wright et al. 1997; Wenglinsky 2000; Puma and Drury 2000: 13–14; Darling-Hammond 2000; Lankford et al. 2002; Ingersoll 2002; *Campaign for Fiscal Equity* 2002; Wayne 2002).

72. On California see Ogawa et al. 1999; CSR Research Consortium 2002; Jepsen and Rivkin 2002. On New York see Goodnough 2001.

73. Sanders and Rivers 1996; see also Mendro et al. 1998; Bembry et al. 1998.

74. On new teachers see Johnson et al. 2001; Recruiting New Teachers 1999; Am. Council on Education 1999: 13–15. On professional development see Elmore and Burney 1997; McLaughlin and Talbert 2001; Elmore 2002; Cohen and Hill 2001.

75. Natl. Commission on Teaching . . . 1996: 15; see also Wilson et al. 2002.

76. New York, which has had a curriculum-based examination in place for years, has the highest average SAT scores of any state once racial, class, and gender characteristics are controlled (Graham and Husted 1993). For similarly positive results of curriculum-based exams, including for poor or low-achieving students, see Bishop and Mane 2001.

77. "Voices from the Front" 1999; see also Kohn 1999; Sacks 2001. More sober critics include Koretz and Barron 1998; Klein et al. 2000; Linn 2000; Resnick 2001; Amrein and Berliner 2002.

78. Hartocollis 2001; Alexakis 2001.

79. Hartocollis 2001; Zernike 2000; see also Manzo 2001.

80. Corcoran 1999; see also Darling-Hammond 1994; Newmann et al. 1997; Ladd 1996; Orfield and Kornhaber 2001. On linking standards and incentives for adults as well as students, see Coleman 1997; Porter 1994; Cornett and Gaines 2002.

81. The National Academy of Sciences recently reported that the evidence is insufficient "to determine conclusively what effect, if any, exit examinations have on dropout rates. Indeed, the likelihood is that the effects of these tests will vary significantly, depending on how they are constructed and implemented and on how their results are used. However, . . . high-stakes testing at any level may sometimes be used in ways that have unintended harmful effects on students at particular risk for academic failure because of poverty, lack of proficiency in English, disability, and membership in population subgroups that have been educationally disadvantaged." The NAS does conclude that "retention in grade is a very strong predictor of dropping out" (Beatty et al. 2001: 7).

For arguments that high-stakes tests increase dropout rates, see Haney 2000; Jacob 2001; Lillard and DeCicca 2001. For disagreement see Bishop and Mane 2001; Toenjes and Dworkin 2002.

Retention may help some students *if* accompanied by extra help, small classes, and innovative teaching methods (Roderick et al. 1999; Roderick et al. 2000; Lorence et al. 2002). But such programs are scarce in poor districts with many underachieving students and weaker teachers.

82. Testing is also connected with the politics of school finance: one savvy superintendent favors his state's high-stakes test because "you have to respond to the

needs of the public. It's going to be very difficult for the policy makers to continue to pump resources into public education if the perception is that the schools are producing graduates who are not capable of doing the work that's out there in the new economy" (Goldscheider 2001; see also Alexakis 2001; F. Hess, 2002a; and Hill and Lake 2002 on the politics of standards). Testing can also create powerful evidence for increased funds to some districts.

83. On complaints see Viadero 1999a: 14; Robelen 2000; Office for Civil Rights 2000. Quotations in Robelen 2000: 14; Delgado 1999.

84. *GI Forum et al. v. Texas* . . . 2000 (emphasis in original); Viadero 1999a; Hartocollis 1999: B1.

85. Thompson 1999; Archer 1999; Bryk et al. 1998.

86. The law is at www.ed.gov/legislation/ESEA 02. Quotation is in Viadero 2000c: 20; for evidence, see Hannaway and McKay 2001.

87. Corcoran 1999.

88. Heubert and Hauser 1999: 5–8. For other good guidelines, with similar conclusions, see Center for School Change 1999; Natl. Assn. of State Boards of Education 1997; Am. Educational Research Assn. 2000; Learning First Alliance 2001; and Achieve 2001. Behn 1997 suggests how to implement such guidelines.

89. In Corcoran 1999. The conservative Chester Finn concurs with the liberal professor: "It's unjust, even immoral, for a state to crack down on the kids while leaving their instructors and schools untouched" (Finn 2001). Newmann et al. 2001b show that with good instruction, poor children can do more "authentic intellectual work" *and* attain higher standardized test scores.

90. Heubert and Hauser 1999: 5. On what the federal law can accomplish, see "Forum: The Feds Step In" 2002.

91. SRI International and Bay Area Research Group 2001; see also DC Voice 2001.

92. Reynolds et al. 2001. These analysts estimate an average return of $7.14 per dollar invested in the program by the time graduates reach adulthood. The return comes from higher salaries and tax payments, fewer remedial services, and less involvement with the criminal justice system (Reynolds et al. 2002). The duration of impacts is less clear for other half-day programs.

93. Barnett 1995: 43. Impact of prekindergarten is in Grissmer et al. 2000: 34–36; 76–93. See also Karoly et al. 1998; Puma and Drury 2000: 28; Heckman and Lochner 2000: 58–64; Gilliam and Zigler 2001; *Ed. Week* 2002. Committee for Economic Development 2002. Weiss 2002 shows the good long-term effects of full-day kindergarten for urban children. Impact of further compensatory education is in Reynolds and Temple 1998. On other nations, see OECD 2001.

94. A recent study, however, partly contradicts this view; whites who attended Head Start are more likely to complete high school and attend college and earn slightly higher wages in their early twenties than comparable whites who did not. Black Head Start graduates were less likely to be charged with or convicted of a crime in their teens and early adulthood (Garces et al. 2000). For similarly encouraging fundings for Early Head Start, see Mathematica Policy Research, Inc. 2002.

95. Schorr 2001.

96. NCES, *Digest of Ed. Statistics* 2001: tables 43, 44; Gallagher et al. 2001.

97. On summer school see Alexander et al. 2001; Entwistle et al. 2002. On af-

terschool programs see Depts. of Education and Justice 1998; Roderick et al. 2000; Gewertz 2000; Snow 1998; Halpern 1999.

98. Krueger and Whitmore 2001, 2002. See also Grissmer et al. 2000: 76–93; J. Finn et al. 2001; NCES 2000c: 31–35; Molnar et al. 2001. When class-size reduction is focused broadly, not just on poor children, its impact is less certain and can have perverse effects, as California's experience demonstrated.

99. Wagner and Vander Ark 2001; Wasley et al. 2000; Stiefel et al. 2000; Lee and Loeb 2000; Hill 2001.

100. McDonnell 1994: 424. High-stakes testing apparently increases motivation and work effort of most, though not all, low-achieving students (Roderick and Engel 2001).

Notes to Chapter 5

1. Smith 1976 (1776): V, 300; Rivera 2000; Moe: 2001 345.

2. Getchell 2001.

3. Keegan 2001: 3.

4. Chubb and Moe 1990: 167, 217 (emphasis in original); see also Hill et al. 1997.

5. The few systematic evaluations of magnet schools usually, but not always, find that magnets slightly foster integration and slightly improve the quality of schooling for their participants (Goldring and Smreker 2000; Meeks et al. 2000).

6. Rossell and Glenn 1988; Schneider et al. 2000; Willie et al. 2002.

7. Keegan 2001: 3.

8. Friedman 1955: 91, 94.

9. Henig 1994: 103; see also Wells 1993: ch. 3.

10. Wells 1993: 32. The Community School of Santa Barbara put it even more grandly in 1970: "The idea is that freedom is a supreme good; that people, including young people, have a right to freedom, and that people who are free will in general be more open, more humane, more intelligent people" (ibid.: 35).

11. Deal and Nolan 1978; Wells 1993: ch. 2.

12. Elmore 1990; Jencks 1970; Cookson 1994: 75.

13. www.friedmanfoundation.org/about/mission.html; www.ij.org/profile/index.html.

14. Reich 2000. John Coons and Stephen Sugarman are also prominent liberal white supporters; they have spent decades designing voucher plans to disproportionately benefit poor children, children with disabilities or limited English proficiency, and children of color (Coons and Sugarman 1999). See also Halstead and Lind 2001.

15. www.baeo.org/about/index.htm; and baeo.org/about/manifesto.htm. On African American supporters, see Wilgren 2000; on Latinos, see Zehr 2001d; www.edreform.com/press/2001/amicus2001.pdf.

16. See Witte 2000; Cookson 1994: 65–68; and Carl 1996 on the politics of Milwaukee's move into vouchers. Opposition came from liberals—teachers' unions, the Democratic party, integrationist proponents of Milwaukee's magnet program—and conservative Republicans, especially parents.

17. On East Harlem, see Fliegel and MacGuire 1993; Meier 1996; on Milwaukee see Leake and Faltz 1993.

18. NCES *Condition of Ed.* 2002: suppl. tables 29–1, 29–2.

19. Glazerman 1997; Schneider et al. 2000.

20. Cullen et al. 2001. Schneider et al. 1998 and Fuller et al. 1999 reach similar conclusions about magnet schools, which provide the most common form of intradistrict choice. See also Gill et al. 2001: 98–99; and Martinez et al. 1996 (for more positive conclusions).

21. Ferguson 1997; Phi Delta Kappa 1995; NBC News/*Wall Street Journal* 1997.

22. Quotations are in Wells 1996: 36; analyses of reasons for interdistrict choice are also in Fuller et al. 1999: 34–35; NCES 1995b; Fossey 1994; Lamdin and Mintrom 1997; Wronkovich et al. 1998. In the first two years of open enrollment in Wisconsin, about 40 percent of transfers went to districts with lower rates of success on measures of achievement or attainment; about two-thirds of the districts to which students applied had average incomes higher than the home districts of those students (Hetzner 2001). Fewer than 1 percent of Wisconsin's students, however, transferred by the third year of the program (Wisconsin Legislative Fiscal Bureau 2001: 18).

Despite its light use, three-quarters of Americans endorsed interdistrict choice in one recent survey (Moe 2001: 334).

23. Arsen et al. 1999; Hetzner 2001.

24. On impact see Fuller et al. 1999; Goldhaber 1999. On Britain see Gorard et al. 2001: quotation on p. 21; Gorard and Taylor 2001. Data on use of school choice option in England is at Department for Education and Skills, United Kingdom, www.dfes.gov.uk/statistics.

25. C. Finn et al. 2001: 37; second quotation from Tom Mooney, president of the Ohio Federation of Teachers, in Stephens 2001.

26. Rauch 2001.

27. Charter Schools Office c. 2002; and Charter Schools Institute 2002 illustrate variations among and enthusiasms of charter school founders. Hill is quoted in Zernike 2001a; see also Rothstein 1998a. Rand study is Gill et al. 2001: 95; see also Miron and Nelson 2001. Finn et al. 2000 provides a more enthusiastic review but he does not account for self-selection among charter students; Wong et al. 2000: 25–26 find much less achievement gain when controlling for students' prior achievement.

28. NCES 2000e.

29. On lack of knowledge, see Public Agenda 1999b: 10; NPR et al. 1999; Democratic Leadership Council 1999a; Moe 2001: 178, 180. In the DLC survey, more respondents thought charter schools were private schools than thought they were publicly funded schools. On support, see those surveys, as well as Democratic Leadership Council 1998; *Wash. Post* et al. 2000; CNN/*USA Today* 2001. Phi Delta Kappa 2000; and Phi Delta Kappa 2001 suggest greater public skepticism about the idea and practices of charter schools.

30. First poll in Finn et al. 1997; the others are RPP Intl. 1999; Teske et al. 2001; New Jersey Dept. of Education 2001. NEA poll is NEA 1998: 132.

31. Wells et al. 2000: 180–188. Quotation is in Rothstein and Nathan 1998.

32. Overall data are in NCES 2000e; Schnaiberg 2000; Fuller et al. 1999: 53; Henig et al. 2001; Gill et al. 2001: 152–55. District-level comparisons are in Cobb and Glass 1999; Gill et al. 2001: 169–72; Wells et al. 2000; Wong et al. 2000.

Lacireno-Paquet et al. 2002 find that market-oriented charter schools enroll fewer students who are not proficient in English and fewer special education students than do comparable regular public schools.

33. On parents' choices see Henig 1996; Fuller et al. 1999; Saporito and Lareau 1999; Lankford and Wyckoff 2000; Fairlie 2003. Washington Web site findings are in Schneider and Buckley 2002.

34. Anglo parents also had much greater success in finding charter schools with test scores higher than those of regular public school students (Weiher and Tedin 2002).

35. Some charter schools, though open to any student, have a distinctive ethnic orientation and are, not surprisingly, dominated by students from that ethnic group. The AGBU Alex and Marie Manoogian School in Michigan has "its roots in Armenian culture," and almost three-quarters of its students are Armenian; 98 percent of the students in the Ha:sañ Preparatory and Leadership Charter School in Arizona are members of the Tohono O'odham Indian tribe (Charter Schools Office c. 2002: 5; Zehr 2001c).

36. Wells 2002 argues that charter schools have not been closed often enough for malfeasance or lack of accomplishment.

37. On finances see Welles 2000; on instability see Snyder 2002. For a more sanguine view of for-profit schools, see Hentschke et al. 2002.

38. Lieberman 1999: 151. For evidence of some responsiveness by some regular schools to charters, see Horn and Miron 2000; Wong et al. 2000; Teske et al. 2001; RPP Intl. 2001; Hess et al. 2001; Mintrom 2001; Maranto 2001; and Hoxby forthcoming 2003. Wells 1998; Olson 2000b; and Arsen et al. 2001 find that public schools show little if any responsiveness or that charters harm regular schools as much as help them.

39. On innovation see Finn et al. 2000 (which includes the quotation); Corwin and Flaherty 1995; Mintrom 2001. On lack of innovation, see Arsen et al. 1999; Teske et al. 2001. For founders' views see NCES 2000e: 42–43.

The most recent federal survey shows that, compared with regular public schools, elementary-level charter schools are much more likely to offer programs before and after the regular school day and much more likely to offer special instructional programs such as Montessori and ungraded classrooms. They are less likely to offer programs for the gifted and talented. At the secondary level, charters are less likely than regular schools to offer Advanced Placement courses, and much less likely to offer programs for gifted and talented students. More regular public school teachers than charter school teachers have participated in professional development activities on the use of computers in instruction (NCES 2002).

40. Schnaiberg 1999.

41. Olson 2000c: 24.

42. Hannaway 1998: 24. Chester Finn describes this as a "hopeful but precarious time" for charters; he worries about lack of national and state-level leadership, adverse publicity and overregulation. These will, he fears, result from "bad apples," the difficulties of beginning a charter school, "relentless and inventive . . . enemies," debilitating internal divisions over accountability, and the incoherence that usually attends a "grass-roots effort" (www.edexcellence.net/gadfly/gadfly.html, October 24, 2001).

States are putting more effort into removing the "bad apples"; whether regulation stifles innovation more than it maintains accountability remains to be seen (Sandham 2001).

43. Fiske and Ladd 2000, quotation on pp. 225–26.

44. Ladd and Fiske 2001: 59, 60.

45. Candisky 2001; "The Education . . .:" 2001.

46. Moe 1995.

47. *Zelman v. Simmons-Harris* 2002. A useful immediate set of responses is in Pew Forum on Religion and Public Life 2002. On use of choice programs to foster group identities or religious values, see Ravitch 1996; Galston 2002. On private schools and racial integration and tolerance, see Reardon and Yun 2002, and Campbell 2001.

48. Roughly a million children are now home schooled (advocates claim up to two million), generally because their parents believe that no school sufficiently accommodates their religious or philosophical commitments (Bureau of the Census 2001; Stevens 2001).

49. www.ij.org/profile/index.html.

50. Ceaser and McGuinn 1998: 92; see also Gintis 1995. Abernathy 2001 provides a simulation showing that if vouchers expanded, parents using them would indeed become more involved with their children's school—but less involved with the educational system at large.

51. Peterson and Campbell 2001: 1. The authors characterize voucher supporters' views here, although they generally share these views. See also the rest of that volume; Viteritti 1999; Howell and Peterson 2002. Authors in Ravitch and Viteritti 1997; and Peterson and Hassel 1998 also generally support broad choice plans.

52. Iris Young, personal communication with authors, Aug. 2000.

53. Glazer 2001: 37.

54. Opponents or skeptics include Levin 1983; Henig 1994; Witte 2000; and most authors in Rasell and Rothstein 1993.

55. For suggestions about how, see Sugarman and Kemerer 1999; Coons and Sugarman 1999; Godwin and Kemerer 2002.

56. Witte 2000: 132; Greene et al. 1999; Rouse 1998.

57. Greene and Peterson 1996; Witte 1996. The *Wall Street Journal*, happily pouring oil on the fire, reported a few months later that "the two men have come to despise each other, with Mr. Witte at the Milwaukee U. [*sic*] calling his foe a 'snake' and Mr. Peterson shooting back that Mr. Witte's work is 'lousy.' 'It's escalated to the point where I don't trust him enough to talk to him on the telephone,' Mr. Witte says. 'He'd be recording the conversation, and so would I'" (Davis 1996).

58. When the legislature expanded the Milwaukee program after five years to permit 15,000 students to participate, it dropped the requirement for evaluation (partly because of the Witte-Peterson imbroglio). So we have no achievement data on the larger number of participants. On receiving schools see Wisconsin Legislative Audit Bureau 2000.

59. Gill et al. 2001: 84–85; GAO 2001b.

60. Applicants participated in a lottery to determine who would receive vouchers, thus producing an experimental group who could change to a private school and a control group who also wanted to change but were not given the means to do so. Comparing test results for the two groups, Peterson and his coauthors con-

cluded that "school voucher programs may have the capacity to shrink the black-white test-score gap for participating students"; David Myers of Mathematica Policy Research, who did the initial statistical work, however, was more cautious about whether real change occurred. There may also be methodological flaws in these studies that would keep them from being truly randomized field experiments. Many students dropped out of the private schools or testing program, and it is plausible that the least successful students disappeared. We are also told little about how *schools* selected among vouchered students; it is plausible that those accepted into the schools of the highest quality, or accepted at all, had the fewest academic or social problems to begin with. In short, the experimental and control groups may not be as similar as they appear to be on the basis of the initial random distribution, and the groups may be increasingly *less* comparable across years. Finally, no one can explain why black students, but not Anglo or Hispanic students, showed achievement gains and why gains varied across ages, grades, and subjects of study (Howell et al. 2001, quotation on p. 152; Mathematica Policy Research Inc. 2000; Howell et al. 2002; Mayer et al. 2002; Howell and Peterson 2002. For a critique see Gill et al. 2001: 86–87).

61. "Blacks v. Teachers" 2001: 27.

62. Most students in private voucher programs end up in religious schools for several reasons. On the supply side, the vast majority of private schools are parochial, many nonparochial private schools have relatively high tuition, and at least some nonparochial private schools are not eager for voucher students. On the demand side, many parents prefer religious education for their children.

On parents see Teske and Schneider 2001; Howell 2002. On Edgewood see Greene and Hall 2001. On Florida, see Canedy 2002. Quotation in St. Angelo 2001.

63. Greene 2001a. Greene 2001b finds dramatic improvement in schools threatened with vouchers for their students. Camilli and Bulkley 2001; Kupermintz 2001 and Carnoy 2001 dispute his findings. See Belfield and Levin 2002; Hoxby forthcoming 2003; F. Hess 2002b for evidence of small but consistent improvements in public schools facing competition. Quotation is in Gill et al. 2001: 86; see also McEwan 2000; Simon and Lovrich 1996.

64. First quotation is from McEwan and Carnoy 2000: 227. Attendance and achievement are from Carnoy 1995; Keller 2001; see also Parry 1997; Gauri 1999; Hsieh and Urqiola 2002. *Economist* quotation is in "Back to School" 2001.

65. Phi Delta Kappa surveys, as well as Joint Center for Political and Economic Studies 1998: table 1; Zogby Intl. 1998; *Family Circle* 1994; Hochschild and Scott 1998: tables A4, A5.

66. For the most recent surveys, or surveys with non-Anglo oversamples, see polls by Joint Center in most years since 1990; Phi Delta Kappa 1999, 2001; Public Agenda 1999b: 14; *Wash. Post* et al. 1999, 2001; NBC News/*Wall Street Journal* 1999, 2000; Pew Research Ctr. 1999b, 2000; CBS News/*New York Times* 2001; Gallup/CNN/*USA Today* 2001; Gallup 2002; Moe 2001. McGuinn 2001; and Reid 2001 analyze divisions within the black community over vouchers and charter schools.

67. On direct choice see Public Agenda 1995a; Phi Delta Kappa 1999. On presidential action, vouchers tied with three other proposals for last place out of 13 items (CBS News 1999). In 2002 respondents ranked vouchers "to leave failing public schools for private schools" sixth in priority for "improving public education." Only 5 percent endorsed this—about as many as endorsed more school

construction or involvement of for-profit corporations (Public Education Network and *Ed. Week* 2002: 8).

In 1996 majorities of New York City residents agreed that the school chancellor and board of education were doing only a "fair" or "poor" job, yet only 12 percent thought the city should provide vouchers for private or parochial schools. (A third called for more money, and another third called for an "overhaul" of the current public school system) (Marist Institute for Public Opinion 1996: 9).

68. Public Agenda 1999b: table 1; Moe 2001: ch. 6. NPR et al. 1999 and Phi Delta Kappa 1995 report somewhat lower proportions of "don't know's."

69. Moe 2001: data in table 3.7; quotation on p. 345.

70. Catterall and Chapleau 2000; "Voucher Foes . . ." 2000; Wildman 2001. Vouchers or tax credits for private and parochial schools also lost by as much as two to one in ballot initiatives in Maryland (1972), Michigan (1978), Washington, D.C. (1981), Oregon (1990), California (1993), Washington (1996), and Colorado (1992 and 1998).

71. Another three governors rate a support level of "yes, qualified" (Moffit et al. 2001: table 3). Headline is in Rothstein 2001.

72. Schemo 2001. Similarly, "Baltimore school officials said yesterday they will offer 194 places this year for 30,000 students who are in schools designated as low-performing and are eligible to transfer to a better school." Hundreds of students in Camden, New Jersey, were also eligible to move in the summer of 2002, but no public school or charter school reported space for any of them (Bowie 2002; Newman 2002; see also Robelen 2002).

73. The letter is by Gould 2000. The original proponents of vouchers in Milwaukee complained of "yuppy resistance"; the associate director of President George Bush's Office on Competitiveness agreed that Republican leaders liked choice, but that rank-and-file party loyalists who have moved to the suburbs or small urban enclaves did not (Cookson 1994: 68). In California's 1993 voucher vote, residents of precincts with high-quality public schools (as measured by housing price premiums) were especially likely to oppose the proposition (Brunner et al. 2001). Bush is quoted in Wildman 2001: 15.

74. *Simmons-Harris et al . . .* 1999: 728–729. To his dismay a Republican mayor in New Jersey ran into the same political calculation: "'[Republican Governor Christie] Whitman didn't push as hard as I thought [after she proposed a voucher plan to the state legislature]. She feels complacency on this issue'" (Winerip 1998). See, most fully, Ryan and Heise 2002.

75. Moe 2001: 87.

Notes to Chapter 6

1. Rojas 2000: 29; *Plyler v. Doe* 1982; Edelman 2002: 149.

2. On bilingual education see Pyle 1996; Horvitz 2001. On children with disabilities see Lanigan et al. 2001: 220–25; Gorman 2001: 235–40. First quotation on ability grouping is from a meeting of the Montclair (New Jersey) board of education, Apr. 27, 1993; second is from Special Board Conference meeting, Montclair, May 3, 1993 (Shore 1998: 53, 57).

3. Students in southern and border states were, of course, assigned to schools depending on who they were until the federal government intervened to abolish

segregated school systems. But the government intervened on behalf of neighborhood schools, or more generally on behalf of mixing children in a single school and
classroom regardless of differences in race.

4. Lieberman 2001: 41; Fuchs and Fuchs 1998: 313.

5. Office of Special Education Programs (OSEP) 2001: II 21–29; U. S. Commission on Civil Rights 1997: ch. 3; NCES *Digest of Ed. Statistics 2001:* table 52.

Among five nations that identify students as "learning disabled," the United
States came in second, after Finland, in the proportion of students so identified.
(The other nations, all with barely a quarter as many students identified, were Ire-
land, the Netherlands, and Flemish Belgium). A higher proportion of American
students than in any of 18 other nations with comparable data received "additional
resources to access the curriculum" (OECD 2000: 58, 68–69; 75–76).

6. Estimates rise as high as $60 billion, but no one can determine the costs
more closely. By some measures the costs of special education have doubled during the 1990s.

7. Sack 2000: 1.

8. Crucial early court decisions were *Pennsylvania Association for Retarded Chil-
dren . . .* 1972 and *Mills v. Board . . .* 1972. Crucial laws were the Education of the
Handicapped Act (1970), Section 504 of the Rehabilitation Act in 1973, the Amer-
icans with Disabilities Act in 1990, and the Education for All Handicapped
Children Act (PL 94-142) in 1975. The latter was amended in 1990, becoming the
Individuals with Disabilities Education Act (IDEA), and again in 1997. On inter-
actions among advocates, courts, and legislatures see Melnick 1994: Part III; and
U.S. Commission on Civil Rights 1997: ch. 2.

9. OSEP 2001: A-80, 81; NCES *Digest of Ed. Statistics 2001:* table 53.

10. Staples 1997: 65.

11. Osborne 2000: 56, 59.

12. First and last quotations are in Dolnick 1993: 38, 46; second is in Natl.
Assn. of the Deaf 1994.

13. Quotation is in Horn and Tynan 2001: 31; on underachieving children,
see Kelman and Lester 1997; Sleeter 1986. Parrish 1995a, 1995b introduce the ar-
cane issues in special education finance.

In a recent survey of parents of children in special education programs, almost
three times as many (29 percent) thought schools were too slow to identify children who need extra services as thought schools were too quick to do so (11 percent). A third agreed that "some parents push their children into special education
just to get extra help and resources" even if the placement is not warranted, and
another 13 percent claimed not to know (Public Agenda 2002b).

It can be very difficult for students to return to mainstream classes from special education placements. For an illustration, see Fine 2002.

14. Van Dyke et al. 1995: 476.

15. Ibid., quotations on p. 477. Fuchs and Fuchs 1994 provide an insightful,
although disapproving, analysis of the movement for full inclusion.

16. Brantlinger 1997: table 2; Van Dyke et al. 1995: 475.

17. Quotation from McDonnell et al. 1997: 55. Data are from NCES *Digest
of Ed. Statistics 2001:* table 55; and *Ed. Week* 1998: 64–65.

18. *Ed. Week* 1998: 64. Across the nation just over 12 percent of the children
in the 100 largest school districts had IEPs in 1999. Fewer than 8 percent did in

Detroit, but more than 18 percent did in Pinellas County, Florida, and 20.3 percent in Albuquerque (NCES 2001b: table 3).

19. OSEP 1996: ch. 4.

20. In 1999–2000, African Americans were 20 percent of all students, but 34 percent of those in programs for the retarded, 27 percent of those in programs for people with serious emotional disturbance or behavioral disorders, and 18 percent of students with specific learning disabilities. Fewer white students than one would expect proportionally were in programs for the retarded or emotionally disturbed (OSEP 2001: II 26-28; see also Civil Rights Project 2001).

21. Ladner and Hammons 2001.

22. OSEP 1997: I 19-21, I 41-48; U.S. Commission on Civil Rights 1997: 55-57; Hehir and Gamm 1999: 229-30; Donovan and Cross 2002.

23. Blackorby and Wagner 1996; McDonnell et al. 1997: 97, 134.

24. First study is Hanushek et al. 2003b. For older findings that separate classes produce better outcomes or mixed results see Kavale 1990; and Hocutt 1996 (and citations therein). Second study is in Cullen 1996; and Cullen and Figlio 1998: 20. Older findings that mainstreaming generally produces better results include Madden and Slavin 1983; Baker et al. 1994; Reynolds and Wolfe 1999.

25. U.S. Congress 1997: 11.

26. *Oberti v. Board . . . 1993*; and *Sacramento . . . v. Holland . . . 1994.*

27. Lipsky and Gartner 1997: 72; The Arc 1997; www.thearc.org/posits/ed.html. Other groups supporting full inclusion are the Assn. for Persons with Severe Handicaps, and the National Family Assn. for the Deaf-Blind.

28. Learning Disabilities Assn. of America. 1993. This view is shared by groups such as Children and Adults with Attention Deficit Disorders and the Natl. Assn. of the Deaf. Lipsky and Gartner 1997, ch. 13, summarizes various groups' positions on inclusion; see also Fuchs and Fuchs 1998. Over twice as many parents of students in special education agree that mainstreaming helps special-needs students as say that it harms them (Public Agenda 2002b).

29. Natl. Assn. of Elementary School Principals 1995; quotation is from the spokesperson. AFT statement is quoted in Murphy 1994: 56-57; its policy statement on full inclusion lists its problems from the perspectives of both students and teachers (AFT 1994). The NEA and the National School Boards Assn. also have formal policy statements opposing full inclusion.

30. Stainback and Stainback 1992: 34; Murphy 1994: 56.

31. On the right level of spending, see *Los Angeles Times* Poll 1995; Phi Delta Kappa 1996; NPR et al. 1999; Horace Mann Education Corporation 1999. For estimate of costs and priorities, see Phi Delta Kappa 1996.

32. Duff 2001: 151; Pallmaffy 2001: 1; Hotakainen et al. 1994.

33. On the physically handicapped, see Phi Delta Kappa 1992, 1995. On others, see Phi Delta Kappa 1992, 1995, 1998; NPR et al. 1999; *Los Angeles Times* 1998 (California Adults and Parents).

34. Teachers are in *Los Angeles Times* 1998 (California Teacher Union Members); Phi Delta Kappa 1998 teachers survey. Students are in Ferguson 1997.

35. The figures are 67 percent and 56 percent, respectively (CBS News 1999). The same pattern holds for children with learning disabilities (Phi Delta Kappa 1995).

36. CBS News 1999; quotation in Hotakainen et al. 1994.

37. A recent example of anxieties about discipline are in Phi Delta Kappa 1999; the results are the same in virtually every survey.

38. Fine 2001; Blum 2000; Greenberger 2001b: 1. In the survey of parents of children in special education, more chose "better programs and policies" than chose "more funding" when asked how special education could best be improved (Public Agenda 2002b).

39. There are no more precise figures. The Natl. Clearinghouse for English Language Acquisition (NCELA) 2002 states that 4.4 million students have limited proficiency in English; a decade earlier, when immigration levels were much lower, the Council of Chief State School Officers used the figure of 5.5 million (1990). NCELA also provides data on languages of LEP students and the growth in their number since the 1980s.

40. Ruiz-de-Velasco and Fix 2000: 11–12.

41. About a quarter of the students in New Mexico also are limited in English proficiency (NCELA 2002). On district variation see NCES 2001b: table 15. On California see Tafoya 2002.

42. The Dept. of Education estimates that 184,000 of the 2.9 million children in bilingual or ESL programs also have disabilities. Zehr 2001a analyzes one of the few programs designed to help these children.

43. In fact economists Mark Lopez and Marie Mora (1998) find that "it is socio-economic factors, and not necessarily participation in the [bilingual education] program, that explains a large portion of the poor performance of bilingual education students."

44. On poverty and Title I, see Planning and Evaluation Service 1993: 326–348; Planning and Evaluation Service and Office of Bilingual Education and Minority Language Affairs (OBEMLA) 1995. On federal funds, see GAO 1999: 2.

45. Van Hook 2002: quotations on p. 185, emphases in original.

46. M. Lopez 1999: note 3.

47. Schildkraut 2000: 10. For the early history, see Moran 1988; Renyi 1993; Rothstein 1998b; and citations in August and Hakuta 1997: 367. On immigrants and native language training, see Zimmerman 2002.

48. *Lau v. Nichols* 1974.

49. Crawford 1999: 62–100; August and Hakuta 1997: app. A; count of laws is updated from map in *Education Week*, April 1, 1998, p. 4.

50. Ross 1998: 133–134.

51. Report is GAO 1994b; quotation is from Porter 1996: 261. On movement into regular classes, see American Institutes for Research 1977–78; Ross 1998: 134. In the first results in California of a new test on English proficiency, 24 percent of students in bilingual classes scored in one of the two "advanced" categories, but only 9 percent are moved into mainstream classes each year. Critics argued that this gap showed that bilingual teachers seek to retain students; supporters responded that the test results were misleading and superficial (Yi and Ragland 2002).

52. 1992 data are in Fleischman and Hopstock 1993; current data in NCELA 2002. On bilingualism and teachers, see NCES, *Condition of Ed. 1997*: suppl. table 45-2; GAO 1999: 3–8; Bradley 1999.

53. August and Hakuta 1997: 22; Rivera-Batiz 1996: 31–32; NCES *Condition of Ed. 1997*: suppl. tables 4-1, 4-2; GAO 1994a.

54. OBEMLA 1998: 1; see also Cummins 1986; August and Hakuta 1997: chs.

2 and 3. On quick transitions see Porter 2000; Rossell and Baker 1996; Chavez and Amselle 1997. OBEMLA is now the Office of English Language Acquisition (OELA). Its position on bilingual education is less expansive.

55. Unz is in Wildermuth 1998; for the Academy see August and Hakuta 1997: 138 (internal citation not included), 171, 373. On research design see also Crawford 1999: ch. 5; Stewart 1993: 150–154; on comparisons among programs, see also El Paso (Texas) Independent School District 1989; Wrobel and O'Brien 1998.

56. First study is Greene 1998, quotation on p. 2; Greene 1997: 11; personal correspondence from Jay Greene, February 18, 2000, on file with authors. Second is M. Lopez 1999, quotations on pp. 3–4. Lopez and Mora 1998 provide the results for earnings; quotation from abstract.

57. Noonan 2000; Steinberg 2000; Zehr 2001b.

58. Research is in Howard 2001; Genesee and Gandera 1999. Quotation is in Hipp 2001. See Cooper 2000 for endorsement.

59. August and Hakuta 1997: ch. 7; see also Genesee 1999.

60. Rodriguez 1998: 16; Greenberger 2001a.

61. Sanko 2001; Acuna 1998; Schulte and Keating 2001a.

62. "Trinkets" is from Traub 1999 (paraphrasing a teacher; he disagrees with this argument); state librarian is De Cos 1999: 13–14. Others are more blunt; one citizen assured a journalist that "this is very much about money" (Billingsley 1996).

63. Billingsley 1996; Unz 1999: 24–25; Pardington 2002.

64. Survey data are in Decker 1998a; see also Decker 1998b. Quotations from Wisckol 1999. Parents' and students' responses are in *Los Angeles Times* 1998 (California Adults and Parents, California Children).

65. "Survey Results . . ." 2001; Unz quoted in O'Brien 1998: 10. A few years earlier, he had strongly opposed California's Proposition 187.

66. On Yarborough and Johnson, see Stein 1986: 31–32. On Nixon, see Davies 2002; "Dole Wants . . ." 1995; Riley 2000. On Bush, see O'Sullivan 2000; Anderson 2001.

67. Rodriguez 1998: 18.

68. On Chicago, see Rossi 1998. While a mayoral candidate, Michael Bloomberg endorsed New York's policy on the grounds that "speaking multiple languages is great and we should not forget our roots. But without a comprehension of English, it will be difficult to share in the American dream" (Soifer 2002).

69. *Los Angeles Times* 1998: 46. This survey offers a small but telling illustration of how difficult it is to know what evidence to trust, and perhaps of the temptation to shift pieces of evidence to fit one's preferred position. The well-respected and mildly conservative journal, the *Public Perspective* ("A Major *Los Angeles Times* Poll . . ." 1998), reported the survey's results but with a curious twist: it reported the level of Californians' support for bilingual education on the question that *did not* include an explanation, and support for the English immersion alternative on the question that *did* include an explanation. Since respondents endorsed both programs more after they had received an explanation than before, the *Public Perspective* inadvertently (??) exaggerated the gap between support for more and less separation.

70. Davis and Smith 1999. Other surveys find similar support for short-term bilingual classes or even English-only classes (Phi Delta Kappa 1993; *Time/CNN*/Yankelovich Partners 1993a, 1995; Gallup/CNN/*USA Today* 1998).

71. Public Agenda 1998a: 23–27; Metropolitan Life Survey 1993: 9.

72. "State's Rights . . .", 2001.

73. Jesness 1998.

74. Ruiz-de-Velasco and Fix 2000: 14–15.

75. We are endorsing what one political philosopher calls "language rationalization" because it "can enhance social mobility, facilitate democratic deliberation, encourage the formation of a common political identity, and increase the efficiency of public institutions." He remains agnostic about whether language rationalization should outweigh official multilingualism or language maintenance; we consider the latter in the next chapter (Patten 2001: quotation on p. 701).

76. Viadero 1999b, quoting Kenji Hakuta; see also M. Lopez 1999: 24.

77. See Oakes et al. 1992: 577–82 on the history of tracking. Estimates are in NCES 1994: tables 5, 6; Weiss et al. 1994; Rees et al. 1996: 84.

78. On reasons for placement, see NCES 1994: table 13; 2000b: 29–38; McGrath and Kuriloff 1999; Useem 1992. On fluidity see Lucas 1999: ch. 2; Loveless 1999.

79. Mirel 1999.

80. Scott and Bernhardt 2000.

81. NCES 2000c. On distribution into tracks, see Rees et al. 1996: 84; NCES *Digest of Ed. Statistics 1996*: table 132; 1997b: table 135.

82. On distribution by race, see Gamoran and Mare 1989: table 1; Oakes et al. 1992: 576 (for reviews of older studies); Jones et al. 1995: table 2; Argys et al. 1996: tables 1A, 1B; Education Trust 1998a: 11–13; NCES *Digest of Ed. Statistics 1997*: table 135. For disagreement about racial bias, see Pallas et al. 1994. Quotation is in Dickens 1996: 473; see also *Harvard Law Review* 1989; Mickelson and Heath 2001; Losen 1999; Weiner 2001.

83. First quotation from Miller 1995: 237–240. Reported studies are in Haller 1985; and Gamoran and Mare 1989; second quotation is from Ferguson 1998: 329; see also 336. Ferguson is himself African American. See also Lucas and Gamoran 1993; Jones et al. 1995.

84. Data on college prep are in NCES *Digest of Ed. Statistics 1997*: table 135. On class bias in placement, see Jones et al. 1995; Dauber et al. 1996; Lucas 1999: chs. 3, 6.

85. The problem is that too few classrooms abjure ability grouping for there to be good control or comparison groups. Standard methods for trying to overcome this problem are weak because children vary so much across the groups in ways that line up with group placement that one cannot tell why those in one group are doing better or worse than those in another. As Robert Slavin (1990a: 505) puts it, "When comparing high- to low-ability groups, pretest or covariate differences of one or two standard deviations are typical. . . . Are the San Francisco Forty-Niners better than the Palo Alto High School football team, controlling for height, weight, speed, and age? Such questions fall into the realm of the unknowable." Ronald Ferguson (1998: 335) similarly concludes that "without studies that use control or comparison groups, one simply cannot know how much reading group placement affects student achievement."

86. Slavin 1990b; Epstein and MacIver 1992; Gamoran 1992: 812.

87. On gifted students, see Kulik 1992; Figlio and Page 2002. On enriched classes and math classes, see Mosteller et al. 1996: 9–17; Argys et al. 1996; Ferguson 1998: 330–40; see also Gamoran and Mare 1989; Lucas 1999: 123–27.

88. Donovan and Cross 2002: ES-4 (see also Baker 2001); Wright et al. 1997.

89. Exchange (between Maureen Hallinan and Jeannie Oakes) 1994 provides an illuminating discussion of this dilemma.

90. Quotation is from Ferguson 1998: 330–35; Epstein and MacIver 1992; see also Lou et al. 1996. On students in low tracks, see Camarena 1990; Gamoran 1993a; Accelerated Schools Project 2000. Epple et al. 2002; and Figlio and Page 2002 argue that tracking indirectly benefits all students because it attracts high-income students to a school.

91. Gamoran 1993b: quotation on p. 44; Ferguson 1998: 338; see also Oakes 1985: esp. p. 129; Dreeben and Gamoran 1986; Gamoran 1986; Oakes et al. 1992: 587.

92. On teaching see Ingersoll 1999; on low achievers, see Good 1987; Weiss 1997: 4.

93. NCES 1995a: tables A2.2b, A2.2c; Camara and Schmidt 1999: 6–7. On advanced courses see NCES 1999.

94. On course offerings, see Monk and Rice 1997; Jones et al. 1995; Spade et al. 1997; Raudenbush et al. 1998. On poor schools, see Oakes et al. 1992: 589; NCES 1995a: table A2.2b. On less-educated parents, see NCES 2000b: 21.

95. Gerwin 2001; Moses and Cobb 2001: 5. On the similar project of "algebra for all," see Ham and Walker 1999; Gamoran and Hannigan 2000.

96. http://apcentral.collegeboard.com/article/0,1281,150-156-0-2055,00.html. Data are not available by economic class status. Perhaps twice as many students take AP courses as take the tests at their end. Cone 1992 analyzes benefits and difficulties of opening up AP courses to new students.

97. Bathen 1999; Sahagun and Weiss 1999; Viadero 2001a. In response to the lawsuit, in 2000 the California legislature authorized grants so that poor schools can develop AP courses, teachers can be appropriately trained, and poor students are encouraged to take them. As of the summer of 2002, the lawsuit was on hold until the new program could be implemented and its results known (www.leginfo.ca.gov; www.aclu-sc.org/litigation/docket.html).

98. Gallup Organization 1954; Harris 1965; *Newsweek* 1981; *USA Today* 1985; Public Agenda 1994; Phi Delta Kappa 1997. Beliefs about children's giftedness are in Shell Oil Company 1998; Public Agenda 1998b.

99. NPR et al. 1999; see also Phi Delta Kappa 1982, 1985, 1988; *U.S. News & World Report* 1996. Focus groups are in Public Agenda 1995b: 7, 8.

100. On educators see Public Agenda 1997: tables 3, 7. List is from Jeannie Oakes's Foreword in Wheelock 1992: 2; on states see Loveless 1999.

101. NEA 1999: resolutions B-14 and B-20; Shanker 1994; Natl. Council for the Social Studies 1992; Natl. Research Council 1996: 222.

102. Loveless 1999: 110–11, 137; see also White et al. 1996.

103. Shore 1998.

104. Jencks and Phillips 1998: 52.

Notes for Chapter 7

1. Ravitch 1997; Kiss 1999: 198; Bruni 1998; "Arkansas . . ." 2001.

2. First quotation in Clabaugh 1993: 117. The Commission was appointed by the American Assn. of Colleges for Teacher Education (quoted in McCormick 1984: 94).

3. Manzo 1997; Haberman and Post 1998: 97; see also Banks 1995; 1999. Reich 2002 analyzes the links between liberalism and multiculturalism.

4. The more generic the question's focus on "teaching respect for people of different racial and ethnic groups," the higher the rate of support, sometimes reaching 90 percent or more. See Phi Delta Kappa 1993; Public Agenda 1994; National Conference 1994; CBS News/*New York Times* 1993; Survey Research Center 1993; Bureau of Sociological Research/Dept. of Sociology 1994.

On diverse cultural traditions, see Phi Delta Kappa 1994. Racial differences on this item were small; better-educated and young adults were more sympathetic to "diverse traditions" than their opposites.

5. On traditional subjects see *Time*/CNN/Yankelovich Partners 1994. On whether schools do enough, see Davis and Smith 1999; Phi Delta Kappa 1992; Metropolitan Life Survey 1996: 7–13. In general young adults (of all races) held views closer to the black perspective than did their elders.

6. Some, however, continue to oppose it. Kenneth Weinig, founding headmaster of the Independence School in Delaware, identifies multiculturalism as the first of "the 10 worst educational disasters of the 20th century;" in his view, its "result . . . will be a nation of ethnic divisions, closer to a Bosnia" than to a mosaic or melting pot (Weinig 2000).

7. These are the researchers', not respondents', phrases (Stevenson and Gonzalez 1992; see also Merelman 1995; Bennett 2001).

8. Survey data are in Public Agenda 1998a: table 5; see also table 6. Commonality and identity politics are defined in Gitlin 1993: 172, 174; see Olneck 1993 for a more sympathetic analysis of identity politics in multicultural education.

9. Quotations in Bennett 2001: 172, 173; Ravitch 2001: 28.

10. Hilliard 1992: 370–71; Delpit 1992: 248. Irvine and York (1995: 489) similarly argue that "the cultures of students of color or their 'way of life' are often incongruous with expected middle-class cultural values, beliefs, and norms of schools. These cultural differences often result in cultural discontinuity . . . and has [*sic*] led researchers to conclude that cultural differences . . . are major contributors to the school failure of students of color."

11. Delpit 1992: 247; Foster 1995: 575.

12. Asante 1991: 171 (see also Lee 1995: 21); Johnson 1990.

13. Harding 1970: 279; Asante 1991: 171.

14. "Emancipatory narratives" comes from Swartz 1992: 342; quotation is from Swartz 1993: 495. See Sleeter and Grant 1987 for a similar continuum. Sleeter 1994 ties their typology directly to the ideology of the American dream.

15. Swartz 1993; Banks 1997; Watkins 1994.

16. Bigelow 1998b: 47; Bigelow 1998a: 62; see also McLaren 1997. Survey data are in Public Agenda 1998a: tables 5, 6.

17. In a survey of 900 professors of education, over a third agreed that "designing a core body of knowledge amounts to unfairly imposing one group's cultural values on others." "I find . . . myself to be keyed into a particular culture, a particular ethnicity," reported one. "And I don't want to impose mine on people whose culture is different." Two-fifths agreed that public schools' primary goal for immigrants should be to help "maintain their own language and culture, even if it takes them longer to absorb America's language and culture" (Public Agenda 1997: 22–23).

18. Raz 1994: 77. Even Elizabeth Kiss modifies the comment quoted at the beginning of this chapter—that "a society is not truly democratic" if some members must "deny or hide a deeply felt identity"—with the caveat "unless expression of that identity is itself incompatible with democratic equality."

19. Macedo 1997: 269–70; Olneck 1993: 238–39. Alternative terms are "bicultural-bilingual" or "developmental bilingual."

20. Del Valle 1998: 193; Glazer 1998.

21. Trueba 1988; UC Linguistic Minority Research Institute 1997: sec. VII; Guthrie 1997.

22. Pewewardy 1997: 2; Delgado-Gaitan 1994: 56, 82.

23. Hernandez-Chavez 1977. The canonical proponent of this view is Randolph Bourne: "Foreign cultures have not been melted down or run together, made into some homogeneous Americanism, but have remained distinct but cooperating to the greater glory and benefit, not only of themselves but of all the native 'Americanism' around them. What we emphatically do not want is that these distinctive qualities should be washed out into a tasteless, colorless fluid of uniformity. . . . These nuclei of nationalistic culture . . . make for the intelligence and social values which mean an enhancement of life. And just because the foreign-born retains this expressiveness is he likely to be a better citizen of the American community" (Bourne 1977 [c. 1918]: 253–55).

Within the huge literature on this topic, see particularly Young 1990; Galston 2002; and Kymlicka 1996. Moran 1987 argues that debates over bilingual education and English-only movements are really status conflicts between old and new Americans.

24. Levinson 1999a: 54; Schmidt 1989–90: 236; see also Flores Macias 1979; Levinson 1999b, esp. p. 94.

25. Taylor and Gutmann 1994: 25; Attinasi 1997: 281. See also Zentella 1997; Galindo 1997; Darder 1997; Ruiz 1997: 319; Schmidt 2000.

26. A final illustration: "To construct a democratic society free from vestiges of oppression, a bilingual education program . . . must be rooted in the cultural capital of subordinate groups and . . . their own language" (Macedo 2000: 210).

27. Davis and Smith 1999; Public Agenda Online 2002; *Time*/CNN/ Yankelovich Partners 1995; *Wash. Post* et al. 1999. On Texas, see Brooks 1998. Small sample sizes for non-Anglo groups suggest caution in interpreting many of these results; however, similar patterns appear in *Time*/CNN/Yankelovich Partners 1993a; and Roper Organization 1982. That, along with non-survey-based political activities and contexts, suggests that these results can be trusted.

28. Many Latinos also hold broader views compatible with, though not directly focused on, cultural maintenance programs. Almost a third think that urban minority schools should focus literature and history courses on minority writers and heroes; even more agree that such courses will motivate students to learn and enhance their self-esteem. Hispanics respond more positively to the image of "multicultural" than do blacks or whites and are more likely to describe themselves as group oriented rather than individualistic. On courses see Public Agenda 1998a: 29–30; other results in the text and this note are in Post-Modernity Project 1996.

29. *Wash. Post* et al. 1999. Other non-Anglo groups might also hold mixed views when given the same choices; we know of no evidence on this point.

30. Patten 2001: 701.

31. Ibid., p. 701.

32. Marable (1995: 111) himself endorses "radical democratic multicultural-ism" rather than Afrocentrism. Michael Harris (1992: 306) goes a step farther: "It is not psychologically healthy for Blacks to position themselves within the context of the postcolonial and postslavery systems of Western societies when interpreting their reality, because these systems continue to contain interpretations and values that are hostile and often destructive to people of African descent."

33. Gill 1991: 572; Swartz 1992: 341. Sefa Dei 1994 interprets African values and their relationship to American Afrocentrism.

34. Hilliard et al. 1990: xxi; Nobles 1990: 20–21; Edelin 1990: 43 (emphasis in original); Banks 1992: 263. See also Asante 1999; and citations in Hilliard et al. 1990, and Binder 1999.

35. Ravitch 2001: 29.

36. Binder 2000.

37. On courses see Public Agenda 1998a: 29–30. Immigrant and Hispanic parents generally resemble black parents on these issues, whereas Anglo parents do not. On identity and nationalism, see Jackson and Gurin 1987; Tate 1996; Dawson 2001: ch. 3; Hochschild 2003.

38. On distinct cultures see Davis and Smith 1999: 959 (see also p. 519). About the same proportion of whites and even more Hispanics concur. On separate schools see Joint Center for Political and Economic Studies 1992; Dawson 2001: 331; *Los Angeles Times* Poll 1991.

Some whites may endorse separate schools as a route back to segregation. Others may do so for more complicated reasons: as the (white) philosopher of education Walter Feinberg put it, "There are incidents or occasions where these schools are justified, where corrective measures are necessary. In general, they ought not to be the rule. But when we are pushed toward that position, it says something terribly bad about our society" (Chira 1993).

39. "Proposal for . . ." 1991; Binder 1999: 233.

40. Brown 2000 seeks to "bridge the distance between the liberal critique and the Afrocentric response."

41. Weyrich 1999. The Free Congress Foundation is a self-described politically and culturally conservative think tank whose "main focus is on the Culture War" (www.freecongress.org/fcf/).

42. Withdrawal is Weyrich's preferred solution: "What I mean by separation is, for example, what the homeschoolers have done. Faced with public school systems that no longer educate but instead 'condition' students with the attitudes demanded by Political Correctness, they have seceded" (Weyrich 1999). See also Detwiler 2000; Carter 1987.

43. Mashberg and Yablonski 1999 summarize the constitutional cases.

44. Gallup Organization 1982, 1991, 2001b; Bishop 1998; Fox News 1999; "Believer Nation . . ." 2000: 33; People for the American Way Foundation 2000: 35–44.

45. "Opinions of Candidates . . ." 1999. Gore's aide soon amended his statement to say that the vice president endorsed teaching creationism in religion, not science, courses.

46. Williamsburg Charter Foundation 1987; *Time*/CNN/Yankelovich Clancy

Shulman 1991; *Time*/CNN/Yankelovich Partners 1993b; Public Agenda 1994; Gallup Organization 1996; Servin-Gonzalez and Torres-Reyna 1999: 621; Moore 1999; NBC News/*Wall Street Journal* 1999; Gallup/CNN/*USA Today* 1999; CNN/*USA Today* 1999; People for the American Way Foundation 2000. On alternative textbooks see Losh-Hesselbart 1999: 9.

47. Johnson is in Binder 2001. The judge's statement is in a 1982 preliminary injunction against the school curriculum of Mobile County, Alabama; it is quoted in *Smith v. Board . . .* 1987, fn. 1. Institute for Creation Research is quoted in People for the American Way Foundation 1999: 15.

48. Clines 1999; Cumming 2001. Tim LaHaye, the fundamentalist analyst and author, argues that secular humanism has led to "the dreadful increase in venereal disease in our country, the rise of sexual perversion, the aborting of millions of babies, the escalating crime rate, and practically every social evil facing our society today" (Bates 1994: 53).

49. Herbert Anderson, in "Public Pulse" 2000.

50. The 1968 decision was *Epperson et al. v. Arkansas*, the 1987 decision was *Edwards v. Aguillard*.

51. McMurtrie 2001 summarizes creation science; Gieryn et al. 1985 give the perspective of sociologists of science; Numbers 1992 provides its history; Pennock 2001 engages debates over creationism. On implications for schooling, see Gibeaut 1999; Press and Matalin 1999.

52. The most recent Supreme Court decision was *Tangipahoa Parish . . .* 2000. In Nov. 2001 the Alabama state board of education voted unanimously for new phrasing that is not quite as strong. The evaluation and quotation from Alabama are in Lerner 2000. On other states see Binder 2001; Hoff 2000; Deckman 1999.

53. Belluck 2000: 1; Raymo 1999.

54. The issue does not concern only biology. "Scientific disciplines with a historical component such as astronomy, geology, biology, and anthropology cannot be taught with integrity if evolution is not emphasized" (Natl. Science Teachers Assn. 1997: 3).

55. Bates 1994: 72, 80, 204–5.

56. *Mozert v. Hawkins . . .* 1986, 1987. The two internal quotations are from a cited Supreme Court decision. Macedo 1995 develops the distinction between civil and religious tolerance.

57. Judge Cornelia Kennedy, concurring in *Mozert v. Hawkins . . .* 1987. See Stolzenberg 1993 for disagreement with this view. Dent 1988; Levinson 1993; and Tomasi 2002 also argue for greater accommodation of "opting-out" parents.

58. Rizk 1995; Eisgruber 1996.

59. Aleinikoff 1998.

Notes for Chapter 8

1. Clinton 1995; Bush 2001; Brinkley 2000: 30; Walzer 1995: 187–88.

2. Treas 1995; Frey and DeVol 2000; Hodgkinson 2000.

3. These figures assume that the racial and ethnic categories that we now use will remain meaningful over the next century. That is unlikely, especially if intermarriage continues to grow at the same rate that it has over the past few decades.

Nationally at least 8 percent of children have parents of two races or ethnicities (www.census.gov/population/socdemo/race/interractab4.txt, and . . . interactab5.txt). Almost twice that proportion of recent births in California are multiracial or multiethnic ("Integration, Census" 2000).

4. On California, see E. Lopez 1999: 7–10; Reyes 2001: 5–13. On other states and cities, see Olson 2000a: 35; Vernez and Krop 1999: table 1; Lambert 2000. Los Angeles and Miami have even higher proportions of immigrants of the first or second generation than New York. Hodgkinson 2000 surveys the implications of these demographic changes for schools.

5. By one prediction the dependency ratio in the United States will increase from about 63:100 in 1992 to about 83:100 in 2030 (Bureau of the Census 2000; see also Treas 1995). By another calculation the ratio of working age adults to the total population will rise slightly until 2010 (to 103.1 of the 1997 ratio of 100), then decline steeply through 2040 (to 95.2 of the 1997 ratio of 100) (Toder and Solanki 1999: 5–10).

6. Frey 2000: 23; Skertic 2001.

7. Toder and Solanki 1999: 3. In California the older the survey respondents, the more they report being "extremely concerned" about health-care costs, and the less they are "extremely concerned" about public schools or higher education (Field Institute 2002a).

8. Poterba 1997: 60–61. See chapter 3 on weak support among elderly Anglos for increases in school funding; older African Americans and Latinos continue to support high levels of funding for schools (Tedin et al. 2001).

9. Antitax groups in southern California, for example, have argued against bond issues to build new schools by asserting that if immigration were curtailed, these new public expenditures would be unnecessary (Folmar 1999).

10. On interracial coalitions see Hochschild and Rogers 2000; Wilson 1999; Warren 2001.

11. The initial paragraph held that "the People of California . . . have suffered and are suffering economic hardship caused by the presence of illegal aliens in this state. That they have suffered and are suffering personal injury and damage caused by the criminal conduct of illegal aliens in this state. That they have a right to the protection of their government from any person or persons entering this country unlawfully. Therefore, the People of California declare their intention to . . . prevent illegal aliens in the United States from receiving benefits or public services in the State of California" (Inniss 1996: 617).

12. Quotation in Wisckol 1999. The Mexican ambassador to the United States complained that "there is an equation now in California that goes: Illegal immigrants equal to Mexicans, equal to criminals, equal to someone who wants social services" (Rosenblum 1999: 371). Referendum results are in "Heading North" 1994; Campbell and Wong 1998.

13. Ness and Nakao 1996; "Elections '96 . . ." 1996; see also Cain et al. 2000.

14. *Los Angeles Times* Poll 1993a, 1994.

15. *Los Angeles Times* Poll 1999; Public Policy Institute of California 1998: 23–24; 1999: 24.

16. Public Policy Institute of California 2001: 19.

17. *Los Angeles Times* Poll 1999. Both proportions have declined since 1993, substantially for Anglos (*Los Angeles Times* Poll 1993b). In 1999 about 40 percent

of Latinos concurred that Los Angeles had too many immigrants; in 1993 almost two-thirds did.

18. For example, even more Californians in all three racial or ethnic groups had agreed two years earlier, in 1997, that immigrant children have a harmful effect on the schools of the state (*Los Angeles Times* Poll 1997). On immigrants' impact see *Los Angeles Times* Poll 1999.

19. Tobar 1998.

20. Field Institute 2002b: 1. Close to a majority of registered Latinos describe themselves as "middle of the road," and the rest are roughly split between conservatives and liberals (Field Institute 2000: 1, 5). They are thus available to be mobilized by either major political party—a classic case for the operation of pluralist electoral politics (Dahl 1961).

21. Roughly eight million of the 31 million Hispanics in the United States are registered to vote. Perhaps another seven million are eligible to vote, and more will become so as Latinos become naturalized citizens. (That is happening slowly, but perhaps at an increasing rate [Ramakrishnan 2002]). As the president of the Assn. of Hispanic Advertising Agencies put it, "From local to national campaigns, candidates must recognize Latinos, understand our needs and, more importantly, to include us. We are, after all, the mainstream of America" ("Latino Advertisers . . ." 1999).

22. "As GOP Reaches Out . . ." 2000. Even the president of Orange County's Republican club, who had supported Proposition 187, opposed its proposed successor on the grounds that "a wedge issue like this drives people apart. . . . We need to work to bring people together" (Wisckol 1999).

23. "Editorial: Bush on Education" 1999. Vice President Gore supported bilingual education more strongly and urged more funding, but he focused more on improving teachers' training to help children learn English quickly than on children's right to bilingualism or cultural maintenance. Pachon is in Greenhouse 2000.

24. Public Policy Institute of California 1999, 2001: 9, 10. On immigrants' attachment to schooling see Garcia Castro 1982; Pessar 1987.

25. Iowans will, nevertheless, remain individualists: they define a successful multicultural education, as a local superintendent puts it, as one in which students "look at the individual and not necessarily the ethnicity." All quotations from Reid 2000.

26. McDonnell et al. 2000: 8.

27. Public Policy Institute of California 1999: 10–12; *Los Angeles Times* Poll 2000.

28. Gamoran 2001 similarly forecasts continued class inequalities but diminishing racial inequalities in schooling.

29. Noguera and Akom 2000.

References

Abbott v. Burke II (1990). 119 NJ 287; 575 A.2d 359.

Abell Foundation (2001). *Teacher Certification Reconsidered.* Baltimore.

Abernathy, S. (1996). *Preliminary Capacity Study: Intra-district Vouchers and Sheff v. O'Neill.* Princeton U., Woodrow Wilson School of Public and Intl. Affairs.

—— (2001). *Exit, Voice, and Choice: Parents, Principals, and Market Reforms in Public Education.* Ph.D. dissertation, Princeton U., Dept. of Politics.

Abramson, A., et al. (1995). "The Changing Geography of Metropolitan Opportunity." *Housing Policy Debate* 6(1): 45–72.

Accelerated Schools Project (2000). "Research Background on Accelerated Schools." www.stanford.edu/group/ASP/research_base.html.

Acemoglu, D., and J.-S. Pischke (2001). "Changes in the Wage Structure, Family Income, and Children's Education." *European Economic Review* 45(4–6): 890–904.

Achieve (2001). "Tips for Policymakers." www.achieve.org/achieve.nsf/PolicyTips?OpenForm.

Ackerman, L. (2001). Letter to the Editor. *Los Angeles Times, Orange County Ed.,* Apr. 29: Metro B10.

Acuña, R. (1998). Letter to the Editor. *The Nation,* June 29: 2.

Adams, J. Jr. (1997). "School Finance Policy and Students' Opportunities to Learn: Kentucky's Experience." *The Future of Children: Financing Schools* 7(3): 79–95.

Advisory Commission on Intergovernmental Relations (1993). *Changing Attitudes Toward Government and Taxes 1993.* Wash., DC.

Advisory Council to the New York State Board of Regents Subcommittee on Low-Performing Schools (1994). *Perform or Perish.* NY State Education Dept.

Ahearn, J. (1995). "Grass-Roots Rethinking on School Integration Has Value." *Bergen Record,* Nov. 30: NO7.

Albert Shanker Institute (1999). *Standards-Based Education Reform: Teachers' and Principals' Perspectives.* Wash., DC.

Aleinikoff, T. A. (1998). "A Multicultural Nationalism?" *American Prospect* 9(36): 80–86.

Alexakis, G. (2001). "Test Prep." *Wash. Monthly,* Mar.: 29–36.

Alexander, K., et al. (2001). "Schools, Achievement, and Inequality." *Educational Evaluation and Policy Analysis* 23(2): 171–91.

Allen, K., and M. Kirby (2000). *Unfinished Business: Why Cities Matter to Welfare Reform*. Brookings Institution Press.

American Assn. of University Women (1998). "Survey of Candidates for Wake County Commissioner on Issues Affecting Education," www.rtpnet.org/~aauw/1998–1999/Survey/Intro98.html.

American Civil Liberties Union (2000). "In Groundbreaking Settlement, California Must Guarantee Equal Education for All." www.aclu.org/news/2000/n032100a.html.

American Council on Education (1999). *To Touch the Future: Transforming the Way Teachers Are Taught*. Wash., DC.

American Educational Research Assn. (2000). "Position Statement Concerning High Stakes Testing in Pre-K–12 Education." www.aera.net/about/policy/stakes.htm.

American Federation of Teachers (1994). "Resolution on Inclusion of Students with Disabilities." www.aft.org/about/resolutions/1994/inclusion.html.

—— (2000). *Building a Profession: Strengthening Teacher Preparation and Induction*. K–16 Teacher Education Task Force.

American Federation of Teachers and National Education Assn. (1998). *Public School Renovation, Construction and Modernization Survey*. Jan. 5–10. Wash., DC.

American Institutes for Research (1977–78). *Evaluation of the Impact of ESEA Title VII Spanish/English Bilingual Education Program*. Palo Alto, CA.

Amrein, A., and D. Berliner (2002). "High-Stakes Tests, Uncertainty, and Student Learning." *Education Policy Analysis Archives* 10(18). http://epaa.asu.edu/epaa/v10n18.

Anderson, G. (1999). "The Politics of Participatory Reforms in Education." *Theory into Practice* 38(4): 191–95.

Anderson, J. (1998). "Comprehensive School Reform Will Need Comprehensive Support." *Ed. Week*, June 24: 52, 38.

Anderson, N. (2001). "House Bill Would Downplay Bilingualism." *Los Angeles Times*, May 15: part A1, p. 18.

Angrist, J., and V. Lavy (1999). "Using Maimonides' Rule to Estimate the Effect of Class Size on Scholastic Achievement." *Quarterly Journal of Economics* 114(2): 533–75.

Anyon, J. (1997). *Ghetto Schooling*. Teachers College Press.

Applebome, P. (1995). "A Wave of Suits Seeks a Reversal of School Busing." *New York Times*, Sept. 26: A1, B6.

Archer, J. (1999). "Sanders 101." *Ed. Week*, May 5: 26–28.

—— (2000). "Ohio High Court Again Overturns Finance System." *Ed. Week*, May 17: 1, 25.

—— (2002). "Focusing In on Teachers." *Ed. Week*, April 3: 36–39.

Argys, L., et al. (1996). "Detracking America's Schools: Equity at Zero Cost?" *Journal of Policy Analysis and Management* 15(4): 623–45.

"Arkansas: House Measure Targets Evolution Theory" (2001). *Chicago Tribune*, Mar. 22: 16.

Armor, D. (1995). *Forced Justice: School Desegregation and the Law*. Oxford U. Press.

Arsen, D., et al. (1999). *School Choice Policies in Michigan*. Michigan State U., Education Policy Ctr.

———— (2001). "A Work in Progress." *Education Next*, Winter: 14–19.

"As GOP Reaches Out to Immigrants Some Find It a Stretch" (2000). *Associated Press*, June 26.

Asante, M. (1991). "The Afrocentric Idea in Education." *Journal of Negro Education* 60(2): 170–80.

———— (1999). *African American Culture*. Peoples Publishing Group.

Ashenfelter, O., and C. Rouse (2000). "Schooling, Intelligence, and Income in America." In *Meritocracy and Economic Inequality*, ed. K. Arrow et al. Princeton U. Press: 89–117.

Asimov, N. (2000). "State Offers Schools Cash to Improve." *San Francisco Chronicle*, July 13: A1.

Attinasi, J. (1997). "Racism, Language Variety, and Urban Minorities." In *Latinos and Education*, ed. A. Darder et al. Routledge: 279–301.

August, D., and K. Hakuta (1997). *Improving Schooling for Language-Minority Children*. Natl. Academy Press.

"Back to School" (2001). *Economist*, June 16: 38.

Baker, B. (2001). "Gifted Children in the Current Policy and Fiscal Context of Public Education." *Educational Evaluation and Policy Analysis* 23(3): 229–50.

Baker, E., et al. (1994). "The Effects of Inclusion on Learning." *Educational Leadership* 52(4): 33–35.

Banks, J. (1995). "Multicultural Education." In *Handbook of Research on Multicultural Education*, ed. J. Banks. Simon & Schuster Macmillan: 2–24.

————, ed. (1997). *Multicultural Education: Issues and Perspectives*. Wiley.

———— (1999). "Multicultural Education in the New Century." *School Administrator* 56(5): 8–10.

Banks, W. C. (1992). "The Theoretical and Methodological Crisis of the Africentric Conception." *Journal of Negro Education* 61(3): 262–72.

Bankston, C. III, and S. Caldas (2002). *A Troubled Dream: The Promise and Failure of School Desegregation in Louisiana*. Vanderbilt U. Press.

Barber, B. (1992). *An Aristocracy of Everyone: The Politics of Education and the Future of America*. Oxford U. Press.

Barnett, W. S. (1995). "Long-Term Effects of Early Childhood Programs on Cognitive and School Outcomes." *The Future of Children* 5(3): 25–50.

Barro, R., and J.-W. Lee 2001. "International Data on Educational Attainment." *Oxford Economic Papers* 3: 541–63.

Barton, P. (2001). *Raising Achievement and Reducing Gaps*. Natl. Education Goals Panel.

Bates, S. (1994). *Battleground: One Mother's Crusade, the Religious Right, and the Struggle for Our Schools*. Henry Holt.

Bathen, S. (1999). "Education: The Deeper Inequality Behind the AP-Course Suit." *Los Angeles Times*, Oct. 17: 1ff.

Beattie, I. (2002). "Are All 'Adolescent Econometricians' Created Equal?" *Sociology of Education* 75(1): 19–43.

Beatty, A., et al., eds. (2001). *Understanding Dropouts*. Natl. Academy Press.

Behn, R. (1997). "Linking Measurement and Motivation." In *Advances in Educational Administration: Improving Educational Performance*, ed. P. Thurston and J. Ward. JAI Press: 15–58.

Belden Russonello, & Stewart (2000). *Making the Grade: Teachers' Attitudes Toward Academic Standards and State Testing.* Wash., DC.

Belfield, C., and H. Levin (2002). *The Effects of Competition on Educational Outcomes.* Columbia U., Natl. Ctr. for the Study of Privatization in Education (forthcoming 2003, *Review of Educational Research*).

"Believer Nation: A Roper Center Data Review" (2000). *Public Perspective* 11(3): 24–35.

Belluck, P. (2000). "Science Expands, Religion Contracts." *New York Times*, Aug. 13: wk 1, 5.

Bembry, K., et al. (1998). *Policy Implications of Long-Term Teacher Effects on Student Achievement.* Dallas Public Schools.

Benjamin, G., and R. Nathan (2001). *Regionalism and Realism: A Study of Governments in the New York Metropolitan Area.* Brookings Institution Press.

Bennett, C. (2001). "Genres of Research in Multicultural Education." *Review of Educational Research* 71(2): 171–217.

Berends, M., et al. (2002) *Facing the Challenges of Whole-School Reform: New American Schools after a Decade.* Rand Corporation.

Bergstrom, T., et al. (1982). "Micro-based Estimates of Demand Functions for Local School Expenditures." *Econometrica* 50(5): 1183–1206.

Berliner, D., and B. Biddle (1995). *The Manufactured Crisis: Myths, Fraud, and the Attack on America's Public Schools.* Addison-Wesley.

Berne, R., and L. Stiefel (1999). "Concepts of School Finance Equity." In *Equity and Adequacy in Education Finance*, ed. H. Ladd et al. Natl. Academy Press: 7–33.

Betts, J. (1995). "Does School Quality Matter?" *Review of Economics and Statistics* 77(2): 231–50.

——— (2000). *The Changing Role of Education in the California Labor Market.* Public Policy Institute of California.

Betts, J., and R. Costrell (2001). "Incentives and Equity under Standards-Based Reform." In *Brookings Papers on Education Policy 2001*, ed. D. Ravitch. Brookings Institution Press: 9–74.

Biblarz, T., and A. Raftery (1999). "Family Structure, Educational Attainment and Socioeconomic Success." *American Journal of Sociology* 105(2): 321–65.

Bigelow, B. (1998a). "Good Intentions Are Not Enough: Recent Children's Books on the Columbus-Taino Encounter." In *Rethinking Columbus*, ed. B. Bigelow and B. Peterson. Rethinking Schools Ltd.: 62–68.

——— (1998b). "Once Upon a Genocide: Columbus in Children's Literature." In *Rethinking Columbus*, ed. B. Bigelow and B. Peterson. Rethinking Schools Ltd.: 47–55.

Billingsley, K. (1996). "Hispanic Parents Battling to Stop Bilingual Classes." *Wash. Times*, Feb. 18: A5.

Binder, A. (1999). "Friend and Foe: Boundary Work and Collective Identity in the Afrocentric and Multicultural Curriculum Movements in American Public Education." In *The Cultural Territories of Race*, ed. M. Lamont. U. of Chicago Press: 221–48.

——— (2000). "Why Do Some Curricular Challenges Work While Others Do Not? The Case of Three Afrocentric Challenges." *Sociology of Education* 73(2): 69–91.

——— (2001). "Identity Trouble in Sacrosanct Battles: Elite and Grassroots Factions Confront Each Other in the Scientific Creationist Movement." *Sociology of Religion* 27(2): 45–62.

Binstock, R., and C. Day (1996). "Aging and Politics." In *Handbook of Aging and the Social Sciences, 4th ed.*, ed. R. Binstock and L. George. Van Nostrand Reinhold: 362–87.

Bishop, G. (1998). "The Religious Worldview and American Beliefs about Human Origins." *Public Perspective* 9(5): 39–44.

Bishop, J. (1997). "The Effect of National Standards and Curriculum-Based Exams on Achievement." *American Economics Assn. Papers and Proceedings* 87(2): 260–64.

Bishop, J., and F. Mane (2001). "The Impacts of Minimum Competency Exam Graduation Requirements on College Attendance and Early Labor Market Success of Disadvantaged Students." In *Raising Standards or Raising Barriers?*, ed. G. Orfield and M. Kornhaber. Century Foundation Press: 51–83.

Blackorby, J., and M. Wagner (1996). "Longitudinal Postschool Outcomes of Youth with Disabilities." *Exceptional Children* 62(5): 399–413.

"Blacks v. Teachers" (2001). *Economist*, Mar. 10–16: 27–28.

Blanding, M. (2001). "Shift into Diverse." *Boston Magazine*, May: 120, 98.

Blau, F., and L. Kahn (2001). *Do Cognitive Test Scores Explain Higher U.S. Wage Inequality?* National Bureau of Economic Research.

Blum, J. (2000). "D.C. Schools Still Neglect Some in Special Education." *Wash. Post*, Oct. 2: A1.

Board of Education of Oklahoma City v. Dowell (1991). 498 U.S. 237.

Bosworth, M. (2001). *Courts as Catalysts: State Supreme Courts and Public School Finance Equity.* SUNY Press.

Bourne, R. (1977 [orig. c. 1918]). "Trans-National America." In *Randolph Bourne: The Radical Will*, ed. O. Hansen. Urizen Books: 248–64.

Bowie, L. (2002). "Schools Setting Limit on Transfers." *Baltimore Sun*, July 10: B1.

Braddock, J. I., et al. (1994). "Why Desegregate? The Effect of School Desegregation on Adult Occupational Desegregation of African Americans, Whites, and Hispanics." *Intl. Journal of Contemporary Sociology* 31(2): 273–83.

Bradley, A. (1999). "States' Uneven Teacher Supply Complicates Staffing of Schools." *Ed. Week*, Mar. 10: 1, 10–11.

Brantlinger, E. (1997). "Using Ideology: Cases of Nonrecognition of the Politics of Research and Practice in Special Education." *Review of Educational Research* 67(4): 425–59.

Briffault, R. (1992). "The Role of Local Control in School Finance Reform." *Connecticut Law Review* 24(3): 773–811.

Brinkley, A. (2000). "Remarks by Newly Elected Members." *Bulletin of American Academy of Arts and Sciences* (Jan.–Feb.): 29–31.

Brittain, J. (1993). "Educational and Racial Equity Toward the Twenty-First Century—A Case Experiment in Connecticut." In *Race in America*, ed. H. Hill and J. Jones., Jr. U. of Wisconsin Press: 167–83.

Bronner, E. (1999). "After 45 Years, Resegregation Emerges in Schools, Study Finds." *New York Times*, June 13.

Brooks, A. P. (1998). "Poll: Texans Favor Bilingual Education." *Austin American-Statesman*, June 28: B1.

Brown, E. (2000). "Black Like Me? 'Gangsta' Culture, Clarence Thomas, and Afrocentric Academies." *New York U. Law Review* 75(2): 308–53.

Brown v. Board of Education I (1954). 347 U.S. 484.

Brown v. Board of Education II (1955). 349 U.S. 294.

Bruni, F. (1998). "Bilingual Education Battle Splits Santa Barbara." *New York Times*, May 27: A12.

Brunner, E., et al. (2001). "Capitalization and the Voucher: An Analysis of Precinct Returns from California's Proposition 174." *Journal of Urban Economics* 50(3): 517–36.

Bryk, A., and B. Schneider (2002). *Trust in Schools: A Core Resource for Improvement.* Russell Sage Foundation Press.

Bryk, A., et al. (1998). *Academic Productivity of Chicago Public Elementary Schools.* Consortium on Chicago School Research.

Buckman, R. (1995). "IPS Kids Bused to Lawrence Falter on Tests." *Indianapolis Star*, Apr. 15.

Bureau of Sociological Research/Dept. of Sociology (1994). Nebraska Annual Social Indicators Survey. U. of Nebraska-Lincoln.

Bureau of the Census (1975). *Historical Statistics of the United States, Colonial Times to 1970.* U.S. Government Printing Office.

——— (2000). *Projections of the Total Resident Population by 5-Year Age Groups, and Sex with Special Age Categories: Middle Series.* U.S. Government Printing Office.

——— (2001). *Home Schooling in the United States: Trends and Characteristics.* U.S. Government Printing Office.

——— (2002). *Statistical Abstract of the United States, 2001.* U.S. Government Printing Office.

Burkett, E. (1998). "Don't Tread on My Tax Rate." *New York Times Magazine*, Apr. 26: 42–45.

Burrows, F. (1972). "School Busing: Charlotte, N.C." *Atlantic Monthly*, Nov.: 17–22.

Burtless, G., ed. (1996). *Does Money Matter? The Effect of School Resources on Student Achievement and Adult Success.* Brookings Institution Press.

Bush, G. W. (2001). *Remarks by the President in Submitting Education Plan to Congress.* Dept. of State Intl. Information Programs.

——— (2000). "No Child Left Behind." www.whitehouse.gov/news/reports/no-child-left-behind.html.

Business Roundtable (2001). *What Parents, Students, and Teachers Think about Standards, Tests, Accountability . . . and More.* Wash., DC.

Cain, B., et al. (2000). *Ethnic Context, Race Relations, and California Politics.* Public Policy Institute of California.

Camarena, M. (1990). "Following the Right Track: A Comparison of Tracking Practices in Public and Catholic Schools." In *Curriculum Differentiation*, ed. R. Page and L. Valli. SUNY Press: 159–82.

Camara, W., and A. Schmidt (1999). *Group Differences in Standardized Testing and Social Stratification.* College Entrance Examination Board.

Cameron, S., and J. Heckman (2001). "The Dynamics of Educational Attainment for Black, Hispanic, and White Males." *Journal of Political Economy* 109(3): 455–99.

Camilli, G., and K. Bulkley (2001). "Critique of 'An Evaluation of the Florida A-Plus Accountability and School Choice Program.'" *Education Policy Analysis Archives* 9(7). epaa.asu.edu/epaa/v9n7.

Campaign for America's Children (2000). "Left. Right." *New York Times.* Nov. 9.: B5.

Campaign for Fiscal Equity v New York (2001). 719 N.Y.S.2d 475; 2001 N.Y. Misc. Lexis 1.

——— (2002). 2002 N.Y. App. Div. Lexis 7252.

Campbell, A., and C. Wong (1998). *"Racial Threat" and Direct Democracy: Contextual Effects in Two California Initiatives.* Annual mtg., Midwest Political Science Assn.

Campbell, D. (2001). "Making Democratic Education Work." In *Charters, Vouchers, and Public Education,* ed. P. Peterson and D. Campbell. Brookings Institution Press: 241–67.

Candisky, C. (2001). "Supreme Court to Rule on Vouchers." *Columbus Dispatch,* Sept. 26.

Canedy, D. (2002). "Florida Court Bars Use of Vouchers." *New York Times,* Aug. 6: A10.

Card, D. (1999). "The Causal Effect of Education on Earnings." In *Handbook of Labor Economics,* ed. O. Ashenfelter and D. Card. Elsevier: 1802–63.

Card, D., and T. Lemieux (2001). "Dropout and Enrollment Trends in the Postwar Period." In *Risky Behavior Among Youth,* ed. J. Gruber. U. of Chicago Press: 438–82.

Card, D., and A. Payne (1998). *School Finance Reform, the Distribution of School Spending, and the Distribution of SAT Scores.* National Bureau of Economic Research.

Carl, J. (1996). "Unusual Allies: Elite and Grass-roots Origins of Parental Choice in Milwaukee." *Teachers College Record* 98(2): 266–85.

Carnoy, M. (1995). "Is School Privatization the Answer?" *Ed. Week,* July 12: 52, 40.

——— (2001). *School Vouchers: Examining the Evidence.* Economic Policy Institute.

Carter, R. (1996). "The Unending Struggle for Equal Educational Opportunity." In *Brown v. Board of Education: The Challenge for Today's Schools,* ed. E. Lagemann and L. Miller. Teachers College Press: 19–26.

Carter, S. (1987). "Evolutionism, Creationism, and Treating Religion as a Hobby." *Duke Law Journal* (6): 977–96.

Castles, F. (1989). "Explaining Public Education Expenditures in OECD Nations." *European Journal of Political Research* 17(4): 431–48.

Catterall, J., and R. Chapleau (2000). *Voting on Vouchers: A Socio-Political Analysis of California Proposition 38.* Teachers College, Natl. Ctr. for the Study of Privatization in Education.

CBS News (1999). Poll. Jan.

CBS News/*New York Times* (1993). Survey. Mar. 28–31.

——— (2001). Poll. Mar. 8–12.

Ceaser, J., and P. McGuinn (1998). "Civic Education Reconsidered." *Public Interest* (133): 84–103.

Ctr. for School Change (1999). "Assessment of Student Achievement Criteria." U. of Minnesota, Hubert Humphrey Institute.

Ctr. on Education Policy and American Youth Policy Forum (2000). "Do You Know the Good News about American Education?" www.ctredpol.org/publications.htm.

"Charlotte Contemplates Life After School Busing" (1999). *New York Times*, Sept. 13: A15.

Charter Schools Institute (2002). *Charter Schools in New York*. SUNY.

Charter Schools Office (c. 2002). *Miracles in Profile*. Central Michigan U.

Chase, B. (1997–98). "The New NEA: Reinventing Teacher Unions for a New Era." *American Educator*, 12–15.

Chavez, L., and J. Amselle (1997). "Bilingual Education Theory and Practice." *Bulletin*, Feb.: 101–6.

Chira, S. (1993). "Rethinking Deliberately Segregated Schools." *New York Times*, July 11: 4–20.

Chubb, J., and T. Moe (1990). *Politics, Markets, and America's Schools*. Brookings Institution Press.

Civil Rights Project (2001). *Minority Issues in Special Education*. Harvard Law School.

Civil Rights Project and Achieve, Inc. (2001). *Dropouts in America*. Harvard U.

Clabaugh, G. (1993). "The Limits and Possibilities of 'Multiculturalism.'" *Educational Horizons*, Spring: 117–19.

Clines, F. (1999). "Capitol Sketchbook: In a Bitter Cultural War, An Ardent Call to Arms." *New York Times*, June 17: A26.

Clinton, W. (1993). Remarks by the President to the Annual Conference of the Democratic Leadership Council, White House. Dec. 3.

——— (1995). "Remarks Honoring Franklin D. Roosevelt in Warm Springs, Georgia, April 12." *Weekly Compilation of Presidential Documents* 31(15): 614–18.

Clotfelter, C. (1999). "Public School Segregation in Metropolitan Areas." *Land Economics* 75(4): 487–504.

——— (2001). "Are Whites Still 'Fleeing'? Racial Patterns and Enrollment Shifts in Urban Public Schools, 1987–1996." *Journal of Policy Analysis and Management* 20(2): 199–221.

Clough, R., and S. Uchitelle (1995). *Voluntary Interdistrict Coordinating Council for the Settlement Agreement, Complete Twelfth Report to the U.S. District Court, Eastern District of Missouri*. St. Louis, Missouri.

CNN/*USA Today* (1994). Gallup, CNN, *USA Today* Poll. Apr. 22–24.

——— (1998). Survey. July 7–8.

——— (1999). Poll. July 16–18.

——— (2000). Poll. Apr. 7–9.

——— (2001). Poll. Jan. 5–7.

CNN/*USA Today*/Gallup Organization (1999). "Education: Major Proposals." www.publicagenda.org/issues/angles_graph.cfm?issue_type=education&id=2&graph=mp15.gif.

Cobb, C., and G. Glass (1999). "Ethnic Segregation in Arizona Charter Schools." *Education Policy Analysis Archives* 7(1). http://epaa.asu.edu/epaa/v7n1.

Cochran-Smith, M., and M. Fries (2001). "Sticks, Stones, and Ideology; The Discourse of Reform in Teacher Education." *Educational Researcher* 30(8): 3–15.

Cogan, L., et al. (2001). "Who Takes Math and in Which Track? Using TIMSS to Characterize U.S. Students' Eighth-Grade Mathematics Learning Opportunities." *Educational Evaluation and Policy Analysis* 23(4): 323–41.

Cohen, D., and H. Hill (2001). *Learning Policy: When State Education Reform Works.* Yale U. Press.

Coleman, J. (1997). "Output-Driven Schools: Principles of Design." In *Redesigning American Education*, ed. J. Coleman et al. Westview.

Coleman, J., et al. (1966). *Equality of Educational Opportunity.* U.S. Government Printing Office.

Combs, B. (1991). "Creative Constitutional Law: The Kentucky School Reform Law." *Harvard Journal on Legislation* 28(2): 367–78.

Committee for Economic Development (2002). *Preschool for All: Investing in a Productive and Just Society.* Wash., DC.

Cone, J. (1992). "Untracking Advanced Placement English." *Phi Delta Kappan*, May: 712–17.

Connecticut Conference of Municipalities (1997). *Education-Related Disparities in Connecticut.* New Haven.

Cook, M., and W. Evans (2000). "Families or Schools? Explaining the Convergence in White and Black Academic Performance." *Journal of Labor Economics* 18(4): 729–54.

Cook, T. (1984). "What Have Black Children Gained Academically from School Integration?" In *School Desegregation and Black Achievement*, ed. T. Cook et al. U.S. Dept. of Education: 6–42.

Cookson, P. (1994). *School Choice: The Struggle for the Soul of American Education.* Yale U. Press.

Coons, J., and S. Sugarman (1999). *Education by Choice: The Case for Family Control.* Educator Intl. Press.

Cooper, K. (2000). "Riley Endorses Two-Way Bilingual Education." *Wash. Post*, Mar. 16: A02.

Corcoran, D. (1999). "Requiring Standard Tests for Graduation." *New York Times*, Aug. 4: B8.

Corcoran, T. (1995). *Changes in Classroom Practices under KERA.* Annual mtg., American Educational Research Assn.

Corcoran, T., and N. Scovronick (1998). "More than Equal: New Jersey's Quality Education Act." In *Strategies for School Equity*, ed. M. Gittell. Yale U. Press: 53–69.

Cornett, L. and G. Gaines (2002). *Quality Teachers: Can Incentive Policies Make a Difference.* Southern Regional Education Board.

Cortez, A. (1998). "Power and Perseverance: Organizing for Change in Texas." In *Strategies for School Equity*, ed. M. Gittell. Yale U. Press: 181–99.

Corwin, R., and J. Flaherty (1995). *Freedom and Innovation in California's Charter Schools.* Southwest Regional Laboratory.

Council of Chief State School Officers (1990). *School Success for Limited English Proficient Students.* Wash., DC.

Crawford, J. (1999). *Bilingual Education: History, Politics, Theory, and Practice 4th ed.* Bilingual Educational Services, Inc.

Crosby, S. (2001). "Wheel of Fortune." *CommonWealth*, Fall: 7–12.

CSR Research Consortium (2002). *What We Have Learned About Class Size Reduction in California.* Sacramento, California, Dept. of Education.

Cullen, J., and D. Figlio (1998). *Local Gaming of State School Finance Policies: How Effective Are Intergovernmental Incentives?* U. of Michigan, Dept. of Economics.

Cullen, J., et al. (2001). *The Impact of School Choice on Student Outcomes: An Analysis of the Chicago Public Schools.* U. of Michigan, Dept. of Economics.

Cumming, K. (2001). "Review of the PBS Video 'Evolution' Series." *Acts & Facts of the Institute for Creation Research* 30(12 [Online Issue No. 16]).

Cummins, J. (1986). "Empowering Minority Students." *Harvard Educational Review* 56(1): 18–36.

Cutler, D., and E. Glaeser (1997). "Are Ghettos Good or Bad?" *Quarterly Journal of Economics* 112(3): 827–72.

Cutler, D., et al. (1999). "The Rise and Decline of the American Ghetto." *Journal of Political Economy* 107(3): 455–506.

Dahl, R. (1961). *Who Governs?* Yale U. Press.

Daniels, L. (1983). "In Defense of Busing." *New York Times Magazine*, Apr. 17: 34–37, 92–98.

Danziger, S., and D. Reed (1999). "Winners and Losers: The Era of Inequality Continues." *Brookings Review* 17 (4): 14–17.

Darder, A. (1997). "Creating the Conditions for Cultural Democracy in the Classroom." In *Latinos and Education*, ed. A. Darder et al. Routledge: 331–50.

Darling-Hammond, L. (1994). "National Standards and Assessments: Will They Improve Education?" *American Journal of Education* 102(4): 478–510.

——— (2000). "Teacher Quality and Student Achievement: A Review of State Policy Evidence." *Education Policy Analysis Archives* 8(1). http://epaa.asu.edu/epaa/v8nl.

——— (2001). *The Research and Rhetoric on Teacher Certification: A Response to "Teacher Certification Reconsidered."* Stanford U., School of Education.

Darling-Hammond, L., et al. (2001). "Does Teacher Certification Matter?" *Educational Evaluation and Policy Analysis* 23(1): 57–77.

Darling-Hammond, L., and G. Sykes, eds. (1999). *Teaching as a Learning Profession.* Jossey-Bass.

Datnow, A., et al. (2002). *Extending Educational Reform: From One School to Many.* RoutledgeFalmer.

Dauber, S., et al. (1996). "Tracking and Transitions through the Middle Grades." *Sociology of Education* 69(4): 290–307.

Davies, G. (2002). "The Great Society after Johnson: The Case of Bilingual Education." *Journal of American History* 88(4): 1405–29.

Davis, B. (1996). "Dueling Professors Have Milwaukee Dazed over School Vouchers." *Wall Street Journal*, Oct. 11: 1.

Davis, J. (1997). "The GSS—Capturing American Attitude Change." *Public Perspective* 8(2): 31–34.

Davis, J., and T. Smith (1999). *General Social Surveys, 1972–1998: Cumulative Codebook.* National Opinion Research Ctr.

Davis, J., et al. (2001). *General Social Surveys, 1972–2000: Cumulative Codebook.* National Opinion Research Ctr.

Dawson, M. (2001). *Black Visions: The Roots of Contemporary African-American Political Ideologies.* U. of Chicago Press.

Dayton, J. (1993). "Correlating Expenditures and Educational Opportunity in

School Funding Litigation: The Judicial Perspective." *Journal of Education Finance* 19(2): 167–82.

DC Appleseed Public School Governance Project (1999). *Reforming the DC Board of Education*. Wash., DC.

DC Voice (2001). *Half the Solution: The Supports DC Students Need to Meet High Academic Standards*. Wash., DC.

De Cos, P. (1999). *Educating California's Immigrant Children: An Overview of Bilingual Education*. California State Library.

Deal, T., and R. Nolan, eds. (1978). *Alternative Schools: Ideologies, Realities, Guidelines*. Nelson-Hall.

Decker, C. (1998a). "Bilingual Education Ban Widely Supported." *Los Angeles Times*, April 13: A1.

——— (1998b). "Support Slips for Prop. 226, Not Prop. 227." *Los Angeles Times*, May 23: A1.

Deckman, M. (1999). *Christian Soldiers on Local Battlefields: Campaigning for Control of America's School Boards*. Ph.D. dissertation, American U., Dept. of Political Science.

Del Valle, S. (1998). "Bilingual Education for Puerto Ricans in New York City." *Harvard Educational Review* 68(2): 193–217.

Delaney, D. (1994). "The Boundaries of Responsibility: Interpretations of Geography in School Desegregation Cases." *Urban Geography* 15(5): 470–86.

Delgado, G. (1999). "Commentary: Perspective on Education." *Los Angeles Times*, Mar. 2: B7.

Delgado-Gaitan, C. (1994). "Socializing Young Children in Mexican-American Families." In *Cross-Cultural Roots of Minority Child Development*, ed. P. Greenfield and R. Cocking. Erlbaum: 55–86.

Delli Carpini, M., and S. Keeter (1996). *What Americans Know about Politics and Why It Matters*. Yale U. Press.

Delpit, L. (1992). "Education in a Multicultural Society." *Journal of Negro Education* 61(3): 237–49.

Democratic Leadership Council (1998). *Active Center Holds Survey*. Wash., DC.

——— (1999a). *A Hunger for Reform Survey*. Wash., DC.

——— (1999b). *Community Consensus Survey*. Wash., DC.

Dent, G. (1988). "Religious Children, Secular Schools." *Southern California Law Review* 61(4): 863–941.

Denton, N. (1996). "In Pursuit of a Dream Deferred: Linking Housing and Education." *Minnesota Law Review* 80(4): 795–824.

Dept. of Education and Dept. of Justice (1998). *Safe and Smart: Making After-School Hours Work for Kids*. Wash., DC.

Dept. of Housing and Urban Development (1998). *The State of the Cities 1998*. Wash., DC.

Detwiler, F. (2000). *Standing on the Premises of God: The Christian Right's Fight to Redefine America's Public Schools*. New York U. Press.

Devroye, D., and R. Freeman (2001). *Does Inequality in Skills Explain Inequality of Earnings across Advanced Countries?* National Bureau of Economic Research.

Dewhurst, J. F., et al. (1961). *Europe's Needs and Resources: Trends and Prospects in Eighteen Countries*. Twentieth Century Fund.

Dickens, A. (1996). "Revisiting *Brown v. Board of Education*: How Tracking Has Resegregated America's Public Schools." *Columbia Journal of Law and Social Problems* 29(4): 469–506.

"Dole Wants to End Bilingual Classes in U.S." (1995). *San Francisco Chronicle*, Sept. 5.

Dolnick, E. (1993). "Deafness as Culture." *Atlantic Monthly*, Sept.: 37–53.

Donovan, M. S., and C. Cross, eds. (2002). *Minority Students in Special and Gifted Education*. Natl. Academy Press.

Downs, A. (2000). "Successful School Reform Efforts Share Common Features." *Harvard Education Letter* 16(2): 1–5.

Dreeben, R., and A. Gamoran (1986). "Race, Instruction, and Learning." *American Sociological Review* 51(5): 660–69.

Driscoll, A. (1999). "Risk of High School Dropout among Immigrant and Native Hispanic Youth." *Intl. Migration Review* 33(4): 857–75.

"Dropout Rates in the United States: 2000." (2001). *Education Statistics Quarterly* 13(4).

Duff, A. (2001). "How Special Education Policy Affects Districts." In *Rethinking Special Education for a New Century*, ed. C. Finn et al. Fordham Foundation and Progressive Policy Institute: 135–59.

Dutton, S., et al. (1998). "Racial Identity of Children in Integrated, Predominantly White, and Black Schools." *Journal of Social Psychology* 138(1): 41–53.

Dyer, R. A. (2000). "Most Latinos Back TAAS Exit Exam Despite Bias Fears." *Fort Worth Star-Telegram*, July 24: 11.

Easterlin, R. (1981). "Why Isn't the Whole World Developed?" *Journal of Economic History* 41(1): 1–19.

Eaton, S. (2001). *The Other Boston Busing Story: What's Won and Lost Across the Boundary Line*. Yale U. Press.

Edelin, R. (1990). "Curriculum and Cultural Identity." In *Infusion of African and African American Content in the School Curriculum*, ed. A. Hilliard III et al. Aaron Press: 37–45.

Edelman, M. (2002). "Corkin Cherubini." In *Profiles in Courage for Our Time*, ed. C. Kennedy. Hyperion Press: 141–55.

"Editorial: Bush on Education" (1999). *Austin American-Statesman*, Sept. 4: A14.

"Editorial Excerpts from the Nation's Press on Segregation Ruling" (1954). *New York Times*, May 18: 19.

Edmunds, R. (1979). "Some Schools Work and More Can." *Social Policy* 9(5): 28–32.

Education Commission of the States (1983). *Action for Excellence*. Denver, CO.

Education Trust (1998a). *Education Watch 1998: The Education Trust State and National Data Book, vol. II*, Wash., DC.

——— (1998b). "Good Teaching Matters: How Well-Qualified Teachers Can Close the Gap." *Thinking K–16* 3(2): 1–14.

——— (2000). "Honor in the Boxcar." 4(1). www.edtrust.org/main/main/reports.asp.

Ed. Week (1998). *Quality Counts '98: The Urban Challenge. Ed. Week* and Pew Charitable Trusts.

——— (2000). *Quality Counts 2000: Who Should Teach? Ed. Week* and Pew Charitable Trusts.

——— (2002). *Quality Counts 2002: Building Blocks for Success: State Efforts in Early-Childhood Education. Ed. Week* and Pew Charitable Trusts.

Edwards v. Aguillard (1987). 482 U.S. 578.

Eisgruber, C. (1996). "The Constitutional Value of Assimilation." *Columbia Law Review* 96(1): 87–102.

El Paso (Texas) Independent School District (1989). *Bilingual Education Evaluation: The Fifth Year in a Longitudinal Study.* Office of Research and Evaluation.

Elam, S., ed. (1989). *The Gallup/Phi Delta Kappa Polls of Attitudes Toward the Public Schools, 1969–88.* Phi Delta Kappa Educational Foundation.

"Elections '96: State Propositions: A Snapshot of Voters" (1996). *Los Angeles Times,* Nov. 7: A29.

Ellwood, D., and T. Kane (2000). "Who Is Getting a College Education? Family Background and the Growing Gaps in Enrollment." In *Securing the Future,* ed. S. Danziger and J. Waldfogel. Russell Sage Foundation Press: 282–324.

Elmore, R. (1990). "Choice as an Instrument of Public Policy: Evidence from Education and Health Care." In *Choice and Control in American Education, vol. 1: The Theory of Choice and Control in American Education,* ed. W. Clune and J. Witte. Falmer: 285–318.

—— (1996). "Getting to Scale with Good Educational Practice." *Harvard Educational Review* 66(1): 1–26.

—— (2000). *Building a New Structure for School Leadership.* Albert Shanker Institute.

—— (2002). *Bridging the Gap Between Standards and Achievement.* Albert Shanker Institute.

Elmore, R., and D. Burney (1997). *Investing in Teacher Learning: Staff Development and Instructional Improvement in Community School District #2, New York City.* Natl. Commission on Teaching and America's Future, and Consortium for Policy Research in Education.

Entwistle, D., and K. Alexander (1992). "Summer Setback: Race, Poverty, School Composition, and Mathematics Achievement in the First Two Years of School." *American Sociological Review* 57(1): 72–84.

Entwistle, D., et al. (2002). "Baltimore Beginning School Study in Perspective." In *Looking at Lives: American Longitudinal Studies of the Twentieth Century,* ed. E. Phelps et al. Russell Sage Foundation Press: 167–93.

Epperson et al. v. Arkansas (1968). 393 U.S. 97; 89 S. Ct 266.

Epple, D., et al. (2002). "Ability Tracking, School Competition, and the Distribution of Educational Benefits." *Journal of Public Economics* 83(1): 1–48.

Epstein, J., and D. MacIver (1992). *Opportunities to Learn: Effects on Eighth Graders of Curriculum Offerings and Instructional Approaches.* Johns Hopkins U., Ctr. for Research on Elementary and Middle Schools.

Erlichson, B., and M. Goertz (2001). *Implementing Whole School Reform in New Jersey: Year Two.* Rutgers U., Bloustein School of Planning and Public Policy.

Evans, W., et al. (1997). "School House, Court Houses, and State Houses after *Serrano.*" *Journal of Policy Analysis and Management* 16(1): 10–31.

—— (1999). "The Impact of Court-Mandated School Finance Reform." In *Equity and Adequacy in Education Finance,* ed. H. Ladd et al. Natl. Academy Press: 72–98.

—— (2001). "The Property Tax and Education Finance." In *Property Taxation and Local Government Finance,* ed. W. Oates. Lincoln Institute of Land Policy: 209–35.

Exchange (between Maureen Hallinan and Jeannie Oakes) (1994). *Sociology of Education* 67(2): 79–91.

Fairlie, R. (2003). "Racial Segregation and the Private/Public School Choice." In *School Choice and Student Diversity*. ed. Janelle Scott and H. Levin. Teachers College Press.

Family Circle (1994). Family Index Project Survey. June–Aug.

Farley, R., and W. Frey (1994). "Changes in the Segregation of Whites from Blacks During the 1980s." *American Sociological Review* 59(1): 23–45.

Ferdinand, P. (1998). "Education Funding Issue Colors New England Fall." *Wash. Post*, Oct. 18: A3.

Ferguson, G. (1997). *Searching for Consensus in Education Reform*. American Viewpoint, Inc.

Ferguson, J. (1997). "What Students Say about Mainstreaming." *American School Board Journal*, Dec.: 18–21.

Ferguson, R. (1991). "Paying for Public Education: New Evidence for How and Why Money Matters." *Harvard Journal on Legislation* 28(2): 465–98.

——— (1998). "Can Schools Narrow the Black-White Test Score Gap?" In *The Black-White Test Score Gap*, ed. C. Jencks and M. Phillips. Brookings Institution Press: 318–74.

Ferguson, R., and H. Ladd (1996). "How and Why Money Matters: An Analysis of Alabama Schools." In *Holding Schools Accountable*, ed. H. Ladd. Brookings Institution Press: 265–98.

Field Institute (2000). *A Digest Examining California's Expanding Latino Electorate*. San Francisco.

——— (2002a). *California Opinion Index: How Concerned Californians Are about Major Issues Facing the State*. San Francisco.

——— (2002b). *A Digest of California's Political Demography*. San Francisco.

Figlio, D., and M. Page (2002). "School Choice and the Distributional Effects of Ability Tracking." *Journal of Urban Economics* 51(3): 497–514.

Finance Project (2000). *Improving Educational Achievement*. www.financeproject.org/achievement.htm.

Fine, L. (2001). "Report by City Leaders Criticizes D.C.'s Special Education Services." *Ed. Week*, Jan. 17: 12.

——— (2002). "Disparate Measures." *Ed. Week*, June 19: 30–34.

Finn, C. (1997). "Learning-Free Zones." *Policy Review*, Sept.–Oct.: 34–38.

——— (2001). "Appraising State Standards, Tests, and Accountability Systems." *Education Gadfly* 1(25). www.edexcellence.netgadfly/vo1/gadfly25.html#checker.

Finn, C. et al. (1997). *Charter Schools in Action: Final Report*. Hudson Institute.

——— (2000). *Charter Schools in Action: Renewing Public Education*. Princeton U. Press.

——— (2001). "Charter Schools: Taking Stock." In *Charters, Vouchers, and Public Education*, ed. P. Peterson and D. Campbell. Brookings Institution Press: 19–42.

Finn, J., et al. (2001). "The Enduring Effects of Small Classes." *Teachers College Record* 103(2): 145–83.

Firestone, W., et al. (1997). *From Cashbox to Classroom: The Struggle for Fiscal Reform and Educational Change in New Jersey*. Teachers College Press.

"Fiscal 2002 Education Appropriations and President's Fiscal 2003 Proposals" (2002). *Ed. Week*, June 19: 26–27.

Fiske, E. (1982). "Education: Sputnik Recalled: Science and Math in Trouble Again." *New York Times*, Oct. 5: C1ff.

Fiske, E., and H. Ladd (2000). *When Schools Compete: A Cautionary Tale*. Brookings Institution Press.

Flathman, R. (1996). "Liberal versus Civic, Republican, Democratic, and Other Vocational Educations." *Political Theory* 24(1): 4–32.

Fleischman, H., and P. Hopstock (1993). *Descriptive Study of Services to Limited English Proficient Students, vol. 1*. Development Associates.

Fliegel, S., and J. MacGuire (1993). *Miracle in East Harlem: The Fight for Choice in Public Education*. Times Books.

Flores Macias, R. (1979). "Choice of Language as a Human Right." In *Bilingual Education and Public Policy in the United States*, ed. R. Padilla. Eastern Michigan State U.: 39–57.

Folmar, K. (1999). "Racial Issues Creep into Bond Battles." *Los Angeles Times*, Sept. 14: B1ff.

Forbes, H. D. (1997). *Ethnic Conflict: Commerce, Culture, and the Contact Hypothesis*. Yale U. Press.

Fordham Foundation (1999). "The Teachers We Need and How to Get More of Them." www.edexcellence.net/library/teacher.html.

"Forum: The Feds Step In" (2002). *Education Next* 2(1): 29–41.

Fossey, R. (1994). "Open Enrollment in Massachusetts: Why Families Choose." *Educational Evaluation and Policy Analysis* 16(3): 320–34.

Foster, M. (1995). "African American Teachers and Culturally Relevant Pedagogy." In *Handbook of Research on Multicultural Education*, ed. J. Banks and C. Banks. Macmillan: 570–81.

Fox News (1999). Fox News/Opinion Dynamics Poll. Aug. 25–26.

Frahm, R. (1996a). "Residents as Divided as Court on *Sheff: Courant*-ISI Connecticut Poll." *Hartford Courant*, Aug. 16: A1.

——— (1996b) "Q and A with the Governor." *Hartford Courant*, July 14: A4.

Franklin, B. (1962 [1749]). "Constitutions of the Publick Academy in the City of Philadelphia." In *Benjamin Franklin on Education*, ed. J. Best. Teachers College Press: 152–58.

——— (1987 [1749]). "Proposals Relating to the Education of Youth in Pennsylvania." In *Writings*, ed. J. A. Lemay. Library of America: 323–44.

Freeman v. Pitts (1992). 503 U.S. 467.

Freivogel, W. (2002). "St. Louis: Desegregation and School Choice in the Land of Dred Scott." In *Divided We Fail: Coming Together through Public School Choice*, Century Foundation Task Force on the Common School. Century Foundation Press: 209–235.

Frey, W. (2000). "The New Urban Demographics." *Brookings Review*, Summer: 20–23.

Frey, W., and R. DeVol (2000). *America's Demography in the New Century: Aging Baby Boomers and New Immigrants as Major Players*. Milken Institute.

Friedman, M. (1955). *Capitalism and Freedom*. U. of Chicago Press.

Fry, R., et al. (2000). *Growing Inequality in Collegiate Attainment: Evidence on the Role of Family Income*. Educational Testing Service.

Fuchs, D., and L. Fuchs (1994). "Inclusive Schools Movement and the Radicalization of Special Education Reform." *Exceptional Children* 60(4): 294–310.

———— (1998). "Competing Visions for Educating Students with Disabilities." *Childhood Education* 74(5): 309–16.

Fuerst, J. S., and R. Petty (1992). "Quiet Success: Where Managed Integration Works." *American Prospect* 3(10) 65–73.

Fuhrman, S., ed. (1993). *Designing Coherent Education Policy.* Jossey-Bass.

———— (1999). *The New Accountability.* U. of Pennsylvania, Consortium for Policy Research in Education.

Fuller, B., et al. (1999). *School Choice: Abundant Hopes, Scarce Evidence of Results.* Policy Analysis for California Education; U. of California, Berkeley; and Stanford U.

Furstenberg, F., Jr., and J. Kmec (2002). "Racial and Gender Differences in the Transition to Adulthood." In *Advances in Life-Course Research 7: New Frontiers in Socialization.* ed. R. Settersten and T. Owens. Elsevier: 435–70.

Galindo, R. (1997). "Language Wars: The Ideological Dimensions of the Debates on Bilingual Education." *Bilingual Research Journal* 21(2–3): 163–201.

Gallagher, J., et al. (2001). *Education for Four-Year-Olds: State Initiatives.* U. of North Carolina, Frank Porter Graham Child Development Ctr.

Gallagher, K., and J. Bailey, eds. (2000). *The Politics of Teacher Education Reform: The National Commission on Teaching and America's Future.* Corwin Press.

Gallup/CNN/*USA Today* (1998). Poll. May 8–10.

———— (1999). Poll. June 25–27.

———— (2001). Poll. Apr. 20–22.

Gallup Organization (1954). Gallup Poll—American Institute of Public Opinion. *Gallup Poll Monthly.* July 2–7.

———— (1973). Poll. Aug. 3–6.

———— (1975). Poll. Sept. 12–15.

———— (1982). Poll. July 23–26.

———— (1991). Gallup Poll. *Gallup Poll Monthly.* Nov. 21–24.

———— (1996). Gallup Poll. Apr. 25–28.

———— (1997). *The Gallup Poll Social Audit on Black/White Relations in the United States.* Princeton, NJ.

———— (2001a). *Americans Strongly Behind Mandatory School Testing.* Princeton, NJ.

———— (2001b). Poll. Feb. 19–21.

———— (2002). Gallup Poll: "The Racial Divide." June 21–23.

Galston, W. (1989). "Civic Education in the Liberal State." In *Liberalism and the Moral Life,* ed. N. Rosenblum. Harvard U. Press: 89–101.

———— (2002). *Liberal Pluralism: The Implications of Value Pluralism for Political Theory and Practice.* Cambridge U. Press.

Galuszka, P. (1997). "Kentucky's Class Act." *Business Week,* Apr. 7: 90–94.

Gamoran, A. (1986). "Instructional and Institutional Effects of Ability Grouping." *Sociology of Education* 59(4): 185–98.

———— (1992). "The Variable Effects of High School Tracking." *American Sociological Review* 57(6): 812–28.

———— (1993a). "Alternative Uses of Ability Grouping in Secondary Schools." *American Journal of Education* 102(1): 1–22.

———— (1993b). "Is Ability Grouping Equitable?" *Education Digest* 58(7): 44–46.

———— (2001). "American Schooling and Educational Inequality: A Forecast for the 21st Century." *Sociology of Education,* extra issue: 135–53.

Gamoran, A., and E. Hannigan (2000). "Algebra for Everyone?" *Educational Evaluation and Policy Analysis* 22(3): 241–54.

Gamoran, A., and R. Mare (1989). "Secondary School Tracking and Educational Inequality." *American Journal of Sociology* 94(5): 1146–83.

Garces, E., et al. (2000). *Longer Term Effects of Head Start*. National Bureau of Economic Research.

Garcia Castro, M. (1982). "Women in Migration: Colombian Voices in the Big Apple." *Migration Today* 10(3–4): 23–32.

Garfinkel, I., et al., eds. (1996). *Social Policies for Children*. Brookings Institution Press.

Gauri, V. (1999). *School Choice in Chile*. U. of Pittsburgh Press.

Gendron, E. (1972). "Busing in Florida: Before and After." *Integrated Education*: 3–7.

General Accounting Office (1994a). *Hispanics' Schooling: Risk Factors for Dropping Out and Barriers to Resuming Their Education*. Wash., DC.

——— (1994b). *Limited-English Proficiency: A Growing and Costly Educational Challenge Facing Many School Districts*. Wash., DC.

——— (1995a). *School Facilities: America's Schools Not Designed or Equipped for Twenty-First Century*. Wash., DC.

——— (1995b). *School Facilities: Condition of America's Schools*. Wash., DC.

——— (1999). *Public Education: Title I Services Provided to Students with Limited English Proficiency*. Wash., DC.

——— (2001a). *BIA and DOD Schools: Student Achievement and Other Characteristics Often Differ from Public Schools'*. Wash., DC.

——— (2001b). *School Vouchers: Publicly Funded Programs in Cleveland and Milwaukee*. Wash., DC.

Genesee, F., ed. (1999). *Program Alternatives for Linguistically Diverse Students*. U. of California, Santa Cruz, Ctr. for Research on Education, Diversity, and Excellence.

Genesee, F., and P. Gandera (1999). "Bilingual Education Programs: A Cross-National Perspective." *Journal of Social Issues* 55(4): 665–85.

Gerber, E., et al. (2000). *Stealing the Initiative: How State Government Responds to Direct Democracy*. Prentice-Hall.

Gerwin, C. (2001). "Algebraic Solution." *CommonWealth*, Winter: 6(1).

Getchell, K. (2001). "Advocates in Action." *School Choice Advocate*, Aug.: 4–5.

Gewertz, C. (2000). "After the Bell Rings." *Ed. Week*, Feb. 2: 34–36.

——— (2002). "McGreevey Creates Panel to Iron Out *Abbott* Wrinkles." *Ed. Week*, Feb. 27: 13, 18.

GI Forum et al. v. Texas Education Agency et al. (2000). 87 F. Supp. 2d 667.

Gibeaut, J. (1999). "Evolution of a Controversy." *American Bar Association Journal*, 50–55.

Gieryn, T., et al. (1985). "Professionalization of American Scientists: Public Science in the Creation/Evolution Trials." *American Sociological Review* 50(3): 392–409.

Gill, B., et al. (2001). *Rhetoric Versus Reality: What We Know and What We Need to Know About Vouchers and Charter Schools*. Rand Corporation.

Gill, W. (1991). "Jewish Day Schools and Afrocentric Programs as Models for Educating African American Youth." *Journal of Negro Education* 60(4): 566–80.

Gilliam, W., and E. Zigler (2001). "A Critical Meta-analysis of All Evaluations of

State-Funded Preschool from 1977 to 1998." *Early Childhood Research Quarterly* 15(4): 441–73.

Gintis, H. (1995). "The Political Economy of School Choice." *Teachers College Record* 96(3): 492–511.

Gitlin, T. (1993). "The Rise of 'Identity Politics.'" *Dissent*, Spring: 172–77.

Gittell, M., ed. (1998). *Strategies for School Equity: Creating Productive Schools in a Just Society*. Yale U. Press.

Glazer, N. (1998). "Pluralism and the New Immigrants." *Society* 35(2): 232–38.

——— (2001). "Seasons Change." *Education Next*, Fall: 34–37.

Godwin, K. and F. Kemerer (2002). *School Choice Tradeoffs: Liberty, Equality, and Diversity*. University of Texas Press.

Goertz, M. (1998). "Steady Work: The Courts and School Finance Reform in New Jersey." In *Strategies for School Equity*, ed. M. Gittell. Yale U. Press: 101–14.

Goldberg, C. (1997). "School Tax Law Splits 'Haves' and 'Have Nots.'" *New York Times*, Dec. 19: A34.

Goldhaber, D. (1999). "School Choice: An Examination of the Empirical Evidence on Achievement, Parental Decision Making, and Equity." *Educational Researcher* 28(9): 16–25.

Goldhaber, D., and D. Brewer (2000). "Does Teacher Certification Matter?" *Educational Evaluation and Policy Analysis* 22(2): 129–45.

Goldin, C., and L. Katz (1997). *Why the United States Led in Education: Lessons from Secondary School Expansion, 1910 to 1940*. National Bureau of Economic Research.

——— (1999). "Human Capital and Social Capital: The Rise of Secondary Schooling in America, 1910–1940." *Journal of Interdisciplinary History* 24(4): 683–723.

Goldring, E., and C. Smreker (2000). "Magnet Schools and the Pursuit of Racial Balance." *Education and Urban Society* 33(1): 17–35.

Goldscheider, E. (2001). "Overseeing Schools in Springfield." *Boston Globe*, Aug. 26: B8.

Good, T. (1987). "Two Decades of Research on Teacher Expectations." *Journal of Teacher Education* 38(4): 32–47.

Goodman, D. (1999). "America's Newest Class War." *Mother Jones*, Sept.–Oct.: 68–75.

Goodnough, A. (2001). "Most Eighth Graders Again Fail New York Statewide Exams." *New York Times*, Oct. 24: A20.

Gorard, S., et al. (2001). "School Choice Impacts: What Do We Know?" *Educational Researcher* 30(7): 18–23.

Gorard, S., and C. Taylor (2001). "Specialist Schools in England." *School Leadership and Management* 21(4): 365–81.

Gorman, S. (2001). "Navigating the Special Education Maze." In *Rethinking Special Education for a New Century*, ed. C. Finn et al. Fordham Foundation and Progressive Policy Institute: 233–58.

Gould, P. (2000). Letter to the Editor. *Ed. Week*, Sept. 20: 35.

Graham, A., and T. Husted (1993). "Understanding State Variation in SAT Scores." *Economics of Education Review* 12(3): 197–202.

Green, R. (2000). "Desegregation Effort Called 'Dismal.'" *Hartford Courant*, Aug. 7: A3.

Green v. Board of Education of New Kent County (1968). 391 U.S. 430.

Greenberger, S. (2001a). "Bilingual Ed Loses Favor with Some Educators." *Boston Globe*, Aug. 5: A1.

———— (2001b). "Lack of Certified Teachers Hampers Special-Ed Classes." *Boston Globe*, Sept. 23: B1, 8.

Greene, J. (1997). "A Meta-analysis of the Rossell and Baker Review of Bilingual Education Research." *Bilingual Research Journal* 21(2 and 3): 103–22.

———— (1998). *A Meta-analysis of the Effectiveness of Bilingual Education.* U. of Texas at Austin, Government Dept.

———— (2001a). *An Evaluation of the Florida A-Plus Accountability and School Choice Program.* Manhattan Institute for Policy Research.

———— (2001b). "Reply to 'Critique of "An Evaluation of the Florida A-Plus Accountability and School Choice Program" by Gregory Camilli and Katrina Bulkley in *Education Policy Analysis Archives.*'" Manhattan Institute.

Greene, J., and D. Hall (2001). *The CEO Horizon Scholarship Program: A Case Study of School Vouchers in the Edgewood Independent School District, San Antonio, Texas.* Mathematica Policy Research, Inc.

Greene, J., and P. Peterson (1996). "School Choice Data Rescued from Bad Science." *Wall Street Journal*, Aug. 14: A12.

Greene, J., et al. (1999). "Effectiveness of School Choice: The Milwaukee Experiment." *Education and Urban Society* 31(2): 190–213.

Greenhouse, S. (2000). "Guess Who's Embracing Immigrants Now." *New York Times*, Mar. 5: wk4.

Grissmer, D., et al. (1997). "Does Money Matter for Minority and Disadvantaged Students?" In *Developments in School Finance*, ed. W. Fowler, U.S. Dept. of Education, Office of Educational Research and Improvement: 13–30.

———— (1998). "Why Did the Black-White Score Gap Narrow in the 1970s and 1980s?" In *The Black-White Test Score Gap*, ed. C. Jencks and M. Phillips. Brookings Institution Press: 182–226.

———— (2000). *Improving Student Achievement: What State NAEP Scores Tell Us.* Rand Corporation.

Guryan, J. (2001a). *Desegregation and Black Dropout Rates.* National Bureau of Economic Research.

———— (2001b). *Does Money Matter? Regression-Discontinuity Estimates from Education Finance Reform in Massachusetts.* National Bureau of Economic Research.

Guthrie, J. (1997). "Bilingual Education Split Not on Strict Ethnic Lines." *San Francisco Examiner*, Nov. 2: C1, 5.

Gutmann, A. (1987). *Democratic Education.* Princeton U. Press.

Haberman, M., and L. Post (1998). "Teachers for Multicultural Schools: The Power of Selection." *Theory into Practice* 37(2): 96–104.

Haller, E. (1985). "Pupil Race and Elementary School Ability Grouping." *American Educational Research Journal* 22(4): 465–83.

Hallow, R. (1997). "NAACP to Air Disputes over Mandatory Busing." *Wash. Times*, June 24: A4.

Halpern, R. (1999). "After-School Programs for Low-Income Children." *Future of Children* 9(2): 81–95.

Halstead, T., and M. Lind (2001). *The Radical Center.* Doubleday.

Ham, S., and E. Walker (1999). *Getting to the Right Algebra: The Equity 2000 Initiative in Milwaukee Public Schools.* Manpower Demonstration Research Corporation.

Hamilton, H., and S. Cohen (1974). *Policy Making by Plebiscite: School Referenda.* Heath.

Haney, W. (2000). "The Myth of the Texas Miracle in Education." *Educational Policy Analysis Archives* 8(41). http://epaa.asu.edu/epaa/v8n41.

Hannaway, J. (1998). *Governance in Education: A Review.* Urban Institute.

Hannaway, J., and S. McKay (2001). "Taking Measure." *Education Next* 1(3): 9–12.

Hanushek, E. (1998). "Conclusions and Controversies about the Effectiveness of School Resources." *Federal Reserve Board of New York Economic Policy Review* 4(1): 11–27.

Hanushek, E., and S. Rivkin (1997). "Understanding the Twentieth-Century Growth in U.S. School Spending." *Journal of Human Resources* 32(1): 35–68.

Hanushek, E., and J. Somers (2001). "Schooling, Inequality, and the Impact of Government." *American Economic Review* 91(2): 24–28.

Hanushek, E., et al. (2003a). "Does the Ability of Peers Affect Student Achievement?" *Journal of Applied Econometrics.*

——— (2003b). "Inferring Program Effects for Specialized Populations: Does Special Education Raise Achievement for Students with Disabilities?" *Review of Economics and Statistics.*

Harding, V. (1970). "Beyond Chaos: Black History and the Search for the New Land." In *Amistad,* ed. J. Williams and C. Harris. Vintage: 267–92.

Harp, L. (1990). "Kentucky Districts Seen Jumping on Reform Bandwagon." *Ed. Week,* Aug. 1: 36.

——— (1991). "After First Year, Kentucky Reforms Called 'On the Move.'" *Ed. Week,* Apr. 10: 1, 20–22.

——— (1997). "In Kentucky, Education Reform Puts the Emphasis on Writing Well." *Lexington Herald-Leader,* Apr. 15.

Harris, L., and Associates (1965). Harris Survey. Sept.

——— (1970). Survey Mar.

——— (1972). Survey Feb. 28–Mar. 7.

——— (1978). San Bernardino, California, Community Survey. Mar.

Harris, M. (1992). "Africentrism and Curriculum." *Journal of Negro Education* 61(3): 301–16.

Harrison, E. (1992). "Kentucky's Education Reforms Fail Early Tests." *Los Angeles Times,* July 19: A20.

Hartford Courant (1993). Connecticut Poll. Jan. 26–Feb. 3.

Hartocollis, A. (1999). "The Man behind the Exams." *New York Times,* Apr. 1: B1, B10.

——— (2001). "Schools Told Not to Boycott Albany Tests." *New York Times,* Oct. 31: A15.

Harvard Law Review (1989). "Note: Teaching Inequality: The Problem of Public School Tracking." 102(6): 1318–41.

Hauser, R., et al. (2001). *High School Dropout, Race-Ethnicity, and Social Background from the 1970s to the 1990s.* U. of Wisconsin at Madison, Center for Demography and Ecology.

Haynes, V. D. (1995). "America Rethinks School Desegregation." *Times-Picayune*, Nov. 19: A1.

Hayward, C. (2000). *De-Facing Power*. Cambridge U. Press.

Hazelwood School District et al. v. Kuhlmeier et. al. (1988). 484 U.S. 260.

"Heading North" (1994). *Economist*, Nov. 19: 29–30.

Heckman, J., and L. Lochner (2000). "Rethinking Education and Training Policy." In *Securing the Future: Investing in Children from Birth to College*, ed. S. Danziger and J. Waldfogel. Russell Sage Foundation Press: 47–83.

Hehir, T., and S. Gamm (1999). "Special Education: From Legalism to Collaboration." In *Law and School Reform*, ed. J. Heubert. Yale U. Press: 205–43.

Heidenheimer, A. (1981). "Education and Social Security Entitlements in Europe and America." In *The Development of Welfare States in Europe and America*, ed. P. Flora and A. Heidenheimer. Transaction: 269–304.

Hendrie, C. (1998a). "A Denver High School Reaches Out to the Neighborhood It Lost to Busing." *Ed. Week*, June 17: 1, 22–23.

——— (1998b). "New Magnet School Policies Sidestep an Old Issue: Race." *Ed. Week*, June 10: 10–12.

——— (1998c). "Taxes, Transfer Program on the Table in St. Louis Desegregation Settlement." *Ed. Week*, Aug. 5: 8.

Henig, J. (1994). *Rethinking School Choice*. Princeton U. Press.

——— (1996). "The Local Dynamics of Choice: Ethnic Preferences and Institutional Responses." In *Who Chooses? Who Loses? Culture, Institutions, and the Unequal Effects of School Choice*, ed. B. Fuller et al. Teachers College Press: 95–117.

——— (2001). *Growing Pains: An Evaluation of Charter Schools in the District of Columbia, 1999–2000*. George Washington U., Ctr. for Washington Area Studies.

Henig, J., et al. (1999). *The Color of School Reform: Race, Politics, and the Challenge of Urban Education*. Princeton U. Press.

Hentschke, G., et al. (2002). *Education Management Organizations*. Reason Public Policy Institute.

Hernandez, R. (1995). "NAACP Suspends Yonkers Head." *New York Times*, Nov. 1: B1, 4.

Hernandez-Chavez, E. (1977). "Meaningful Bilingual Bicultural Education: A Fairy Tale." *NABE Journal* 1(3): 39–54.

Herr, K. (1999). "The Symbolic Uses of Participation: Co-opting Change." *Theory into Practice* 38(4): 235–40.

Hertert, L. (1995). "Does Equal Funding for Districts Mean Equal Funding for Classroom Students? Evidence from California." In *Where Does the Money Go? Resource Allocations in Elementary and Secondary Schools*, ed. L. Picus and J. Wattenbarger. Corwin: 71–84.

Hess, F. (1999a). "A Political Explanation of Policy Selection: The Case of Urban School Reform." *Policy Studies Journal* 27(3): 459–73.

——— (1999b). *Spinning Wheels: The Politics of Urban School Reform*. Brookings Institution Press.

——— (2002a). "Reform, Resistance, . . . Retreat? The Predictable Politics of Accountability in Virginia," with Comments by Alan Wurtzel and Iris Rotberg. In *Brookings Papers on Education Policy 2002*, ed. D. Ravitch. Brookings Institution Press: 69–122.

———— (2002b). *Revolution at the Margins: The Impact of Competition on Urban School Systems*. Brookings Institution Press.

Hess, F., et al. (2001). "Responding to Competition: School Leaders and School Culture." In *Charters, Vouchers, and Public Education*, ed. P. Peterson and D. Campbell. Brookings Institution Press: 215–38.

Hess, G. (2002). "Accountability and Support in Chicago: Consequences for Students," with Comments by Stanley Litow and Richard Elmore. In *Brookings Papers on Education Policy 2002*, ed. D. Ravitch. Brookings Institution Press: 339–87.

Hetzner, A. (2001). "Open Enrollment Surprises Some Schools." *Milwaukee Journal Sentinel*, Feb. 18: A1 ff.

Heubert, J., and R. Hauser, eds. (1999). *High Stakes: Testing for Tracking, Promotion, and Graduation*. National Academy Press.

Hill, P. (2001). "High Schools and Development of Healthy Young People." Brookings Institution, Brown Center on Education Policy.

Hill, P., and R. Lake (2002). "Standards and Accountability in Washington State," with Comments by Michael Petrilli and Michael Cohen. In *Brookings Papers on Education Policy 2002*, ed. D. Ravitch, Brookings Institution Press: 199–234.

Hill, P., et al. (1997). *Reinventing Public Education: How Contracting Can Transform America's Schools*. U. of Chicago Press.

———— (2000). *It Takes a City: Getting Serious about Urban School Reform*. Brookings Institution Press.

Hilliard, A., III, (1992). "Behavioral Style, Culture, and Teaching and Learning." *Journal of Negro Education* 61(3): 370–77.

Hilliard, A., III, et al., eds. (1990). *Infusion of African and African American Content in the School Curriculum*. Aaron Press.

Hills v. Gautreaux (1976). 425 U.S. 284.

Hipp, L. (2001). "Dual-Language Classes Teach Content, Culture." *Houston Chronicle*, Dec. 1.

Ho, A. (1999). *Did School Finance Reforms Achieve Better Equity?* Iowa State U., Dept. of Political Science.

Hochschild, J. (1984). *The New American Dilemma: Liberal Democracy and School Desegregation*. Yale U. Press.

———— (1995). *Facing Up to the American Dream: Race, Class, and the Soul of the Nation*. Princeton U. Press.

———— (2003). "The Future of Inequality in American Politics." In *The Future of Democratic Politics*, ed. G. Pomper and M. Weiner. Rutgers U. Press.

Hochschild, J., and R. Rogers (2000). "Race Relations in a Diversifying Nation." In *New Directions: African Americans in a Diversifying Nation*, ed. J. Jackson. Natl. Planning Assn.: 45–85.

Hochschild, J., and B. Scott (1998). "Poll Trends: Governance and Reform of Public Education in the United States." *Public Opinion Quarterly* 62(1): 79–120.

Hocutt, A. (1996). "Effectiveness of Special Education: Is Placement the Critical Factor?" *The Future of Children* 6(1): 77–102.

Hodgkinson, H. (1999). *All One System: A Second Look*. Institute for Education Leadership and National Ctr. for Public Policy and Higher Education.

———— (2000). *Secondary Schools in a New Millenium: Demographic Certainties, Social Realities*. National Assn. of Secondary School Principals.

Hoff, D. (2000). "State Capitals Again Stirred by Evolution." *Ed. Week*, Mar. 8: 1, 16–17.

Hoff, D., and K. Manzo (1999). "States Committed to Standards Reforms Reap NAEP Gains." *Ed. Week*, Mar. 10: 1, 12–13.

Hokenmaier, K. (1998). "Social Security vs. Educational Opportunity in Advanced Industrial Societies." *American Journal of Political Science* 42(2): 709–11.

Holmes, S. (1999). "Debate Rekindled as Boston Moves Beyond Busing." *New York Times*, Mar. 14: 20.

Horace Mann Education Corporation. (1999). Education Survey. Aug. 20–21.

Horn, J., and G. Miron (2000). *An Evaluation of the Michigan Charter School Initiative*, Western Michigan U., Evaluation Ctr.

Horn, W., and D. Tynan (2001). "Time to Make Special Education 'Special' Again." In *Rethinking Special Education for a New Century*, ed. C. Finn et al. Fordham Foundation and Progressive Policy Institute: 23–51.

Horvitz, L. (2001). "Report: Bilingual Classes Neglected." *Orlando Sentinel*, Nov. 13.

Hotakainen, R. (1995). "Resignation Clouds Fate of State Board." *Minneapolis Star Tribune*, Sept. 10: 1Aff.

Hotakainen, R., et al. (1994). "Average Kids Are Losing; Soaring Special Education Costs Squeeze Minnesota School Budgets." *Minneapolis Star Tribune*, Dec. 3: ME.

House, G. (2000). "Re-Creating a School System: Lessons Learned in Memphis about Whole-School Reform." *Ed. Week*, Apr. 5: 38, 41.

Houston, P. (1997). "Raising the Caution Flag on the Standards Movement." *Ed. Week*, June 4: 44.

Hout, M. (forthcoming 2003). "Educational Progress for African Americans and Latinos in the United States from the 1950s to the 1990s: The Interaction of Ancestry and Class." In *Ethnicity and Social Mobility in the US and the UK*, ed. G. Loury et al. Cambridge U. Press.

Howard, E. (2001). "Two-Way (Dual) Immersion." ERIC/CLL Resource Guides Online. www.cal.org/ericcll/faqs/rgos/2way.html.

Howell, W. (2002). *Dynamic Selection Effects in School Voucher Programs*. U. of Wisconsin at Madison, Dept. of Political Science.

Howell, W., and P. Peterson (2002). *The Education Gap: Vouchers and Urban Schools*. Brookings Institution Press.

Howell, W., et al. (2001). "Effects of School Vouchers on Student Test Scores." In *Charters, Vouchers, and Public Education*, ed. P. Peterson and D. Campbell. Brookings Institution Press: 136–59.

——— (2002). "School Vouchers and Academic Performance: Results from Three Randomized Field Trials." *Journal of Policy Analysis and Management* 21(2): 191–217.

Hoxby, C. (2000). *Peer Effects in the Classroom: Learning from Gender and Race Variation*. National Bureau of Economic Research.

——— (forthcoming 2003). "School Choice and School Productivity." In *The Economics of School Choice*, ed. C. Hoxby. U. of Chicago Press.

Hsieh, C.-T., and M. Urqiola (2002). *When Schools Compete, How Do They Compete?* Teachers College, Natl. Ctr. for the Study of Privatization in Education.

Humphrey, D., et al. (1999). *Teacher Development: A Literature Review*. SRI Intl.

Iatarola, P., and L. Stiefel (forthcoming 2002). "Intradistrict Equity of Public Education Resources and Performance." *Economics of Education Review*.

"Identity Crisis: Can Teacher Unions Really Promote Reform?" (2001). *Education Next* 1(3): 38–54.

"Improving Our Schools" (2001). *Polling Report* 17(15): 1, 7.

Ingersoll, R. (1999). "The Problem of Underqualified Teachers in American Secondary Schools." *Educational Researcher* 28(2): 26–37.

———— (2002). *Out-of-Field Teaching, Educational Inequality, and the Organization of Schools.* U. of Washington, Ctr. for the Study of Teaching and Policy.

Inniss, L. (1996). "California's Proposition 187—Does It Mean What It Says? Does It Say What It Means?" *Georgetown Immigration Law Journal* 10 (4): 577–622.

Institute for Policy Studies and *The Nation* (2000). Survey. Sept. 21–25.

"Integration, Census" (2000). *Migration News.* http://migration.ucdavis.edu/mn/pastissues/feb2000mn_past.html.

Irvine, J., and D. York (1995). "Learning Styles and Culturally Diverse Students." In *Handbook of Research on Multicultural Education*, ed. J. Banks and C. Banks. Macmillan: 484–97.

Jackson, J., and G. Gurin (1987). *National Survey of Black Americans, 1979–1980.* Inter-University Consortium for Political and Social Research.

Jacob, B. (2001). "Getting Tough? The Impact of High School Graduation Exams." *Educational Evaluation and Policy Analysis* 23(2): 99–121.

Jacoby, T. (1999). "Beyond Busing." *Wall Street Journal*, July 21: A22.

Jargowsky, P. (1997). *Poverty and Place: Ghettos, Barrios, and the American City.* Russell Sage Foundation Press.

Jefferson, T. (1856 [1818]). "Report of the Commissioners Appointed to Fix the Site of the University of Virginia &c." In *Early History of the University of Virginia, as Contained in the Letters of Thomas Jefferson and Joseph Cabell.* J. W. Randolph: 432–47.

Jencks, C. (1970). *Education Vouchers: A Report on Financing Education by Payments to Parents.* Ctr. for the Study of Public Policy.

Jencks, C., and S. Mayer (1990). "The Social Consequences of Growing Up in a Poor Neighborhood." In *Inner-City Poverty in the United States*, ed. L. Lynn and M. McGeary. Natl. Academy Press: 111–86.

Jencks, C., and M. Phillips (1998). "America's Next Achievement Test." *American Prospect* 9 (40): 44–53.

Jencks, C., et al. (1972). *Inequality.* Basic Books.

Jepson, C., and S. Rivkin (2002). *Class Size Reduction, Teacher Quality, and Academic Achievement in California Public Elementary Schools.* Public Policy Institute of California.

Jesness, J. (1998). "What's Wrong with Bilingual Education? Repair It, Don't Replace It." *Ed. Week*, Aug. 5: 46–47, 72.

Johnson, D. (1990). "Milwaukee Creating 2 Schools Just for Black Boys." *New York Times*, Sept. 30: 1, 26.

Johnson, L. B. (1965). "Commencement Address at Howard University: 'To Fulfill These Rights,' June 4, 1965." In *Public Papers of the Presidents of the United States.* U.S. Government Printing Office: 635–40.

Johnson, S., et al. (2001). "Retaining the Next Generation of Teachers: The Importance of School-Based Support." *Harvard Education Letter* 17(4): 8, 6.

Johnston, R. (1997). "Texas Lawmakers Wrestle with Tax-Reform Efforts." *Ed. Week*, May 14: 8, 14.

——— (1998). "Frustrated with State, Texas Districts Back Reviving Finance Suit." *Ed. Week*, May 20: 19, 22–23.

Joiner, R. L. (1994). "Black Mayors Driving Away from Busing." *Emerge*, Mar. 31: 52.

Joint Ctr. for Political and Economic Studies (1992). *Voices of the Electorate among the African-American Population*. Wash., DC.

——— (1997). *1997 National Opinion Poll: Children's Issues*. Wash., DC.

——— (1998). *1998 National Opinion Poll: Education*. Wash., DC.

——— (1999). *1999 Opinion Poll: Education*. Wash., DC.

Jones, J., et al. (1995). "Individual and Organizational Predictors of High School Track Placement." *Sociology of Education* 68(4): 287–300.

Jordon, M. (1993). "Kentucky's Retooled Classrooms 'Erase the Board Clean.'" *Wash. Post*, Apr. 23: A3.

Judson, G. (1994a). "Communities Veto Integration Plan." *New York Times*, Nov. 26: 1ff.

——— (1994b). "Integration by Choice: Connecticut Struggles." *New York Times*, Oct. 7: B1.

Kahlenberg, R. (2001). *All Together Now: Creating Middle-Class Schools through Public School Choice*. Brookings Institution Press.

——— (2001). "The Fall and Rise of School Segregation." *American Prospect*, 12(9): 41–43.

Karen, D. (2002). "Changes in Access to Higher Education in the United States: 1980–1992." *Sociology of Education* 75(3): 191–210.

Karoly, L. et al. (1998). *Investing in Our Children: What We Know and Don't Know about the Costs and Benefits of Early Childhood Interventions*. Rand Corporation.

Kavale, K. (1990). "Effectiveness of Special Education." In *Handbook of School Psychology*, 2nd ed., ed. C. Reynolds and T. Gutkin. Wiley: 868–98.

Keedle, J. (2000). "Missing the Bus: Desegregation's Continued Failure." *Hartford Advocate*, Oct. 19.

Keegan, L. G. (2001). "'Our Gang' . . . A Reformer's Take on Injecting Sanity into the Education Wars." *School Choice Advocate*, Aug.: 1, 3, 6.

Keith, N. (1999). "Whose Community Schools?" *Theory into Practice* 38(4): 225–34.

Keller, B. (2001). "Chile's Longterm Voucher Plan Provides No Pat Answers." *Ed. Week*, Apr. 11: 8.

Kelley, C. (1998). "The Kentucky School-Based Performance Award Program: School-Level Effects." *Educational Policy* 12(3): 305–24.

Kelman, M., and G. Lester (1997). *Jumping the Queue: An Inquiry into the Legal Treatment of Students with Learning Disabilities*. Harvard U. Press.

Kennedy, J. (1963). Radio and Television Report to the American People on Civil Rights, June 11. In *Public Papers of the Presidents of the United States*. U.S. Government Printing Office: 468–71.

Kentucky Commission on Human Rights (1983). *School and Housing Desegregation Are Working Together in Louisville and Jefferson County*. Louisville, Kentucky.

Kerchner, C., et al. (1998). "'New and Improved' Teacher Unionism: But Will It Wash?" *Educational Leadership*, Feb. 1: 21ff.

Kersten, K. (2001). "Academy Teaches History with Integrated Approach." *Minneapolis Star Tribune*, June 22: 21A.

Kettering Foundation (1971). *Attitudes toward the Public Schools*. Apr. 23–26.

Keyes v. School District No. 1 of Denver, Colorado (1973). 413 U.S. 189.

Kirp, D. (1998). "New Hope for Failing Schools." *The Nation*, June 1: 20–22.

Kiss, E. (1999). "Democracy and the Politics of Recognition." In *Democracy's Edges*, ed. I. Shapiro and C. Hacker-Cordon. Cambridge U. Press: 193–209.

Klein, S., et al. (2000). "What Do Test Scores in Texas Tell Us?" *Educational Policy Analysis Archives* 8(49). http://epaa.asu.edu/epaa/v8n49.

Knapp, M. (1997). "Between Systemic Reforms and the Mathematics and Science Classroom." *Review of Educational Research* 67(2): 227–66.

Kohn, A. (1999). *The Schools Our Children Deserve: Moving beyond Traditional Classrooms and "Tougher" Standards*. Houghton Mifflin.

Koretz, D. (1997). "Indicators of Educational Achievement." In *Indicators of Children's Well-Being*, ed. R. Hauser et al. Russell Sage Foundation Press: 208–34.

Koretz, D., and S. Barron (1998). *The Validity of Gains in Scores on the Kentucky Instructional Results Information System (KIRIS)*. Rand Corporation.

Krueger, A. (1998). "Reassessing the View That American Schools Are Broken." *Federal Reserve Board of New York Economic Policy Review*, Mar.: 29–43.

——— (1999). "Experimental Estimates of Education Production Functions." *Quarterly Journal of Economics* 114(2): 497–532.

Krueger, A., and M. Lindahl (2001). "Education for Growth: Why and for Whom?" *Journal of Economic Literature* 39(4): 1101–36.

Krueger, A., and D. Whitmore (2001). "The Effect of Attending a Small Class in the Early Grades on College-Test Taking and Middle School Test Results." *Economic Journal* 111(468): 1–28.

——— (2002). "Would Smaller Classes Help Close the Black-White Achievement Gap?" In *Bridging the Achievement Gap*. ed. J. Chubb and T. Loveless. Brookings Institution Press.

Kulik, J. (1992). *An Analysis of the Research on Ability Grouping*. U. of Connecticut, Natl. Ctr. on the Gifted and Talented.

Kupermintz, H. (2001). "The Effect of Vouchers on School Improvement: Another Look at the Florida Data." *Education Policy Analysis Archives* 9(8). http://epaa.asu.edu/epaa/v9n8.

Kymlicka, W. (1996). *Multicultural Citizenship*. Oxford U. Press.

Labaree, D. (1997). *How to Succeed in School without Really Learning*. Yale U. Press.

Lacireno-Paquet, N., et al. (2002). "Creaming versus Cropping: Charter School Enrollment Practices in Response to Market Incentives." *Educational Evaluation and Policy Analysis* 24(2): 145–58.

Ladd, H., ed. (1996). *Holding Schools Accountable: Performance-Based Reform in Education*. Brookings Institution Press.

Ladd, H., and E. Fiske (2001). "The Uneven Playing Field of School Choice: Evidence from New Zealand." *Journal of Policy Analysis and Management* 20(1): 43–64.

Ladd, H., and J. Hansen (1999). *Making Money Matter: Financing America's Schools*. Natl. Academy Press.

Ladner, M., and C. Hammons (2001). "Special but Unequal: Race and Special Education." In *Rethinking Special Education for a New Century*, ed. C. Finn et al. Fordham Foundation and Progressive Policy Institute: 85–110.

Lambert, B. (2000). "Forty Percent in New York Born Abroad." *New York Times*, July 24: B1, 5.

Lamdin, D., and M. Mintrom (1997). "School Choice in Theory and Practice: Taking Stock and Looking Ahead." *Education Economics* 5(3): 211–44.

Lanigan, K., et al. (2001). "Nasty, Brutish . . . and Often Not Very Short: The Attorney Perspective on Due Process." In *Rethinking Special Education for a New Century*, ed. C. Finn et al. Fordham Foundation and Progressive Policy Institute: 213–31.

Lankford, H., and J. Wyckoff (1995). "Where Has the Money Gone? An Analysis of School District Spending in New York." *Educational Evaluation and Policy Analysis* 17(2): 195–218.

——— (1999). *The Effect of School Choice and Residential Location on the Racial Segregation of Students.* SUNY-Albany.

——— (2000). *Why Are Schools Racially Segregated? Implications for School Choice Policies.* Conference on Social Choice and Racial Diversity, Teachers College.

Lankford, H., et al. (2002). "Teacher Sorting and the Plight of Urban Schools." *Educational Evaluation and Policy Analysis* 24(1): 37–62.

"Latino Advertisers Launch Voter Drive" (1999). *Politico* 2(50). www.politicomagazine.com.

Lau v. Nichols (1974). 414 U.S. 563.

Leake, D., and C. Faltz (1993). "Do We Need to Desegregate All of Our Black Schools?" *Educational Policy* 7(3): 370–87.

Learning Disabilities Assn. of America (1993). "Inclusion: Position Paper." www.ldanatl.org/positions/inclusion.html.

Learning First Alliance (2001). *Standards and Accountability: A Call by the Learning First Alliance for Mid-Course Corrections.* Wash., DC.

"Learning: PBS Studies Public Education" (2001). *Boston Herald*, Aug. 12: M05.

Lee, E. (1995). "Taking Multicultural, Anti-racist Education Seriously: An Interview with Enid Lee." In *Rethinking Schools: An Agenda for Change*, ed. D. Levine et al. Free Press: 9–16.

Lee, M. J. (1999). "How *Sheff* Revives *Brown*: Reconsidering Desegregation's Role in Creating Equal Educational Opportunity." *New York U. Law Review* 74(2): 485–528.

Lee, V., and S. Loeb (2000). "School Size in Chicago Elementary Schools." *American Educational Research Journal* 37(1): 3–31.

Leland, J., and V. Smith (1997). "Echoes of Little Rock." *Newsweek*, Sept. 29: 52–58.

Lemay, J. (1991). *The American Dream of Captain John Smith.* U. Press of Virginia.

Lennon, C. (2000). *You Can't Bus Parental Attitudes: Parenting and the Battle over Segregation and Inequality in Connecticut's Schools.* Ph.D. dissertation, Columbia U., Dept. of Anthropology.

Lerner, L. (2000). *Good Science, Bad Science: Teaching Evolution in the States.* Fordham Foundation.

Levin, H. (1983). "Educational Choice and the Pains of Democracy." In *Public Dollars for Private Schools: The Case of Tuition Tax Credits*, ed. T. James and H. Levin. Temple U. Press.

——— (1987). "Education as a Public and Private Good," with Comments by Anita

Summers and Albert Shanker. *Journal of Policy Analysis and Management* 6(4): 628–47.

Levinson, M. (1999a). "Liberalism, Pluralism, and Political Education: Paradox or Paradigm?" *Oxford Review of Education* 25(1 & 2): 39–58.

——— (1999b). *The Demands of Liberal Education*. Oxford U. Press.

Levinson, S. (1993). "Some Reflections on Multiculturalism, 'Equal Concern and Respect,' and the Establishment Clause of the First Amendment." *University of Richmond Law Review* 27(5): 989–1021.

Lewin, T. (1998). "Patchwork of School Financing Schemes Offers Few Answers and Much Conflict." *New York Times*, Apr. 8: B9.

Libov, C. (1988). "Racial Report on Schools: The Fallout." *New York Times*, Jan. 31: Sec. 11 CN, 1.

Lieberman, J. (1999). "Schools Where Kids Succeed." *Readers' Digest*, Jan.: 145–51.

Lieberman, L. (2001). "The Death of Special Education." *Ed. Week*, Jan. 17: 60, 40–41.

Lieberman, M. (1993). *Public Education: An Autopsy*. Harvard U. Press.

Lillard, D., and P. DeCicca (2001). "Higher Standards, More Dropouts?" *Economics of Education Review* 20(5): 459–73.

Linn, R. (2000). "Assessments and Accountability." *Educational Researcher* 29(2): 4–16.

Lipsky, D., and A. Gartner (1997). *Inclusion and School Reform*. Paul Brookes.

Lissitz, R. (1994). *Assessment of Student Performance and Attitude, Year IV—1994; St. Louis Metropolitan Area Court Ordered Desegregation Effort*. Report Submitted to Voluntary Interdistrict Coordinating Council.

Loeb, S., and J. Bound (1996). "The Effect of Measured School Inputs on Academic Achievement." *Review of Economics and Statistics* 78(4): 653–64.

Lopez, E. (1999). *Major Demographic Shifts Occurring in California*. California Research Bureau.

Lopez, M. (1999). *Does Bilingual Education Affect Educational Attainment and Labor Market Outcomes?* University of Maryland, School of Public Affairs.

Lopez, M., and M. Mora (1998). "The Labor Market Effects of Bilingual Education among Hispanic Workers." *READ Perspectives* 5(2).

Lorence, J., et al. (2002). "Grade Retention and Social Promotion in Texas, 1994–99: Academic Achievement among Elementary School Students," with Comments by Andrew Rotherham and Lorrie Shepard. In *Brookings Papers on Education Policy 2002*, ed. D. Ravitch. Brookings Institution Press: 13–67.

Los Angeles Times (1998). *A Study of California's Public Schools*. Nov.–Dec. 1997.

Los Angeles Times Poll (1991). Race Relations and Judge Thomas Nomination—#259. Sept. 21–25.

——— (1993a). Asians in Southern California—#318. Aug. 7–10.

——— (1993b). Los Angeles Mayor's Race, Schools and Immigration—#306. Jan. 28–Feb. 2.

——— (1994). Future of Los Angeles County—#338. June 17–20.

——— (1995). National Issues—#352. Jan. 19–22.

——— (1997). California Adults, Parents and Children: Education in California—#403. Nov. 18–Dec. 12.

——— (1999). City of Los Angeles Survey—#424. Mar. 20–27.

——— (2000) Exit Poll: California Primary Election—#439. March 7.

Losen, D. (1999). "Silent Segregation in Our Nation's Schools." *Harvard Civil Rights-Civil Liberties Law Review* 34(2): 517–45.

Losh-Hesselbart, S. (1999). "Religion in the Public Schools." *Florida Public Opinion* 3(1): 2–12.

Lou, Y., et al. (1996). "Within-Class Grouping: A Meta-analysis." *Review of Educational Research* 66 (4): 423–58.

Loveless, T. (1999). *The Tracking Wars: State Reform Meets School Policy.* Brookings Institution Press.

———, ed. (2000). *Conflicting Missions: Teachers' Unions and Educational Reform.* Brookings Institution Press.

——— (2001). *How Well Are American Students Learning?* Brookings Institution Press.

Lucas, S. (1999). *Tracking Inequality: Stratification and Mobility in American High Schools.* Teachers College Press.

Lucas, S., and A. Gamoran (1993). *Race and Track Assignment: A Reconsideration with Course-Based Indicators.* University of Wisconsin, Dept. of Sociology.

Ludwig, J., and L. Bassi (1999). "The Puzzling Case of School Resources and Student Achievement." *Educational Evaluation and Policy Analysis* 21(4): 385–403.

Ludwig, J., et al. (2001). "Urban Poverty and Educational Outcomes." In *Brookings-Wharton Papers on Urban Affairs.* ed. W. Gale and J. Pack. Brookings Institution Press: 147–201.

Lundberg, P. (2000). "State Courts and School Funding: A Fifty-State Analysis." *Albany Law Review* 63(4): 1101–46.

Lynch, J. (2001). "The Age-Orientation of Social Policy Regimes in OECD Countries." *Journal of Social Policy* 30(3): 411–36.

Macedo, D. (1997). "English Only: The Tongue-Tying of America." In *Latinos and Education,* ed. A. Darder et al. Routledge: 269–78.

——— (2000). "The Colonialism of the English-Only Movement." *Educational Researcher* 29(3): 15–24.

Macedo, S. (1995). "Liberal Civic Education and Religious Fundamentalism: The Case of God v. John Rawls?" *Ethics* 105(3): 468–96.

Macedo, S. and Y. Tamir, eds. (2002). *Moral and Political Education: Nomos XLIII.* New York University Press.

MacManus, S., and P. Turner (1996). *Young vs. Old: Generational Combat in the Twenty-first Century.* Westview.

Madden, J. (2000). *Changes in Income Inequality within U.S. Metropolitan Areas.* Upjohn Institute for Employment Research.

Madden, N., and R. Slavin (1983). "Mainstreaming Students with Mild Handicaps." *Review of Educational Research* 53(4): 519–69.

"A Major *Los Angeles Times* Poll: California Parents and Teachers" (1998). *Public Perspective* 9(5): 27

Malcom X, (1965). *Autobiography of Malcolm X.* Ed. by A. Haley. Ballantine.

Malen, B. (1999). "The Promises and Perils of Participation on Site-Based Councils." *Theory into Practice* 38(4): 209–16.

Manzo, K. (1997). "Hispanics Want School Courses to Reflect Their History, Culture." *Ed. Week,* May 14: 1, 24.

——— (2001). "Protests over State Testing Widespread." *Ed. Week,* May 16: 1, 26.

Marable, M. (1995). *Beyond Black and White: Transforming African-American Politics.* Verso.

Maraniss, D. (1990). "Integration: Its Promise and Failings." *Wash. Post*, Mar. 4: A1, 22.

Maranto, R. (2001). "Finishing Touches." *Education Next* 1(4): 20–25.

Margolis, E., and S. Moses (1992). *The Elusive Quest: The Struggle for Equality of Educational Opportunity*. Apex.

Marist Institute for Public Opinion (1996). *Mayor Giuliani's Job Performance, Re-election Prospects, Quality of City Life, NYC Public Schools*. Marist College.

Martinez, V., et al. (1996). "Public School Choice in San Antonio." In *Who Chooses? Who Loses?* ed. B. Fuller et al. Teachers College Press: 50–69.

Mashberg, G., and E. Yablonski (1999). "Balancing Religious, Academic Freedoms in Public Education." *New York Law Journal*, July 19: F6.

Massey, D. (1996). "The Age of Extremes: Concentrated Affluence and Poverty in the Twenty-First Century." *Demography* 33(4): 395–412.

Mathematica Policy Research, Inc. (2000). *Voucher Claims of Success Are Premature in New York City*. Princeton, NJ.

———— (2002). *Making a Difference in the Lives of Infants and Toddlers and Their Families: The Impacts of Early Head Start*. Princeton, NJ

Maybank, R. (1996). "Clergy, Educators Blast State Plan to Take Over City Schools." *Baltimore Afro-American*, Aug. 10.

Mayer, D., et al. (2002). *School Choice in New York City after Three Years: An Evaluation of the School Choice Scholarships Program*. Harvard U., Program on Education Policy and Governance.

Mayer, S. (2001). "How Did the Increase in Economic Inequality between 1970 and 1990 Affect American Children's Educational Attainment?" *American Journal of Sociology* 107(1): 1–32.

McCormick, T. (1984). "Multiculturalism: Some Principles and Issues." *Theory into Practice* 23(2): 93–97.

McDermott, K. (1999). *Controlling Public Education*. U. Press of Kansas.

———— (2000). "Barriers to Large-Scale Success of Models for Urban School Reform." *Educational Evaluation and Policy Analysis* 22(1): 83–89.

McDermott, K., et al. (2002). "Have Connecticut's Desegregation Policies Produced Desegregation?" *Equity & Excellence in Education* 35(1): 18–27.

McDonnell, L. (1994). "Assessment Policy as Persuasion and Regulation." *American Journal of Education* 102(4): 394–420.

McDonnell, L., et al., eds. (1997). *Educating One and All: Students with Disabilities and Standards-Based Reform*. Natl. Academy Press.

———— (2000). *Rediscovering the Democratic Purposes of Education*. U. Press of Kansas.

McEwan, P. (2000). "The Potential Impact of Large-Scale Voucher Programs." *Review of Educational Research* 70(2): 103–49.

McEwan, P., and M. Carnoy (2000). "The Effectiveness and Efficiency of Private Schools in Chile's Voucher System." *Educational Evaluation and Policy Analysis* 22(3): 213–39.

McGrath, D., and P. Kuriloff (1999). "'They're Going to Tear the Doors off This Place:' Upper-Middle-Class Parent School Involvement and the Educational Opportunities of Other People's Children." *Educational Policy* 13(5): 603–29.

McGuinn, P. (2001). *Race, School Vouchers, and Urban Politics: The Disconnect between African-American Elite and Mass Opinion*. Annual mtg., American Political Science Assn.

McKean, J. B. (2000). Letter to the Editor. *Ed. Week*, Feb. 2: 44.

McLaren, P. (1997). *Revolutionary Multiculturalism: Pedagogies of Dissent for the New Millennium*. Westview.

McLaughlin, M., and J. Talbert (1993). "How the World of Students and Teachers Challenges Policy Coherence." In *Designing Coherent Education Policy*, ed. S. Fuhrman. Jossey-Bass: 220–49.

——— (2001). *Professional Communities and the Work of High School Teaching*. U. of Chicago Press.

McMurtrie, B. (2001). "Darwinism under Attack." *Chronicle of Higher Education*, Dec. 21: A8–11.

McQuillan, P., and K. Englert (2001). "The Return to Neighborhood Schools, Concentrated Poverty, and Educational Opportunity." *Hastings Constitutional Law Quarterly* 28(4): 739–70.

Meeks, L. et al. (2000). "Racial Desegregation: Magnet Schools, Vouchers, Privatization, and Home Schooling." *Education and Urban Society* 33(1): 88–101.

Meier, D. (1996). *The Power of Their Ideas: Lessons for America from a Small School in Harlem*. Beacon Press.

Meier, K. J., et al. (1989). *Race, Class, and Education: The Politics of Second-Generation Discrimination*. U. of Wisconsin Press.

Melnick, R. S. (1994). *Between the Lines: Interpreting Welfare Rights*. Brookings Institution Press.

Mendro, R. et al. (1998). *An Application of Multiple Linear Regression in Determining Longitudinal Teacher Effectiveness*. Dallas Public Schools.

Merelman, R. (1995). *Representing Black Culture: Racial Conflict and Cultural Politics in the United States*. Routledge.

Metropolitan Life Survey (1993). *The American Teacher 1993: Teachers Respond to President Clinton's Education Proposals*. Metropolitan Life Insurance Co.

——— (1995). *The American Teacher, 1984–1995: Old Problems, New Challenges*, Metropolitan Life Insurance Co.

——— (1996). *Students Voice Their Opinions on: Learning about Multiculturalism*. Metropolitan Life Insurance Co.

——— (2000). *Are We Preparing Students for the Twenty-first Century?* Metropolitan Life Insurance Co.

Mickelson, R., and D. Heath (1999). "The Effects of Segregation on African American High School Seniors' Academic Achievement." *Journal of Negro Education* 68(4): 566–86.

Milken Family Foundation (1997). Education Technology Survey. May 29–31.

Miller, L. (1995). *An American Imperative: Accelerating Minority Educational Advancement*. Yale U. Press.

Miller, P. (1954). *The New England Mind: The Seventeeth Century*. Harvard U. Press.

Miller Brewing Company (1983). Miller Lite Report on American Attitudes Toward Sports 1983. Oct. 1–30, 1982.

Miller-Kahn, L., and M. L. Smith (2001). "School Choice Policies in the Political Spectacle." *Education Policy Analysis Archives* 9(50). http://epaa.asu.edu/epaa/v9n50.

Milligan, S. (2001). "Jeffords' Special-Ed Plan Revived as Power Shifts, Democrats Press for Full Funding." *Boston Globe*, June 4: A1.

Milliken v. Bradley I (1974). 418 U.S. 717.

Mills v. Board of Education of the District of Columbia (1972). 348 F. Supp. 866.

Minorini, P., and S. Sugarman (1999a). "Educational Adequacy and the Courts." In *Equity and Adequacy in Education Finance*, ed. H. Ladd et al. Natl. Academy Press: 175–208.

———— (1999b). "School Finance Litigation in the Name of Educational Equity." In *Equity and Adequacy in Education Finance*, ed. H. Ladd et al. Natl. Academy Press: 34–71.

Minow, M. (1991). "School Finance: Does Money Matter?" *Harvard Journal on Legislation* 28(2): 395–400.

Mintrom, M. (2001). "Policy Design for Local Innovation: The Effects of Competition in Public Schooling." *State Politics and Policy Quarterly* 1(4): 343–63.

Mirel, J. (1999). *The Rise and Fall of an Urban School System: Detroit, 1907–81.* U. of Michigan Press.

———— (2001). *The Evolution of the New American Schools.* Fordham Foundation.

Miron, G., and C. Nelson (2001). *Student Academic Achievement in Charter Schools: What We Know and Why We Know So Little.* Teachers College, Natl. Ctr. for the Study of Privatization in Education.

Missouri v. Jenkins (1995). 515 U.S. 70.

Moe, T. (1995). "Private Vouchers." In *Private Vouchers*, ed. T. Moe. Hoover Institution Press: 1–40.

———— (2001). *Schools, Vouchers, and the American Public.* Brookings Institution Press.

Moffit, R., et al., eds. (2001). *School Choice 2001:What's Happening in the States.* Heritage Foundation.

Molnar, A., et al. (2001). *2000–2001 Evaluation Results of the Student Achievement Guarantee in Education (SAGE) Program.*, U. of Wisconsin-Milwaukee, School of Education.

Monk, D., and J. Rice (1997). "The Distribution of Mathematics and Science Teachers across and within Secondary Schools." *Educational Policy* 11(4): 479–98.

Montgomery, L. (2002). "Md. Seeks 'Adequacy,' Recasting School Debate." *Wash. Post*, Apr. 22: A1.

Moody, C., and J. Ross (1980). "Costs of Implementing Court-Ordered Desegregation." *Breakthrough* (Journal of U. of Michigan, School of Education) 9(1).

Moore, D. (1999). *Americans Support Teaching Creationism as Well as Evolution in Public Schools.* Gallup News Service.

Moran, R. (1987). "Bilingual Education as a Status Conflict." *California Law Review* 75(1): 321–62.

———— (1988). "The Politics of Discretion: Federal Intervention in Bilingual Education." *California Law Review* 76(6): 1249–1352.

———— (1996a). "Courts and the Construction of Racial and Ethnic Identity: Public Law Litigation in the Denver Schools." In *Legal Culture and the Legal Profession*, ed. L. Friedman and H. Scheiber. Westview: 153–79.

———— (1996b). "In the Multicultural Battle, Victory Is to the Weak." *Institute of Governmental Studies (IGS) Public Affairs Report*, Jan.: 1, 14–16.

Morgan, D. (2001). "The New School Finance Litigation." *Northwestern U. Law Review* 96(1): 99–189.

Morgan, E. (1975). *American Slavery, American Freedom: The Ordeal of Colonial Virginia.* Norton.

Moses, R., and C. Cobb (2001). *Radical Equations: Math Literacy and Civil Rights.* Beacon Press.

Mosteller, F., et al. (1996). "Sustained Inquiry in Education: Lessons from Skill Grouping and Class Size." *Harvard Educational Review* 66(4): 797–842.

Mozert v. Hawkins County Board of Education (1986). 647 F. Supp. 1194.

———— (1987). 827 F. 2d. 1058.

Murphy, T. (1994). "Handicapping Education." *Natl. Review*, Sept. 12: 56–59.

Murray, S., et al. (1998). "Education-Finance Reform and the Distribution of Education Resources." *American Economic Review* 88(4): 789–812.

NAACP Legal Defense and Educational Fund (1989). *The Unfinished Agenda on Race in America, vol. 1.* New York.

"NAACP Sets Advanced Goals" (1954). *New York Times*, May 18: 16.

Natl. Assn. of Elementary School Principals (1995). "Rethink Full Inclusion, Say Principals in Nationwide Poll." *NAESP News*, Apr. 7.

Natl. Assn. of State Boards of Education (1997). *The Full Measure: Report of the NASBE Study Group on Statewide Assessment Systems.* Alexandria, VA.

Natl. Assn. of State Budget Officers (1999). *State Expenditures Report 1998.* Wash., DC.

Natl. Assn. of the Deaf (1994). Position Statement on Full Inclusion (July 1994). www.nad.org/infocenter/newsroom/papers/fullinclusion.html, accessed July 15, 1999 (no longer available).

Natl. Ctr. for Education Statistics (1994). *Curricular Differentiation in Public High Schools.* U.S. Dept. of Education.

———— (1995a). *National Education Longitudinal Study of 1988: Trends among High School Seniors, 1972–1992.* U.S. Dept. of Education.

———— (1995b). *Use of School Choice.* U.S. Dept. of Education.

———— (1999). *Answers in the Toolbox: Academic Intensity, Attendance Patterns, and Bachelor's Degree Attainment.* U.S. Dept. of Education.

———— (2000a). *Condition of America's Public School Facilities: 1999.* U.S. Dept. of Education.

———— (2000b). *Mapping the Road to College: First-Generation Students' Math Track, Planning Strategies, and Context of Support.* U.S. Dept. of Education.

———— (2000c). *Monitoring School Quality: An Indicators Report.* U.S. Dept. of Education.

———— (2000d). *School-Level Correlates of Academic Achievement.* U.S. Dept. of Education.

———— (2000e). *The State of Charter Schools 2000.* U.S. Dept. of Education.

———— (2001a). *The 1998 High School Transcript Study Tabulations.* U.S. Dept. of Education.

———— (2001b). *Characteristics of the 100 Largest Public Elementary and Secondary School Districts in the United States: 1999–2000.* U.S. Dept. of Education.

———— (2001c). *Nation's Report Card: Fourth-Grade Reading 2000.* U.S. Dept. of Education.

———— (2001d). *Outcomes of Learning: Results from the 2000 Program for International Student Assessment of 15-Year-Olds in Reading, Mathematics, and Science Literacy.* U.S. Dept. of Education.

———— (2001e). *Nation's Report Card: Mathematics Highlights 2000.* U.S. Dept. of Education.

—— (2002). *Schools and Staffing Survey 1999–2000: Overview of the Data for Public, Private, Public Charter, and Bureau of Indian Affairs Elementary and Secondary Schools.* U.S. Dept. of Education.

—— (various years). *The Condition of Education [Year].* U.S. Dept. of Education.

—— (various years). *Digest of Education Statistics [Year].* U.S. Dept. of Education.

Natl. Ctr. for Public Policy and Higher Education (2000). *Measuring Up 2000: The State-by-State Report Card for Higher Education.* San Jose, CA.

Natl. Clearinghouse for English Language Acquisition. (2002). "Ask NCELA: Frequently Asked Questions." www.ncbe.gwu.edu/askncela/faqs.htm.

Natl. Commission on Excellence in Education (1983). *A Nation at Risk: The Imperative for Educational Reform.* U.S. Government Printing Office.

Natl. Commission on Governing America's Schools (1999). *Governing America's Schools: Changing the Rules.* Education Commission of the States.

Natl. Commission on Teaching and America's Future (1996). *What Matters Most: Teaching for America's Future.* Teachers College.

Natl. Conference (1994). *Taking America's Pulse: The Full Report of the National Conference Survey on Inter-group Relations.* New York.

Natl. Council for the Social Studies, Ad Hoc Committee on Ability Grouping (1992). "Ability Grouping in the Social Studies." *Social Education*, Sept.: 268–70.

Natl. Education Association (1998). *New Rules, New Roles? The Professional Work Lives of Charter School Teachers.* Wash., DC.

—— (1999). "1999–2000 Resolutions." www.nea.org/resolutions/99/99b-14.html, accessed August 2000 (no longer available).

Natl. Education Goals Panel (1994). *Natl. Education Goals Report: Building a Nation of Learners.* U.S. Government Printing Office.

—— (2001). *March toward Excellence: School Success and Minority Student Achievement in Dept. of Defense Schools.* U.S. Dept. of Education.

Natl. Research Council (1996). *National Science Education Standards.* Natl. Academy Press.

Natl. School Boards Foundation (1999). *Leadership Matters: Transforming Urban School Boards.* Alexandria, VA.

Natl. Science Foundation (1983). *Educating Americans for the Twenty-First Century.* Wash., DC.

Natl. Science Teachers Assn. (1997). NSTA Position Statement: The Teaching of Evolution. www.nsta.org/159&id=10.

NBC News/*Wall Street Journal* (1997). Poll Mar. 6–10.

—— (1998). Poll. Apr. 18–20.

—— (1999). Poll. Sept. 9–12.

—— (2000). Poll. Aug. 10–11.

Ness, C., and A. Nakao (1996). "Opponents File Suit to Block Prop. 209." *San Francisco Examiner*, Nov. 6: A1ff.

New Jersey Dept. of Education (2001). *Evaluation of New Jersey Charter Schools.* Office of Charter Schools.

Newman, M. (1999). "The Cost of Educating a Pupil Varies Widely among School Districts." *New York Times*, Mar. 28: NJ8.

—— (2002). "Federal Law on Failing Schools Has States Scrambling to Comply." *New York Times*, July 4.

Newmann, F., et al. (1997). "Accountability and School Performance: Implications from Restructuring Schools." *Harvard Educational Review* 67(1): 41–74.

——— (1999). *The Quality of Intellectual Work in Chicago Schools.* Consortium on Chicago School Research.

——— (2001a). "Instructional Program Coherence." *Educational Evaluation and Policy Analysis* 23(4): 297–321.

——— (2001b). *Authentic Intellectual Work and Standardized Tests: Conflict or Coexistence?* Consortium on Chicago School Research.

Newsweek (1981). *Newsweek* Survey. Mar. 11–17.

——— (1988). "Black and White: A *Newsweek* Poll." Feb. 19–22: 23.

Nie, N., et al. (1996). *Education and Democratic Citizenship in America.* U. of Chicago Press.

Nobles, W. (1990). "The Infusion of African and African American Content." In *Infusion of African and African American Content in the School Curriculum,* ed. A. Hilliard III et al. Aaron Press: 5–24.

Noguera, P., and A. Akom (2000). "The Significance of Race in the Racial Gap in Academic Achievement." www.inmotionmagazine.com/pnaa.html.

Noonan, K. (2000). "I Believed That Bilingual Education Was Best . . . Until the Kids Proved Me Wrong." *Wash. Post,* Sept. 3: B1, 2.

Norman, G. (2000). "The New Vermont: Give It to Canada!" *Weekly Standard,* June 26: 22–25.

NPR/Kaiser Family Foundation/J. F. Kennedy School of Government, Harvard U. (1999). Education Survey. June 25–July 19.

Numbers, R. (1992). *The Creationists.* Knopf.

Nunn, C., et al. (1978). *Tolerance for Nonconformity.* Jossey-Bass.

Oakes, J. (1985). *Keeping Track: How Schools Structure Inequality.* Yale U. Press.

Oakes, J., et al. (1992). "Curriculum Differentiation." In *Handbook of Research on Curriculum,* ed. P. Jackson. Macmillan: 570–608.

Oberti v. Board of Education of Clementon School District (1993). 995 F.2d 1204.

O'Brien, T. (1998). "Taking the Initiative." *West,* Jan. 11: 8–13.

Office for Civil Rights (2000). *The Use of Tests When Making High-Stakes Decisions for Students: Draft.* U.S. Dept. of Education.

Office of Bilingual Education and Minority Languages (1998). "About Us: Office of Bilingual Education and Minority Language Affairs." www.ed.gov/offices/OBEMLA/aboutus.html; www.ed.gov/offices/OBEMLA/faq.html. accessed July 30, 1999 (no longer available).

Office of Educational Research and Improvement (1996). *Assessment of School-Based Management.* U.S. Dept. of Education.

Office of Special Education Programs (various years). *Annual Report to Congress on the Implementation of the Individuals with Disabilities Education Act.* U.S. Dept. of Education.

Ogawa, R., et al. (1999). "California's Class-Size Reduction Initiative." *Educational Policy* 13(5): 659–73.

Oliver, E. (2001). *Democracy in Suburbia.* Princeton U. Press.

Olneck, M. (1993). "Terms of Inclusion: Has Multiculturalism Redefined Equality in American Education?" *American Journal of Education* 101(3): 234–60.

Olson, C., and D. Ackerman (2000). *High School Inputs and Labor Market Outcomes for Male Workers in Their Mid-Thirties.* U. of Wisconsin, Institute for Research on Poverty.

Olson, L. (1993). "Off and Running." *Ed. Week*, Apr. 21: 4–11.

——— (1998a). "Failing Schools Challenge Accountability Goals." *Ed. Week*, Mar. 25: 1, 14.

——— (1998b). "Will Success Spoil Success for All?" *Ed. Week*, Feb. 4: 42–45.

——— (1999a). "Pay-Performance Link in Salaries Gains Momentum." *Ed. Week*, Oct. 13: 1, 18.

——— (1999b). "Researchers Rate Whole-School Reform Models." *Ed. Week*, Feb. 17: 1, 14, 15.

——— (2000a). "Children of Change." *Ed. Week*, Sept. 27: 30–41.

——— (2000b). "Gauging the Impact of Competition." *Ed. Week*, May 24: 1, 18–20.

——— (2000c). "Redefining 'Public' Schools." *Ed. Week*, Apr. 26: 1, 24–27.

Olson, L., and A. Bradley (1992). "Boards of Contention." *Ed. Week*, Apr. 29: 2–10.

"Open Letter" (1997). *Baltimore Sun*, Apr. 1.

"Opinions of Candidates on Teaching Creationism Alarm Some Scientists" (1999). *St. Louis Post-Dispatch*, Aug. 27: A6.

O'Reilly, K. (1995). *Nixon's Piano: Presidents and Racial Politics from Washington to Clinton.* Free Press.

Orfield, G. (1978). *Must We Bus? Segregated Schools and National Policy.* Brookings Institution Press.

Orfield, G., and N. Gordon (2001). *Schools More Separate: Consequences of a Decade of Resegregation.* Harvard U., Civil Rights Project.

Orfield, G., and M. Kornhaber, eds. (2001). *Raising Standards or Raising Barriers? Inequality and High-Stakes Testing in Public Education.* Century Foundation Press.

Orfield, G., and J. Yun (1999). *Resegregation in American Schools.* Harvard U., Civil Rights Project.

Orfield, G., et al. (1992). *Desegregation and Educational Change in San Francisco: Findings and Recommendations on Consent Decree Implementation.* Submitted to Judge William H. Orrick, U.S. District Court, San Francisco, California.

——— (1996). *Dismantling Desegregation: A Quiet Reversal of Brown v. Board of Education.* New Press.

Orfield, M. (1998). *The Myth of the Suburban Monolith.* Harvard U., Civil Rights Project.

——— (2002). *American Metropolitics: The New Suburban Reality.* Brookings Institution Press.

Organization for Economic Cooperation and Development (2000). *Special Needs Education: Statistics and Indicators.* Paris.

——— (2001). *Starting Strong: Early Childhood Education and Care.* Paris.

——— (various years). *Education at a Glance: OECD Indicators.* Paris.

Orr, M. (1998). "The Challenge of School Reform in Baltimore: Race, Jobs, and Politics." In *Changing Urban Education*, ed. C. Stone. U. Press of Kansas: 93–117.

——— (1999). *Black Social Capital: The Politics of School Reform in Baltimore, 1986–1998.* U. Press of Kansas.

Orr, M., et al. (2000). *Concentrated Poverty and Educational Achievement: Politics and Possibility in the Baltimore Region.* U. of Maryland, Dept. of Government and Politics.

Osborne, L. (2000). "The Little Professor Syndrome." *New York Times Magazine*, June 18: 55–59.

O'Sullivan, J. (2000). "Doubletalk on the GOP Platform." *Chicago Sun-Times*, Aug. 22: 27.

Pallas, A., et al. (1994). "Ability-Group Effects." *Sociology of Education* 67(1): 27–46.

Pallmaffy, T. (2001). "The Evolution of the Federal Role." In *Rethinking Special Education for a New Century*, ed. C. Finn et al. Fordham Foundation and Progressive Policy Institute: 1–21.

Pankratz, R., and J. Petrosko, eds. (2000). *All Children Can Learn: Lessons from the Kentucky Reform Experience*. Jossey-Bass.

Pappas, D. (1997). *Changing the Nature of the School Desegregation Debate: The Non-Educational Benefits of the Wilmington, Delaware, Metropolitan Desegregation Plan*. B.A. thesis, Princeton U., Woodrow Wilson School of Public and Intl. Affairs.

Pardington, S. (2002). "Multilingual Pupils Pose a Challenge to Educators." *Contra Costa Times*, Jan. 13.

Paris, D. (1995). *Ideology and Educational Reform*. Westview.

Parker, W. (2000). "The Future of School Desegregation." *Northwestern University Law Review* 94(4): 1157–227.

Parrish, T. (1995a). *Criteria for Effective Special Education Funding Formulas*. Palo Alto, CA, Ctr. for Special Education Finance.

——— (1995b). "What Is Fair? Special Education and Finance Equity." *School Business Affairs* 61(8): 22–9.

Parry, T. (1997). "Theory Meets Reality in the Education Voucher Debate: Some Evidence from Chile." *Education Economics* 5(3): 307–31.

Patten, A. (2001). "Political Theory and Language Policy." *Political Theory* 29(5): 691–715.

Payne, C. (2001). "Building-Level Obstacles to Urban School Reform." In *Education Policy for the Twenty-First Century: Challenges and Opportunities in Standards-Based Reform*, ed. L. Joseph. U. of Illinois Press.

Payne, E., et al. (1978). "Student Perceptions: The Value of Desegregation." *Theory into Practice* 17(2): 172–78.

Payne, K., and B. Biddle (1999). "Poor School Funding, Child Poverty, and Mathematics Achievement." *Educational Researcher* 28(6): 4–13.

Pearce, D. (1981). "Deciphering the Dynamics of Segregation: The Role of Schools in the Housing Choice Process." *Urban Review* 13(2): 85–101.

Penn, M. (1999). "A Hunger for Reform." *Blueprint* [magazine of the Democratic Leadership Council], Fall.

Pennock, R., ed. (2001). *Intelligent Design, Creationism, and Its Critics*. MIT Press.

Pennsylvania Assn. for Retarded Children (PARC) v. Pennsylvania (1972). 343 F. Supp. 279.

People for the American Way Foundation (1999). "Sabotaging Science: Creationist Strategy in the 1990s." www.pfaw.org/issues/education/creationist-strategy.pdf.

——— (2000). "Evolution and Creationism in Public Education." www.pfaw.org/issues/education/creationism-poll.pdf.

Pessar, P. (1987). "The Dominicans: Women in the Household and the Garment Industry." In *New Immigrants in New York*, ed. N. Foner. Columbia U. Press: 103–29.

Peterson, P., and D. Campbell (2001). "Introduction: A New Direction in Public

Education?" In *Charters, Vouchers, and Public Education*, ed. P. Peterson and D. Campbell. Brookings Institution Press: 1–16.

Peterson, P., and B. Hassel (1998). *Learning from School Choice*. Brookings Institution Press.

Petrosko, J., and R. Pankratz (2000). "Public Opinion and Kentucky's School Reform." In *2000 Review of Research on the Kentucky Education Reform Act*, ed. Kentucky Institute for Education Research.

Petrosko, J., et al. (2000). "Executive Summary." In *2000 Review of Research on the Kentucky Education Reform Act*, ed. Kentucky Institute for Education Research.

Pew Forum on Religion & Public Life (2002). *Judgment Day for School Vouchers*. pewforum.org/events/print.php?EventID=30.

Pew Research Ctr. (1997a). Trust in Government Survey. Nov. 14–18.

———— (1997b). Values Update Survey. Nov. 5–17.

———— (1999a). People and the Press 1999 Values Update Survey. Sept. 28–Oct. 10.

———— (1999b). People and the Press Political Typology Survey. July 14–Sept. 9.

———— (2000). People and the Press Campaign 2000 Typology Survey. Aug. 24–Sept. 10.

Pewewardy, C. (1997). "Melting Pot, Salad Bowl, Multicultural Mosaic, Crazy Quilt, Orchestra, or Indian Stew: For Native Peoples, It's Your Choice! Or Is It?" *Indian Country Today (Lakota Times)*, Jan. 20: A7ff.

Phi Delta Kappa (various years). Attitudes toward the Public Schools [Year] Survey.

———— (various years). Teachers' Attitudes toward the Public Schools [Year] Survey [name varies across years].

Phillips, M. (2001). *Do African American and Latino Children Learn More in Predominantly White Schools?* UCLA, School of Public Policy and Social Research.

Picus, L., and J. Bryan (1997). "The Economic Impact of Public K–12 Education in the Los Angeles Region." *Education and Urban Society* 29(4): 442–52.

Planning and Evaluation Service (1993). *Prospects: The Congressionally Mandated Study of Educational Growth and Opportunity, Interim Report*. U.S. Dept. of Education.

Planning and Evaluation Service, and Office of Bilingual Education and Minority Language Affairs (1995). *Prospects: First Year Report on Language Minority and Limited English Proficient Students*. U.S. Dept. of Education.

Plyler v. Doe (1982). 457 U.S. 202.

Pogue, T. (2000). "No Silver Bullet: Questions and Data on Factors Affecting Educational Achievement." Finance Project. www.financeproject.org/achievement.htm.

Porter, A. (1994). "National Standards and School Improvement in the 1990s." *American Journal of Education* 102(4): 421–49.

Porter, R. (1996). *Forked Tongue: The Politics of Bilingual Education*. Transaction.

———— (2000). *Educating Language Minority Children*. Transaction.

Portz, J. (1999). *School Reform and Policy Choice*. Northeastern U., Dept. of Political Science.

Post-Modernity Project (1996). *The State of Disunion, volume 2: Summary Tables*. In Medias Research Educational Foundation.

Poterba, J. (1997). "Demographic Structure and the Political Economy of Public Education." *Journal of Policy Analysis and Management* 16(1): 48–66.

Press, B., and M. Matalin (1999). "Should Science or Religion Be Taught in the Public Schools?" Aug. 17. CNN.

Preston, J. (1998). "Plan by Whitman on Urban Schools Backed by Court." *New York Times*, May 22: 1, B6.

Pride, R. (2000). "Public Opinion and the End of Busing." *Sociological Quarterly* 41(2): 207–25.

Program on Intl. Policy Attitudes of U. of Maryland (2000). Education Survey. June 23–July 9, 1999.

"Proposal for Black/Latino Boys High School Considered" (1991). *New York Metro*, Jan. 22.

Public Agenda (1992). *Educational Reform: The Players and the Politics.* New York.

———— (1994). *First Things First: What Americans Expect from the Public Schools.* New York.

———— (1995a). *Assignment Incomplete: The Unfinished Business of Education Reform.* New York.

———— (1995b). *The Basics: Parents Talk about Reading, Writing, Arithmetic, and the Schools.* New York.

———— (1996). *Given the Circumstances: Teachers Talk about Public Education Today.* New York.

———— (1997). *Different Drummers: How Teachers of Teachers View Public Education.* New York.

———— (1998a). *A Lot to Be Thankful For.* New York.

———— (1998b). *Playing Their Parts: Parental Involvement in Public Schools Survey.* New York.

———— (1998c). *Reality Check: Parent Survey.* New York.

———— (1998d). *Time to Move On: An Agenda for Public Schools.* New York.

———— (1999a). *Cities, Suburbs, and Schools: Would Citizens in Chicago, Cleveland, and Milwaukee Support Greater Collaboration?* New York.

———— (1999b). *On Thin Ice: How Advocates and Opponents Could Misread the Public's Views on Vouchers and Charter Schools.* New York.

———— (2000a). "Clarifying Issues: Education." www.publicagenda.org/clarifying_issues/PDFs/education_ci2000.pdf.

———— (2000b). *National Poll of Parents of Public School Students.* New York.

———— (2002a). "Reality Check 2002." *Ed. Week*; March 6: S1–S8.

———— (2002b). *When It's Your Own Child.* New York.

Public Agenda Online (2002). "Education: Red Flags." www.publicagenda.org/issues/angles_graph.cfm?issue_type=education&id=339&graph=rf8.gif.

Public Education Network and *Ed. Week* (2002). "Accountability for All." *Polling Report* 18(9): 1, 7–8.

Public Policy Institute of California (1998). *The Changing Political Landscape of California, October.* San Francisco.

———— (1999). *The Changing Political Landscape of California, January.* San Francisco.

———— (2001). *Statewide Survey: Californians and Their Government, December.* San Francisco.

"Public Pulse" (2000). *Omaha World-Herald*, Aug. 20: 10B.

Puma, M., and D. Drury (2000). *Exploring New Directions: Title I in the Year 2000.* Natl. School Boards Assn.

Purdy, M. (1996). "Web of Patronage in Schools Grips Those Who Can Undo It." *New York Times*, May 14: A1, B4.

Purdy, M., and M. Newman (1996). "Students Lag in Districts Where Patronage Thrives." *New York Times*, May 13: A1, B4.

Pyle, A. (1996). "80 Students Stay Out of School in Latino Boycott." *Los Angeles Times*, Feb. 14: 1.

Ramakrishnan, K. (2002). *Voters from Different Shores.* Ph.D. dissertation, Princeton U., Dept. of Politics.

Rand Research Brief: Education (1998). *Reforming America's Schools: Observations on Implementing "Whole School Designs."* Rand Corporation.

Rasell, E., and R. Rothstein (1993). *School Choice: Examining the Evidence.* Economic Policy Institute.

Rauch, J. (2001). "Charter Schools: New Hope For America's Latinos." *Jewish World Review*, Oct. 1.

Raudenbush, S., et al. (1998). "Inequality of Access to Educational Resources: A National Report Card for Eighth-Grade Math." *Educational Evaluation and Policy Analysis* 20(4): 253–67.

Ravitch, D. (1996). "Somebody's Children: Educational Opportunity for All American Children." In *Social Policies for Children*, ed. I. Garfinkel et al. Brookings Institution Press: 83–111.

——— (1997). "In Memoriam: Albert Shanker, 1928–1997." *The New Leader*, Feb. 24: 3–4.

——— (2001). "Ex Uno Plures." *Education Next*, 27–29.

Ravitch, D., and J. Viteritti (1997). *New Schools for a New Century.* Yale U. Press.

——— (2001). *Making Good Citizens: Education and Civil Society.* Yale U. Press.

Raymo, C. (1999). "Darwin's Dangerous De-evolution." *Boston Globe*, Sept. 6: C2.

Raz, J. (1994). "Multiculturalism: A Liberal Perspective." *Dissent* (Winter): 67–79.

"Reactions to House Vote on Impeachment Investigation" (2000). *AP, Dateline: Concord, NH*, Apr. 14.

"Reading without Money" (2001). *Weekly Standard*, Dec. 24: 13.

Reardon, S., and T. Eitle (1998). *Patterns and Trends in Diversity and Segregation among Suburban Districts, 1990–1994.* Harvard U., Civil Rights Project.

Reardon, S., and J. Yun (2001). "Suburban Racial Change and Suburban School Segregation, 1987–1995." *Sociology of Education* 74(2): 79–101.

——— (2002). *Private School Racial Enrollments and Segregation*, Harvard U., Civil Rights Project.

Reardon, S., et al. (2000). "The Changing Structure of School Segregation." *Demography* 37(3): 351–64.

Recruiting New Teachers (1999). *Learning the Ropes: Urban Teacher Induction Programs and Practices within the United States.* Belmont, MA.

Reed, D. (1997). "Court-Ordered School Finance Equalization." In *Developments in School Finance, 1996*, ed. W. Fowler, Jr. U.S. Dept. of Education: 91–120.

——— (1998). "Twenty-five Years after *Rodriguez*: School Finance Litigation and the Impact of the New Judicial Federalism." *Law and Society Review* 32(1): 175–220.

———— (2001). *On Equal Terms: The Constitutional Politics of Educational Opportunity.* Princeton U. Press.

Rees, D., et al. (1996). "Tracking in the United States: Descriptive Statistics from NELS." *Economics of Education Review* 15(1): 83–89.

Reich, R. (2000). "The Case for 'Progressive' Vouchers." *Wall Street Journal*, Sept. 6: A26.

———— (2002). *Bridging Liberalism and Multiculturalism in American Education.* U. of Chicago Press.

Reid, K. (2000). "Iowa Grapples with Growing Diversity." *Ed. Week*, Oct. 11: 1, 22.

———— (2001). "Minority Parents Quietly Embrace School Choice." *Ed. Week*, Dec. 5: 1, 20.

Reinhard, B. (1998). "In Troubled Schools, Policy and Reality Collide." *Ed. Week*, Mar. 25: 15.

Renyi, J. (1993). *Going Public: Schooling for a Diverse Democracy.* New Press.

Resnick, L. (2001). "The Mismeasure of Learning." *Education Next* 1(3): 78–83.

Reyes, B. (2001). *A Portrait of Race and Ethnicity in California.* Public Policy Institute of California.

Reynolds, A., and J. Temple (1998). "Extended Early Childhood Intervention and School Achievement." *Child Development* 69(1): 231–46.

Reynolds, A., and B. Wolfe (1999). "Special Education and School Achievement." *Educational Evaluation and Policy Analysis* 21(3): 249–69.

Reynolds, A., et al. (2001). "Long-Term Effects of an Early Childhood Intervention on Educational Achievement and Juvenile Arrest." *JAMA: Journal of the American Medical Assn.* 285(18): 2339–46.

———— (2002). *Age 21 Cost-Benefit Analysis of the Title I Chicago Child-Parent Centers.* U. of Wisconsin, Institute for Research on Poverty.

Rhodebeck, L. (1998). "Competing Problems, Budget Constraints, and Claims for Intergenerational Equity." In *New Directions in Old Age Policies*, ed. J. Steckenrider and T. Parrott. SUNY Press: 154–84.

Rich, W. (1996). *Black Mayors and School Politics.* Garland.

Richard, A. (2002). "Broad Effort to Mix Students by Wealth Under Fire in N.C." *Ed. Week*, May 22: 1, 18.

Riley, R. (2000). "Excellencia para Todos—Excellence for All: The Progress of Hispanic Education and the Challenges of a New Century." www.ed.gov/Speeches/03-2000/000315.html.

Ringquist, E., and J. Garand (1999). "Policy Change in the American States." In *American State and Local Politics: Directions for the Twenty-first Century*, ed. R. Weber and P. Brace. Chatham House: 268–99.

Rivera, J. (2000). "Bush, Seeking Catholic Votes, Says He Backs School Vouchers." *Baltimore Sun*, May 27: 3A.

Rivera-Batiz, F. (1996). *The Education of Immigrant Children: The Case of New York City.* New School for Social Research, Intl. Ctr. for Migration, Ethnicity, and Citizenship.

Rizk, C. (1995). "Plan to Teach Church Kids Separately Angers Parents." *Detroit News*, Dec. 24.

Robelen, E. (2000). "Parents Seek Civil Rights Probe of High-Stakes Tests in La." *Ed. Week*, Oct. 11: 14.

——— (2002). "Few Choosing Public School Choice for This Fall." *Ed. Week*, Aug. 7: 1, 38–39.

Robinson v. Cahill (1973). 62 N.J. 473, 303 A.2d 1353.

Roch, C., and R. Howard (2001). *Litigation, State Courts, and Legislatures: The Case of Education Finance Reform.* Annual mtg., Midwest Political Science Assn.

Roderick, M., and M. Engel (2001). "The Grasshopper and the Ant: Motivational Responses of Low-Achieving Students to High-Stakes Testing." *Educational Evaluation and Policy Analysis* 23(3): 197–227.

Roderick, M., et al. (1999). *Ending Social Promotion: Results from the First Two Years.* Consortium on Chicago School Research.

——— (2000). *Update: Ending Social Promotion.* Consortium on Chicago School Research.

Rodriguez, G. (1998). "English Lesson in California." *The Nation*, Apr. 20: 15–19.

Rojas, P. (2000). "Storming Denver: Padres Unidos Battles for Better Education." *Colorlines*, Summer: 28–29.

Roos, P. (1998). "Intradistrict Resource Disparities." In *School Equity: Creating Productive Schools in a Just Society*, ed. M. Gittell. Yale U. Press: 40–52.

Roper Organization (1982). Roper Report. June 5–12.

Rose, H., and J. Betts (2001). *Math Matters: The Link between High School Curriculum, College Graduation, and Earnings.* Public Policy Institute of California.

Rose v. Council for Better Education, Inc., et al. (1989). 790 S.W.2d 186.

Rosenblum, K. (1999). "Rights at Risk: California's Proposition 187." In *Illegal Immigration in America*, ed. D. Haines and K. Rosenblum. Greenwood: 367–82.

Ross, C., and B. Broh (2000). "The Roles of Self-Esteem and the Sense of Personal Control in the Academic Achievement Process." *Sociology of Education* 73(4): 270–84.

Ross, T. (1998). "Grassroots Action in East Brooklyn: A Community Organization Takes Up School Reform." In *Changing Urban Education*, ed. C. Stone. U. Press of Kansas: 118–38.

Rossell, C., and K. Baker (1996). "The Educational Effectiveness of Bilingual Education." *Research in the Teaching of English* 30(1): 7–74.

Rossell, C., and C. Glenn (1988). "The Cambridge Controlled Choice Plan." *Urban Review* 20(2): 75–94.

Rossi, R. (1998). "School Bd. Limits Bilingual Program." *Chicago Sun-Times*, Feb. 26: 1.

Rothstein, R. (1997). *Where's the Money Going? Changes in the Level and Composition of Education Spending, 1991–1996.* Economic Policy Institute.

——— (1998a). "Charter Conundrum." *American Prospect*, 9 (39): 46–60.

——— (1998b). *The Way We Were? The Myths and Realities of America's Student Achievement.* Century Foundation Press.

——— (2000a). "Equalizing Education Resources on Behalf of Disadvantaged Children." In *A Notion at Risk: Preserving Public Education as an Engine for Social Mobility*, ed. R. Kahlenberg. Century Foundation Press: 31–92.

——— (2000b). "Positive Trends Hidden in SAT and ACT Scores." *New York Times*, Aug. 30: B10.

——— (2001). "Yes, Vouchers Are Dead, and Alternatives Flawed." *New York Times*, June 20: A14.

Rothstein, R., and K. H. Miles (1995). *Where's the Money Gone? Changes in the Level and Composition of Education Spending.* Economic Policy Institute.

Rothstein, R., and J. Nathan (1998). "Charters and Choice." *American Prospect* 9 (41): 74–77.

Rouse, C. (1998). "Private School Vouchers and Student Achievement: An Evaluation of the Milwaukee Parental Choice Program." *Quarterly Journal of Economics* 113(2): 553–602.

RPP Intl. (1999). *The State of Charter Schools 2000: Fourth-Year Report.* U.S. Dept. of Education.

——— (2001). *Challenge and Opportunity: The Impact of Charter Schools on School Districts.* U.S. Dept. of Education.

Rubinfeld, D., and R. Thomas (1980). "On the Economics of Voter Turnout in Local School Elections." *Public Choice* 35(3): 315–31.

Rubinowitz, L., and J. Rosenbaum (2000). *Crossing the Class and Color Lines: From Public Housing to White Suburbia.* U. of Chicago Press.

Ruffins, P. (1999). "What Ever Happened to Integration?" *Black Issues in Higher Education*, Jan. 7: 18–21.

Ruiz, R. (1997). "The Empowerment of Language-Minority Students." In *Latinos and Education*, ed. A. Darder et al. Routledge: 319–28.

Ruiz-de-Velasco, J., and M. Fix (2000). *Overlooked and Underserved: Immigrant Students in U.S. Secondary Schools.* Urban Institute.

Rusk, D. (2002). "Trends in School Segregation." In *Divided We Fail: Coming Together through Public School Choice*, Century Foundation Task Force on the Common School. Century Foundation Press: 61–65.

Ryan, J. (1999). "*Sheff*, Segregation, and School Finance Litigation." *NYU Law Review* 74(2): 529–73.

Ryan, J., and M. Heise (2002). "The Political Economy of School Choice." *Yale Law Journal* 111(8): 2043–2136.

Sack, J. (1998). "In Vermont's Funding Shakeup, a Bitter Pill for the 'Gold Towns.'" *Ed. Week*, Oct. 28: 1, 23.

——— (2000). "IDEA Opens Doors, Fans Controversy." *Ed. Week*, 1, 22–27.

Sacks, D. (1990). "Is Florio's Plan Stiff Medicine or Poison?" *New York Times*, July 11: A19.

Sacks, P. (2001). *Standardized Minds: The High Price of America's Testing Culture and What We Can Do to Change It.* Perseus Books.

Sacramento City Board of Education v. Rachel Holland et. al. (1994). 512 U.S. 1207.

Sahagun, L., and K. Weiss (1999). "Bias Suit Targets Schools without Advanced Classes." *Los Angeles Times*, July 28: 1ff.

San Antonio Independent School District v. Rodriguez (1973). Mar. 21 411 U.S. 1.

Sanders, W., and J. Rivers (1996). *Cumulative and Residual Effects of Teachers on Future Student Academic Achievement.* University of Tennessee, Value-Added Research and Assessment Ctr.

Sandham, J. (2001). "Challenges to Charter Laws Mount." *Ed. Week*, May 2: 1, 24–25.

Sanko, J. (2001). "Bilingual Education Foe Gets Support." *Rocky Mountain News*, Dec. 1.

Saporito, S., and A. Lareau (1999). "School Selection as a Process." *Social Problems* 46(3): 418–39.

Sashkin, M., and J. Egermeier (1993). *School Change Models and Processes.* U.S. Dept. of Education.

Schemo, D. (2000). "Students in U.S. Do Not Keep Up in Global Tests." *New York Times,* Dec. 6: A1, 18.

———— (2001). "Officials Say School Choice Often Just Isn't an Option." *New York Times,* Dec. 22: A11.

Schildkraut, D. (2000). *The English Language and American Identity* Ph.D. dissertation, Princeton U., Dept. of Politics.

Schmader, T., et al. (2001). "Coping with Ethnic Stereotypes in the Academic Domain." *Journal of Social Issues* 57(1): 93–111.

Schmidt, R. (1989–90). "Uniformity or Diversity? Recent Language Policy in California Public Education." *California History* (Winter): 231–39.

———— (2000). *Language Policy and Identity Politics in the United States.* Temple U. Press.

Schmidt, W., et al. (2001). *Why Schools Matter: A Cross-National Comparison of Curriculum and Learning.* Jossey-Bass.

Schnaiberg, L. (1999). "Seeking a Competitive Advantage." *Ed. Week,* Dec. 8: 1, 12–14.

———— (2000). "Research on Charters and Integration Is Limited." *Ed. Week,* May 10: 20.

Schneider, M., and J. Buckley (2002). "What Do Parents Want from Schools? Evidence from the Internet." *Eductional Evaluation and Policy Analysis* 24(2): 133–34.

Schneider, M., et al. (2000). *Choosing Schools: Consumer Choice and the Quality of American Schools.* Princeton U. Press.

———— (1998). *Tiebout, School Choice, Allocative and Productive Efficiency.* SUNY at Stony Brook, Dept. of Political Science.

Schofield, J. (1995a). "Improving Intergroup Relations Among Students." In *Handbook of Research on Multicultural Education,* ed. J. Banks and C. Banks. Macmillan: 635–46.

———— (1995b). "Review of Research on School Desegregation's Impact on Elementary and Secondary School Students." In *Handbook of Research on Multicultural Education,* ed. J. Banks and C. Banks. Macmillan: 597–616.

Schorr, L. (2001). "Tinkering with Head Start." *Ed. Week,* Mar. 28: 56, 41.

Schrag, P. (2001). "Defining Adequacy Up." *The Nation,* Mar. 12: 18–20.

Schulte, B., and D. Keating (2001). "Pupils' Poverty Drives Achievement Gap." *Wash. Post,* Sept. 2: A1, 12–13.

Schuman, H., et al. (1997). *Racial Attitudes in America: Trends and Interpretations.* Harvard U. Press.

Scott, M., and A. Bernhardt (2000). *Pathways to Educational Attainment: Their Effect on Early Career Development.* Teachers College, Institute on Education and the Economy.

Seattle v. State of Washington (1978). 90 Wash. 2d 476, 585 P.2d. 71.

Sefa Dei, G. (1994). "Afrocentricity: A Cornerstone of Pedagogy." *Anthropology and Education Quarterly* 25(1): 3–28.

Serrano v. Priest I (1971). 96 Cal. Rptr. 601.

Servin-Gonzalez, M., and O. Torres-Reyna (1999). "The Polls—Trends: Religion and Politics." *Public Opinion Quarterly* 63(4): 592–621.

Sexton, R. (1998). "The Pritchard Committee and Kentucky School Reform." In

School Equity: Creating Productive Schools in a Just Society, ed. M. Gittell. Yale U. Press: 200–209.

Shanker, A. (1994). "Reform: The Public Speaks." American Federation of Teachers. www.aft.org/stand/previous/1994/101694.html.

Shapiro, R., and J. Young (1990). "Public Opinion Toward Social Welfare Policies: The United States in Comparative Perspective." *Research in Micropolitics* 3:143–86.

Sharpes, D. (1987). *Education and the U.S. Government.* Croom Helm.

Shearson Lehman Brothers (1992). *Financial Success and the American Dream.* New York.

Sheff v. O'Neill I (1996). 238 Conn. 1; 678 A.2d 1267.

Sheff v. O'Neill II (1999). 45 Conn. Supp. 630; 733 A 2d.925.

Shell Oil Company (1998). Shell Poll. July 17–20.

Shen, F., and C. Babington (1996). "Maryland, Baltimore Plan Overhaul of City Schools." *Wash. Post*, Jan. 22: D1.

Shipps, D. (1998). "Corporate Influence on Chicago School Reform." In *Changing Urban Education*, ed. C. Stone, U. Press of Kansas: 161–83.

Shore, A. (1998). *Detracking: The Politics of Creating Heterogeneous Ability Classrooms.* B.A. thesis, Princeton U., Woodrow Wilson School of Public and Intl. Affairs.

Sidener, J. (1995). "Courts, Schools Targeted." *Arizona Republic*, Aug. 26: A1.

Sigelman, L., et al. (1996). "Making Contact? Black-White Social Interaction in an Urban Setting." *American Journal of Sociology* 101(5): 1306–32.

Silva, F., and J. Sonstelie (1995). "Did *Serrano* Cause a Decline in School Spending?" *Natl. Tax Journal* 47(2): 199–216.

Silver, L., (1997). "My Lesson in School Politics." *New York Times*, Sept. 10: A23.

Simmons-Harris et al. v. Zelman et al. (1999). 54 F. Supp. 2d 725.

Simon, C., and N. Lovrich (1996). "Private School Enrollment and Public School Performance." *Policy Studies Journal* 24(4): 666–75.

"Site-Based Management in Minneapolis Public Schools" (1994 [amended 1995, 1997]). Minneapolis Public Schools.

Skertic, M. (2001). "More Young People Are Multiracial." *Chicago Sun-Times*, Mar. 13: 5.

Slavin, R. (1990a). "Ability Grouping in Secondary Schools: A Response to Hallinan." *Review of Educational Research* 60(3): 505–7.

——— (1990b). "Achievement Effects of Ability Grouping in Secondary Schools." *Review of Educational Research* 60(3): 471–99.

Sleeter, C. (1986). "Learning Disabilities: The Social Construction of a Special Education Category." *Exceptional Children* 53(1): 46–54.

——— (1994). "Multicultural Education and the American Dream." *Race, Sex and Class* 2(1): 31–53.

Sleeter, C., and C. Grant (1987). "An Analysis of Multicultural Education in the United States." *Harvard Educational Review* 57(4): 421–44.

Sloane, W. (1996). "*Sheff* Decision Is Opportunity to Reinvent the School System." *Hartford Courant*, Sept. 2.

Smith, A. (1976 [1776]). *An Inquiry into the Nature and Causes of the Wealth of Nations.* U. of Chicago Press.

Smith, M., and J. O'Day (1991). "Educational Equality: 1966 and Now." In *Spheres of Justice in Education*, ed. D. Verstegen and J. Ward. Harper-Collins: 53–100.

——— (1991). "Systemic School Reform." In *The Politics of Curriculum and Testing*, ed. S. Fuhrman and B. Malen. Falmer Press: 233–68.

Smith, S. (forthcoming 2003). *Boom for Whom?: Education, Desegregation, and Development in Charlotte*. SUNY Press.

Smith v. Board of School Commissioners (1987). 827 F. 2d. 684.

Snow, C. (1998). *Preventing Reading Difficulties in Young Children*. Natl. Academy Press.

Snyder, S. (2002). "As Edison Schools Strives for Philadelphia Role, Failures Crop Up Elsewhere." *Knight Ridder Tribune Business News*, Feb. 1.

Soifer, D. (2002). "English Learners Not Left Behind with New Plan." *School Reform News* (of Lexington Institute), Jan.

Solmon, L., and M. Podgursky (c. 1999). *The Pros and Cons of Performance-Based Compensation*. Milken Foundation.

Sonstelie, J., and P. Richardson, eds. (2001). *School Finance and California's Master Plan for Education*. Public Policy Institute of California.

Spade, J., et al. (1997). "Tracking in Mathematics and Science." *Sociology of Education* 70(2): 108–27.

SRI Intl. and Bay Area Research Group (2001). *When Theory Hits Reality: Standards-Based Reform in Urban Districts*. Menlo Park, California.

St. Angelo, G. (2001). "President's Comments." *School Choice Advocate*, Dec.: 2.

St. John, N. (1975). *School Desegregation: Outcomes for Children*. Wiley.

Stainback, W., and S. Stainback (1992). *Curriculum Considerations in Inclusive Classrooms*. Paul Brookes.

Staples, B. (1997). "Special Education Is Not a Scandal." *New York Times Magazine*, Sept. 21: 64–5.

"State's Rights, Federalism Clash in Bilingual Education Debate" (2001). Associated Press, Jan. 5.

Stedman, J. (1994). *Goals 2000: Overview and Analysis*. Congressional Research Service.

Steger, W., and J. Bowermaster (1993). *Crossing Antarctica*. Knopf.

Stein, C. (1986). *Sink or Swim: The Politics of Bilingual Education*. Praeger.

Steinberg, J. (2000). "Increase in Test Scores Counters Dire Forecasts for Bilingual Ban." *New York Times*, Aug. 18: 1, 22.

Stephens, S. (2001). "Charter Schools Sorely Test Dayton." *Cleveland Plain Dealer*, May 21.

Stevens, M. (2001). *Kingdom of Children: Culture and Controversy in the Homeschooling Movement*. Princeton U. Press.

Stevenson, Z., Jr., and L. Gonzalez (1992). "Contemporary Practices in Multicultural Approaches to Education Among the Largest American School Districts." *Journal of Negro Education* 61(3): 356–69.

Stewart, D. (1993). *Immigration and Education*. Lexington Books.

Stiefel, L., et al. (2000). "High School Size: Effects on Budgets and Performance in New York City." *Educational Evaluation and Policy Analysis*. 22(1): 27–39.

Stolzenberg, N. M. (1993). "'He Drew a Circle That Shut Me Out': Assimilation, Indoctrination, and the Paradox of Liberal Education." *Harvard Law Review* 106 (3): 581–667.

Stone, C., ed. (1998a). *Changing Urban Education.* U. Press of Kansas.

—— (1998b). "Civic Capacity and Urban School Reform." In *Changing Urban Education*, ed. C. Stone. U. Press of Kansas: 250–73.

Stone, C., et al. (2001). *Building Civic Capacity: The Politics of Reforming Urban Schools.* U. Press of Kansas.

Sugarman, R. (1995). "New York City's District School Board Members Are Flunking Out." *New York Daily News*, May 30: 4ff.

Sugarman, S., and F. Kemerer, eds. (1999). *School Choice and Social Controversy.* Brookings Institution Press.

Sugrue, T. (1996). *The Origins of the Urban Crisis: Race and Inequality in Postwar Detroit.* Princeton U. Press.

Sullivan, J. (1995). "Merger to Aid Desegregation Is Denounced." *New York Times*, Sept. 28: B1, 6.

Summers, A., and A. Johnson (1996). "The Effects of School-Based Management Plans." In *Improving America's Schools: The Role of Incentives*, ed. E. Hanushek. Natl. Academy Press: 75–96.

Survey Research Ctr. (1993). Georgia Poll, May. U. of Georgia.

"Survey Results: Should Colorado's Bilingual Education Program Be Dismantled?" (2001). *Rocky Mountain News*, Dec. 1.

Sutton, T. (2001). *Holding Schools Accountable: The Effects of Top-Down Testing and Management Mandates on Ohio Schools.* Annual mtg., Midwest Political Science Assn.

Swann v. Charlotte-Mecklenburg Board of Education (1971). 402 U.S. 1.

Swanson, C., and D. Stevenson (2002). "Standards-Based Reform in Practice." *Educational Evaluation and Policy Analysis* 24(1): 1–27.

Swartz, E. (1992). "Emancipatory Narratives: Rewriting the Master Script in the School Curriculum." *Journal of Negro Education* 61(3): 341–55.

—— (1993). "Multicultural Education: Disrupting Patterns of Supremacy in School Curricula, Practices, and Pedagogy." *Journal of Negro Education* 62(4): 493–506.

Swenson, K. (2000). "School Finance Reform Litigation: Why Are Some State Supreme Courts Activist and Others Restrained?" *Albany Law Review* 63(4): 1147–82.

Tafoya, S. (2002). *The Linguistic Landscape of California.* Public Policy Institute of California.

Tangipahoa Parish Board of Education v. Freiler (2000). 530 U.S. 1251; 120 S.Ct. 2706.

Task Force on Federal Elementary and Secondary Education Policy (1983). *Making the Grade.* Twentieth Century Fund.

Tate, K. (1996). *National Black Election Study, 1996.* Inter-University Consortium for Political and Social Research.

Taylor, C. (2000). "Standards, Tests, and Civil Rights." *Ed. Week*, Nov. 15: 40–41, 56.

Taylor, C., and A. Gutmann, eds. (1994). *Multiculturalism: Examining the Politics of Recognition.* Princeton U. Press.

"Teachers against Reform" (2000). *Wash. Post*, July 7: A26.

Tedin, K. (1994). "Self-Interest, Symbolic Values, and the Financial Equalization of the Public Schools." *Journal of Politics* 56(3): 628–49.

Tedin, K. et al. (2001). "Age, Race, Self-Interest, and Financing Public Schools through Referenda." *Journal of Politics* 63(1): 270–94.

Teske, P., and M. Schneider (2001). "What Research Can Tell Policymakers about School Choice." *Journal of Policy Analysis and Management* 20(4): 609–31.

Teske, P., et al. (2001). "Can Charter Schools Change Traditional Public Schools?" In *Charters, Vouchers, and Public Education*, ed. P. Peterson and D. Campbell. Brookings Institution Press: 188–214.

"The Education of a President" (2001). *Wall Street Journal*, June 19: A22.

Thompson, S. (1999). "Confessions of a 'Standardisto.'" *Ed. Week*, Oct. 6: 46, 49.

Time/CNN/Yankelovich Clancy Shulman (1991). Oct. 10.

Time/CNN/Yankelovich Partners (1993a). Sept. 8–9.

—— (1993b). Poll. Jan. 23–25.

—— (1994). Poll. Dec. 7–8.

—— (1995). Poll. Poll. Sept. 27–28.

Tobar, H. (1998). "In Contests Big and Small, Latinos Take Historic Leap." *Los Angeles Times*, Nov. 5: A1.

Toder, E., and S. Solanki (1999). *Effects of Demographic Trends on Labor Supply and Living Standards*. Urban Institute Press.

Toenjes, L., and A. G. Dworkin (2002). "Are Increasing Test Scores in Texas Really a Myth, or Is Haney's Myth a Myth?" *Education Policy Analysis Archives* 10(17). epaa.asu.edu/epaa/v10n17.

Tomasi, J. (2002). "Civic Education and Ethical Subservience." In *Moral and Political Education*, ed. S. Macedo and Y. Tamir. New York U. Press: 193–220.

Transportation Research Board (2002). *The Relative Risks of School Travel*. National Academy Press.

Traub, J. (1994). "Can Separate Be Equal?" *Harper's Magazine*, June: 36–47.

—— (1999). "The Bilingual Barrier." *New York Times Magazine*, Jan. 31: 32–35.

Treas, J. (1995). "Older Americans in the 1990s and Beyond." *Population Bulletin* 50(2): 2–43.

Trent, W. (1997). "Outcomes of School Desegregation." *Journal of Negro Education* 66(3): 255–57.

Trueba, H. (1988). "English Literacy Acquisition: From Cultural Trauma to Learning Disabilities in Minority Students." *Journal of Linguistics and Education* I(2): 125–52.

Tucker, C. (1993). "Ousting School Board May Not Be So Simple." *Atlanta Journal and Constitution*, Jan. 20: A13.

"2001 College Bound Seniors Are the Largest, Most Diverse Group in History" (2001). College Board, New York. www.collegeboard.com/press/article/0,1443,10429,00.html.

Tyack, D., and L. Cuban (1995). *Tinkering toward Utopia: A Century of Public School Reform*. Harvard U. Press.

"Union Dues" (2000). *New Republic*, June 5: 10–11.

University of California Linguistic Minority Research Institute (1997). *Review of the Research on Instruction of Limited English Proficient Students*. U. of California at Davis, Education Policy Ctr.

Unz, R. (1999). "California and the End of White America." *Commentary*, Nov.: 17–28.

Useem, E. (1992). "Middle Schools and Math Groups: Parents' Involvement in Children's Placement." *Sociology of Education* 65(4): 263–79.

U.S. Commission on Civil Rights (1967). *Racial Isolation in the Public Schools*. United States Government Printing Office.

—— (1997). *Equal Education Opportunity and Nondiscrimination for Students with Disabilities.* United States Government Printing Office.

U.S. Congress (1997). Individuals with Disabilities Education Act Amendments of 1997. May 9.

U.S. News and World Report (1996). Poll. Mar. 16–18.

U.S.A. Today (1985). Survey. Apr. 25.

Van Arsdell, M. (1976). *District IX CCC Hearings.* Boston, City-wide Educational Coalition.

Van Dyke, R., et al. (1995). "How to Build an Inclusive School Community." *Phi Delta Kappan*, Feb.: 475–79.

Van Fleet, A. (1977). "Student Transportation Costs Following Desegregation." *Integrated Education* 15(6): 75–77.

Van Hook, J. (2002). "Immigration and African American Educational Opportunity." *Sociology of Education* 75(2): 169–89.

Verba, S. (2001). *Political Equality: What Is It? Why Do We Want It?* Harvard U., Dept. of Government.

Vernez, G., and R. Krop (1999). *Projected Social Context for Education of Children: 1990–2015.* College Entrance Examination Board.

Verstegen, D., and R. King (1998). "The Relationship Between School Spending and Student Achievement." *Journal of Educational Finance* 24(2): 243–62.

Verstegen, D., and T. Whitney (1997). "From Courthouses to Schoolhouses: Emerging Judicial Theories of Adequacy and Equity." *Educational Policy* 11(3): 330–52.

Viadero, D. (1999a) "OCR Probing Social Promotion in Chicago." *Ed. Week*, Dec. 8: 6.

—— (1999b). "Research Board Urges Broad Approach to Bilingual Education." *Ed. Week*, Aug. 4: 12.

—— (2000a). "Minority Gaps Smaller in Some Pentagon Schools." *Ed. Week*, Mar. 29: 1, 20–21.

—— (2000b). "Schooled Out of Poverty." *Ed. Week*, Dec. 13: 35–41.

—— (2000c). "Testing System in Texas Yet to Get Final Grade." *Ed. Week*, May 31: 1, 20–21.

—— (2001a). "AP Program Assumes Larger Role." *Ed. Week*, Apr. 25.

—— (2001b). "Whole-School Projects Show Mixed Results." *Ed. Week*, Nov. 7: 1, 24–25.

—— (2002). "N. H. Court: Accountability a Constitutional Duty." *Ed. Week*, May 1: 18, 21.

Vincent, C., and J. Martin (2000). "School-Based Parents' Groups." *Journal of Education Policy* 15(5): 459–80.

Viteritti, J. (1999). *Choosing Equality : School Choice, the Constitution, and Civil Society.* Brookings Institution Press.

"Voices From the Front" (1999). *Wash. Post*, Jan. 17: B3.

"Voucher Foes, Backers Agree: Issue Is Not Going Away" (2000). *Associated Press State and Local Wire*, Nov. 8.

Wagner, T. (1996). "Creating Community Consensus on Core Values." *Ed. Week*, Oct. 9: 36, 38.

Wagner, T., and T. Vander Ark (2001). *Making the Grade: Reinventing America's Schools.* Routledge.

Walberg, H., and R. Greenberg (1998). "The Diogenes Factor." *Ed. Week*, Apr. 8: 52, 36.

Waldmeir, P. (1996). "Royal Oak Drops Plans for Customized School Services, but Issue Remains." *Detroit News*, Jan. 8.

Walker, R. (1989). "Entire Kentucky School System Is Ruled Invalid." *Ed. Week*, June 14: 1–14.

Walters, S. (2000). "School Aid System Passes Court Test." *Milwaukee Journal Sentinel*, July 12.

Walzer, M. (1995). "Education, Democratic Citizenship, and Multiculturalism." *Journal of Philosophy of Education* 29(2): 181–89.

Warren, M. (2001). *Dry Bones Rattling: Community Building to Revitalize American Democracy.* Princeton U. Press.

Wash. Post et al. (1995). *The Four Americas: Government and Social Policy through the Eyes of America's Multi-racial and Multi-ethnic Society*, Wash., DC.

——— (1999). Survey of Latinos in America. June 30–Aug. 30.

——— (2000). Education Survey. May 11–22.

——— (2001). Racial Attitudes Survey. Mar. 8–Apr. 22.

Wasley, P., et al. (2000). *Small Schools, Great Strides: A Study of New Small Schools in Chicago.* Bank Street College of Education.

Watkins, W. (1994). "Multicultural Education." *Educational Theory* 44(1): 99–117.

Wayne, A. (2002). "Teacher Inequality: New Evidence on Disparities in Teachers' Academic Skills." *Education Policy Analysis Archives* 10(30). epaa.asu.edu/epaa/v10n30.

Wegner, E., and J. Mercer (1975). "Dynamics of the Desegregation Process." In *The Polity of the School*, ed. F. Wirt. Lexington Books: 123–43.

Weiher, G., and K. Tedin (2002). "Does Choice Lead to Racially Distinctive Schools?" *Journal of Policy Analysis and Management* 21(1): 79–92.

Weiner, K. (2001). *Legal Rights, Local Wrongs: When Community Control Collides with Educational Equity.* SUNY Press.

Weinig, K. (2000). "The Ten Worst Educational Disasters of the Twentieth Century: A Traditionalist's List." *Ed. Week*, June 14: 31, 34.

Weiss, A. (2002). *Enhancing Urban Children's Early Success in School: The Power of Full-Day Kindergarten Annual mtg.*, American Educational Research Association.

Weiss, I. (1997). *The Status of Science and Mathematics Teaching in the United States: Comparing Teacher Views and Classroom Practice to National Standards.* U. of Wisconsin, Wisconsin Ctr. for Education Research.

Weiss, I., et al. (1994). *Report of the 1993 National Survey of Science and Mathematics Education.* Horizon Research.

Weizel, R. (2002). "Swifter School Action Sought." *Boston Globe*, Apr. 21: B6, 8.

Welles, E. (2000). "The ABCs of Profit." *Inc.* 22(18): 88–94.

Wells, A. (1993). *Time to Choose: America at the Crossroads of School Choice Policy.* Hill and Wang.

——— (1995). "Reexamining Social Science Research on School Desegregation." *Teachers College Record.* 96(4): 691–706.

——— (1996). "African-American Students' View of School Choice." In *Who Chooses? Who Loses?*, ed. B. Fuller et al. Teachers College Press: 25–49.

——— (1998). *Beyond the Rhetoric of Charter School Reform: A Study of Ten California School Districts.* UCLA, School of Education.

————, ed. (2002). *Where Charter School Policy Fails*. Teachers College Press.

Wells, A., and R. Crain (1994). "Perpetuation Theory and the Long-Term Effects of School Desegregation." *Review of Educational Research* 64(4): 531–55.

———— (1997). *Stepping over the Color Line: African American Students in White Suburban Schools*. Yale U. Press.

Wells, A., et al. (2000). "Charter Schools and Racial and Social Class Segregation." In *A Notion at Risk: Preserving Public Education as an Engine for Social Mobility*, ed. R. Kahlenberg. Century Foundation Press: 169–221.

Wenglinsky, H. (1998). "Finance Equalization and Within-School Equity." *Educational Evaluation and Policy Analysis* 20(4): 269–83.

———— (2000). *How Teaching Matters: Bringing the Classroom Back into Discussions of Teacher Quality*. Educational Testing Service.

Wessmann v. Gittens (1998). 160 F. 3d 790.

Westbrook, R. (1996). "Public Schooling and American Democracy." In *Democracy, Education, and the Schools*, ed. R. Soder. Jossey-Bass: 125–150.

Weyrich, P. (1999). "A Moral Minority? An Open Letter to Conservatives from Paul Weyrich." Free Congress Foundation. www.freecongress.org/fcf/specials/weyrichopenletter.htm.

Wheelock, A. (1992). *Crossing the Tracks: How Untracking Can Save America's Schools*. New Press.

White, K. (1998). "Ohio Voters Reject Sales-Tax Hike for Schools." *Ed. Week*, May 13: 17, 21.

———— (1999a). "High-Poverty Schools Score Big on Kentucky Assessment." *Ed. Week*, May 5: 18, 20.

———— (1999b). "LA Board Names CEO with Broad Powers." *Ed. Week*, Oct. 20: 3.

White, P., et al. (1996). "Upgrading the High School Math Curriculum." *Educational Evaluation and Policy Analysis* 18(4): 285–307.

Wildermuth, J. (1998). "Diverse Voices Heard on Race at Stanford Forum." *San Francisco Chronicle*, Jan. 31: A13.

Wildman, S. (2001). "Credit Is Due." *New Republic*, Feb. 26: 15–16.

Wilgren, J. (2000). "Young Blacks Turn to School Vouchers as Civil Rights Issue." *New York Times*, Oct. 9: A1, 18.

Will, G. (1990). "Beggars and Judicial Imperialism." *Wash. Post*, Feb. 1: A21.

Williams, J. (1995). "The Court's Other Bombshell." *Wash. Post*, July 2: C1, 4.

Williams, T., and H. W. Crew (1994). "The World of *Brown*'s Children." *The Nation*, May 23: 700–703.

Williamsburg Charter Foundation (1987). Survey on Religion and Public Life. Dec. 1–15.

Willie, C., et al. (2002). *Student Diversity and School Improvement*. Bergin & Garvey.

Wilson, S., et al. (2001). "Teacher Preparation Research." *Journal of Teacher Education* 53(3): 190–204.

Wilson, W. J. (1999). *The Bridge over the Racial Divide*. U. of California Press.

Winerip, M. (1998). "Schools for Sale." *New York Times Magazine*, June 14: 42ff.

Wirt, F., and M. Kirst (1997). *The Political Dynamics of American Education*. McCutchan.

Wisckol, M. (1999). "GOP Distances Itself from 'Son of 187.'" *Orange County Register*, Dec. 12.

Wisconsin Legislative Audit Bureau (2000). *Milwaukee Parental Choice Program: An Evaluation*. Wisconsin State Legislature.

6929